Human Rights Between Universality and Islamic Legitimacy

STUDIES IN COMPARATIVE POLITICAL THEORY

Series editor: Diego A. von Vacano, Texas A&M University

Consulting editors: Andrew March, Harvard University, and Loubna El Amine, Northwestern University

Human Rights Between Universality and Islamic Legitimacy
Mahmoud Bassiouni

Democracy after Virtue: Toward Pragmatic Confucian Democracy
Sungmoon Kim

Tantric State: A Buddhist Approach to Democracy and Development in Bhutan
William J. Long

Misplaced Ideas? Political-Intellectual History in Latin America
Elías J. Palti

Human Rights Between Universality and Islamic Legitimacy

MAHMOUD BASSIOUNI

Translated by

CIARAN CRONIN

OXFORD
UNIVERSITY PRESS

OXFORD
UNIVERSITY PRESS

Oxford University Press is a department of the University of Oxford. It furthers the University's objective of excellence in research, scholarship, and education by publishing worldwide. Oxford is a registered trade mark of Oxford University Press in the UK and certain other countries.

Published in the United States of America by Oxford University Press
198 Madison Avenue, New York, NY 10016, United States of America.

Library of Congress Cataloging-in-Publication Data
Names: Bassiouni, Mahmoud, author.
Title: Human rights between universality and Islamic legitimacy / Mahmoud Bassiouni.
Description: New York, NY : Oxford University Press, 2024. |
Series: Studies in comparative political theory
Identifiers: LCCN 2024017247 (print) | LCCN 2024017248 (ebook) |
ISBN 9780197753897 (hardback) | ISBN 9780197753910 (epub)
Subjects: LCSH: Human rights—Islamic countries. | Group identity—Islamic countries. |
Islam and politics. | Muslims—Europe—History—19th century. |
Islamic countries—Foreign relations—Europe. |
Europe—Foreign relations—Islamic countries.
Classification: LCC JC599.I67 B37 2024 (print) | LCC JC599.I67 (ebook) |
DDC 305.6/97094—dc23/eng/20240604
LC record available at https://lccn.loc.gov/2024017247
LC ebook record available at https://lccn.loc.gov/2024017248

DOI: 10.1093/oso/9780197753897.001.0001

Printed by Integrated Books International, United States of America

MIX
Paper
FSC FSC® C183721

Contents

Acknowledgments vii

Human Rights as a Question of Identity 1

PART I. CONTEXTS OF MUSLIM HUMAN RIGHTS DISCOURSE

1. Contemporary Context 13
2. Historical Context 21
3. Theological Context 27

PART II. RECONSTRUCTING THE MUSLIM DISCOURSE ON HUMAN RIGHTS

4. Rejection and Incompatibility 61
5. Appropriation 69
6. Assimilation 82
7. Summary and Outlook 101

PART III. ISLAMIC FOUNDATIONS OF A UNIVERSAL CONCEPTION OF HUMAN RIGHTS

8. The Purpose of Islamic Law (*maqāṣid al-sharīʿa*) 115
9. A Critical Review 146
10. New Conceptions of the *maqāṣid* 163

PART IV. HUMAN RIGHTS AND HUMAN NEEDS

11. Conceptions of Human Rights 183

Acknowledgments

This book is the result of a process that could not have been initiated, continued, or completed without the support and dedication of numerous individuals. First and foremost, I am indebted to Rainer Forst for his unwavering trust and support, which has gone and continues to go far beyond the scope of this book. He has been involved in this project since its inception, providing valuable guidance and constructive feedback and always offering support, even in cases when we disagreed on points of substance. Ömer Özsoy has consistently demonstrated a vested interest in this project and has frequently provided me with assistance in overcoming academic self-doubt. He also provided me with the invaluable opportunity to participate in the recently established Islamic Theology program at Goethe University Frankfurt, which allowed me to share and discuss my thoughts with fellow colleagues and students.

It is thanks to Mohamed Nagy Ibrahim that this book came into being at all. He devoted his days and nights to guiding me through the depths of Islamic legal theory, and he constantly had to deal with my impatient questions, which he always answered in meticulous detail. Many important ideas first developed in discussions with Tasniem Ibrahim, who always stood by my side with an unwavering commitment to help. Her support was essential to the completion of this book.

I would like to express my sincere gratitude to Diego von Vacano, Loubna El Amine, and Andrew March for including this book in the important Studies in Comparative Political Theory series. Andrew and two anonymous reviewers provided many valuable suggestions during the review process, which led me to revise and expand several parts of the manuscript. I am very grateful and heavily indebted to Ciaran Cronin, who took time out of his busy schedule to translate the original manuscript. His perceptive questions and philosophical expertise facilitated a more refined and articulate expression of my ideas. On the part of Oxford University Press, special thanks are due to Angela Chnapko and Alexcee Bechthold for their unwavering support, patience, and excellent editorial work. I would also like to thank Gigi

Clement and Judith Hoover at Newgen, who have been pivotal in ensuring the smooth production of this book.

I used to think it was a charming gesture when scholars saved their most heartfelt thanks for their spouses at the very end of the acknowledgments. Meanwhile, however, I have come to realize that it has very little to do with charm. This project would have been difficult to complete without the unwavering support, persistent encouragement, and insightful feedback of my wife, Sara Hallouda. She provided me with ample food for thought in long conversations on such romantic topics as Islamic legal methodology and ultimately enabled me to gain a better understanding of my own ideas. For this and for all that cannot be expressed in words, I express my deepest gratitude to her.

I dedicate this book to the memory of my mother, Wafaa Assaf, and my grandmother, Hoda Helmy. Two women with the hearts of a hundred men.

Human Rights as a Question of Identity

It seems appropriate to begin a book on Islam and human rights by pointing out that the purpose of academic research is not to praise or blame but to question, to scrutinize, to understand, and to explain. This is a simple point, of course, but it is worth emphasizing because it is not always apparent in discussions of the topic at hand. Often, discussions of Islam and human rights revolve around showing how archaic or unreasonable Islam is as a whole or in some of its parts, while the other side attempts to demonstrate the superiority of Islam over "Western" ideas. Such efforts are, of course, fraught with prejudice, accusation, sermonizing, and plain ignorance. This tendency is perhaps not surprising given the dominant discursive framework within which contemporary debates about Islam and human rights are conducted. We might call it identity discourse. Identity—or, more precisely, cultural identity—requires differentiation from others. It always involves the question of what *we* have in common and what distinguishes *us* from *others*. This is typically accompanied by a hierarchical mode of thinking that devalues the other in order to elevate the self. Not surprisingly, discourses of cultural identity tend to be charged with strong emotions. Their ultimate purpose is not to engage in a substantive discussion but to develop an understanding of identity that allows one side to distinguish itself from the other. Debates about Islam and human rights are thus embedded in a discursive structure in which one side questions the extent to which *they* have caught up with *our* values, while the other side is busy defending its own, culturally authentic moral standards. As a result, debates about complex issues become bogged down in a quagmire of arrogance, apologetics, and polemics, and thus lose their productive substance.

It is hard to overlook that these debates are characterized by a glaring imbalance of power. This is reflected in the typical juxtaposition of Western progressiveness and Islamic backwardness, or the striking contrast between the peacefulness of the West and the violent nature of Islam, or the dichotomy between Western rationality and Islamic piety, or the often unquestioned assumption that freedom and toleration are defining characteristics of the West

Human Rights Between Universality and Islamic Legitimacy. Mahmoud Bassiouni, Oxford University Press.
© Oxford University Press 2024. DOI: 10.1093/oso/9780197753897.003.0001

that are lacking in Islamic culture. To understand these discursive dynamics, we need to view the contemporary discourse in the light of its colonial and postcolonial history.[1] For apart from its profound effects on the transformation and consolidation of political and economic power structures, the colonial era also gave rise to a fundamental pattern of (self-)perception that persists to this day: Europe, confirmed in its cultural superiority, became the embodiment of the normative. Muslim consciousness, on the other hand, succumbed to the "dialectic of the colonized mind"[2] and tended to seek its identity in the demarcation from Europe, oscillating between admiration and aversion.

Given this relationship of domination, it is important to make a clear distinction between what we might call "identity construction" on the Muslim side and "identity preservation" on the European side. Identity preservation refers to the process of declaring certain social and political values to be essential *attributes* of one's own cultural identity, so that, for example, "being European" means valuing freedom, advocating democracy, and respecting human rights. Normative values thus become cultural attributes of "being oneself." One's own identity thus becomes an umbrella term for normative values and, in turn, the standard for what is to be considered normative. Ultimately—and this is where Islam enters the picture—this is achieved by contrasting "being European" or "Western" with an opposite pole of "otherness" whose attributes contradict the supposed characteristics of the West.[3] The goal of this process is not to create a true image of the other, but to create an image of Islam that serves the purpose of self-definition. Ernest Renan, for example wrote in this vein, "Islam is the complete negation of Europe. Islam is fanaticism . . . contempt for science, suppression of civil society; it is the appalling simplicity of the Semitic spirit cramping the human intellect, closing it against every delicate thought, every fine feeling, every rational inquiry, to confront it with an eternal tautology: *God is God*."[4] The

[1] In particular, the self-perception of Muslims must be viewed in this context: "It is hardly questioned by any but the most stubbornly resistant 'Orientalist' that a good deal of Islamic revivalism . . . is the product of a long colonial and postcolonial history, which has shaped a community's perception of itself in terms of the Other." Akeel Bilgrami, "What Is a Muslim?," in *Identities*, ed. Kwame Anthony Appiah and Henry Louis Gates (Chicago: University of Chicago Press, 1995), 209.

[2] Amartya Sen, *Identity and Violence: The Illusion of Destiny* (New York: W. W. Norton, 2006), 88.

[3] Why it is Islam in particular that embodies this otherness in this context should become clear when we recall that for the better part of a millennium, Islam was the only serious ideological and military rival to Christian Europe. Unlike Buddhist, Hindu, and Confucian cultures, whose religious differences from Christianity were far greater, Islam's geographical proximity posed the only perceptible threat to Europe's ideological and political power structure.

[4] "L'islam est la plus complète négation de l'Europe; l'islam est le fanatisme . . . le dédain de la science, la suppression de la société civile; c'est l'épouvantable simplicité de l'esprit sémitique,

"knowledge" of Islam informed by this hegemonic perspective is less concerned with producing scientific insights than with reflecting one's own identity.[5] As the embodiment of the other, Islam is endowed with attributes whose essential function is to emphasize its difference and imperfection in relation to Europe's own identity. From this perspective, Muslims are caught between a premodern religion and a European modernity that seems attainable only if Muslims adopt the Western canon of values through a long overdue process of enlightenment.

While some Muslims have accepted this scenario with resignation, the vast majority have developed a defensive posture. As Gudrun Krämer observes, this is true even of those Muslims who affirm these values in principle.[6] Their attitudes are rooted in an attempt to counter "Enlightenment arrogance" and to defend themselves against the imposed inferiority and the associated attacks on their identity. This is often expressed in a tendency to define their own identity in opposition to what it should not be, namely Western. According to this position, "Islamic values" should be different from everything the West stands for. Islam thus becomes an essential, if not exclusive, component of cultural identity that must be defended against external attacks. As a result, being a Muslim is no longer just a matter of observing Islamic religious and moral norms but also implies an oppositional political stance. In this sense, Abdolkarim Soroush aptly distinguishes between two forms of Islam: "Islam of identity and Islam of truth. In the former Islam is a guise for cultural identity and a response to what is considered the 'crisis of identity.' The latter refers to Islam as a repository of truths that point toward the path of worldly and otherworldly salvation."[7] The tendency to define

rétrécissant le cerveau humain, le fermant à toute idée délicate, à tout sentiment fin, à toute recherche rationnelle, pour le mettre en face d'une éternelle tautologie: *Dieu est Dieu.*" Ernest Renan, "The Share of the Semitic People in the History of Civilization," in Renan, *Studies of Religious History and Criticism*, trans. O. B. Frothingham (New York: F. W. Cristern, 1964), 164–165 (translation amended).

5 Rudi Paret, a renowned German Orientalist, unequivocally attested to this: "The goal and purpose of our scholarly work is to break through the intellectual horizon set by our own environment and to cast an eye on the world of the Orient, in order to learn to better understand, through a foreign entity, the possibilities of human existence and thus, ultimately, ourselves." Quoted in Reinhard Schulze, "'Orientalistics' and Orientalism," in *Islam in the World Today: A Handbook of Politics, Religion, Culture, and Society*, ed. Werner Ende and Udo Steinbach Ithaca, NY: Cornell University Press, 2011, 760.

6 Gudrun Krämer, "The Contest of Values: Notes on Contemporary Islamic Discourse," in *The Cultural Values of Europe*, ed. Hans Joas and Klaus Wiegandt Liverpool: Liverpool University Press, 2008, 338.

7 Abdolkarim Soroush, *Reason, Freedom, and Democracy in Islam: Essential Writings of Abdokarim Soroush* (Oxford: Oxford University Press, 2000), 23.

one's identity in terms of difference from the West is not, of course, a specifically Muslim phenomenon. Rather, as Sen notes, it is a general pattern of reactive identities.[8] Among other things, this "reactive self-perception" leads people to reject or at least negatively label certain values and ideas because they are perceived as Western, even though they may have been historically prevalent in their own culture. Instead, they construct their "own domain of sovereignty"[9] in the realms of morality and religion in an attempt to compete with the West. Since the scientific and technical achievements of the West must inevitably be acknowledged and imitated, the primary objective is to prove one's independence in the spiritual and moral field and to take a stand against the "cultural and intellectual invasion of the Islamic world."[10] As part of this effort, the West is all too readily portrayed as a place of moral anarchy, dysfunctional families, and consumerism; as a place where freedom means nothing more than sexual licentiousness; and as a homogeneous entity in which human rights and democracy are merely the means to an enduring cultural imperialism. But however much the process of Muslim identity construction is carried out in opposition to the West, it is not carried out in isolation from it. For the compass of identity construction remains fixed on the West, even if the circle is drawn with the largest possible radius. Similarly, the idea of conceiving one's "own" Islamic values is nothing more than a reactionary drive to withstand the Western challenge.

From what has been said so far, it is clear that the discourse of identity, in which discussions about Islam are predominantly situated, contributes very little to scientific research. It is a political—that is, power-dependent—discourse in which positions are articulated out of a certain relationship of domination. For the dominant group, it serves to reinforce the status of its identity (identity preservation), while for the dominated group, it provides a framework for figuring out its identity (identity construction). The structure of the discourse thus already predetermines the roles and self-understandings of its participants. Accordingly, the purpose of the identity discourse is not an open, discursive engagement with sociopolitical concerns but the demonstration of one's own cultural superiority or independence.

The debate about the compatibility of Islam and human rights is a clear example of this phenomenon. Krämer has clearly grasped the situation when

[8] See Sen, *Identity and Violence*, 89–93.

[9] Partha Chattergee, *The Nation and Its Fragments*, 6, quoted in Sen, *Identity and Violence*, 90.

[10] To paraphrase the title of Muḥammad al-Ṭāhir ʿAzwi, *al-Ghazw al-Thaqāfi wʾal-Fikri lil-ʿĀlam al-Islāmi* [The Cultural and Intellectual Invasion of the Islamic World] (Mīlah: Dār al-Huda, 1999).

she states that the "issue of human rights . . . has become the epitome of a controversy, if not a culture war [*Kulturkampf*], in which each side seeks to demonstrate its cultural superiority, its humanity and its humanism."[11] The typical course of a Muslim-Western discussion of human rights is thus easy to reconstruct. It usually begins with the observation that Islamic countries do not and have never been able to respect human rights, leading the observer to conclude "that this cannot be attributed solely to particularly unfavorable socio-structural conditions, but must have something significant to do with mentality and (political) culture, and ultimately with Islam."[12] As a first defensive response to these accusations, Muslims then ask their Western interlocutors whether there have "ever been worse violations of human rights, in quantity as well as quality, than during the two World Wars, with the use of chemical and nuclear weapons; during the Stalinist terror regime and the Holocaust; under apartheid in South Africa and ethnic cleansing in Bosnia and Kosovo?"[13] After noting that none of these atrocities were committed by Muslims, the respondent then attempts to demonstrate the superiority of a Muslim conception of human rights. Overall, it is hard to avoid the conclusion that so-called intercultural discussions of human rights have done little to reconcile the parties involved.[14] This is because, for the most part, such dialogues have rarely been conducted on an intercultural basis. Instead, they have had an *intra*cultural focus, with each side trying to defend and promote its own point of view.

This also and especially applies to the Muslim discourse on human rights, which has done little to advance an intercultural understanding of human rights. One is almost inclined to say that it has been more concerned with adopting particularistic positions and producing justifications for them. Although the notion of a "human right" has been known since the early phase of Islam under the heading of "rights of human beings" (*ḥaqq ādamī*) or "rights of legal agents" (*ḥaqq al-mukallaf*), the theoretical foundations of human rights have received very little attention. As a result, it is difficult to

11 Gudrun Krämer, *Gottes Staat als Republik* (Baden-Baden: Nomos, 1999), 147.

12 Ibid., 12.

13 Murad Hofmann, *Religion on the Rise: Islam in the Third Millennium* (Beltsville, MD: Amana, 2001), 73.

14 Jochen Hippler describes the Muslim-Western dialogue as follows: "It has often amounted to nothing more than alibi events, ritual declarations of good will, propaganda for one's own position, and a superficial exchange of courtesies. . . . Each side tends to adopt an overt or veiled patronizing attitude, often paying attention to the other side's statements only when they fit (positively or negatively) into its own view of the world." Jochen Hippler, *Der Westen und die islamische Welt: Eine muslimische Position* (Stuttgart: Institut für Auslandsbeziehungen, 2004), 8–9.

find a fully developed, theoretically grounded Islamic conception of human rights. This is largely because Muslim understandings of human rights do not emerge primarily from an analytical engagement with their own tradition. Rather, they are rooted in colonial and postcolonial narratives of justification, which are typically characterized by a "pronounced tendency toward defense and counter-attack, apologetics and polemics."[15]

A first, defensive justificatory narrative dismisses the concept of human rights as a Western and thus alien idea that violates the cultural integrity of Muslims and must be condemned as an expression of an enduring colonial ideology. Although its proponents do not deny that human beings have rights, they claim that human rights can only be derived from the Islamic *sharīʿa*, on the assumption that the latter already provides a just order by definition. Only a return to the Islamic tradition, the argument goes, guarantees an authentic cultural identity. Here, Islam doesn't serve as a normative guideline for the construction of values. Instead, it serves as a symbolic point of reference to guarantee cultural autonomy.

This quest for cultural self-assertion takes a very different form in another justificatory narrative. Here, human rights are no longer seen as something alien to Islamic culture but as an integral part of it, if not an invention of Islam itself. Once again, the idea is to protect the Islamic tradition from cultural and intellectual Westernization, but this time by emphasizing Islam's compatibility with and superiority over Western ideas. A common strategy is to claim that every laudable modern institution found in the West today was first invented and implemented by Muslims. Thus, Islam emancipated women, established democracy, tolerated religious pluralism, and protected human rights long before the West did. To realize human rights, therefore, all that is needed is a proper implementation of true Islam. This line of reasoning has produced a flood of literature that dominates Islamic human rights discourse to this day. It has resulted in an artificial idealization of the Islamic past and an intellectual attitude that ignores the tensions between the Islamic tradition and human rights.

Instead of anachronistically projecting them into the Islamic past, proponents of a third justificatory approach seek to identify alternative starting points for a modern understanding of human rights in Islam. Their main goal is to find ways to make human rights compatible with the Islamic tradition. This can involve a variety of methodological approaches,

[15] Krämer, *Gottes Staat als Republik*, 147.

ranging from linguistic to hermeneutic critiques of traditional Islamic understandings. Many of these approaches scour the Islamic tradition for a primary value, such as tolerance, dignity, or autonomy, to use as a "gateway" through which human rights can find their way into Islam. This trend has become more pronounced in light of post-9/11 criticism of Islam. It has also reinforced a semantics of "authenticity" and the idea that "true Islam" is realized in one moral vision or another.

As a closer look at these justificatory narratives reveals, the formation process of Muslim understandings of human rights is caught between two different normative demands: that of Islamic legitimacy on the one hand, and that of universality on the other. In order to avoid the impression that the acceptance of human rights is merely a matter of adopting "Western" ideas, human rights must be derived from and justified within the Islamic tradition. At the same time, the Islamic discourse on human rights faces the challenge of developing a conception that can also be accepted from a non-Muslim perspective, since human rights claim universal validity, which implies that they should be enjoyed and respected by all human beings. Human rights represent a set of normative claims that, on the one hand, grant human beings a certain scope of action and, on the other hand, specify certain forms of behavior. In doing so, they enter a moral terrain to which various religious and cultural orders lay claim. In order to live up to their claim to universal validity, human rights must be justified in such a way that their binding force can be accepted by all people, regardless of their cultural affiliation or religious convictions. This means that Islamic human rights discourse must formulate a justification of human rights that can be accepted and recognized as binding regardless of Islamic religious beliefs. This illustrates the dilemma currently facing Islamic human rights discourse. On the level of *theoretical justification*, it is confronted with the need for religiously independent criteria to ensure that human rights can meet with universal approval and thus do justice to their universal character. On the level of *legitimacy*, on the other hand, human rights must be anchored in the Islamic legal and intellectual tradition in order not to be seen as imposed from the outside. As the title of this book suggests, it is precisely in this sense that human rights are caught in a normative dilemma between universality and Islamic legitimacy.

This book proposes a solution to this intractable dilemma. It attempts to develop a conception of human rights that gives equal weight to the normative claims of universality and Islamic legitimacy. To this end, the book is divided into four parts. The first two parts systematically examine the contemporary Islamic human rights discourse, while the remaining two parts are devoted to the theoretical development of an alternative Islamic conception of human rights.

Part I (chapters 1–3) identifies and discusses various contexts of contemporary Islamic human rights discourse, thereby laying the groundwork for its substantive analysis. Chapter 1 discusses the *contemporary context* and looks at four ways in which Muslims articulate their positions on human rights: as part of the international human rights debate within the United Nations, as a critique of Western human rights policies, as a means of countering external criticism, and as critique of authoritarian state practices. Chapter 2 discusses the *historical context* of contemporary Islamic discourse by drawing attention to an earlier debate about the compatibility of Islam and modernity that took place in the second half of the nineteenth century. It outlines a variety of positions that mirror those of the contemporary discourse in order to show the continuing colonial legacy of the contemporary discursive framework. Chapter 3 deals with the *theological context* of the discourse by taking a closer look at the concepts of *sharīʿa* and Islamic law. It aims to clarify and differentiate these terms, to explain the formation and stagnation of the Islamic legal tradition, and to distinguish between static and dynamic conceptions of Islamic law in order to help explain the differences among the various Muslim positions on human rights.

These positions are the main subject of Part II (chapters 4–7), in which I offer a systematic typology and critical reconstruction of Muslim arguments and approaches. Chapter 4 discusses the arguments of *rejection* and *incompatibility*. While the former rejects the idea of human rights as a Western and thus alien concept that violates the cultural integrity of Muslims, the latter claims that Islam cannot be reconciled with human rights because it is based on a premodern value system. Chapter 5 discusses the argument of *appropriation*, in which human rights are no longer seen as a culturally alien element but as an integral part, if not an invention, of Islam. Chapter 6 examines the *assimilation* argument, according to which Islamic legal sources do not constitute an obstacle to the acceptance of human rights. It distinguishes five methodological approaches (textual, evolutionary, intentional, hermeneutical, and pragmatic) and illustrates how they deal with the issues of apostasy, gender rights, and penal sanctions. Chapter 7 provides a *summary and perspective* of Islamic human rights discourse and identifies two of its most fundamental shortcomings. The first is its failure to develop an autonomous and theoretically coherent conception of human rights. The second shortcoming concerns its inability to justify human rights on a universally acceptable basis: if human rights are to be respected only because faith makes it an obligation, then those who have a different faith or no faith at all will have no compelling reason to respect human rights. Present Islamic justifications are therefore incapable of obligating all human beings to respect human rights equally.

Part III (chapters 8–10) therefore begins the attempt to formulate a conception of human rights that is both grounded in the Islamic legal tradition and capable of achieving universal consensus by drawing on the theory of Islamic legal purposes (*maqāṣid al-sharīʿa*). Chapter 8 reconstructs the central ideas of *classical maqāṣid theory* as discussed by jurists such as al-Juwayni, al-Ghazāli, al-Rāzi, al-Āmidi, and al-Shāṭibi. According to them, Islamic legal norms aim to protect five indispensable, universal, and empirically observable human needs, namely life (*nafs*), reason (*ʿaql*), religion (*dīn*), offspring (*nasl*), and property (*māl*). The chapter discusses how classical jurists justify the protection of these necessities and examines the mechanisms devised for their protection, focusing in particular on the three-tiered conception of legal goods (*maṣāliḥ*) and their collective interdependence, which will be taken up in Part IV and applied to the field of human rights theory. Chapter 9 follows the reconstruction of the classical theory with a *critical review*. It focuses on the question of whether the basic needs identified by the classical Islamic jurists meet the postulated requirements of necessity, universality, and empirical observability. By analyzing the various justifications, the chapter concludes that the classical theory of Islamic legal purposes needs to be revised on both theological and philosophical grounds in order to meet its own requirements. Chapter 10 deals with modern Islamic legal discourse and examines fourteen different proposals for *reconceptualizing Islamic legal purposes*. In a critical vein, the chapter emphasizes the need to take seriously the premises of classical theory in order to enable a coherent and methodologically sound revision of *maqāsid*, rather than relying on arbitrary determinations. To avoid the latter, it is necessary, in other words, to identify those goods that meet the criteria of necessity, universality, and empirical observability, an attempt at which will be made in chapter 12.

Part IV (chapters 11–13) is devoted to the explication of a conception of human rights in a double dialogue with the Islamic legal tradition and contemporary human rights theory. Chapter 11 discusses the major *contemporary conceptions of human rights* (as articulated by Charles Taylor, John Rawls, Charles Beitz, Joseph Raz, Rainer Forst, James Griffin, and John

Tasioulas) in order to critically assess how much they can contribute to a concrete understanding of human rights. Based on this assessment, it argues that human rights can most plausibly be understood as socially constructed institutions designed to protect necessary, objective, and universal human needs from corresponding threats. Chapter 12 analyzes what *human needs* are and which human needs exist. According to the proposed definition, human needs denote the universal, objective, and necessary conditions of human existence. Accordingly, needs are universal in the sense that they exist in all human beings regardless of historical or cultural differences; objective in the sense that their existence can be empirically investigated and confirmed; and necessary in the sense that they include only those goods without which human existence would be threatened. Based on a review of various theories from motivational psychology, sociology, and peace and conflict studies, the chapter identifies five such goods: health, security, belonging, recognition, and meaning. Chapter 13 conceptualizes *human rights as institutions for the protection of these human needs*. It takes the central ideas and methodologies of the theory of Islamic legal purposes and applies them to the theory of human rights in order to (a) explain the moral relevance of human rights, (b) show how the content of human rights can be determined, and (c) analyze the relationship and interdependence between different categories of human rights. By critically engaging with the ideas of James Nickel, Thomas Pogge, and Henry Shue, it defends and develops a three-tiered conception of human rights analogous to the three-tiered conception of Islamic legal goods presented in Part III.

PART I
CONTEXTS OF MUSLIM HUMAN RIGHTS DISCOURSE

> Among the difficulties that prevent people from processing knowledge . . . are the large number of written texts, the difference in the terminology used . . . and the divergence in the methods employed.[1]

All three of the obstacles that the famous Arab social historian Ibn Khaldūn identified in the fourteenth century as hindering scholarly work and understanding prove to be just as problematic for someone working on "Islam and human rights" today. It is no easy task to provide a systematic account of a discussion characterized by such a plurality of views and positions. Nevertheless, there is a common thread running through the discussion, namely the initial question of whether and how the idea of human rights can be reconciled with Islam. The confusion begins when we consider the various attempts that have been made to answer this question. In order to create a reasonably manageable structure, it has become common practice in the literature to present three or four Muslim positions on human rights[2] as ideal types, in ascending order of their degree of compatibility with human rights.[3]

[1] ʻAbd al-Raḥmān Ibn Khaldūn, *Muqaddimat Ibn Khaldūn*, ed. ʻAli ʻAbd al-Wāḥed Wāfi (Cairo: Maktabat al-Usra, 2006), 3:1107. Translations from works for which no English translation is cited are those of the author.

[2] When I use the term "human rights" without further qualification, I am referring to the contemporary canon of human rights contained in the relevant international legal documents, that is, the Universal Declaration of Human Rights, the International Covenant on Civil and Political Rights, and the International Covenant on Economic, Social and Cultural Rights.

[3] Thus Heiner Bielefeldt, *Philosophie der Menschenrechte* (Darmstadt: Primus, 1998), for example, distinguishes conservative, pragmatic, and liberal positions; Lorenz Müller, *Islam und Menschenrechte* (Hamburg: Deutsches Orient Institut, 1996) distinguishes Islamists, modernists, and secularists; Bassam Tibi, *Im Schatten Allahs* (Düsseldorf: Ullstein, 2003), on the other hand, makes a distinction between conservatives, fundamentalists, and secularists. These positions are not arranged either conceptually or substantively in accordance with any clearly defined principle.

There is nothing inherently wrong with this approach. However, its informative value is diminished by the fact that it completely ignores the frameworks and contexts of these respective positions. In other words, it ignores explanatory factors that determine whether a position affirms or denies the compatibility of Islam with human rights, or assigns a positive or negative value to them.

In order to arrive at more meaningful results and a more systematic understanding, therefore, we need to clarify some preliminary questions and examine the contexts that significantly shape the modern discussion of Islam and human rights. First, I will consider the *contemporary context* and identify various debates and processes in which Muslims are currently articulating their positions on human rights (chapter 1). In a second step, I will attempt to situate the basic dynamics of contemporary Muslim human rights discourse in its *historical context* (chapter 2). My aim is to show that the debate on the compatibility of Islam and human rights is not a new phenomenon. Rather, it is, in a broader sense, a continuation of an earlier debate that took place in the late nineteenth and early twentieth centuries, which centered on the question of whether or not Islam was compatible with modernity. As the common question about "compatibility" indicates, both the debate over human rights and the debate over the somewhat fuzzier concept of modernity revolve around the ability of Muslims to culturally process foreign ideas or, more precisely, ideas that they experience as alien. This cultural process usually takes place within a *theological context*, which I will explore in more detail in chapter 3. The theological context is particularly important because different understandings and evaluations of human rights are largely a function of different understandings of the Islamic legal tradition. In Part II, therefore, I will present these understandings in order to systematize the various Muslim positions on the basis of their conception of Islamic law.

1
Contemporary Context

Looking at the debate on Islam and human rights, we can identify four main settings in which Muslim positions on human rights are articulated. First, Muslim positions are part of the international human rights debate. Second, Muslims express their position as a critique of Western human rights policies. Third, Muslim arguments can be understood as a response to Western criticism. Finally, Muslims invoke the language of human rights to challenge authoritarian state practices. In what follows, I will highlight only these discursive contexts in order to provide a coherent classification of the various Muslim arguments and positions. The reader should always bear in mind that when I refer to "Muslims" or "Islamic states," I am not directly referring to "Islam" in the religious and philosophical sense. The debate about the compatibility of Islam and human rights takes place on two different levels: on the theoretical level, it asks whether Islam in its religious and philosophical dimensions is compatible with human rights; on the practical level, it focuses on whether human rights are valid, upheld, or violated in so-called Islamic states. The fact that the practical level is also treated under the heading of "Islam" and human rights is due to the erroneous tendency to interpret the politics of the Arab or Islamic world exclusively as the expression of transhistorical forces, in this case Islam.[1]

Muslims as Participants in the International Human Rights Debate

In the international human rights debate within the framework of the United Nations, Islamic countries tend to take both a general and a specific stance. At the general level, they articulate views shared by other non-Western countries on issues such as economic rights, decolonization, international justice, and cultural sovereignty. On the other hand, the views they articulate have

[1] See Aziz al-Azmeh, *Islams and Modernities* (London: Verso, 1993), 59.

Human Rights Between Universality and Islamic Legitimacy. Mahmoud Bassiouni, Oxford University Press.
© Oxford University Press 2024. DOI: 10.1093/oso/9780197753897.003.0002

a specifically religious—in this case Islamic—character. However, as Fred Halliday notes, the latter represent only a small part of the international debate: "The arguments most frequently heard have little to do with religion or culture. Some pertain to the arguments, heard throughout the Third World, on redistribution of wealth, equity in international trade and so on."[2] Accordingly, a quantitative evaluation of the ratification behavior within the United Nations shows that the behavior of members of the Organization of Islamic Cooperation (OIC) is no different from that of other UN member states.

Figure 1.1 shows that Islamic states do not adopt a hard position on the ratification of treaties. Only the optional protocols to the International Covenant on Civil and Political Rights (ICCPR) and the Convention on the Elimination of All Forms of Discrimination against Women (CEDAW)[3] have been ratified by proportionally fewer OIC member states. Since this study does not explicitly address the question of whether or not human rights are actually being upheld in Islamic countries, I will refer here only to further studies on the subject.[4]

Criticism of Western Human Rights Policies

"Why should we accept declarations of human rights drafted by the same powers that colonized and pillaged our countries?"[5] "Why did the CIA overthrow a democratically elected government in Iran in 1953? Why did the West intervene so late in Kosovo? Why the one-sided support for Israel? Why the 1993 coup in Algeria after democratic elections? Why Chechnya?

[2] Fred Halliday, "Relativism and Universalism in Human Rights: The Case of the Islamic Middle East," *Political Studies* 43 (1995): 157.

[3] Mashood Baderin points out that the reservations of certain Muslim countries concerning some of the articles of the CEDAW, such as Articles 7, 9, and 15, are rooted in the fact that they conflict with national law in the respective countries and not with Islamic law per se. Only the reservations concerning Articles 2 and 16 of the Convention were justified by appeal to Islamic law. See Mashood A. Baderin, *International Human Rights and Islamic Law* (Oxford: Oxford University Press, 2003), 62.

[4] See especially Mashood A. Baderin, "A Macroscopic Analysis of the Practice of Muslim State Parties to International Human Rights Treaties: Conflict or Congruence?," *Human Rights Law Review* 1, no. 2 (2001): 265–303. Also Abdullahi A. An-Na'im, "The Position of Islamic States regarding the Universal Declaration of Human Rights," in *Innovation and Inspiration: Fifty Years of the Universal Declaration of Human Rights*, ed. Peter Baehr, Cees Flinterman, and Mignon Senders (Amsterdam: Royal Netherlands Academy of Arts and Sciences, 1999), 177–192; Susan Waltz, "Universal Human Rights: The Contribution of Muslim States," *Human Rights Quarterly* 26, no. 4 (2004): 799–844.

[5] Shirin Sinnar, "Reflections on the 50th Anniversary of the Universal Declaration of Human Rights," *Commentary* 19 (1998): 1–5, quoted in Hofmann, *Religion on the Rise*, 71.

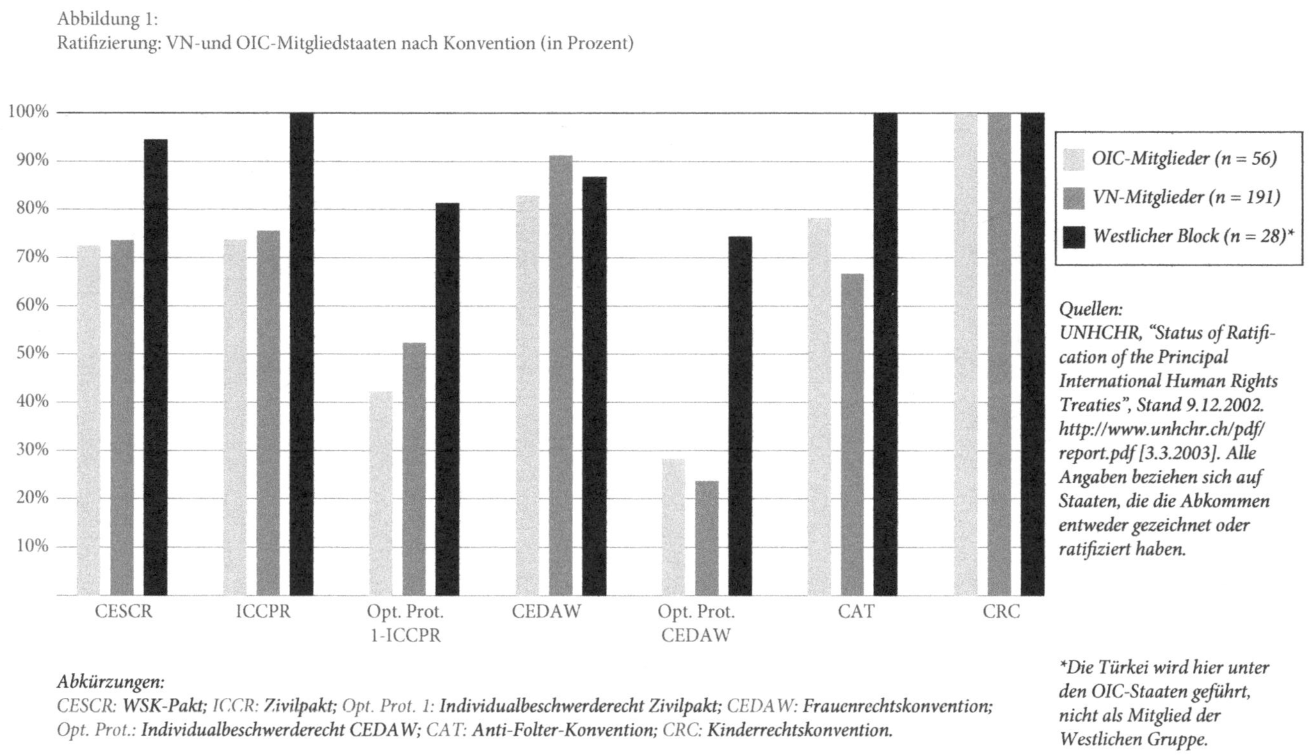

Figure 1.1 Ratification behavior of UN and OIC member states (in percentages).

Source: Anna Würth, *Dialog mit dem Islam als Konfliktpräventation? Zur Menschenrechtspolitik gegenüber islamisch geprägten Staaten* (Berlin: Deutsches Institut für Menschenrechte, 2003), 25.

Why support the Taliban or Saddam Hussein in the war with Iran? And what about the current situation with Iraq? . . . Isn't it true that Israel has not implemented a single UN resolution since 1967?"[6] The list of such and similar accusations could fill pages. And it is accusations like these that constitute the most serious obstacle to the unconditional recognition of human rights in Muslim societies. Samuel Huntington points this out when he writes, "Non-Westerners do not hesitate to point to the gaps between Western principle and Western action. Hypocrisy, double norms, and 'but nots' are the price of universal pretensions. Democracy is promoted but not if it brings Islamic fundamentalists to power; non-proliferation is preached for Iran and Iraq, but not for Israel. . . . Double norms in practice are the inevitable price of universal norms of principle."[7]

It should be noted that the reservations of many people in Islamic countries are not directed against human rights or their observance as such, but against the governments "that occasionally speak of 'human rights,' but otherwise willingly turn a blind eye to human rights violations or even commit such violations themselves."[8] In their view, "Western principles" such as freedom and justice are applied in the West itself, but not in dealings with the rest of the world.[9] For Abdoldjavad Falaturi, the lack of respect for human rights in the rest of the world reveals an ambiguity in the concept of "human being": "There seem to be two categories of human beings: those to whom the Universal Declaration of Human Rights applies (the members of Western civilization), and those who do not belong to this category (the majority of the inhabitants of our planet, i.e. those who currently belong mainly to the Third World)."[10] Similarly, Rāshid al-Ghannūshi describes the Universal Declaration as "illusory" and criticizes it for using the term "human being" in a misleading way, since it seems to apply only "to French, English, or Western citizens in general."[11] Similarly, Murad Hofmann

[6] Katajun Amirpur, "Sind Islam und Menschenrechte vereinbar? Zeitgenössische Menschenrechtsbegründungen: Von der demokratieorientierten Deutung des Korans zur Akzeptanz außer-religiöser Werte," in *Facetten islamischer Welten. Geschlechterordnungen, Frauen- und Menschenrechte in der Diskussion*, ed. Mechthild Rumpf, Ute Gerhard, and Mechtild M. Jansen (Bielefeld: transcript, 2003), 174.

[7] Samuel Huntington, *The Clash of Civilizations and the Remaking of World Order* (New York: Simon & Schuster, 1996), 184.

[8] Amirpur, "Sind Islam und Menschenrechte vereinbar?," 174.

[9] See Hippler, *Der Westen und die islamische Welt*, 65–72.

[10] Abdoldjavad Falaturi, *Westliche Menschenrechtsvorstellungen und Koran* (Cologne: GMSG, 2002), 6.

[11] Rāshid al-Ghannūshi, *al-Ḥurriyāt al-ʿAmma fi-l-Dawla al-Islāmiyya* (Beirut: Markaz Dirasāt al-Waḥda al-ʿArabiyya, 1993), 34.

sarcastically describes human rights as "blond and blue-eyed."[12] Tariq Ramadan comments, "As in the time of Athens—a model?—people are content to ensure that [human rights] are more or less successfully realized for a small number—in the industrialized countries—and to deal with them as needed beyond these borders."[13] The political instrumentalization of human rights referred to in these comments instills mistrust in Western governments and their human rights agenda and illustrates that their policies are not based on principles, but on interests.[14] In Parvez Manzoor's trenchant phrase: out of the Machiavellian bag of *raison d'état* jumps the utopian cat of human rights.[15] As a review of the Cold War confirms, human rights have always been a central part of the political rhetoric of the great powers.[16] For example, the first half of Article 13 (2) of the Universal Declaration of Human Rights, which states that "everyone has the right to leave any country, including his own," was used to criticize the former Soviet Union for its refusal to grant Russian Jews the right to emigrate. The second half of this article, "and to return to his country," is still officially rejected by Washington with regard to the right of the Palestinians.[17] It would be wrong to assume that the instrumentalization of human rights is directed only against Islamic states or is the exclusive preserve of Western states. But it should be noted that the historical and continuing discrepancy between Western human rights claims and practices toward the Islamic world is one of the main causes of Muslim skepticism about human rights and provides a politically convenient reason for their rejection. At least on a practical level, this state of affairs is a major obstacle to the universalization of human rights.

[12] Hofmann, *Religion on the Rise*, 71.

[13] Tariq Ramadan, *Islam: Le Face à Face des Civilisations. Quel Projet Pour Quelle Modernité?* (Lyon: Tawhid, 1996), 367.

[14] For an instructive discussion using the United States as an example, see Stephen B. Cohen, "Conditioning US Security Assistance on Human Rights Practices," *American Journal of International Law* 76, no. 2 (1982), 246–279. For a more recent analysis, see Barbara Ann Rieffer-Flanagan, "Rhetoric versus Reality: American Foreign Policy and Religious Freedom in the Middle East," in *Routledge Handbook on Human Rights and the Middle East and North Africa*, ed. Anthony Tirado Chase (London: Routledge, 2016), 317–328.

[15] Parvez S. Manzoor, "Human Rights: Secular Transcendence or Cultural Imperialism?," *Muslim World Book Review* 15, no. 1 (1994): 3.

[16] This is the subject of Tony Evans, "Power, Hegemony and the Universalization of Human Rights," *Human Rights Fifty Years On: A Reappraisal*, ed. Tony Evans (Manchester: Manchester University Press, 1998), 1–23.

[17] Noam Chomsky provides an analysis of these and other "double norms" in "The United States and the Challenge of Relativity," in Evans, *Human Rights Fifty Years On*, 24–56.

Response to Western Criticism

Muslim statements on human rights are mostly reactive, which is often reflected in the apologetic stance they take in Islamic-Western human rights discourse. The act of rejecting Western criticism follows seamlessly from the critique of Western human rights practice outlined above, which is used to "neutralize" external criticism. Accordingly, Muslims usually try to prove that what the West accuses them of is not true. Among the defenders of the compatibility of Islam and human rights, some try to relativize as much as possible certain legal provisions that are allegedly contrary to human rights, while others try to highlight the passages in Islamic source texts that are compatible with human rights. Thus, a common denominator of all Muslim positions discussed in this study is the effort to prove that Western accusations and criticisms of Islam are false. Such apologetic discourse thus becomes a matter of proving that Muslims are *not incapable* of protecting human rights. Some writers even go out of their way to emphasize that Islam "naturally" guarantees human rights, and that it had done so before and more effectively than the West: "Islam has preceded all international declarations, charters and covenants. In the domain of human rights, Islam has defined and ingrained such rights since fourteen hundred years ago. The UDHR (Universal Declaration of Human Rights), covenants, and international charters are just echoing and reiterating what Islam had already established in this domain."[18]

Such arguments are more illustrations of external pressure to profess human rights than attempts to deal with the actual content of human rights. Their purpose is to fend off international criticism. In Halliday's words, they "can be seen not as, disembodied or theological, interpretations of a holy text, but as political responses, in a context of the promotion of power domestically and internationally."[19] The identity discourse mentioned in the introduction plays an important role here. Muhammad Sid Ahmed sums up the situation clearly when he says, "Human rights are an expression of identity, of self, and here is the great crisis."[20]

[18] Sulieman Abdul Rahman al-Hageel, *Human Rights in Islam and Refutation of the Misconceived Allegations Associated with These Rights* (Riyadh: Imam Muhammad Bin Saud Islamic University, 1999), 17.

[19] Halliday, "Relativism and Universalism in Human Rights," 161.

[20] Quoted in Kevin Dwyer, *Arab Voices: The Human Rights Debate in the Middle East* (London: Routledge, 1991), 61.

Criticism of Authoritarian State Practices

Historically, the human rights paradigm has been at the forefront of social struggles against oppressive political, social, or economic practices and structures. Human rights have been, and continue to be, fought for in contexts characterized by different forms of domination. As the Iranian Green Movement in 2009 and the events of the Arab Spring in 2011 have shown, Muslim-majority societies are no exception. Throughout the Islamic world, the language of human rights has been used to articulate a variety of political and economic grievances against existing authoritarian regimes, culminating in calls for their overthrow. For example, in her widely circulated video that helped spark the protests in Egypt, Asma Mahfouz called on her fellow citizens to join her in Tahrir Square on January 25 to "demand our rights, our fundamental human rights."[21] Along with concepts such as freedom, dignity, and social justice, the language of human rights was used to challenge the existing status quo and to protest violence, oppression, exploitation, and humiliation.[22] Even before the mass uprisings in the Arab world, Islamist parties such as the Muslim Brotherhood invoked the language of human rights to challenge the authoritarian structures of the state and its repressive policies.[23] With its rise to power, the Brotherhood initially embraced the concept of human rights and proclaimed its unqualified commitment to protecting them,[24] a commitment that gradually weakened and gave way to an increasingly qualified and conditional endorsement, resulting in significant restrictions and curtailments.[25] As postrevolutionary developments in Egypt and elsewhere show, the struggle against authoritarian state practices

[21] The video and parts of the translated transcript can be found at Democracy Now, "Asmaa Mahfouz and the YouTube Video That Helped Spark the Egyptian Uprising," February 8, 2011, https://www.democracynow.org/2011/2/8/asmaa_mahfouz_the_youtube_video_that.

[22] See the collections of photos taken during the protests in Tahrir Square compiled by Karima Khalil, *Messages from Tahrir: Signs from Egypt's Revolution* (Cairo: American University of Cairo Press, 2011). For an account of how social and political debates in Muslim-majority societies are framed and informed by the human rights paradigm, see Anthony Tirado Chase, *Human Rights, Revolution, and Reform in the Muslim World* (Boulder, CO: Lynne Rienner, 2012).

[23] Carrie Rosefsky Wickham, *The Muslim Brotherhood: Evolution of an Islamist Movement* (Princeton, NJ: Princeton University Press), 46.

[24] The founding statement of its Freedom and Justice Party begins, "In the spirit of the January 25 Revolution . . . that opened the horizon for bright hope for this country to shift towards freedom, democracy, justice and full human rights, our 'Freedom and Justice Party'—being inspired in its programs and mechanisms by the demands of this great revolution, while seeking the achievements of the sublime objectives of this revolution . . ." See "The Founding Statement of the Freedom and Justice Party," June 1, 2011, https://ikhwanweb.com/the-founding-statement-of-the/.

[25] See Moataz El Figiery, *Islamic Law and Human Rights: The Muslim Brotherhood in Egypt* (Newcastle: Cambridge Scholars, 2016).

and structures is ongoing, and social and religious minorities, both Muslim and non-Muslim,[26] continue to demand recognition and equal treatment. Although the continued and renewed entrenchment of authoritarian structures paints a rather bleak picture, it is important to keep in mind that human rights progress has always been and will continue to be subject to a dialectic of oppression and emancipation.[27] Despite their apparent failure to disrupt authoritarian state structures, the Arab and Iranian uprisings have sparked a significant expansion of the human rights movement by transforming the human rights paradigm into a dominant frame in which ordinary people—not just educated elites—voice their grievances against oppressive social and political practices.[28] It should come as no surprise, then, that dominant political authorities have resorted to identity narratives to undermine local human rights activism by portraying it as part of a subversive foreign agenda.[29]

[26] See Joshua Castellino and Kathleen A. Cavanaugh, *Minority Rights in the Middle East* (Oxford: Oxford University Press, 2013).

[27] For an assessment of the Arab Spring that takes the broader historical perspective into consideration, see Micheline R. Ishay, *The Levant Express: The Arab Uprisings, Human Rights and the Future of the Middle East* (New Haven, CT: Yale University Press, 2019).

[28] See Asef Bayat, *Revolutionary Life: The Everyday of the Arab Spring* (Cambridge, MA: Harvard University Press, 2021).

[29] See Narges Bajoghli, *Iran Reframed: Anxieties of Power in the Islamic Republic* (Stanford, CA: Stanford University Press, 2019); Nathaniel Greenberg, *How Information Warfare Shaped the Arab Spring: The Politics of Narrative in Tunisia and Egypt* (Edinburgh: Edinburgh University Press, 2019).

2
Historical Context

Historically, the dynamics underlying contemporary Muslim human rights discourse and the related question of identity can be traced back to the second half of the nineteenth century. Faced with European superiority and aware of their own need for reform, Muslim intellectuals pondered how to explain the stagnation of Islamic societies and what initiatives were needed to bring about the desired progress. Many Muslims were troubled not only by Europe's material superiority, but also by the sense of inferiority they felt in the face of Europe's ideological defamation of Islamic societies. "Any person," wrote the French philosopher Ernest Renan in 1883, "with a modicum of instruction in the affairs of our time clearly sees the current inferiority of Muslim countries, the decadence of the states governed by Islam, the intellectual nonentity of the races that derive their culture and education solely from this religion."[1] Thus the idea of reform derived its impetus from an ideological challenge that saw the causes of Muslim stagnation as residing in Islam and identified the latter as inhibiting, or even blocking, the progress of Islamic societies. Accordingly, the crisis of the Muslim search for identity unfolded in response to the question of how to define oneself in relation to Europe and what role Islam should play in this regard. In a broader sense, Muslims were confronted with the basic questions of political philosophy: What principles should we live by, and where do we derive these principles from? Can the principles of a modern society be derived from Islam? Or is it necessary to refer to the ideas and institutions of Europe? To what extent can we then still define ourselves as Muslims in relation to Europe? In response to these questions, three broad currents of thought can be identified.

[1] Ernest Renan, "Islam and Science," in Renan, *What Is a Nation? And Other Political Writings*, trans. and ed. M. F. N. Giglioli (New York: Columbia University Press, 2018), 265. In general, Renan considered the Muslim mind to be inherently incapable of science and philosophy: "Indeed, the distinguishing trait of the Muslim is his hatred of science, his persuasion that research is useless, frivolous, almost ungodly" (274). Renan draws the corresponding conclusion: "To liberate the Muslim from his religion is the best service that one can render him" (*Émanciper le musulman de sa religion est le meilleur service qu'on puisse lui rendre*). For this quote (missing in the English translation), see Ernest Renan, "L'Islamisme et la Science," in Renan, *Discours et Conférences* (Paris: Calmann Lévy, 1887), 403.

Human Rights Between Universality and Islamic Legitimacy. Mahmoud Bassiouni, Oxford University Press.
 DOI: 10.1093/oso/9780197753897.003.0003

Trialogue of Identities

Echoing the European position, a *secularist* school of thought believed that Muslims, by virtue of their religion, were intellectually incapable of developing progressive thought in the European sense.[2] According to this view, Islam was fundamentally incompatible with science and modern civilization. Muslims should therefore accept European modernity as the ultimate frame of reference and assimilate to Europe as much as possible. Politically, this assimilationist stance became most prominent in Turkey. In contrast, a second, much broader current of thought, which might be called *traditionalist*, argued that the plight of Muslims was due to colonization and oppression by the European West. According to this view, the stagnation of Islamic societies was caused by the exercise of European imperial power, to which Muslims had fallen victim, so that adopting European ideas would be tantamount to intellectual capitulation. Instead, Muslims should seek and rediscover their strength in their own past. The only way to express one's true identity, according to this argument, is to return to one's own tradition.

As is readily apparent, these two arguments amount to either blindly accepting the legacy of Muslim civilization, with all its social and institutional peculiarities, or rejecting it altogether, along with all its values. Whatever their differences in content, however, the two positions have one thing in common: both see liberation from Muslim inferiority as the imitation of a model—Europe, on the one hand, and one's own tradition, on the other. It is therefore appropriate to describe the secularist argument as imitating Europe and the traditionalist argument as imitating history.[3] The position commonly called *modernist* seeks to avoid this imitative attitude.[4] Islamic modernism saw itself as a middle way between the historical-imitative spirit, which sought to revive Muslim identity through a return to the past and equated the cultural "self" and any change toward the cultural "other"

[2] This current essentially refers to the nineteenth-century graduate group of the Syrian Protestant School (now the American University of Beirut), which was dedicated to the mission of enlightening Muslims and persuading them to transform Islam as Europe had transformed Christianity. Among its proponents were Shibli Shumayyil (1850–1917), Farah Antun (1874–1922), George Zaidan (1861–1914), Yaqub Suruf (1852–1917), Salma Musa (1887–1958), and Nicola Haddad (1878–1954). See Albert Hourani, *Arabic Thought in the Liberal Age: 1798–1939* (London: Oxford University Press, 1962), ch. 10.

[3] See ʿAbdul Ḥamīd Abū Sulaymān, *Crisis in the Muslim Mind* (Herndon, VA: International Institute of Islamic Thought, 1993), 3–4.

[4] However, the name of this position is not uniform. In the scholarly literature, it is also referred to as "Islamic Reformism" or "Salafiyya."

with right and wrong, and the European-imitating spirit, which sought total cultural assimilation and unreflectively embraced Europeanization in all its forms. Islamic modernism can be seen as a position of recognition. It hardly questioned the desirability and acceptability of modern ideas and institutions. On the contrary, it asserted that they were here to stay and did its best to demonstrate that Islamic beliefs and the guiding ideals of modern society are not at odds. The key to this argument was a more nuanced understanding of the Islamic tradition, coupled with a distinction between what is essential, stable, and unchangeable and what is nonessential, temporary, and open to change.

Religious Understanding in Time and Place

To understand the dimension of the modernist reform effort, we must keep in mind the circumstances that gave rise to the idea of reform. The call for reform has been a constant feature of the history of Muslim thought. It was advocated by thinkers such as al-Ghazāli (d. 1111/505)[5] and Ibn Taimiyya (d. 1328/728). As Soroush points out, however, these and other reformers were more concerned with "rescuing religion from the clutches of the unenlightened and the peddlers of religion."[6] The reform efforts of Islamic modernists, in contrast, focused on restoring and renewing the meaning of religion in a rapidly changing world. They were faced with the dilemma that no religion could be considered relevant if it blindly accepted every innovation at the expense of its own consistency and served only to legitimize a fait accompli, while a stubborn insistence on permanence would make religious life impossible in the modern world; in the end, both paths lead to the irrelevance of religion. Muhammad Iqbal (d. 1938) had this dilemma in mind when he wrote that a religion "must possess eternal principles to regulate its collective life, for the eternal gives us a foothold in the world of perpetual change. But eternal principles when they are understood to exclude all possibilities of change which, according to the Qur'an, is one of the

[5] In order to place classical Islamic thinkers in their historical context, I list in parentheses the year of their death according to the Gregorian and the Islamic calendars. The primary function of the Islamic calendar year is to indicate the historical distance from the time of the founding of Islam. The Islamic calendar begins with the Prophet's emigration from Mecca to Medina (year 622 according to the Gregorian calendar).

[6] See Soroush, *Reason, Freedom, and Democracy in Islam*, 28.

greatest 'signs' of God, tend to immobilize what is essentially mobile in its nature."[7] Accordingly, the task of Muslim intellectuals was to reconcile stability and change.[8] To do so, they had to distinguish between the constant and the variable components of religion, between the profane and the sacred, between form and substance, and, more broadly, between religion and religious understanding.

Islamic modernism assumed that the supposed intellectual backwardness of Muslims was rooted in an ossified, inflexible understanding of Islam based primarily on blind obedience (*taqlīd*) to the now outdated system of norms elaborated by Islamic jurisprudence. It therefore called for an internal reform of the Islamic normative order in the light of reason to allow for a more liberal and contemporary reading of Islam's foundational texts (the Qur'an and the Sunnah). In addition to Jamal al-Dīn al-Afghāni (d. 1897), who came from Persia but was active throughout the Islamic world, the dominant figure in this movement was the Egyptian theologian Muḥammad 'Abdūh (d. 1905) and later his disciple Muḥammad Rashīd Riḍa (d. 1935).[9] They called for reopening the door of independent reasoning (*ijtihād*) in order to free Islam from nonessential elements that had become entrenched over time. As Hofmann notes, Islamic modernists realized that "a revival of Islam was possible only if, together with the sacrifice of many medieval glosses and casuistry, a clear distinction was made between the true sources of Islam: the Qur'an and the authentic Sunnah of the Prophet . . . on the one hand, and the marvelous edifice of Islamic jurisprudence and scholarship, on the other—the latter being the result of human efforts, and therefore fallible, as specific responses to specific problems."[10] According to the modernists, traditional understandings of Islam fail to recognize the fundamental difference between values, principles, and goals established by the religious sources regardless of time and place, on the one hand, and interpretations, applications, and methods tied to people's respective local and historical understandings, on the other. For them, the stagnation of religious thought was a result of Muslims' inability to recognize the contextual and temporal character of Islamic jurisprudence as such. They argued that it was essential to recognize that interpretations of religious sources do not emerge in a

[7] Muhammad Iqbal, *The Reconstruction of Religious Thought in Islam* (Stanford, CA: Stanford University Press, 2012), 119.
[8] Ibid.
[9] For a comprehensive collection of writings on Islamic modernism, see Charles Kurzman, ed., *Modernist Islam 1840–1940: A Sourcebook* (Oxford: Oxford University Press, 2002).
[10] Murad Hofmann, *Islam: The Alternative* (Beltsville, MD: Amana, 2003), 59.

vacuum but always reflect particular historical, cultural, social, and political circumstances. Individuals and societies differ from time to time and place to place according to their circumstances, needs, and challenges. If religion is to retain its social functionality, religious understanding must adapt to its context. While Islamic values and principles must remain unchanging, they must be constantly imbued with new substance to meet the quantitative and qualitative changes of each age. If religion was to continue to guide society in times of social change, religious understanding would have to be reinterpreted as a matter of urgency. If this process of reinterpretation were to come to a halt, the inevitable result would be the development of impotent, religiously encrusted social mechanisms that would ultimately lead to social stagnation. Thus, according to the modernists, the stagnation of Muslim societies was due not to the values and goals embodied in Islam but to the way they were perceived and applied. Thus it was not Islam per se that needed reforming but Muslim thought. "The real issues here are those of the particular and the general, the methodology of Islamic thought, the lack of appreciation of the elements of time and place in the composition of society, and the concept of revelation as a source of knowledge complementing both reason and nature so that humanity can fulfill its role of doing good on earth."[11] According to ʿAbdūh, when it came to identifying the stable and the mutable components of religion, an important systematic distinction had to be made between norms that regulate ritual action (*ʿibadāt*) and those that regulate interpersonal relations (*muʿāmalāt*). While the Islamic sources prescribed specific norms for the former, they established only general principles for the latter, and it was left to people to give concrete substance to these principles in the context of their respective living conditions.[12] In fact, ʿAbdūh argued, in the realm of interpersonal relations, Islam recognizes no authority other than that of reason, and institutions commonly regarded as possessing religious authority, such as the caliphate and various ecclesiastical offices, were, in ʿAbdūh's opinion, purely secular institutions devoid of dogmatic authority.[13] "This was," Hofmann writes, "revolutionary, for Muslims were supposed to reaccustom themselves to the idea (familiar to early Islam) that the Qu'ran has not regulated *each and everything*, but only those things which God thought necessary to regulate; that there are areas of

[11] Abū Sulaymān, *Crisis in the Muslim Mind*, 54.
[12] See Hourani, *Arabic Thought in the Liberal Age*, 148.
[13] See Al-Azmeh, *Islams and Modernities*, 93.

activity consciously left to human regulation, and also areas which must not be limited by any human regulation whatsoever."[14] In order to understand and make sense of these ideas, we need to take a closer look at the theological context and the concept of Islamic *sharīʿa.*

[14] Hofmann, *Islam: The Alternative*, 59.

3

Theological Context

The term *sharīʿa* is on everyone's lips. For some, it symbolizes order and justice; for others, it is synonymous with barbarism and oppression. Some associate it with a sense of stability and security, while others fear a return to the Middle Ages. The term is used by both Muslims and non-Muslims to politicize and polemicize. However, "many of those who call for or place their hopes in the 'application of Shari'ah' have no legal knowledge and no precise idea of what 'Shari'ah' might mean in particular."[1] This observation may not come as a surprise, since public debates generally revolve not around the precise meaning of the term but rather around the assertion of the superiority of one's own identity.[2] Problematically, this tendency is not limited to public discourse but also pervades much of the discourse in Islamic studies, which, influenced by paradigms of Orientalism, all too often serves to entrench culturalist and identitarian patterns of thought.[3]

In order to provide a more nuanced understanding, I will attempt to present a systematic account of the Islamic *sharīʿa*. It is important to keep in mind that understanding the Islamic *sharīʿa* has a crucial bearing on how we understand the entire system of Islamic thought and belief. In this sense, Joseph Schacht is right when he emphasizes that "Islamic law is the epitome of Islamic thought, the most typical manifestation of the Islamic way of life, the core and kernel of Islam itself. . . . [I]t is impossible to understand Islam without understanding Islamic law."[4]

1 Krämer, *Gottes Staat als Republik*, 50.

2 On this, see Anver M. Emon, "On the Pope, Cartoons, and Apostates: Shari'a 2006," *Journal of Law and Religion* 22, no. 2 (2007): 303–321.

3 See Abbas Poya and Maurus Reinkowski, eds., *Das Unbehagen in der Islamwissenschaft: Ein klassisches Fach im Scheinwerferlicht der Politik und der Medien* (Bielefeld: transcript, 2008).

4 Joseph Schacht, *An Introduction to Islamic Law* (Oxford: Clarendon Press, 1964), 1. This statement was originally made by Gotthelf Bergsträsser, Schacht's teacher, who noted that "Islamic law, in its broad sense, which includes the regulation of worship, is the epitome of the genuine Islamic spirit, the most decisive expression of Islamic thought, the very essence of Islam." Gotthelf Bergsträsser, *Grundzüge des Islamischen Rechts*, rev. and ed. Joseph Schacht (Berlin: de Gruyter, 1935), 1.

Human Rights Between Universality and Islamic Legitimacy. Mahmoud Bassiouni, Oxford University Press.
 DOI: 10.1093/oso/9780197753897.003.0004

Sharīʿa and *Fiqh*

The semantic meaning of the term *sharīʿa* is "the path that leads to the water source."[5] In a metaphorical sense, this path can be understood as leading humanity to eternal bliss and happiness through religious and ethical principles.[6] However, this conceptualization of *sharīʿa* contributes little to its structural understanding. To get a better idea of what the term entails, we need to approach it analytically. In its most general sense, the term refers to a system of norms (*aḥkām*).[7] Since any system of norms can be called a *sharīʿa* in the Arabic language,[8] we need an attribute to distinguish one *sharīʿa* from another. Thus when we speak of the "Islamic *sharīʿa*," we are referring to an Islamic system of norms. This system includes three different categories of norms: (a) norms of faith, which formulate the content of the faith that Muslims should internalize; (b) ethical norms, which state what moral qualities or virtues (gratitude, patience, mercy, etc.) human beings should possess; and (c) norms of action, which in turn are divided into norms of ritual action (*ʿibādāt*) and norms regulating interpersonal relations (*muʿāmalāt*) (Figure 3.1).[9]

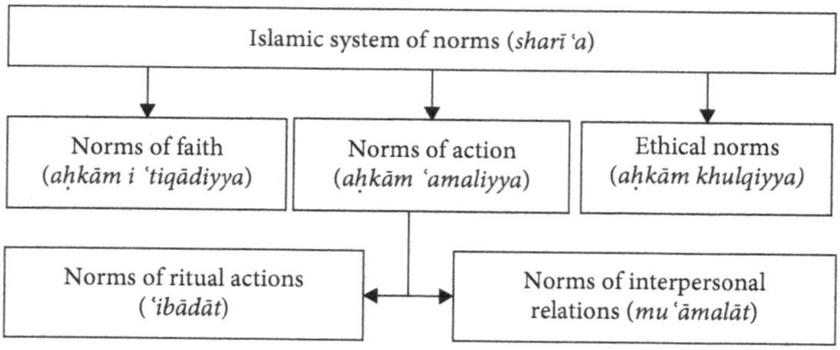

Figure 3.1 *Sharīʿa* as a system of norms.

[5] Muḥammad Ibn Yaʿqūb al-Fīrūzābādi, *al-Qāmūs al-Muḥīṭ* (Beirut: Dār al-Kutub al-ʿIlmiyya, 1995), 659.

[6] Ali Merad, "Die Sharīʿa—Weg zur Quelle des Lebens," in *Freiheit der Religion: Christentum und Islam unter dem Anspruch der Menschenrechte*, ed. Johannes Schwartländer (Mainz: Matthias-Grünewald-Verlag, 1993), 392–393.

[7] Bernard Weiss, *The Spirit of Islamic Law* (Athens: University of Georgia Press, 2006), 7–8, 17–18.

[8] In Arabic, for example, it is common to speak of a Christian or Mosaic *sharīʿa*. The term is also commonly used in nonreligious contexts. For example, a famous play by the Egyptian poet Aḥmad Shawqi (d. 1932) is called *Sharīʿat ul-Ghāb* (The Law of the Jungle).

[9] See Mohammad Hashim Kamali, *Principles of Islamic Jurisprudence* (Cambridge, UK: Islamic Texts Society, 2003), 26; Nyazee, *Theories of Islamic Law*, 20ff.; Tariq Ramadan, "The Way (*Al-Shariʿah*) of Islam," in *The New Voices of Islam: Rethinking Politics and Modernity: A Reader*, ed. Mehran Kamrava (Berkeley: University of California Press, 2006), 92.

The norms of faith (*aḥkām iʿtiqādiyya*) primarily entail strict monotheism, that is, belief in one God (*tawḥīd*), his revelations, prophets, and messengers, angels, the Day of Judgment, and predestination. The discipline that deals with the study of the foundations of the Islamic faith is called *ʿilm al-kalām* (Islamic scholastic theology). Ethical norms (*aḥkām khulqiyya*) deal with the moral qualities, motives, and consequences of human action. Their primary focus is on the inner dimension of the human being, and they are devoted to the development and attainment of a higher level of morality and a deeper spiritual awareness. Both *ʿilm al akhlāq* (virtue ethics) and *taṣawwuf* (Sufism) deal with this area. The norms of action (*aḥkām ʿamaliyya*), on the other hand, are the subject of a discipline called *fiqh*, which essentially means "understanding."

The basic concern of *fiqh* is to answer the fundamental questions "What should we do?" and "How should we live?" Norms of ritual action (*ʿibādāt*) specify how a Muslim should perform ritual actions, such as how to pray or fast and how often. Norms of interpersonal relations (*muʿāmalāt*) deal with social relations and regulate the relations of individuals to each other, the relations of individuals to the state, and relations between states.[10] While *fiqh* seeks to provide answers to the practical questions "What should we do?" and "How should we live?," the discipline of *uṣūl al-fiqh* asks where and how answers to these questions can be found. It identifies the sources from which and the methods through which norms are established, derived, or modified.

Fiqh is thus a part of the Islamic *sharīʿa*, but only that part which relates directly to the practical life of human beings. When we speak of "Islamic law" in the strict sense, we are referring to that part of the Islamic *sharīʿa* that deals with the rules of conduct governing interpersonal relations (*muʿāmalāt*).[11] Since the Islamic system of norms includes spiritual, ethical, and ritual norms in addition to legal norms, it would be erroneous to equate the Islamic *sharīʿa* with Islamic law.[12] Rather, Islamic law is part of an overarching concept that unifies and regulates various areas of human life. The often heard assertion that Islam is a religion that encompasses all spheres of life is therefore correct, but it should be understood in a differentiated manner. If the comprehensive character of the Islamic *sharīʿa* is taken to mean that it does

[10] Imran Ahsan Khan Nyazee, *Outlines of Islamic Jurisprudence* (Islamabad: Advanced Legal Study Institute, 2000), 132.

[11] Mohamed Ibrahim, *Al Qurān aus Sicht des Uṣūl al Fiqh als erste Hauptquelle der Rechtsfindung im Islam* (Darmstadt: Averroes Institut für wissenschaftliche Islamforschung, 2007), 3.

[12] This is discussed in greater detail by Mathias Rohe, *Islamic Law in Past and Present* (Leiden: Brill, 2015), 10–21, who distinguishes broader and narrower understandings of the *sharīʿa*.

not distinguish between various areas of life, then this must be emphatically questioned. Many Muslims unreflectively assume that there is no difference between the private and the public, between religion and politics, or between faith and thought; Islam, they say, is all-encompassing. This idea, which Orientalists are only too happy to confirm, gives the impression that the comprehensive character of the Islamic *sharīʿa* amounts to a sacralization of all spheres of life. In order to guard against such erroneous conclusions, it is necessary to show how the law differs from the other normative categories of the *sharīʿa*.

Differentiation of Islamic Law

Legal norms represent one of the two parts of the norms of action, namely the part that regulates interpersonal relations. This specification is important because combining ritual and interpersonal norms into a single group of norms obscures a fundamental difference in frame of reference and character between the two branches. Norms that regulate ritual or liturgical actions refer to a constant and unchanging relationship between God and human beings and outline the formal and quantitative aspects of ritual devotion. For the most part, these aspects are not rationally comprehensible. For example, we cannot rationally explain why Muslims should pray five times a day rather than, say, four times. Nor can we rationally justify why the morning prayer consists of two, the noon prayer of four, and the evening prayer of three segments (*rakʿa*), or why the social tax (*zakāh*) is 2.5 percent and not, say, 3 or 5 percent.[13] These rationally unintelligible norms (*aḥkām ghayru maʿqūlat al-maʿna*) must be accepted and followed by every pious Muslim regardless of insight into their reason. Since only Muslims are considered norm addressees in this context, ritual norms can be conceptualized as communal norms. Interpersonal norms, on the other hand, are concerned with the constantly evolving and changing relationships between people and can therefore be conceptualized as societal norms. Unlike ritual norms, they have the additional quality of being justifiable or rationally intelligible.[14] Rational intelligibility implies that each norm has a justification that can be understood

[13] Note that this is not a question of the meaning and purpose of a ritual institution itself, such as the meaning and benefits of fasting, but only of the formal conditions of its exercise.

[14] See Michael Mumisa, *Islamic Law: Theory and Interpretation* (Beltsville, MD: Amana, 2002), 141, 164, 173; Kamali, *Principles of Islamic Jurisprudence*, 271.

through the use of reason, so that it can be obeyed on the basis of rational insight.[15] According to Ibrahim, therefore, in dealing with this group of norms, "it does not matter whether one is a devout Muslim or not a Muslim at all. Nor does it matter whether one believes that the Qur'an is the word of God, that it was invented by Mohammad, or that it was copied from the Jews and Christians. The only attribute that the reader should possess is that he or she is endowed with reason and is able to consider these norms rationally."[16] The question of the justifiability of norms, which we will encounter frequently in the course of this book, is significant because it has a direct bearing on whether norms are modifiable or immutable, and thus is closely related to the capacity of Islamic law to change and develop. Mir-Hosseini makes the following observation: "In contrast to the rules of *'ibadāt*, which regulate the relationship between God and human beings and thus leave little room for rationalization and explanation, the rules of *mu'āmalāt*, which regulate the relationships between human beings, are generally almost completely open to rational considerations. Since human affairs are in a state of constant flux and development, these rules must be reinterpreted in accordance with the actual conditions of life at any given time."[17] In the realm of interpersonal relations, it is generally assumed that everything is permissible unless it is explicitly or unambiguously forbidden (*al ibāḥa aṣlun fi'l-ashyā'*).[18] In contrast to ritual norms, human reason is thus granted a wide discretion, limited only by explicit prohibitions. Norms governing interpersonal relations can thus be divided into a flexible (*mutaghayyir*) and a fixed (*thābit*) dimension (Figure 3.2).[19]

[15] According to the jurist Sayf al-Dīn al-Āmidi (d. 1233/631), the assumption that Islamic legal norms are groundless is untenable because it contradicts the consensus of all Islamic jurists and the observable practice and character of the legislator (God), who calls Himself wise (*ḥakīm*). This implies that God does nothing without a reason, so we must assume that His norms are well-founded. The only question that remains open is whether these reasons are understandable or not. According to al-Āmidi, the latter must be ruled out because it would amount to a requirement to follow legal norms blindly (*ta'abbud*). In the first place, such a requirement is contradicted by the fact that, on closer examination, the legislative practice provides more reasons to assume that the legislation in question is justifiable than that it is arbitrary. Second, the justifiability of legal norms makes them more consistent with the ethical principles and customs of reasonable people, which, third, helps to ensure their acceptance and observance. See Sayf al-Dīn al-Āmidi, *al-Aḥkām fī Uṣūl al-Aḥkām* (Beirut: Dār al-Kutub al-'Ilmiyya, 2005), 3:232–233, 249–250.

[16] Ibrahim, *Al Qurān aus Sicht des Uṣūl al Fiqh als erste Hauptquelle der Rechtsfindung im Islam*, 4.

[17] Ziba Mir-Hosseini, "Neue Überlegungen zum Geschlechterverhältnis im Islam: Perspektiven der Gerechtigkeit und Gleichheit für Frauen," in Rumpf, Gerhard, and Jansen, *Facetten islamischer Welten*, 63.

[18] Mumisa, *Islamic Law*, 128.

[19] See Yūsuf al-Qaraḍāwi, "'Awāmil al-Si'a w'al-Murūna fī al-Sharī'a al-Islāmiyya," in *Wujūb Taṭbīq al-Sharī'a al-Islāmiyya w'al-Shubuhāt Alati Tuthār Ḥawl Taṭbīqiha*, ed. Manā' al-Qaṭṭān (Riyadh: Jāmi'at al-Imām Muḥammad Ibn Sa'ūd al-Islāmiyya, 1984), 113–115.

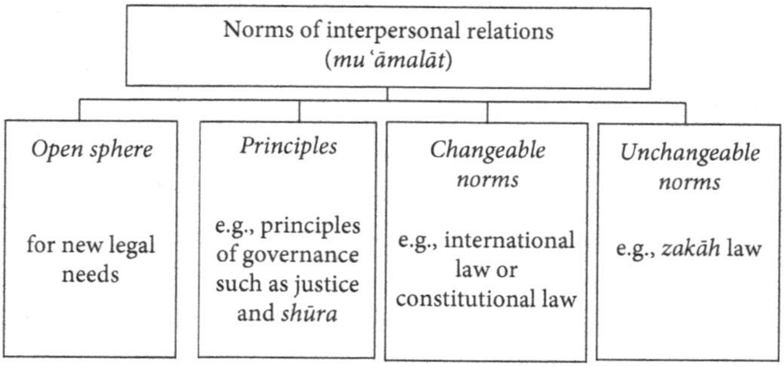

Figure 3.2 Norms of interpersonal relations.

Unchangeable norms are essentially commandments and prohibitions that are explicitly regulated in the Qur'an and the Sunnah. As part of the *mu'āmalāt*, they must also be rationally justified and have a "necessary link between the norm and its cause" (*al-ḥukm yadūr ma' al-'illa 'adaman wa wu'jūdan*).[20] An example of this is the prohibition on the consumption of alcoholic beverages based on the Qur'anic verse 5:90. The reason for this prohibition is an empirically verifiable property of alcoholic beverages, namely that they are intoxicating. When an alcoholic beverage, such as wine, ceases to be intoxicating because it has been transformed into vinegar, the prohibition is automatically lifted. Consequently, a norm remains unchangeable until it is no longer tied to the rational context for which it was established.

Changeable norms are norms that are not explicitly regulated by the Qur'an or the Sunnah and relate to legal needs that have evolved historically, so they cannot claim to be timelessly valid or binding. For example, the concepts of *dār al-islām* (realm of Islam) and *dār al-ḥarb* (realm of war) in international law arose in a historical context in which Muslims were at war with the Persian and Byzantine empires, and the geopolitical assumption (widespread in the Middle Ages) was that peace was merely the absence of war.[21] Such legal institutions, which have evolved out of specific historical circumstances, are tied to the conditions and requirements of a particular social structure, and must be modified in the event of social change to meet

[20] Mumisa, *Islamic Law*, 104–105.

[21] For an accessible account, see Khaled Abou El Fadl, *The Great Theft: Wrestling Islam from the Extremists* (San Francisco: HarperCollins, 2005), 220–249; Tariq Ramadan, *Western Muslims and the Future of Islam* (Oxford: Oxford University Press, 2004), 62–77.

new social demands and circumstances.[22] Accordingly, we must distinguish between historical models and timeless principles. *Principles* are guidelines for action and define fundamental maxims and values that must be fulfilled in every age. How and in what form this is done, however, remains open. In other words, it is not the principles themselves but their implementation that changes over time. In this sense, Ramadan observes, "Faithfulness to principles cannot involve faithfulness to historical models because times change, societies and political and economic systems become more complex, and in every age it is in fact necessary to think of a model appropriate to each social and cultural reality."[23]

To avoid the danger of viewing one's own reality through foreign lenses, it is therefore necessary to distinguish between principles and their specific historical and cultural expressions. Moreover, as interpersonal relationships evolve and become more complex and multifaceted—in other words, as people's need for rules of conduct increases—an *open sphere* (*mantiqat al-ʿafw*) ultimately provides an opportunity to develop norms to satisfy newly emerging legal needs.[24] For "neither Qur'an nor *sunnah* . . . provide direct guidance for traffic law in space or on the ski-slopes, nor for copyright on the internet, not to speak of surrogate motherhood, genetic engineering, in-vitro fertilization and the like."[25]

We are now in a better position to address the initial question of how law as part of the Islamic *sharīʿa* differs from other categories of norms.[26] In

[22] As regards the *dār al-islām* and *dār al-ḥarb*, this social change goes so far that Mumisa notes, "In fact, today we can say that many Muslim countries could be classified as enemy countries [*dār al-ḥarb*] while some non-Muslims have become friendly countries since it is becoming increasingly difficult to exercise free thinking as well as practice Islam in some Muslim countries while non-Muslim countries have become truly pluralistic." Mumisa, *Islamic Law*, 183–184.

[23] Ramadan, "The Way (*Al-Shariʿah*) of Islam," 70.

[24] al-Qaraḍāwi, "ʿAwāmil al-Siʿa w'al-Murūna fī al-Sharīʿa al-Islāmiyya," 71.

[25] Hofmann, *Religion on the Rise*, 179.

[26] The issue of how Islamic law interacts with the other normative categories of the Islamic *sharīʿa* cannot be dealt with in depth here. The importance of this issue requires a separate, in-depth study. In the most basic sense, norms are rules of conduct. Their purpose is to guide or regulate human action. The question, then, is what role the various categories of norms play in guiding human action. Within the framework of the Islamic *sharīʿa*, practical norms can be identified as the category that is limited to regulating external actions, both in ritual matters (*ʿibādāt*) and in social interactions (*muʿāmalāt*). Ethical norms, on the other hand, focus on the moral disposition and are concerned with the *inner* motivation of human action. In this sense, practical norms and morality enter into a reciprocal relationship, allowing both dimensions of human action to be coordinated and harmonized in order to bind the actor to a norm out of personal insight. Of course, a norm may be followed without insight into its moral content—for example, out of fear of the consequences of noncompliance. This applies to both the ritual and secular spheres of life. However, this external motivation is a very superficial and fragile basis for norm compliance. Internalizing the moral substance of a norm, on the other hand, can help stabilize an actor's motivation and thereby strengthen the validity of a given norm. Meanwhile, norms of faith provide their addressees with a religious motive

summary, Islamic jurisprudence (*fiqh*) can be said to prescribe a normative domain in which human reason may not make any changes (*'ibādāt*), while at the same time leaving open a space of freedom that can be regulated only with the aid of human reason (*mu'āmalāt*). What distinguishes the various categories of the Islamic *sharī'a* is how they respond to changes in time and space.

Faith norms, ritual norms, and ethical norms remain constant and have absolute validity regardless of changes in time and space. The requirement to believe in divine unity applies to Muslims in twenty-first-century Antarctica just as it did to Muslims in the seventh-century Arabian Peninsula. Both also observe the same practices of ritual devotion and are bound by the same ethical values. In contrast, norms of interpersonal relations are subject to temporal and spatial variation, since their potential impact and ability to guide human behavior are directly linked to variable and changeable human needs. Therefore, the claim that Islamic law is valid and applicable to all times and places is true only if people continuously play their part in setting legal norms and engage in a constant process of reasoning and interpretation (*ijtihād*), so that the law can meet people's legal needs. If this does not happen, the law stagnates while human life continues to evolve.

The Stagnation of Islamic Law

The word *ijtihād* (literally: "effort") is a *terminus technicus* in Islamic jurisprudence for the effort to reach an independent judgment in legal matters. In the context of the development of Islamic law, *ijtihād* refers to a hermeneutical process by which norms are derived from the Qur'an and Sunnah, taking into account geographical and historical changes in order to meet contemporary legal needs. It is relatively easy to show that *ijtihād* has not been continuous throughout the history of Muslim thought. Mir-Hosseini attributes this to the fact that Muslim jurists "over time transformed what was essentially a temporary phenomenon into a legal principle of permanent validity. . . . They did this, firstly, by transforming social norms into ideals of the Shari'ah and, secondly, by treating all regulations . . . as if they belonged to the category of immutable, rationally inaccessible *'ibadāt.*" In this way,

to obey a norm in order to benefit from it in the hereafter, even if the observance of a norm does not bring any worldly benefit. In this way, the norm's obligatory character is supported by a religious consciousness.

temporally and spatially bound theories and norms, which formed the basis of the social order at a specific period "over time became detached from their social context and historical development and were henceforth regarded as a fixed and eternal law."[27] As a result, historically and culturally conditioned norms of interpersonal relations were subjected to a process that, over time, elevated them to immutable, sacred, even divine laws. The model of Islamic law that emerged from these processes was thus based on a historical subject that took on a life of its own and was henceforth considered timeless and self-evident. The mere observation that such an objectification of historical subjectivity took place, however, only *describes* the process of stagnation that Islamic law underwent, without really explaining how and why this happened over time.

Classical Explanatory Models

In their attempt to explain the stagnation of Islamic law, many commentators overhastily conclude that its cause lies in the historical phenomenon of the "closing of the gates of *ijtihād*," that is, in "the notion that everything worth knowing has already been known and was better understood by earlier generations closer to the source."[28] According to this view, the final Qur'anic revelation, "Today I perfected your religious law for you, and have bestowed upon you the full measure of my blessings" (5:3), led medieval Islamic scholars to the overly triumphalist conclusion that the development of new legal norms was forbidden and to declare that only the imitation (*taqlīd*) of the legal norms of the four schools of law was permissible.[29] Joseph Schacht describes this process as follows:

> By the beginning of the fourth century of the hijra (about A.D. 900) . . . the point had been reached when the scholars of all schools felt that all essential questions had been thoroughly discussed and finally settled, and a consensus gradually established itself to the effect that from that time onwards no one might be deemed to have the necessary qualifications for independent reasoning in law, and that all future activity would have to be

[27] Mir-Hosseini, "Neue Überlegungen zum Geschlechterverhältnis im Islam," 64.
[28] Hofmann, *Islam: The Alternative*, 3.
[29] This refers to the Ḥanafi, Māliki, Shāfiʿi, and Ḥanbali schools of law.

> confined to the explanation, application, and, at the most, interpretation of the doctrine as it had been laid down once and for all. This "closing of the door of ijtihād," as it was called, amounted to the demand for taklīd, a term . . . which now came to mean the unquestioning acceptance of the doctrines of established schools and authorities.[30]

This line of argument, which became established in the classical literature of Islamic studies, assumes that (a) there was a consensus that (b) was developed by Muslim jurists in the tenth century, based on the assumption that (c) all necessary interpretations of the Islamic sources had already been made, and that (d) no one possessed the necessary skills to do so any longer, so that (e) Islamic law had acquired its final form and was thus (f) binding on all subsequent generations. We know from the work of Hallaq that there is no consensus in the history of Muslim thought on the "closing of the gates of *ijtihād*," as just outlined.[31] It has been established that some jurists continued to practice *ijtihād* even after the establishment of the schools of law. Moreover, a chronological analysis of legal literature shows that the term *insidād bāb al-ijtihād* (closing of the gates of *ijtihād*) was not used before the beginning of the twelfth century. The debate over whether the gates were actually closed, and the related question of the existence of *ijtihād*-qualified jurists (*mujtahid*), was so controversial that jurists were unable to reach a consensus on these issues. Muhammad Iqbal, who as early as 1929 called the thesis of the closing of the gates "pure fiction," quotes the fourteenth-century thinker Badr al-Dīn Zarkāshi (d. 1392), who remarked, "If the upholders of this fiction mean that the previous writers had more facilities [to engage in *ijtihād*], while the later authors had more difficulties in their way, it is nonsense; for it does not require much understanding to see that *ijtihād* for later doctors is easier than for earlier doctors. Indeed the commentaries on the Koran and sunnah have been compiled and multiplied to such an extent that the *mujtahid* of today has more material for interpretation than he needs."[32] The gates of *ijtihād*, it seems, were not completely closed—which is not to

[30] Schacht, *An Introduction to Islamic Law*, 70–71. For a similar account, see Noel J. Coulson, *A History of Islamic Law* (Edinburgh: Edinburgh University Press, 1964), 80–81.

[31] Wael B. Hallaq, "Was the Gate of Ijtihad Closed?," *International Journal of Middle East Studies* 16, no. 1 (1984): 3–41.

[32] Iqbal, *The Reconstruction of Religious Thought in Islam*, 141. For another presentation of opposing positions, see Mahmud Shukri al-Alusi, "Ijtihad and the Refutation of Nabhani," in Kurzman, *Modernist Islam 1840–1940*, 158–171.

say, of course, that they were wide open.[33] It is a historically undeniable fact that, with some notable exceptions, the theoretical and practical importance of *ijtihād* declined dramatically from the fourteenth to the nineteenth century, giving way to an imitative mentality that long characterized (and largely continues to characterize) Muslim thought. This mentality, however, was not caused by a particular historical choice but by a variety of factors.[34] In order to understand the stagnation of Islamic law and the resulting impact on Muslim thought, it is important to identify a number of basic processes that were crucial to its development.

The Construction of Authority and Taqlīd

The first question we need to address is how Muslim legal thought succumbed to the *taqlīd* mentality. The term *taqlīd* is used in Islamic jurisprudence to describe the uncritical acceptance of another's opinion or doctrine: "[It] signifies the acceptance of and acting upon another's word without trying to substantiate it. In other words, the determining factor is one's trust in or reverence for the scholar, or his/her own negligence or lack of interest in trying to establish the truth on his/her own."[35] *Taqlīd*, understood as the blind acceptance of another opinion, must be distinguished in this sense from mere adherence to another opinion *(ittibā')*: "*taqlīd* means to follow someone without any justification for doing so, while observance involves following what can be justified through proof. This difference makes the former prohibited and the latter permissible."[36] Thus, when we speak of a *taqlīd mentality*, we mean the basic intellectual attitude of accepting another person's opinion without knowing its justification (*qubūl qawl bilā ḥujja*). The development of this mentality can be traced to a phenomenon in Muslim legal thought that can be described as "intellectual dependence on authority" or, more succinctly, as "belief in authority." This refers to the psychological

[33] For a critical examination of Hallaq's denial of the thesis of "the closing of the gates of *ijtihād*," see Sherman A. Jackson, *Islamic Law and the State: The Constitutional Jurisprudence of Shihāb al-Dīn al-Qarāfī* (Leiden: Brill, 1996), 76–79 and Baber Johansen, *Contingency in a Sacred Law: Legal and Ethical Norms in the Muslim Fiqh* (Leiden: Brill, 1999), 446–463.

[34] In his treatise on the stagnation of Muslim thought, 'Abd al-Raḥmān al-Kawākibi lists fifty-six different reasons for stagnation. See "Summary of the Causes of Stagnation," in Kurzman, *Modernist Islam 1840–1940*, 152–154.

[35] Taha Jabir Al-Alwani, *Issues in Contemporary Islamic Thought* (London: International Institute of Islamic Thought, 2005), 97–98. See also Mumisa, *Islamic Law*, 148.

[36] Al-Alwani, *Issues in Contemporary Islamic Thought*, 98 (quotation adapted to clarify meaning).

tendency to *validate* or, in extreme cases, *justify* one's own opinion by reference to the reputation of respected authorities. This is certainly not a uniquely Muslim phenomenon, since it can be traced back to classical Greek philosophy. Indeed, there are remarkable parallels in this regard between the development of Greek and Muslim thought.

According to Windelband, "the *appeal to authority* often makes its appearance in Greek and Hellenistic philosophy in the sense of a confirmation and strengthening of an author's own views, but not as a decisive and conclusive argument."[37] Although *jurare in verba magistri*, blind faith in the words of the teacher, was common among the subordinate members of the schools, Windelband argues,

> the heads of schools, and in general the men who engaged in independent research, maintained an attitude toward the teachings of the former time that was much more one of criticism than of unconditional subjection; and though in the schools, chiefly the Academic and Peripatetic, the inclination to preserve and maintain the teaching of the founder as an unassailable treasure was fostered by the custom of commenting upon his works, yet in all the conflict as to the criteria of truth the principle had never been brought forward that something must be believed because this or that great man had said it.[38]

Later, according to Windelband, the simple appeal to authority developed into an increasing tendency to see one's own ideas as nothing more than a continuation of older teachings. The assumption was that one could gain greater acceptance for one's work by associating it with the name of one of the icons of wisdom, such as Aristotle, Plato, or Pythagoras. Ultimately, the growing need for authority led individual philosophers to conclude that they were no longer capable of discovering the truth on their own, so they sought help by submitting to the authorities of the past.[39]

Following Windelband, we can identify three stages of belief in authority. The first stage is that of *intellectual confirmation*. The appeal to an authority serves only to confirm one's own view, while maintaining a critical-intellectual relationship to the authority. The second stage is that of

[37] Wilhelm Windelband, *A History of Philosophy* (New York: Macmillan, 1901), 219. I owe the reference to Windelband to Mumisa, *Islamic Law*, 4–5.

[38] Windelband, *A History of Philosophy*, 219–220.

[39] Ibid., 220.

intellectual legitimation, in which one's views are attributed to an authority in order to gain greater acceptance for one's point of view. Finally, the third stage is *intellectual dependence*. Here, one's view is justified by appeal to authority. The appeal to authority, known in eristic dialectics as *argumentum ad verecundiam* (argument from authority), uses the prestige and esteem of an authority to justify one's own view in the following form:

1. Person X holds opinion A ("Einstein believed in God").
2. I respect and admire Person X ("Einstein was a genius").
3. Therefore I hold opinion A ("Therefore I believe in God").

To understand how the construction of belief in authority works in the Muslim context, it is necessary to take a historical look at the development of Muslim legal thought. Then as now, the question of what is permitted and what is forbidden, what we should do and how we should live, played a central role in legal thought. In terms of how these questions were answered, however, we can distinguish four phases. The emergence of Islam (in 610) marked the *first phase* of Muslim legal thought, which lasted until the death of the Prophet (11/633). The main feature of this phase is that every legal question that arose was answered by the norms of the Qur'an and the Sunnah of the Prophet. When people wanted to clarify certain questions, they went to the Prophet and asked him. He would either receive a revelation or answer the question himself. The text of the Qur'an was not revealed all at once or in its entirety, but over a period of twenty-three years, answering people's questions in the context of specific events. In addition, the Prophet's statements and actions, as well as his expressions of approval and disapproval, satisfied people's need for legal and behavioral norms.

The *second phase* in the development of Muslim legal thought began with the death of the Prophet and lasted until the end of the reign of the Rightly Guided Caliphs (11–40/631–661).[40] After the Prophet's death, new questions arose that needed to be answered. With the expansion of the Islamic polity, new social and political constellations emerged that did not exist at the time of the Prophet, as well as legal problems that neither the Qur'an nor the Sunnah addressed. Faced with these practical problems, Muslims had

[40] The term "Rightly Guided" or "Righteous Caliphs" (*al-khulafā' al-rāshidūn*) refers to the Caliphs Abū Bakr, 'Umar, Uthmān, and 'Ali, who ruled the Muslim community after the Prophet's death.

to derive the law according to the needs of their situation. That the Prophet had already trained his companions (*ṣaḥāba*) to think independently during his lifetime, so that he could send them out as judges to the various areas of the Islamic state, is made clear, for example, by the well-known tradition that the Prophet sent Mu'ādh Ibn Jabal to Yemen and asked him, " 'What will you judge by when you decide a case?' He answered: 'By the Book of Allah.' The Prophet asked: 'If you do not find the answer in the Book of Allah, what will you do?' He spoke: 'I will consult the Sunnah of the Prophet of Allah.' The Prophet asked: 'And if you do not find it in the Sunnah of the Prophet of Allah?' He answered: 'Then I will strive to form my own opinion.' "[41] Thus, in addition to the Qur'an and the Sunnah, the sources of jurisprudence included the *ijtihad* of the Prophet's companions.

Whereas during the time of the four Rightly Guided Caliphs the spiritual and political leadership were united in the person of the caliph, during the *third phase*, which began with the rise to power of the Umayyad dynasty (40/661), the spiritual intelligentsia gradually separated from political authority, leading to a crucial development for Muslim thought, to which we will return below. The third phase, which I would like to examine more closely, was characterized by a gradual formalization of legal thought, culminating in the emergence of the famous four schools of law around the middle of the fourth/tenth century.[42] Because of its proximity to the Prophet, legal reasoning at the time of *ṣaḥāba* did not involve the formal process later developed by jurists. It was only with increasing distance that the need to record and systematize the process of legal reasoning was recognized. Therefore, scholars in the *ḥadīth* tradition began to collect and thematically arrange the Sunnah of the Prophet and to record the legal opinions and practices of the *ṣaḥaba*. This "textualization"[43] of legal thought was the first step in the development of a scholarly discipline that was no longer exclusively devoted to the practical task of establishing legal norms but began to reflect theoretically on the sources of legal reasoning and judicial decision-making. Faced with new questions, it became necessary to justify the various legal opinions and to show how one had arrived at one or another opinion and on what sources one had relied on.

[41] Quoted in 'Abd al-Wahhāb Khallāf, *'Ilm Uṣūl al-Fiqh* (Cairo: Maktabat Dār al-Turāth, 1956), 21.
[42] See Christopher Melchert, *The Formation of the Sunni Schools of Law, 9th–10th Centuries* C.E. (Leiden: Brill, 1997).
[43] Wael B. Hallaq, *The Origins and Evolution of Islamic Law* (Cambridge: Cambridge University Press, 2005), 66.

The problem of how to deal with new legal questions initially gave rise to two main methodological currents. The first, rationalist current, known as *ahl al-ra'y*, described as jurists those who, in their search for answers to new legal questions, had transmitted only a few *aḥadīth* (plural of *ḥadīth*) of the Prophet and were more inclined to judge the new legal questions from the point of view of reason. The second, traditionalist current, known as *ahl al-ḥadīth*, attached special importance to the *ḥadīth* tradition and argued that new legal cases should be answered exclusively by referring to the sayings of the Prophet, in addition to the Qur'an.[44] The conflict between these two schools of thought quickly led to the realization that the Qur'an and the Sunnah were only limited sources for new legal questions and could not provide a basis for dealing with or anticipating all social events and problems.[45] This realization would soon give rise to an ambitious scholarly discipline aimed at developing methods for providing consistent answers to new legal questions. The scholars who engaged in this discipline were called *fuqahā'*. All *fuqahā'* had disciples with whom they discussed legal questions and various approaches to answering them, initially in teaching circles. It was not uncommon for scholars to join several teaching circles in search of knowledge.[46] In the period 80 to 250 (700 to 865), several jurists from these circles established themselves as leading figures in their field through their *ijtihād* and were able to gain a large intellectual following. Among these scholars were Abū Ḥanīfa (d. 150/767), al-Thawri (d. 161/777), Mālik (d. 179/795), Awzā'i (d. 157/773), Abū Yūsuf (d. 182/798), al-Shaybāni (d. 189/804), al-Shāfi'i (d. 204/819), and Abū Thawr (d. 240/854), to name a few.

The appearance of these and many other figures also marked the beginning of the *first moment* of belief in authority in Islamic legal history. For here, too, the appeal to authority was initially only a matter of confirming one's own opinion by referring to recognized scholars without losing one's intellectual independence. All scholars had disciples who developed

[44] For a detailed account, see Muhammad Kalisch, "Vernunft und Flexibilität in der islamischen Rechtsmethodik" (PhD diss., TU Darmstadt, 1997), 74–85.

[45] Khallāf, *'Ilm Uṣūl al-Fiqh*, 58.

[46] "On adopting a particular method, each jurist gathered around him a certain following who learned their jurisprudence and method from him. Yet, it was rare that a student or a young jurist would restrict himself to one circle or one teacher, for it was not uncommon for aspiring jurists to attend more than one circle in the same city, and even perhaps several circles. . . . [A]spiring jurists did not confine themselves to circles within one city, but traveled from one region to another in search of reputable teachers. 'Travel in search of knowledge' became an activity indulged in by many, and one of the most impressive features of Islamic scholarship." Hallaq, *Origins and Evolution of Islamic Law*, 153.

independently and produced their own legal opinions and methodologies. Well-known examples are Abū Yūsuf and al-Shaybāni, both of whom were disciples of Abū Ḥanīfa: although they disagreed with 85 percent of his legal decisions, their teachings constitute a large part of Ḥanafi legal doctrine.[47] Jurists such as Ibn Surayj (d. 306/918), Tabari (d. 310/922), Ibn Khuzayma (d. 309/923), and Ibn al-Mundhir (d. 314/928) also held very different views from al-Shāfiʿī, despite their adherence to the Shāfi'i school of law.[48] It is worth noting, however, that none of the scholars to whom a school of law was later attributed ever intended to establish a school of law. As Kalisch notes, a name like Ḥanafi or Shāfi'i initially meant only that the line of succession of a scholar's teachers could be traced back to Abū Ḥanīfa or al-Shāfiʿī.[49]

The fact that none of the scholars, including those whose names are associated with the four Sunni schools of law, ever sought to establish a particular legal school (*madhhab*) raises the question of how and why the schools of law came into being.[50] A short answer to this question is that the formation of schools of law was bound up with the growing need for authority, which brings us to the *second moment* of belief in authority. As we can see from the examples just cited, a large proportion of jurists, despite their individual creativity, tended to attribute their teachings to an authority in order to gain greater recognition for their own views. "By doing so," Hallaq comments, "they could avoid attacks that were the automatic reaction against fissiparous tendencies and could certainly earn immediate recognition once their opinions were put under the aegis of a great jurist."[51] By presenting their own ideas as a mere continuation of the old doctrines, they were also able to introduce new legal doctrines without creating an obvious rupture with the past. This was not done to deceive. Rather, it was based on the pragmatic consideration that opinions that can claim continuity with an authoritative doctrine have a stronger claim to legitimacy than those that mark a clear break with the past.

47 Mumisa, *Islamic Law*, 150.

48 See Hallaq, "Was the Gate of Ijtihad Closed?," 10. Tabari even went so far as to establish his own legal methodology.

49 Kalisch, *Vernunft und Flexibilität in der islamischen Rechtsmethodik*, 86.

50 Said Ramadan, *Islamic Law: Its Scope and Equity* (London: Macmillan, 1961), 83, poses this question and answers it vaguely in terms of the classical concept of consensus. Although he addresses the concept of authority (85), he does not discuss it in detail. For detailed accounts of the role of authority in the development of Islamic law, see Jackson, *Islamic Law and the State*, 73–102; Wael B. Hallaq, *Authority, Continuity and Change in Islamic Law* (Cambridge: Cambridge University Press, 2001); Khaled Abou el Fadl, *Speaking in God's Name: Islamic Law, Authority and Women* (Oxford: Oneworld, 2001).

51 Hallaq, "Was the Gate of Ijtihad Closed?," 11.

Note that authority, in order to be perceived as such, had to have a clear source. This source was a renowned scholar who was elevated to the status of founder of a school through a retrospective process of authority construction. This process involved two steps. First, the alleged founder was detached from the intellectual environment that produced his legal doctrine. (It is well known that none of the scholars credited with outstanding knowledge developed his legal doctrine in a social or intellectual vacuum. For example, the legal doctrine that Abū Ḥanīfa transmitted to his disciples was largely transmitted to him by his own teachers, namely Ibrahīm al-Nakhāʿi [d. 96/714] and Ḥammād b. Abi Sulaymān [d. 120/737], and the same is true of Mālik and al-Shāfiʿi and many others.[52] Nevertheless, the legal doctrine of the supposed founder becomes "independent" in the process of authority construction.) The second step of authority construction consisted in the aforementioned tendency to attribute the intellectual achievements of later jurists to the supposed founder. This is particularly evident in the case of the Ḥanbali school of law, which was founded within a century of the death of its namesake, Ibn Ḥanbal (241/855), who was not a jurist nor did he hand down a legal system, and which can be largely traced back to the teachings of Khallāl (d. 311/923).[53] Thus it was not the actual contributions of the scholars but retrospective processes that conferred the status of founder on one or other of them.[54] The function of the person designated as the founder was to confer legitimacy on a particular legal doctrine, thereby allowing it to generate an aura of authority that ultimately manifested in the formation of the school of law.

While the third phase of Muslim legal thought is characterized by a wide range of legal opinions and *ijtihād*, the *fourth, postformative phase* of schools of law around the middle of the fourth/tenth century marks the beginning of a fundamental transformation in the development of law. After the emergence of the schools of law and the associated development of authoritative structures, Muslim legal thought increasingly confined itself to the achievements of previous generations. Recourse to the Qur'an and Sunnah as sources of legal thought was replaced by the authoritative legal

[52] For a detailed account in the case of the four name-givers, see Hallaq, *Authority, Continuity and Change in Islamic Law*, 26–43.

[53] Hallaq, *Origins and Evolution of Islamic Law*, 160.

[54] The question of why, from among the diversity of legal doctrines and personalities, only a fraction were able to become authoritative legal doctrines cannot be dealt with in detail here. See ibid., 169–172; for jurists whose legal doctrines did not develop into schools of law, see Hallaq, *Authority, Continuity and Change in Islamic Law*, 58–61.

doctrine of the respective school. *Ijtihād*, the use of revelation to derive legal norms, was replaced by *tarjīḥ*, the process of deriving legal norms from the teachings of the schools of law.[55] The voice of revelation was thus silenced and replaced by a historical understanding of law that claimed a monopoly on interpretation. With the aim of defending the doctrines of its own school, legal thought increasingly concentrated on the mechanical reproduction of old legal doctrines and gradually fell into a phase of intellectual dependence. The primary manifestation of the growing importance of the schools of law was the practice of commentary, which henceforth limited the role of the jurist to merely interpreting and explaining the great phenomena of the past. This practice, as al-Alwani notes, led to literal chains of commentaries, in which even the commentaries themselves were explained and explanations were resummarized: "[S]tudies were confined to a few specific textbooks, commentaries on those textbooks, commentaries on the commentaries, and annotations on the commentaries on the commentaries."[56] The task of the jurist thus became largely one of collecting, explaining, and summarizing legal opinions and judgments within his own school of law. Ibn Rushd (Averroes) (d. 595/1198) used the following analogy to describe the role of the jurist:

> We find the (so-called) jurists of our time believing that the one who has memorized the most legal opinions has the greatest legal acumen. Their view is like the view of one who thought that a cobbler is he who possesses a large number of shoes and not one who has the ability to make them. It is obvious that the person who has a large number of shoes will (some day) be visited by one whose feet the shoes do not fit. He will then have to go back to the cobbler who will make shoes that are suitable for his feet.[57]

Unable to arrive at their own legal insights, legal scholars increasingly confined themselves to the authorities of the past, according them an almost sacred status.[58] It became accepted wisdom in the scholarly community that

[55] Kamali, *Principles of Islamic Jurisprudence*, 501.
[56] Al-Alwani, *Issues in Contemporary Islamic Thought*, 108.
[57] Abū al-Walīd Muḥammad Ibn Aḥmad Ibn Rushd, *Bidāyat al-Mujtahid wa Nihāyat al-Muqtaṣid* (Beirut: Dār al-Maʿrifa, 2000), 3:254; translation adopted with slight amendments from Ibn Rushd, *The Distinguished Jurist's Primer*, trans. Imran Ahsan Khan Nyazee (Reading: Garnett, 2006), 2:233. A similar analogy from the Muslim legal literature compares those who merely collect legal opinions and memorize them to pharmacists who merely collect medicines without being able to diagnose a disease.
[58] Hofmann, *Religion on the Rise*, 45n33, refers to this as the "*Qala-qala-qala* syndrome (he-says-he-says)."

independent legal thinkers lacked the expertise to make the right decisions when it came to interpreting the law. As a result, legal thought became increasingly dogmatic and unfolded exclusively within the four schools of law. The schools of law thus became the sole source of legitimacy, while independent legal reasoning became increasingly suspect: "Whoever claims to be able to form his own opinions today will be rejected and ignored, because Muslims today only follow the tradition of one of the four schools."[59] This trend was further reinforced by the development of a terminology that helped the schools of law to delegitimize dissenting opinions. Opinions that deviated from the accepted legal doctrine of a school were classified as false (*fāsid*), weak (*ḍaʿīf*), deviant (*shādh*), or unusual (*gharīb*).[60] The development of such terminology ultimately served to reduce the diversity of views to a single, authoritative opinion. To borrow a term from Abou el Fadl, one might appropriately call this a form of "interpretative despotism."[61] We can also draw on an observation by Schopenhauer, who brilliantly reconstructs how such an interpretive despotism, in which independent thinkers are forced to accept a supposedly universally valid opinion, comes into being:

> We should find that it is two or three persons who, in the first instance, accepted it, or advanced and maintained it; and of whom people were so good as to believe that they had thoroughly tested it. Then a few other persons, persuaded beforehand that the first were men of the requisite capacity, also accepted the opinion. These, again, were trusted by many others, whose laziness suggested to them that it was better to believe at once, than to go through the troublesome task of testing the matter for themselves. Thus the number of these lazy and credulous adherents grew from day to day; for the opinion had no sooner obtained a fair measure of support than its further supporters attributed this to the fact that the opinion could only have obtained it by the cogency of its arguments. The remainder were then compelled to grant what was universally granted, so as not to pass for unruly persons who resisted opinions which every one accepted, or pert fellows who thought themselves cleverer than any one else. Now the affirmation became an obligation. When opinion reaches this stage, adhesion becomes a duty; and henceforward the few who are capable of forming a judgment

[59] Ibn Khaldūn, *Muqaddimat Ibn Khaldūn*, 3:951.
[60] On the development of this terminology, see Hallaq, *Authority, Continuity and Change in Islamic Law*, 121–165.
[61] Abou el Fadl, *Speaking in God's Name*, 92.

hold their peace. Those who venture to speak are such as are entirely incapable of forming any opinions or any judgment of their own, being merely the echo of others' opinions; and, nevertheless, they defend them with all the greater zeal and intolerance. For what they hate in people who think differently is not so much the different opinions which they profess, as the presumption of wanting to form their own judgment; a presumption of which they themselves are never guilty, as they are very well aware.[62]

The Separation of Intellectual and Political Authority

In the previous section, we examined the question of the stagnation of the development of Islamic law. Our thesis was that the stagnation was due to the phenomenon of belief in authority, which includes the moments of intellectual confirmation, intellectual legitimation, and intellectual dependence. In order to outline how the belief in authority arose, we first identified four distinct phases in the development of Islamic law and were able to establish that the belief in authority had relatively early roots in the Islamic intellectual tradition. Furthermore, we found that it was only after a gradual process of authority construction that Muslim legal thought lapsed into a state of intellectual dependency or a *taqlīd* mentality expressed in blind adherence to the schools of law. The postformative phase of the legal schools thus represents the final major phase in the substantive development of Islamic law. The question remains, however, why the need for authority played such an important role in the formation of Islamic law. Although we have been able to reconstruct the development of Muslim legal thought, we still need to ask why its development took this path and not another one.

The answer emerges when we consider a phenomenon that Abū Sulaymān aptly calls the separation of intellectual and political authority (*infiṣām bayna al-qiyāda al-fikriyya wa'l-qiyāda al-siyāsiyya*).[63] This refers to the process by which the religious intelligentsia (*'ulamā'*) became detached from the political leadership, which began at the beginning of the third phase with the rise to power of the Umayyad dynasty. The Umayyads, known for their despotic and arbitrary exercise of power, were able to assert their claim to

[62] Arthur Schopenhauer, *The Art of Controversy*, trans. T. Bailey Saunders (University Park: Penn State Electronic Classics Series, 2005), 32–33.

[63] See Abū Sulaymān, *Azmat al-'Aql al-Muslim* (Herndon, VA: International Institute of Islamic Thought, 1991), 47.

power only after fierce power struggles, which resulted in the division of the Muslim community into different political factions. In their attempt to legitimize their rule, the rulers quickly realized that they needed the support of the religious intelligentsia, which enjoyed a high level of social recognition due to its competence in religious and legal matters.[64] The religious intelligentsia, on the other hand, was wary of getting involved in power politics and distanced itself from the rulers in order to maintain its independence from the state, which led to a split in the leadership of the Muslim community into two parties. *Two types of authority* emerged, each claiming a different sphere. On the one side, there was the political authority of the rulers, who possessed coercive power and exercised effective control over the population. On the other side, there was the moral authority of the religious intelligentsia, which enjoyed high standing among the population on account of its expertise in religious and legal matters, while at the same time being able to confer the religious legitimacy that the political leadership needed to defend its power against competing claims. Of particular importance, in addition to this competence, was the fact that the religious intelligentsia possessed an epistemic authority that entitled it to determine right and wrong, or in other words, to define the law. Thus, legal authority was not vested in the state but in the hands of the *'ulamā'*.

This is an important observation, because we can draw two basic conclusions from it, one formal and one substantive. The formal conclusion is that Islamic law developed independently of the state. Whereas in other legal cultures, law developed out of the political system, the state played virtually no role in the development of Islamic law. Against this background, the question arises as to why the concept of authority played such an important role in the development of Islamic law. Since the legal authority did not lie with the state, there was an authority vacuum that had to be filled by the emergence of an alternative source of authority. This alternative source was found in the institution of the legal school, which, as already described, emerged from a gradual process of authority construction. As Hallaq observes:

> Islamic law did not emerge out of the machinery of the body politic, but rather arose as a private enterprise initiated and developed by pious men who embarked on the study and elaboration of law as a religious activity.

[64] Hallaq, *Origins and Evolution of Islamic Law*, 180.

> Never could the Islamic ruling elite, the body politic, determine what the law was. This significant fact clearly means that, whereas in other legal cultures the body politic was the source of legal authority and power, in Islam this body was largely, if not totally, absent from the legal scene. The rise of doctrinal schools was the compensation, the alternative solution. The lack of governmental legal authority and power [was] made up for by the evolution and full emergence of the *madhhab*, an entity which came to possess even greater legal authority than that produced in other cultures by the body politic.[65]

The phenomenon of separation of authority thus allows us to establish a link between the role of authority and the development of Islamic law. On closer examination, however, a second, more substantive conclusion can be drawn that is instructive with respect to the substantive development of Islamic law. Looking at the relationship between the religious and political leadership, we see that the latter, in its quest to legitimize its power and gain legal influence, pursued a strategy of integrating the religious intelligentsia into the political process. This provoked the resistance of the *'ulamā'*, who sought to protect the integrity of Islam from state intervention.[66] The refusal of religious intellectuals to occupy state positions often led to their oppression and torture,[67] which created a general aversion to the political system among them, which, as Mumisa notes, was reflected in their works: "What one discovers

[65] Ibid., 204. For a deeper examination of this topic, see, more generally, Jackson, *Islamic Law and the State.*

[66] Kamali, *Principles of Islamic Jurisprudence*, 502–503 notes, "[T]he development of uṣūl was influenced by the rift over legitimacy between the *'ulamā'* and rulers. While the *'ulamā'* refused to acknowledge to the rulers the authority to legislate and interpret the *Sharī'ah*, the rulers denied the *'ulamā'* a share in political power. The fact, for example, that Imam al-Shāfi'ī wrote so strongly against *istiḥsān* [a method of legal reasoning based on equity] and equated it with caprice and arbitrary tampering with Sharī'ah was designed partly to deny the political rulers the opportunity to circumvent the *nuṣūṣ* [religious source text] and *ijmā'* [judicial consensus] on grounds of political expediency and preference."

[67] "The strategy of the new political leadership was to contain the religious intelligentsia and to force its members to do as they were told by applying increasing amounts of pressure. Thus the lot of the great Ulama, especially those four who founded the schools of legal thought, consisted of torture and exemplary punishment. Imam Abū Ḥanīfah (d. 150/767) died in prison because he refused to accept a position as a judge in a regime that was not committed to Islam. . . . Imam Mālik (d. 175/795) . . . was so badly beaten that his hand was paralyzed. Likewise, Imam Aḥmad Ibn Ḥanbal (d. 241/855) was forced to undergo a great deal of suffering for his opposition to the political ambitions of those in power. Imam al Shāfi'ī (d. 204/820) was forced to flee from the authorities in Baghdad after he was brought there in chains from Yemen. Finally, he had to take refuge in Egypt, far from the center of power." Abū Sulaymān, *Crisis in the Muslim Mind*, 25–26. Further examples of jurists who were subjected to torture can be found in Abou el Fadl, *Speaking in God's Name*, 70n20 and Hallaq, *Origins and Evolution of Islamic Law*, 180–181.

from a thorough study of the lives and histories of the founders of the schools of jurisprudence is that they all distanced themselves from contemporary rulers and developed their ideas in an atmosphere of abstraction. Few of them, if any, developed a very meaningful political theory, not because they lacked in political understanding, but because they did not want to have anything to do with the political establishment. For this reason, one can hardly find in their writings any detailed discussion on political science."[68]

The religious intelligentsia's aversion to politics led them devote themselves to the study of religious texts, focusing almost exclusively on ritual norms and that part of interpersonal relations that did not concern politics and the norms of government. The public sphere of interpersonal relations—that is, matters of government and politics—was increasingly neglected. Concepts such as the state,[69] community, society, and the public became increasingly irrelevant, and interest in developing norms and institutions of government waned. As Abū Sulaymān observes, "[A]s their political isolation grew, they [scholars] began to shun all but academic pursuits, and taught and wrote on the most personalized aspects of the texts of the Qur'an and the Sunnah, such as worship and transactions, and ignored issues related to politics, government, social organization, and the general nature of the group and society."[70]

This lack of interest is also reflected in the division of scientific disciplines into religious and nonreligious sciences. While the science of Qur'an exegesis (*'ilm al-tafsīr*), the science of *ḥadīth* (*'ilm al-ḥadīth*), and the so-called science of Kalām[71] (*'ilm al-kalām*), as well as Arabic studies, virtue ethics, Sufism, and private law were developed, public law, and especially constitutional law, suffered complete neglect. As Weiss comments on the situation, "A cursory look at the chapter headings of a typical *fiqh* work and at the number of pages encompassed by the various chapters reveals a striking feature of Muslim juristic doctrine, namely the far greater attention and care given to matters of private law than to matters of public law. In the realm of private

68 Mumisa, *Islamic Law*, 158–159.

69 The term "state" (Arabic: *dawla*) was reduced to its literal meaning, namely "transformation." When used with reference to politics, it means "period of government" or period of rule or dynasty. Thus one speaks of *dawlat al-khulafā' al-rāshidīn* (Dynasty of the [four] Rightly Guided Caliphs) or of *al-dawla al-amawiyya* (Umayyad dynasty).

70 Abū Sulaymān, *Crisis in the Muslim Mind*, 36–37.

71 Kalām is the scholarly discipline that is concerned with the rational justification of the Islamic faith. See 'Ali Sāmi al-Nashshār, *Nash'at al-Fikr al-Falsafi fī al-Islām* (Cairo: Dār al-Ma'ārif, 1977), 1:48.

law the jurists strove to be as comprehensive as possible. The drive toward comprehensiveness is not evident in the discussions of public law matters."[72]

Because of the split between moral and political authority, and the resulting rift between the religious and political leadership, Muslim thought remained underdeveloped in the social and political sciences and tended to focus instead on the spiritual and ritual sciences. Al-Alwani provides an apt description of this state of affairs: "I know of no specialized studies in our classical legacy that could be described today as political thought, or as treatises on political systems, international relations, systems of government, the history of diplomacy, political development, methods of political analysis, political theory, political planning, or any of the other categories currently studied as part of contemporary knowledge."[73] This explains, among other things, why Muslim thought was unable to formulate elaborate concepts of justice, equality, and freedom within a sociopolitical framework. In the Muslim intellectual tradition, these issues have tended to be approached from a metaphysical perspective, for example, in the context of the question of divine justice, human equality before God, or human free will. Similarly, there is no elaborate social scientific discussion of the concept of human rights in the Muslim intellectual tradition. While Muslim thought was increasingly confined to the private sphere, social and political affairs fell under the jurisdiction of the political leadership. It is not surprising, therefore, that the legal practice of states in the Islamic world was largely despotic and dictatorial in nature.

Legal Understanding between Text and Context

In our systematic study of the Islamic *sharīʿa*, we defined Islamic law formally as a subsystem within the Islamic system of norms. In the differentiation of Islamic law, we identified the feature that distinguishes it from the other subcategories of the Islamic *sharīʿa*—namely, that Islamic law is a mutable and thus an open system due to its dependence on geographical and historical contexts. In a longer historical excursus, we examined several factors that were formative for the formal and substantive development of Muslim legal thought and that ultimately led to the stagnation of the Islamic legal

[72] Weiss, *Spirit of Islamic Law*, 173.

[73] Al-Alwani, *Issues in Contemporary Islamic Thought*, 229. A similar criticism is voiced by ʿAbd al-Majīd al-Sharfī, *al-Islam bayn al-Risāla wa'l-Tarīkh* (Beirut: Dār al-Talīʿa, 2008), 154–155.

system. The term "stagnation" refers to the standstill or "nonadvancement" of a process (Lat. *procedere*, to proceed or advance). Thus, when we say that Islamic law has stagnated, we mean that a process that was initially in motion came to a halt and ended up in a state of stasis. We have deconstructed this final state in an attempt to show that the Islamic legal tradition is simply the historically and culturally shaped product of a suspended process of normative derivation carried out at a particular time by particular individuals for a particular society. In light of this, we must ask how we should deal with the Islamic legal tradition. What should we understand by the term "Islamic law" today? What exactly do we mean when we speak of Islamic law? Indeed, we must go so far as to ask whether Islamic law exists at all in a unified or definitive form—and if so, what is its normative content?

One approach to answering these questions is to take the Islamic legal tradition as a starting point. According to this approach, Islamic law consists of a collection of precedents and legal decisions formulated by the four schools of jurisprudence, all of which are considered timeless and treated as if they were legal texts. According to this view, Islamic law consists of clearly established and immutable positive decrees that can be implemented without further ado. This view is thus based on an objectivist or ahistorical understanding of Islamic law, in that it grants an inviolable status to the legal corpus that has evolved over centuries and rejects any changes to this historically evolved model. In what follows, we will refer to this as a *static conception of* Islamic law. According to Kalisch, this view is "widespread especially among ordinary people and scholars with inadequate theological training."[74] For the latter "Shari'ah in its traditional form is divine truth itself, just as it is, and in this capacity it is timelessly evident and eternally binding."[75] For such Muslims, Asad notes, any deviation from this model would mean the loss of Islamic authenticity: "Their minds seem to work on the supposition that our recent past was 'Islamic'; and that, therefore, everything that implies a departure from the conventions of our yesterday—both with regard to our social customs and our approach to problems of law—goes against Islam."[76] This notion of authenticity obviously ignores the fact that most traditional norms are inextricably linked to the historical, social, cultural, and political

[74] Kalisch, *Vernunft und Flexibilität in der islamischen Rechtsmethodik*, 5.

[75] Rotraud Wielandt, "Menschenwürde und Freiheit in der Reflexion zeitgenössischer muslimischer Denker," in Schwartländer, *Freiheit der Religion*, 204.

[76] Muhammad Asad, *This Law of Ours and Other Essays* (Kuala Lumpur: Islamic Book Trust, 2000), 12.

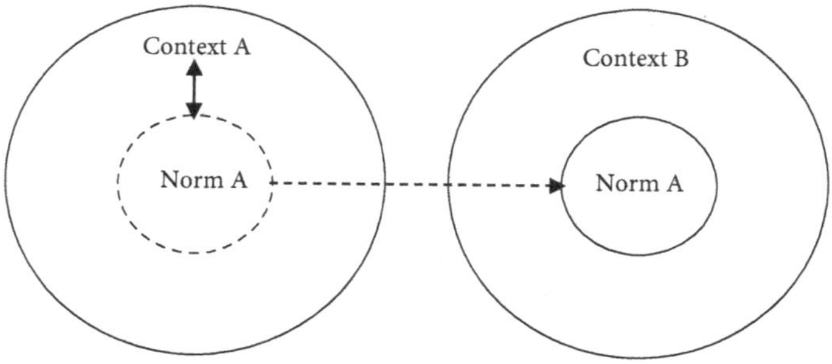

Figure 3.3 Static understanding of law.

conditions in which they were established. They are products of their time and served to provide answers to a particular social and geographical reality that differs substantially from today's. Figure 3.3 provides a visual representation of this state of affairs, in which the interdependence of norm and context (represented by the dashed circle) is canceled out by the norm's becoming autonomous (represented by the solid circle), now asserting a context-independent normativity. The static understanding of Islamic law is thus based on the paradoxical attempt to universalize a local and temporal context. This is tantamount to "attempting to recreate the past within the present without exploring the nature of world historical and social change."[77]

As Mumisa observes, "For the *fuqaha* and writers of these texts, their interpretations of the *Qur'an* and *Sunnah* were an attempt at finding answers for people of their times and not for tomorrow's people and future problems. The re-interpretation of the *Qur'an* and *Sunnah*, therefore, is a challenge which every Muslim society and generation must face since no act of interpretation of Islamic law or any legal system can anticipate solutions for concrete cases which might arise in the future of a society, in perpetual change."[78] In the same context, Nyazee notes, "[T]here is no reason to believe that the last and final word on Islamic law was said several centuries ago and that the legal doctrines developed by the earlier jurists have to be uncritically maintained, *in toto*, by the present generation of Muslims. Every generation, notwithstanding its reverence for its ancestors, has to carry its own cross; has to fall back on its own brain power to solve its problems."[79] Do these remarks

[77] Taha Jabir al-Alwani and Imad al Din Khalil, *The Qur'an and the Sunnah: The Time-Space Factor* (Herndon, VA: International Institute of Islamic Thought, 1991), 26.

[78] Mumisa, *Islamic Law*, 6.

[79] Nyazee, *Theories of Islamic Law*, vii. Iqbal formulates the same concern in similar terms: "The teaching of the Qur'an that life is a process of progressive creation necessitates that each generation,

imply that the Islamic legal tradition is of no importance for the contemporary understanding of Islamic law and can simply be set aside? Certainly not. But the benefit we can derive from the Islamic legal tradition depends on how we approach it. The static approach resembles a museum in which the curator merely stores and displays ancient artifacts in order to preserve the inherited tradition; how and why they came to be is of no interest to the curator. The result is a descriptive understanding of Islamic legal tradition that preserves the façade of Islam's heyday; it reflects a romantic view of the past that lacks practical relevance to the present.

A more fruitful approach, therefore, would be to develop a constructive understanding of the Islamic legal tradition, which entails elaborating the basic principles and higher purposes of the Islamic legal system by situating existing norms in their respective historical and geographical contexts of emergence. Our conceptualization of Islamic law must therefore be based on a *dynamic conception*, which presupposes that Islamic legal norms must be seen as contingent on certain circumstances. According to this conception, Islamic law contains norms that are based on timeless principles but which "may need to be modified under changed circumstances, since the crucial issue is not the individual regulation but the timeless legal idea that underlies it."[80] This applies not only to the norms of historically conditioned legal doctrines but also to the norms of the Qur'an and the Sunnah that pertain to the sphere of interpersonal relations. "We need to acknowledge," Mumisa points out, "that there is a time-space gap not only between us and the classical interpretations, but just as much between us and the *Qur'an* itself. We can't just read the *Qur'an* and understand what we see, because of the gap that divides past and present."[81] This remark is particularly important because many Muslims associate the idea of *ijtihād* with the notion that one can reinterpret religious source texts without critical reference to history. Although this understanding of *ijtihād* postulates an unfettered recourse to the Qur'an and the Sunnah, it takes its orientation from the external wording of the text and is therefore no less static in its *understanding* of the sources than the understanding of Islamic law described above.

guided but unhampered by the work of its predecessors, should be permitted to solve its own problems." Iqbal, *The Revival of Religious Thought in Islam*, 134.

80 Kalisch, *Vernunft und Flexibilität in der islamischen Rechtsmethodik*, 6.
81 Mumisa, *Islamic Law*, 38.

It is undisputed among Muslims that every norm from the Qur'an and Sunnah "is to be regarded as the best regulation at the time and under the concrete circumstances of the revelation or the decree of the Prophet."[82] Problems arise, however, when "circumstances change as a result of changes in time and place, resulting in a changed situation."[83] In this case, the fundamental question arises as to whether a norm retains its claim to validity or not. If we assume that every norm is based on a timeless legal idea, a *ratio legis*, whose realization depends on the existence of certain circumstances, then the norm's claim to validity can be maintained only under the circumstances that lead to the realization of the *ratio legis*. If those circumstances cease to exist, the norm loses its claim to validity and must be modified on the basis of its *ratio legis*. Therefore, it is crucial to understand the purpose of the norm and to find a rule under changed conditions that corresponds to this purpose, even if it contradicts the wording of the Qur'an.[84] "In other words, the legal ruling applied depends upon the particular situation. However, if the circumstances change, it is senseless to insist on maintaining an irrelevant ruling. Rather, a new ruling that takes into account the new conditions must be sought."[85] With regard to the nature of Islamic legal norms, this also implies that they are not fixed but are constantly evolving in tandem with social and historical change, so that their supratemporal legal objective can be realized in a given context despite changing circumstances (Figure 3.4).[86]

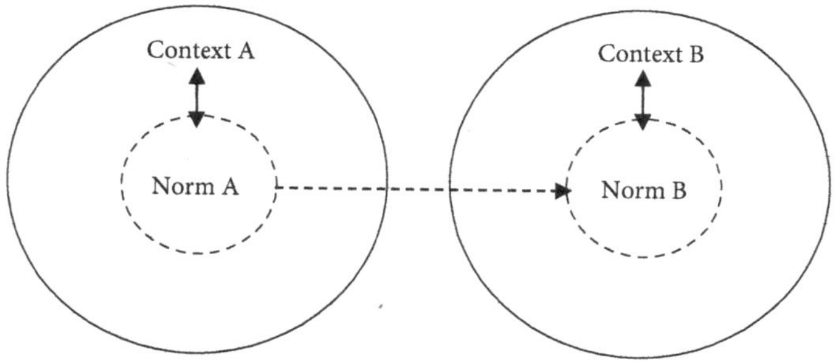

Figure 3.4 Dynamic understanding of law.

[82] Kalisch, *Vernunft und Flexibilität in der islamischen Rechtsmethodik*, 5.
[83] Ibid.
[84] Ibid.
[85] Abū Sulaymān, *Crisis in the Muslim Mind*, 52.
[86] In this sense, Fazlur Rahman emphasizes, "[T]he process of questioning and changing a tradition—in the interests of preserving or restoring its normative quality in the case of its

Thus the dynamic conception makes an inference from the universal and timeless level to the local and temporal context, and not vice versa. The question of the normative content of Islamic law must therefore be answered by looking at the timeless legal idea(s) that underlie the particular legal norms. We will address this issue in detail in a later part of the book in the discussion of the "purposes of Islamic law" (*maqāṣid al-sharīʿa*). In what follows, we will first offer a systematic reconstruction of Muslim human rights discourse on the basis of the static and dynamic conceptions of Islamic law identified here.

normative elements—can continue indefinitely and . . . there is no fixed or privileged point at which the predetermining effective history is immune from such questioning." Fazlur Rahman, *Islam and Modernity: Transformation of an Intellectual Tradition* (Chicago: University of Chicago Press, 1982), 11.

PART II

RECONSTRUCTING THE MUSLIM DISCOURSE ON HUMAN RIGHTS

In what follows, I will analyze how Muslim thinkers, ideologues, researchers, and scholars approach the issue of human rights. In particular, I will examine how different Muslim voices respond to the question of whether Islam and human rights are compatible. Muslim perspectives on the relationship between Islam and human rights are so diverse and complex that it is very difficult to draw a general conclusion on this question. In fact, it is virtually impossible to predict a Muslim's position on human rights based on his or her religious affiliation alone. The fact that I examine only Muslim perspectives on human rights in this section says little about the content of their positions. Thus the reader should not be led to believe that I am offering insight into "the Islamic" position on human rights. Rather, my aim is to provide an overview of the diversity of contemporary Muslim perspectives on human rights. This should always be kept in mind, especially since some authors claim to speak for all Muslims. Fred Halliday puts it well when he writes, "In confronting what is said by governments, individual writers or organizations, one has to take them in their specific context and not assume that they speak for an Islamic world, or tradition, or that theirs is the only possible, or legitimate, interpretation of the religion. We are dealing with a diversity of views and interpretations not a single body of thought. . . . The claim that those invoking Qoran and *shari'a* in some way represent, or speak for, the Islamic world is simply false."[1]

Different Muslim thinkers also have very different educational backgrounds and spheres of activity, which offer a plurality of methodological approaches and, accordingly, different perspectives. It has become quite common in the literature to distinguish between Islamists or

[1] Halliday, "Relativism and Universalism in Human Rights," 156.

fundamentalists, traditionalists or conservatives, modernists or reformers, and secularists or liberals. As these terms suggest, much of the scholarship on Islam and human rights is hampered by conceptual vagueness and the desire to apply concepts informed by a European perspective to non-European processes, with the result that these concepts can mean anything and nothing at the same time. Moreover, it remains open what criteria should be used to distinguish the various positions. Without going into these (rather serious) problems in more detail, I will follow Fred Halliday's approach and distinguish the various positions according to their *argumentative stances*:[2]

1. *Rejection*: the argument that human rights do not conform to Islam and must therefore be rejected.
2. *Incompatibility*: the view that Islam cannot be reconciled with human rights.
3. *Appropriation*: the view that human rights are valid only "within the framework of the *sharīʿa*."
4. *Assimilation*: the argument that there is no problem in reconciling Islam and human rights.

As we saw in the Part I, a statement about the compatibility of Islam and human rights depends to a significant extent on the underlying conception of Islamic law. In chapter 3, I identified two conceptions of Islamic law, which I called *static* and *dynamic*. In brief, the fundamental difference between these two conceptions is that the former rejects a critical, historical view of the Islamic legal tradition and takes Islamic law in its traditional form as given, while the latter adopts a contextual perspective and assumes that Islamic law is capable of development. In what follows, I will systematize these positions on human rights on the basis of their underlying conceptions of Islamic law. My hypothesis will be that the more dynamic the conception of Islamic law that informs a position, the more likely it is that Islam can be reconciled with human rights. Thus, with increasing dynamism, the assessment of the compatibility of Islam and human rights changes.

Taking these aspects into account, our systematization leads to the following constellation (see Figure 4.1): The arguments of *rejection* and *incompatibility* presuppose a static conception of Islamic law; both deny that a synthesis of Islam and human rights is possible. The argument of

[2] Ibid., 154–155.

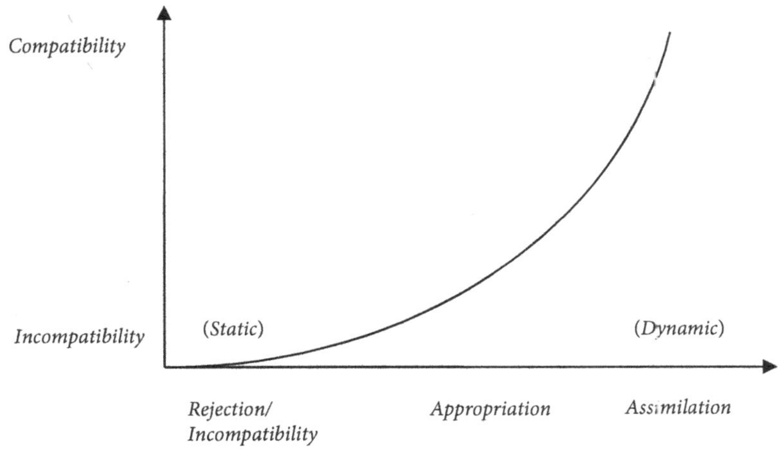

Figure 4.1 Spectrum of compatibility.

appropriation, on the other hand, is based on a quasi-static conception. It sees a chance for a synthesis, but only in those points that do not contradict traditional Islamic law. The argument of *assimilation* starts from a dynamic conception and therefore does not see any contradiction between Islam and human rights. According to this view, any existing contradictions can be eliminated by a new *ijtihād*, since it views legal norms as time-dependent regulations.

So far, this systematization has only listed the different positions without saying anything about their argumentative methods and strategies. Apart from the different methods used by the different positions, it will turn out that there is also a plurality of methodological approaches *within* the positions. These will be discussed in more detail in the sections on the individual positions. By way of illustration, I will discuss how each position deals with the classical problem areas of the Islamic legal tradition, which revolve around the issues of gender equality, the evaluation of corporal punishment (*ḥudūd*), and the problem of religious freedom, especially apostasy (*ridda*). The reason for focusing on these areas rather than others is that they are generally considered to be the classic problem areas of Islamic law that block or complicate the path to acceptance of human rights. It is not my intention to discuss these issues in their own right. I merely use them as examples to illustrate how Muslim positions deal with these conflicts. Thus the presentation is not thematic in the sense that it attempts to analyze the above issues; rather, it focuses on the positions, highlighting the different approaches to the problems and the proposed solutions. Finally, the reader is reminded that this analysis does not and cannot claim to be exhaustive of all Muslim contributions to the human rights discourse, since this would be impossible within the scope of this study. The aim of the following analysis is to provide the reader with a systematic cartography of Muslim positions in the human rights debate, explaining the respective positions by analyzing contributions that *exemplify* a particular argument or approach. The contributions evaluated here therefore serve only as examples.

4

Rejection and Incompatibility

When it comes to the positions of rejection and incompatibility, we are not really dealing with a debate about Islam *and* human rights. It would be more appropriate to call it a debate about Islam *or* human rights. Any attempt to legitimize the concept of human rights from an Islamic perspective would be condemned by both sides, by the former for appealing to Islam and by the latter for advocating human rights. Paradoxical as it may sound, the harshest critics of Islam and its most ardent defenders agree on most points, which is why we will discuss both positions together. Both share the same image of Islam, both are based on the same conception of Islamic law, both deny the possibility of a synthesis of Islam and human rights, and both see Islam as the antithesis of the West.

The rejectionist position dismisses the issue of human rights by stating that Muslims do not need special human rights because they already follow a just order by virtue of their piety: "A Muslim, guided by his true religion, does not need new man-made laws. Allah the Almighty has perfected the religion for us, and completed his blessings and has chosen Islam as our religion. Therefore, whoever goes beyond this is deemed to have diverted from the right path and committed injustice."[1] Any deviation from this ideal is rejected as alien to the system. As Ann E. Mayer observes, "Some Muslims who are opposed to international human rights principles—and, indeed, to any ideas that come from the West—would tend to support the idea that the further an 'Islamic' position diverges from modern, Western norms or the more it resembles the views propounded by premodern Islamic jurists, the closer it comes to representing authentic Islamic doctrine."[2]

[1] In the words of the former Saudi Arabian minister for religious affairs and general secretary of the Muslim World League, Abdulla bin Abdul Mohsin al-Turki, quoted in al-Hageel, *Human Rights in Islam and the Refutation of the Misconceived Allegations Associated with These Rights*, 13.

[2] Ann E. Mayer, "Current Muslim Thinking on Human Rights," in *Human Rights in Africa: Cross-Cultural Perspectives*, ed. Abdullahi An-Na'im and Francis M. Deng (Washington, D.C.: Brookings Institution, 1990), 145.

Human Rights Between Universality and Islamic Legitimacy. Mahmoud Bassiouni, Oxford University Press.
 DOI: 10.1093/oso/9780197753897.003.0005

What is authentically Islamic, according to this view, is everything that is anti-Western. Critics of this position agree with this notion of authenticity and see it as the epitome of Islamic culture. In their view, Muslims are incapable of recognizing human rights because they are held hostage by a religion that is at odds with modernity and its moral values. Fatema Mernissi concludes, "When we speak about the conflict between Islam and democracy, we are in fact talking about an eminently legal conflict. If the basic reference for Islam is the Koran, for democracy it is effectively the United Nations Charter, which is above all a superlaw. The majority of Muslim states have signed this covenant, and thus find themselves ruled by two contradictory laws. One law gives citizens freedom of thought, while the *shari'a* . . . condemns it."[3] While the incompatibility of human rights and Islam is justified on the grounds that the latter is based on a premodern value system, the proponents of the rejectionist position emphasize the cultural relativity of human rights. Not surprisingly, the argument of cultural relativism is usually used by representatives of authoritarian regimes to reject external criticism of internal human rights practices. Reza Afshari is right when he says that "[c]ultural relativists who are active in the politics of their countries are bad human rights advocates."[4] The rejectionist argument is thus purely political, considering human rights as part of an imperialist and ethnocentric project that must be rejected as such. An engagement with the proclaimed confrontation rarely takes place outside this political context.

Apart from the fact that the argument of incompatibility often appears in the political context, it is also and above all part of a discourse that claims to have a social scientific character. In what follows, I will examine the tenability of this claim on the basis of a closer analysis of the argument. To illustrate this position, I will draw on the contribution of Bassam Tibi, who approaches the issue from the perspective of a sociology of religion. First, I will briefly outline Tibi's methodological approach before discussing his thesis of the incompatibility of Islam and human rights in detail.

[3] Fatema Mernissi, *Islam and Democracy: Fear of the Modern World* (New York: Basic Books, 2002), 60.
[4] Reza Afshari, "An Essay on Islamic Cultural Relativism in the Discourse of Human Rights," *Human Rights Quarterly* 16, no. 2 (1994): 273.

The Incompatibility Argument: A Critical Analysis

The Islamic Model for Reality

A characteristic feature of Tibi's approach is the thesis (based on Clifford Geertz's sociology of religion) that every religion, including Islam, is a cultural system. The claim is that religion is constituted by sociocultural symbols that convey an image of reality and construct a plan for dealing with it. However, there is a crucial difference between a "model of something" and a "model for something." The former refers to representations of objects (e.g., in nature), while the latter refers to conceptions of something qua human activity.[5] Models *of* something are concrete because they exhibit a structural correspondence with the represented object, whereas models *for* something are abstract because they refer to human perceptions of reality and its properties. The latter are accessible only through interpretation, not through empirical observation. Accordingly, religion is defined as "(1) a system of symbols which acts to (2) establish powerful, pervasive, and long-lasting moods and motivations in men by (3) formulating conceptions of a general order of existence and (4) clothing these conceptions with such an aura of factuality that (5) the moods and motivations seem uniquely realistic."[6] Religion, according to this definition, is a model for something, that is, a model *for*, rather than a model *of*, reality, that creates motivations that shape people's actions. A religious person who recognizes a divergence between reality and his or her conception of it will experience this as a form of disorder and will seek to restore the order of existence conveyed by the religious symbolic system he or she feels is under threat. Ultimately, according to Tibi, the social change that has taken place cannot be culturally processed.

According to Tibi, "[T]he Islamic religion is unalterable and cannot be adapted to any reality, for it is itself the ultimate religion, revealed by the seal of all prophets."[7] If the ideas conveyed by Islam are inherently unchangeable,

[5] See Clifford Geertz, *The Interpretation of Cultures* (New York: Basic Books, 1973), 93.

[6] Ibid., 90, italicized in original.

[7] Bassam Tibi, *Islam and the Cultural Accommodation of Social Change* (Boulder, CO: Westview Press, 1990), 9. Here Tibi uses the expression "seal of all prophets" (*khatam al-nabiyīn*) (Qur'an 33:40) as proof of Islam's inability to adapt to new social realities. According to Abdullah Yusuf Ali's commentary on the Qur'an, however, this expression implies only that the prophecy has come to an end, which does not exclude later reforms: "When a document is sealed, it is complete, and there can be no further addition. The Holy Prophet Muhammad closed the long line of Messengers. Allah's teaching is and will always be continuous, but there has been and will be no Prophet after Muhammad. *The later ages will want thinkers and reformers, not Prophets.*" Abdullah Yusuf Ali, *The Meaning of the Holy Qur'an* (Beltsville, MD: Amana, 1989), 1069, emphasis added.

even though reality is constantly changing, then, according to Tibi, we must ask ourselves "whether Islam represents an obstacle to change, as it would seem . . . to obstruct rather than facilitate the cultural reception of change."[8] Tibi further argues that Islamic doctrine contains two conflicting notions of development: a forward-looking option that focuses on the future of humanity (the hereafter) and a backward-looking interpretation of history that seeks to restore the early Islamic community of the Prophet after his emigration to Medina in 622. For this world, however, Islam recognizes only the early community of the Prophet as the *communitas perfecta* and the supreme guideline for development. Thus, according to Tibi, the Islamic view of the future is backward-looking because it takes the past reality of the seventh century as the yardstick for all political, social, and economic development (see Figure 4.2).[9] It is this "simultaneity of the non-simultaneous"[10] that Tibi sees as the central problem of Islam.

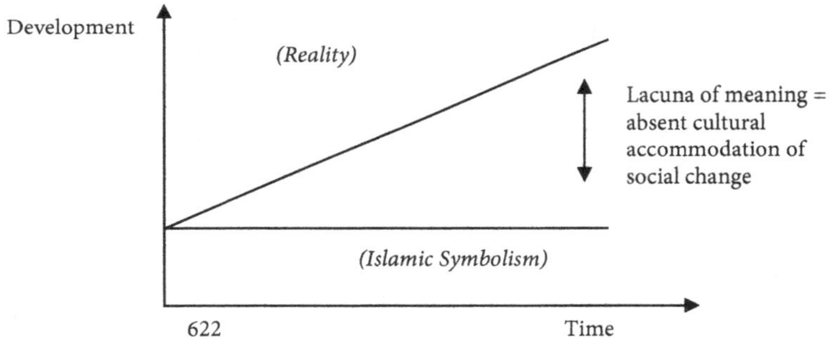

Figure 4.2 The problem of the inability to cope with social change, according to Tibi.

[8] Tibi, *Islam and the Cultural Accommodation of Social Change*, 9.

[9] It is worth noting the contribution of Friedemann Büttner here, who highlights the structural similarities between secular and religious crisis management strategies: "Crisis management strategies always refer at least implicitly . . . to a 'different condition' to be realized in the future. Corresponding models are therefore action-guiding constructs that have a fundamentally similar structure, regardless of whether they have their point of reference in a hypostatized future, like the ideologies of secular modernity, or in an idealized past, like fundamentalist crisis management strategies. Both are *constructs* that are ultimately grounded in religion and serve to politically mobilize people *for an alternative future social reality.* Modernist and fundamentalist attempts at crisis management are functionally equivalent in this respect." Friedemann Büttner, "Der fundamentalistische Impuls und die Herausforderung der Moderne," *Leviathan* 24, no. 4 (1996): 487–488, emphasis in the original.

[10] Bassam Tibi, *Die fundamentalistische Herausforderung: Der Islam und die Weltpolitik* (Munich: Beck, 2002), 49.

As a result, Tibi argues, Islam is unable to process the values of cultural modernity, including democracy and human rights, in terms of its own culture. According to Islamic doctrine, every past, present, and future development is derived from religious sources. Not only are all human actions determined, but all social changes are legitimized through Qur'anic exegesis. Thus God rules the world and directs it according to His will, that is, according to His word as contained in the Qur'an. Islamic law, too, "is divine law revealed by God and [is] not to be conceived of in historical terms," since according to Islamic thought, "it is immutable and eternally valid."[11] Thus Islamic law does not help people to regulate their social relations but serves instead "as an instrument whereby God governs the world."[12] Islamic law thus exacerbates the problems of development, since its fixation on the revealed word of God makes it impossible to adapt to any development. With regard to the guiding assumption that religion can be understood as a model for reality, Tibi concludes that Islam does not offer a new outlook for the future but merely a vision of the future based on a return to the good old days. For Tibi, therefore, the central problem is Islam itself: Muslims cannot cope with cultural change because they cannot change their cultural system, that is, Islam. According to this view, Muslims are prisoners of their own culture and would be acting un-Islamic if they granted themselves a right to resist, since "Islamic doctrine recognizes no such right. The Qur'an (4:59) clearly states: 'O ye who believe! Obey Allah, and obey the messenger and those of you who are in authority.'"[13] According to this interpretation, even a strike would be a form of disobedience forbidden by Islam. Edward Said offers a critical comment on this kind of portrayal of Islam: "If Islam is flawed from the start by virtue of its permanent disabilities, the Orientalist will find himself opposing any Islamic attempts to reform Islam, because, according to his views, reform is a betrayal of Islam.... How can an Oriental slip out from these manacles into the modern world except by repeating with the Fool in King Lear, 'They'll have me whipp'd for speaking true, thou'lt have me whipp'd for lying; and sometimes I am whipp'd for holding my peace.'"[14]

[11] Tibi, *Islam and the Cultural Accommodation of Social Change*, 69.

[12] Ibid., 64.

[13] Tibi, *Im Schatten Allahs*, 62. Ironically, Tibi is as selective in his presentation of Islamic doctrine as the fundamentalists he describes. He rips verses out of their context in the Qur'an in order to lend more authority to his arguments while ignoring verses that contradict his arguments. On the point in question, compare verses 3:79 and 33:67.

[14] Edward Said, *Orientalism* (New York: Vintage Books, 1979), 106.

Islam is described as a more or less uniform system that seems to be defined primarily by opposition to non-Muslims and rejection of their basic values.[15] Thus Tibi like other "Orientalists—from Renan to Goldziher to MacDonald to von Grunebaum, Gibb and Bernard Lewis—[sees] Islam . . . as a 'cultural synthesis' . . . that could be studied apart from the economics, sociology, and politics of the Islamic peoples. . . . The impact of colonialism, of worldly circumstances, of historical development: all these were to Orientalists as flies to wanton boys, killed—or disregarded—for their sport, never taken seriously enough to complicate the essential Islam."[16]

The Incompatibility of Islam and Human Rights

Tibi's central contention is that anyone who adheres to the *sharīʿa* comes into ideological conflict with human rights because Islam and human rights are "like fire and water."[17] Accordingly, only the European tradition of human rights, not *sharīʿa*, can help Muslims integrate into a universally oriented democratic community of values.[18] Tibi rejects the proposal to integrate universal legal norms into Islamic culture on the grounds that they cannot be integrated into the framework of Islamic law because Islam has not developed a concept of the individual subject. Moreover, the religious unity of the *umma* (the Islamic community) forms such a strong collective structure that the idea of a separate individual asserting rights against the state is unthinkable. In support, Tibi cites a statement by Ibn Taimiyya, who died in 1328 but whom he describes as "the leading medieval Islamic jurist to the present day"[19]: "The sultan is the shadow of Allah (*Zhul Allah*) on earth."[20] According to this saying, Tibi argues, a ruler must always be obeyed; to oppose him would be an expression of unbelief. The individual has no rights to which he could appeal against the ruler or the state. All power is vested in the

[15] Dorothee Bölke, "Der islamische Fundamentalismus bei Peter Scholl-Latour, Gerhard Konzelmann und Bassam Tibi," in *Das Schwert des "Experten,"* ed. Verena Klemm and Karin Hörner (Heidelberg: Palmyra, 1993), 227.

[16] Said, *Orientalism*, 105.

[17] Bassam Tibi, "Wie Feuer und Wasser," *Der Spiegel* 3 (1994): 170–172.

[18] Tibi, *Im Schatten Allahs*, 14.

[19] Ibid., 73.

[20] Tibi does not say where this quotation can be found, but simply refers to Ibn Taimiyya's work *al-Siyāsa al-Sharʿiyya* (*Sharīʿa*-Based Politics). However, he apparently considers the quotation from Ibn Taimiyya to be so well known that he scolds a reviewer in his preface for failing to make the connection with the title of his book "In the Shadow of Allah" on the grounds that the reviewer in question had previously claimed that books with "Allah" in their title sell better.

ruler, who in turn receives his power from God.[21] The omnipotence of God is transferred to His governor, and therefore to recognize the existence of any other power would be tantamount to polytheism.

Since, as Tibi claims, the Islamic tradition lacks a conception of the human being as an individual, he asserts that the development of an Islamic notion of human rights is in principle impossible. Instead, he argues for an understanding of the Islamic religion that reduces its influence to the sphere of the inward, since this is the only way to incorporate human rights into Islamic culture. He concludes his argument with a plea for the Europeanization of Islam: "Either Muslims will Islamize Europe or Europe will Europeanize Islam. I repeat: there is no middle way!"[22]

Our initial doubts about the viability of the incompatibility argument are confirmed, if they were not before, by a critical examination of Tibi's argument here. We can temporarily disregard his exclusive reliance on constitutional ideas derived from medieval Muslim jurists to support his argument, because it is not only his selective choice but also his presentation of the literature he cites that is problematic. A closer examination of the quotation on which he bases his argument—"The sultan is the shadow of Allah on earth"—reveals that Tibi misappropriates the quotation. In the eighth section of the second chapter of his work *al-Siyāsa al-Shar'iyya* (on the "Limits and Rights of Human Beings"), Ibn Taimiyya describes the duty of Muslims to appoint a leader. He justifies this by referring to the saying of the Prophet—"When three people set out on a journey, they should appoint one of them as their leader"—and argues that it is necessary to have a person in charge who takes care of the general affairs of a community. At the same time, this person should ensure that the rights of the people are enforced and thus that justice is done. Justice is necessary, he argues, "because we have a divine obligation to enjoin good and forbid evil, which cannot be accomplished without power and authority. . . . This is why it has been narrated that 'the ruler [*ṣulṭān*] is the shadow of God on earth.'"[23] As this quotation makes clear, this metaphor does not come from Ibn Taimiyya himself ("This is why it has been narrated that"). Contrary to Tibi's portrayal, it is also clear that Ibn Taimiyya is not using the metaphor to call for unconditional obedience to a ruler, but

[21] Udo Steinbach, "Die Menschenrechte im Verständnis des Islam," *Verfassung und Recht in Übersee* 8, no. 1 (1975): 48–50.

[22] Tibi, *Im Schatten Allahs*, 508.

[23] Ibn Taimiyya, *al-Siyāsa al-Shar'iyya fī Iṣlāḥ al-Rāʿī w-al-Ra'iyya* (Beirut: Dār al-Afāq al-Jadīda, 1983), 139. The attentive reader will notice a parallel to the Hobbesian theory of the state here.

rather to clarify the duty of the ruler and the state to ensure justice.[24] Thus, as Kassis observes, the term "shadow" takes on a metaphorical protective function in this context.[25] This function becomes apparent when one considers the longer version of the proverb: "The sultan is God's shadow on his earth, in whom every oppressed finds refuge" (*al-ṣulṭān ẓillu-llāhi fī arḍihi ya'wā ilayhi kull maẓlūm*).[26]

Tibi's claim that Islamic jurisprudence has not developed a concept of the subject also proves untenable. For example, Ibn Taimiyya, along with most Islamic legal literature, recognizes that human beings have individual rights. These are generally discussed under the heading "rights of the legal agent" (*ḥaqq al-mukallaf*). Ibn Taimiyya refers to them as *ḥaqq ādamī* or *ḥuqūq al-ādamiyīn*, literally "rights of human beings."[27] One might excuse Tibi's failure to recognize the heterogeneous character of Islamic legal culture. It is ironic, however, that, by arguing from a sociological and anthropological perspective, he elevates himself to an authority on the interpretation of Islam, while categorically branding Muslim authorities (both past and present) as fundamentalists. He speaks from the position of "someone who is totally committed to modernity, who is so confident in his ability to deal with uncertainty and openness that he *himself* becomes the criterion of what is rational: we are the reasonable ones, while the fundamentalists are the irrational ones who deny reality."[28]

[24] In this sense, Ibn Taymiyya's closest disciple, Ibn Qayyim al-Jawziyya (d. 1350/751), applies the metaphor of the shadow to the law, stating that it represents "God's justice among His servants, His mercy towards creation, His shadow on earth." See Ibn Qayyim al-Jawziyya, *A'lām al-Muwaqqi'īn 'an Rabb al-'Ālamīn* (Beirut: Dār al-Kutub al-'Ilmiyya, 1996), 3:11.

[25] Riyadh Aziz Kassis, *The Book of Proverbs and Arabic Proverbial Works* (Leiden: Brill, 1999), 65.

[26] Ibid., 65–66. The protective function of the shadow metaphor is also expressed in the tradition according to which on the Last Day God will say, "Where are those who love one another for the sake of My glory? Today I will protect them in My shade [*al-yawm aẓilluhum fī ẓillī*] when there will be no shade but Mine." See Muḥammad 'Abd al-Fattāḥ, ed., *Mukhtarāt Min Ṣaḥīḥ al-Aḥādīth al-Qudsiyya Ma' al-Arba'īn al-Nawawiyya* (al-Mansura: Dār al-Manāra, 2004), 65–66.

[27] In Arabic, "Adam" is used as a synonym for the human being. See Ibn Taimiyya, *al-Siyāsa al-Shar'iyya*, 60, 123. For the concept of *ḥaqq*, see Muhammed Hashim Kamali, "Fundamental Rights of the Individual: An Analysis of Haqq (Rights) in Islamic Law," *American Journal of Islamic Social Sciences* 10, no. 3 (1993): 340–366.

[28] Büttner, "Der fundamentalistische Impuls und die Herausforderung der Moderne," 474.

5
Appropriation

In contrast to the positions of rejection and incompatibility, the position we will now examine does not categorically reject a synthesis of Islam and human rights. On the contrary, the core claim of the appropriation position is that Islam and human rights are not only compatible, but that human rights can *only* be realized *in Islam*, since they have a religious foundation and are therefore obligatory in character. According to this view, human rights are no longer alien to Islamic culture, but rather an integral part of it, if not an invention of Islam.

This line of argument, and Western attempts to refute it, continue to dominate the Islamic-Western discourse on human rights. This is partly due to the fact that the argument of appropriation has been widely discussed in the Western literature, where it is usually presented as *the* Islamic position on human rights,[1] but also not least because it is represented at the level of international law, with its inclusion in the Universal Islamic Declaration of Human Rights of 1981 and the Cairo Declaration on Human Rights in Islam of 1990. The reactive context in which this argument is presented also contributes to the fact that its underlying motivation is not a substantive engagement with human rights but rather the pressure to formally accept their validity. A closer look at the argument reveals that while it does not deny human rights in principle, it does not grant them unqualified approval either. It might be more accurate to speak of an Islamization of human rights. Instead of rejecting them outright, it integrates human rights into an Islamic framework, more precisely into the classical conception of Islamic law, and thus "redefines" them. It aims to respect the modern conception of human rights (at least in appearance) without rejecting tradition.[2] In what follows,

[1] See, for example, Ann E. Mayer's oft-cited standard work *Islam and Human Rights: Tradition and Politics* (Boulder, CO: Westview Press, 1991), which is based on an analysis of five Muslim contributions to the debate that can be classified as conservative.

[2] See Mohamed Charfi, "Die Menschenrechte im Bezugsfeld von Religion, Recht und Staat in den islamischen Ländern," in Schwartländer, *Freiheit der Religion*, 99–100.

Human Rights Between Universality and Islamic Legitimacy. Mahmoud Bassiouni, Oxford University Press.
 DOI: 10.1093/oso/9780197753897.003.0006

I will examine the success of this strategy through a critical analysis of the main features of the appropriation position.

Human Rights and Copyrights

A typical feature of contemporary Muslim human rights literature is the attempt to support individual human rights norms with quotations from the Qur'an or the Sunnah.[3] Many Muslim scholars and institutions are even keen to emphasize that Islam supported human rights earlier and more effectively than the West. For example, one declaration states that "Islam was the first to recognize basic human rights and almost 14 centuries ago it set up guarantees and safeguards that have only recently been incorporated in the Universal Declaration of Human Rights."[4] Another example is the Universal Islamic Declaration of Human Rights issued by the Islamic Council of Europe in 1981, which begins with the statement "Islam gave to mankind an ideal code of human rights fourteen centuries ago."[5] The following articles are consistently written in such a way that a summary of the relevant right is followed by one or more quotations from the Qur'an or the Ḥadīth. In this way, an attempt is made to demonstrate that human rights were established by Islam long before the Western-inspired human rights discourse, so that from a historical perspective human rights can and should be seen as an Islamic achievement. In this vein, Muḥammad al-Ghazāli refers to human rights as "our property that has been returned to us"[6] and comments, "The

[3] For an overview of the different legal areas and their equivalents in the Qur'an and the Sunnah, see Lise J. Abid, *Menschenrechte im Islam* (Bonn: Huda Schriftenreihe, 2001).

[4] International Commission of Jurists, University of Kuwait, and Union of Arab Lawyers, eds., *Human Rights in Islam: Report of a Seminar Held in Kuwait, December 1980* (Geneva: International Commission of Jursits, 1982), 9.

[5] Examples of such statements could easily be multiplied. Remarkably, they can be found not only in public statements but also in academic articles. See, for example, al-Tāj Ibrāhīm Daf' Allah Aḥmad, "Ḥuqūq al-Insān fī al-Sharī'a al-Islāmiyya fī Ḍaw' Maṣadrīhā al-Qur'ān w-al-Sunnah," *Majallat Kulliyyat al-Tarbiyyah Jām'at al-Azhar* 34, no. 164 (2015): 471: "Islam preceded man-made charters and laws in establishing the principles of human rights and respect for the human personality by guaranteeing freedom of thought, freedom of religion, political freedom, and establishing the principles of consultation, rights, justice and equality among human beings. Islam was the first to establish the principles of human rights in their most complete and comprehensive form."

[6] Muḥammad al-Ghazāli, *Huqūq al-Insān bayna Ta'līm al-Islām wa I'lān al-Umam al-Muttaḥida* (Alexandria: Dār al-Da'wa, 1993), 8. The expression "our property that was returned to us" (*biḍā'atuna ruddat ilaynā*) is taken from verse 12:65 of the Qur'an, which refers to the events in the story of the prophet Joseph. It is also used by Rāshid al-Ghannūshi with regard to the idea of democracy. See *al-Ḥurriyāt al-'Amma fi-l-Dawla al-Islāmiyya*, 88.

principles that we once exported are being exported back to us as if they were a human discovery that we had never known and lived."[7]

Without going into the merits of these claims, I would like to argue that, contrary to what some critics assert,[8] the problem is not so much the absence of human rights in Islamic thought as the tendency toward a "one-sided Islamic occupation of human rights,"[9] which, as Bielefeldt notes, is no less pronounced than Western attempts to essentialize human rights into "Occidental Christian values."[10] Finding evidence of a cultural embedding of human rights is no more problematic in the case of Islam than in the case of Christianity or Confucianism.[11] A problem arises, however, when the cultural embedding of human rights turns into "culturalist claims to exclusivity."[12] Typical of such claims to exclusivity is the attempt to trace human rights back to a particular cultural "root," a metaphor intended to imply that human rights are the apparent "fruits" of a historical maturation that can be understood only in terms of that root.[13] It is then claimed, for example, that human rights have their origin in the biblical narratives and would be inconceivable without the idea that human beings are created in the image of God.[14] Such arguments are based on motifs of cultural identity and carry the danger of normatively and politically motivated retrospective projections. As Dieter Senghaas notes, it is no exaggeration to say "that the implementation of the idea of human rights and the associated idea of the secular state has succeeded in spite of the resistance of the Christian religions and not because of any prescriptions of these religions. To assert the latter would be to turn the actual course of history on its head."[15]

7 Ibid.

8 See Mayer, *Islam and Human Rights*, 54–55.

9 Bielefeldt, *Philosophie der Menschenrechte*, 137.

10 Ibid., 121–129.

11 As Mohamed Charfi notes, "You know, when you support human rights, there is a certain nationalism that comes forward: for an American, human rights are the invention of Jefferson, for a Frenchman it is 1789, for an Englishman it is something else. Well, in these circumstances, I can also cite Omar Ibn al-Khattab, who said, 'How can you enslave people when their mothers brought them into the world free?' So if each human community is going to search in its own history for an origin to human rights, it will always come up with something." Mohamed Charfi, cited in Dwyer, *Arab Voices*, 175. 'Umar Ibn al-Khaṭṭāb was the second Caliph of the Prophet.

12 Bielefeldt, *Philosophie der Menschenrechte*, 127.

13 Heiner Bielefeldt, "Menschenrechtlicher Universalismus ohne eurozentrische Verkürzung," in *Gelten Menschenrechte Universal? Begründungen und Infragestellungen*, ed. Günter Nooke, Georg Lohmann, and Gerhard Wahlers (Freiburg: Herder, 2008), 124.

14 See, for example, Tine Stein, *Himmlische Quellen und irdisches Recht: Religiöse Voraussetzungen des freiheitlichen Verfassungsstaates* (Frankfurt: Campus, 2007), ch. 7.

15 Dieter Senghaas, *Wohin driftet die Welt? Über die Zukunft friedlicher Koexistenz* (Frankfurt: Suhrkamp, 1994), 116.

It is clear that essentialist cultural claims to exclusivity can arise only when modern understandings are read back into history. To illustrate this, consider the abstruse claim that Muslims invented the idea of deliberative democracy and provided the theoretical foundation for discourse ethics, since Islam established the principle of *shūra*, meaning consultation and decision-making, 1,400 years ago. Obviously, the search for possible points of reference for modern thought in one's own tradition is possible only from a modern point of view. As Bielefeldt points out, the same applies to the allocation of human rights in one's own culture:

> *Looking back* from a modern perspective, it is possible to build a bridge between human rights universalism and the biblical notion of creation in God's image or Stoic cosmopolitanism; similarly, analogies to the modern rule of law can be found *retrospectively* in the Magna Charta or other medieval treaties establishing rule; it might also be useful *in retrospect* to compare freedom as a human right with the "freedom of a Christian" proclaimed by the reformers. Thus, neither the idea of creation in the image of God, nor the Stoic proclamation of universal human dignity, nor the Magna Charta, nor the Reformation's sharpened insight into religious freedom is really a "root" of modern human rights in which the potential of human rights was founded once and for all. On the contrary, it is only the modern consciousness of human rights that creates the precondition for the retrospective identification of humanitarian motifs in history, on the basis of which aspects of continuity can be *reconstructed.*[16]

In discussing the origins or emergence of human rights, therefore, it seems more appropriate to consider them as specific responses or reactions to certain historically experienced and recurring threats.[17] As Menke and Pollmann note, it would be impossible to understand the modern idea of human rights without interpreting it explicitly as a response to the experience of the political-moral catastrophe of the Second World War.[18] It is no accident that the preamble to the Universal Declaration of Human Rights speaks of "barbarous acts which have outraged the conscience of mankind." Accordingly, it is not wrong to describe modern human rights as

[16] Bielefeldt, *Philosophie der Menschenrechte*, 128.
[17] For a more in-depth discussion, see chapter 13.
[18] See Christoph Menke and Arnd Pollmann, *Philosophie der Menschenrechte zur Einführung* (Hamburg: Junius, 2007), 11–18.

achievements that "were fought for in protracted political conflicts during the process of modernization in Europe."[19] As such, far from being part of "Europe's original cultural and genetic makeup,"[20] they are the product of a confrontation with historically experienced threats from which institutional consequences were drawn. Recognizing that this process of institutionalization took place largely in Europe does not limit the universal validity of human rights, any more "than the humble rise of Islam in two insignificant desert towns on the edge of the Roman Empire detracted from its consequent universality and sweep."[21] From this perspective, therefore, the claim that Islam invented human rights proves to be a misjudgment. But even from an Islamic theological perspective, the idea that Islam introduced human rights can be shown to be untenable. According to Roger Garaudy, such an attitude contains a triple error: "It ignores the past, previous wisdom and revelation, which are also messages from God; it ignores the future, because it saves us the effort of finding, from eternal principles, ever new solutions to ever new problems that 'God does not stop creating, He who is present in all new things' (Sura 55:29); it ignores the present, because it prevents dialogue in the impoverished certainty that our religion is the best because we are ignorant of the others."[22]

The Sacralization of Human Rights

Along with the origin of human rights, there is considerable disagreement about the philosophical foundation that underpins and justifies them.[23] A characteristic feature of the Muslim justification of human rights is the assumption that rights are granted by God, and by God alone, as the sole legislator.[24] According to this view, every right has its source in Islam as a code of eternal and immutable truths of universal validity. This view is particularly

[19] Senghaas, *Wohin driftet die Welt?*, 112.
[20] Ibid.
[21] Sadik Jalal al-Azm, *Is Islam Secularizable? Challenging Political and Religious Taboos* (Berlin: Gerlach Press, 2014), 8.
[22] Roger Garaudy, "Die Menschenrechte und der Islam: Begründung, Überlieferung, Verletzung," *Concilium* 26 (1990): 127.
[23] For a discussion of different approaches, see Jerome J. Shestack, "The Philosophic Foundations of Human Rights," *Human Rights Quarterly* 20, no. 2 (1998): 201–234, who identifies a total of twelve philosophical "sources" of human rights.
[24] It should be noted that the justification of human rights examined here is characteristic of most Muslim positions that affirm a synthesis of Islam and human rights, not just of the appropriation argument. I will therefore make a critical remark on this once all positions have been reconstructed.

clearly expressed in the Preamble to the Universal Islamic Declaration of Human Rights: "Whereas by virtue of their Divine source and sanction these rights can neither be curtailed, abrogated or disregarded by authorities, assemblies or other institutions, nor can they be surrendered or alienated... we, as Muslims... do hereby... at the beginning of the Fifteenth Century of the Islamic Era, affirm our commitment to uphold the following inviolable and inalienable human rights that we consider are enjoined by Islam."[25]

The idea that human rights have a divine source, which is also shared by other religions,[26] implies first of all that human rights are not something that we have at our disposal and that they do not emerge from a political process. This idea goes along with the argument that rights granted by God that must be observed toward God are in principle more firmly anchored than contractual rights: "Human rights must have a sound basis, a good source, and we believe God is this source. God gives man rights that no one can take away. What parliament decides by a majority of 51 percent today is a right; tomorrow it might not be. Human rights is not a toy to be played with, it needs a warranty and we believe that warranty is God. We differ from others, Muslims and others, because we believe man has rights that do not come from the discussions of intellectuals or parliamentarians, but come from God."[27] Similarly, Mawdudi argues, "When we speak of human rights in Islam, we mean those rights granted by God. Rights granted by Kings or legislative assemblies can be withdrawn as easily as they are conferred, but no individual and no institution has the authority to withdraw the rights conferred by God."[28]

At first glance, these remarks seem only to emphasize the prepolitical character of human rights. However, the problem posed by this conception

[25] Preamble of the Universal Islamic Declaration of Human Rights, September 19, 1981.

[26] See, for instance, Nicholas Wolterstorff, *Justice: Rights and Wrongs* (Princeton, NJ: Princeton University Press, 2008).

[27] Rached Ghannouchi, cited in Dwyer, *Arab Voices*, 41. He expands on this in his *al-Ḥurriyāt al-ʿAmma fi-l-Dawla al-Islāmiyya*, 40–42. Different versions of the same argument can be found in ʿAbd al-Salām al-Tarmānīni, *Ḥuqūq al-Insān fī Nazar al-Sharīʿah al-Islāmiyya* (Beirut: Dār al-Kitāb al-Jadīd, 1976), 19; ʿAlī ʿĪsā ʿUthmān, *Falsafat al-Islām fī al-Insān* (Beirut: Dār al-Adab, 1986), 92–93; Muḥammad ʿImāra, *al-Islām wa Ḥuqūq al-Insān. Ḍarūriyyāt, la Ḥuqūq* (Cairo: Dār al-Shurūq, 2006), 14–15. For more recent articulations, see Badr al-Rashīdī, Muḥammad Fawzy Ḥāmed, and ʿAlī Sājed, "al-Ḥurriyāt wa Ḥuqūq al-Insān bayn al-Islām w-al-Mawāthīq al-Dawliyyah li-Ḥuqūq al-Insān," *Majallat al-ʿUlūm al-Islāmiyya al-Dawliyya* 5, no. 1 (2021): 143–176; Layla al-ʿAqīl, "Ḥuqūq al-Insān fī al-Qurʾān al-Karīm," *Majallat al-ʿUlūm al-Islāmiyya al-Dawliyya* 4, no. 3 (2020): 97–131; Ṣāleḥ Zayd Quṣīla, "Ḥuqūq al-Insān fī al-Tasawwur al-Islāmī w-al-Wāqiʿ al-Insāni," *Majallat al-Ustādh al-Bāḥith li-l-Dirasāt al-Qanūniyya w-al-Siyāsiyya* 4, no. 2 (2019): 674–699.

[28] Abul Aʿla al-Mawdudi, *Human Rights in Islam* (Leicester: Islamic Foundation, 1976), 15.

of human rights becomes apparent when we consider the underlying philosophical premise. It is true that this theocentric conception of human rights does not deny that the establishment and preservation of human rights is a central task of human beings. But the status and associated dignity of human beings is determined solely by the fact that humanity is a divine creation and must be respected as such.[29] Muslims usually support this line of argument with the following passages from the Qur'an:[30]

- "Thy Sustainer said unto the angels: 'Behold, I am about to create a human being out of clay; and when I have formed him fully and breathed into him of my spirit, fall you down before him in prostration!'" (38:71, 72)
- "Thy Sustainer said unto the angels: 'Behold, I am about to establish upon earth one who shall inherit it.' They said: 'Wilt Thou place on it such as will spread corruption thereon and shed blood—whereas it is we who extol Thy limitless glory, and praise Thee, and hallow Thy name?' He answered: 'Verily, I know that which you do not know'" (2:30)
- "Now, indeed, We have conferred dignity on the children of Adam, and borne them over land and sea, and provided for them sustenance out of the good things of life, and favoured them far above most of Our creation." (17:70)
- "Verily, we did offer the trust [*amāna*][31] [of reason and volition] to the heavens, and the earth, and the mountains: but they refused to bear it because they were afraid of it. Yet man took it up." (33:72)

Criticism of the anthropocentrism of human rights does not lead to the rejection of the concept of human rights, but often to the demand that human rights be given a theological foundation.[32] Put in a formula, this means "Divine rights *for* individuals: yes. Rights *of* the individual: no."[33]

[29] An interesting and insightful account of Muslim justifications of human dignity is offered by Rotraud Wieland, "Menschenwürde und Freiheit in der Reflexion zeitgenössischer muslimischer Denker," in Schwartländer, *Freiheit der Religion*, 179–209. For a detailed discussion, see Mohammad Hashim Kamali, *The Dignity of Man: An Islamic Perspective* (Cambridge, UK: Islamic Text Society, 2002).

[30] Unless otherwise stated, all translations of the Qur'an are from Muhammad Asad, *The Message of the Qur'ān* (Bristol: The Book Foundation, 2003).

[31] Muhammad Asad translates the word *amāna* as "reason," "intellect," or "the faculty of volition," that is, as "the ability to choose between two or more possible courses of action or modes of behaviour, and thus between good and evil." Ibid., 732.

[32] Bielefeldt, *Philosophie der Menschenrechte*, 175.

[33] Hofmann, *Religion on the Rise*, 75, my emphasis. The shortcomings of this formula will be discussed below.

The Islamization of Human Rights

What distinguishes the position of appropriation from other Muslim approaches is the tendency to either reject or integrate human rights by juxtaposing them with classical Islamic law. Those human rights that go beyond the framework of the *sharīʿa* are rejected,[34] while those that do not contradict it are redefined and legitimized in Islamic terms. Human rights can thus find their place in the *sharīʿa*, but only as long as they do not contradict it. The *sharīʿa* functions as the exclusive standard for determining the scope and content of human rights.[35] This is particularly evident in the Cairo Declaration of Human Rights, in which the rights to freedom and equality are initially formulated in comprehensive terms but are ultimately limited to "the framework of the *sharīʿa*." Thus, Article 24 affirms, "All the rights and freedoms stipulated in this Declaration are subject to the Islamic Shari'ah."[36] Likewise, the final article, 25 emphasizes, "The Islamic Shari'ah is the only source of reference for the explanation or clarification of any of the articles of this Declaration."[37] The rights contained in the Declaration are therefore subject to a "general clause" which states that the *sharīʿa* remains the ultimate basis for decisions and that, in case of doubt, is superior to any humanly conceived requirement.

Needless to say, some human rights are severely restricted by being forced into the framework of classical Islamic law. Because of their primacy, the provisions of classical Islamic law regarding apostasy (which is punishable by death) and corporal punishment retain their validity. For example, Article 2 of the Cairo Declaration affirms the right to bodily integrity and states that "it is prohibited to take away life except for a Shari'ah-prescribed reason."[38] Article 22 guarantees everyone "the right to express his opinion freely," but only "in such manner as would not be contrary to the principles of the Shari'ah." The same pattern is found in the Universal Islamic Declaration

[34] When I use the term *sharīʿa* in discussing this position, I am referring to the static conception of Islamic law. I use the term because it is commonly used to refer to Islamic law in the debate, to which I am alluding here.

[35] Heiner Bielefeldt, "Muslim Voices in the Human Rights Debate," *Human Rights Quarterly* 17, no. 4 (1995): 605. Sultanhussein Tabandeh even argues that where the Universal Declaration of Human Rights contradicts the *sharīʿa*, it should be rewritten in order to bring it into line with Islam. Sultanhussein Tabandeh, *A Muslim Commentary on the Universal Declaration of Human Rights* (London: F. J. Goulding, 1970).

[36] Cairo Declaration on Human Rights in Islam, August 5, 1990.

[37] Ibid.

[38] Ibid., Article 2.

of Human Rights. The right to life is considered inviolable, even sacred, but with the subsequent limitation that "this sacredness can be touched only by the power of the Shari'ah and the procedures conceded by it."[39] Likewise, the right to freedom "can be restricted or limited by the Shari'ah and the procedures conceded by it."[40] Regarding freedom of opinion, religion, and expression, Article 12 states, "Every man shall have the right to think, believe and express what he thinks and believes without anybody hindering him or intervening, as long as it stays within the framework of the Shari'ah."[41]

The argument of appropriation proves to be particularly detrimental to women's rights, for example in the case of the rules governing legal testimony or those governing marriage and inheritance, as well as in the area of political participation rights. While the Declaration emphasizes that Islam does not distinguish between men and women, and that both are equal before God,[42] a closer look reveals that it does not recognize gender equality at the legal level. Thus while men and women are equal in dignity according to the Declaration, they are unequal in rights. There may be equality before God, but not in the distribution of interpersonal rights and responsibilities. In other words, "for Islam, men and women have the same dignity, but different tasks; they are of the same value, but have different abilities; they are equal before God, but have different roles in life."[43] This view draws on classical Islamic law to defend a notion of humanity that holds that the sexes are unequal[44] and that women are subordinate, mentally and physically weak beings in need of male protection. Proponents of this view claim that the different roles of the sexes in life are a result of their (naturally given) anatomical or physiological differences. Since the female sex has the function of reproducing the human species, it is incumbent upon women to bear and raise children, which means, among other things, that they are also responsible for housework. And since it is the man who is physiologically capable

39 Declaration of Human Rights in Islam, September 19, 1981, Article 1a.

40 Ibid., Article 2a.

41 Ibid., Article 12.

42 Ibid., Article 3b: "Every thought, every legislation, and every situation that justifies discrimination between individuals on the basis of gender, race, color, language, or religion, is a direct impediment to this universal Islamic principle [of equality]"; see also *Cairo Declaration*, Article 1: "All men are equal in terms of basic human dignity and basic obligations and responsibilities, without any discrimination based on race, colour, language, belief, sex, religion, political affiliation, social status or other considerations."

43 Hofmann, *Islam: The Alternative*, 126.

44 The *Islamic Charta* of the Central Council of Muslims in Germany is also subject to this view. Article 13 contains the vague statement "Islamic law demands equal treatment of what is identical and permits unequal treatment of what is not identical."

of heavy physical labor, it is his duty to provide for the family. Accordingly, the unequal legal status of women is derived from these "empirical findings" about the natural differences between the sexes. In fact, some commentators claim that the most important human right of women is the preservation and protection of their chastity,[45] an argument that is mainly used as a justification for denying women a wider range of rights.[46] Riffat Hassan notes, "Many Muslims, when they speak of human rights, either do not speak of women's rights at all or are mainly concerned with the question of how a woman's chastity may be protected. . . . The husband in fact, is regarded as his wife's gateway to heaven or hell and the arbiter of her final destiny. That such an idea can exist within the framework of Islam—which totally rejects the idea of redemption, of any intermediary between a believer and the Creator—represents both a profound irony and a great tragedy."[47]

Although Ann E. Meyer is right when she says that "there is very little in the original Islamic sources that supports these stereotypes,"[48] there is no doubt that this image of women managed to infiltrate Islamic jurisprudence and influenced (and still influences) numerous interpretations of Qur'anic verses.[49] The most famous example is verse 4:34, which in a classical translation (Pickthall) reads, "Men are in charge of women, because Allah hath made the one of them to excel the other, and because they spend of their property (for the support of women)."[50] Zineb Miadi comments that "these verses are often misused by misogynistic Muslims to justify the subservient status of Muslim women, and they support the accusations published in certain Western journals that Islam devalues women."[51] Now, as Krämer notes, this image of women and its theological glorification is by no means specific to Islam, as a cursory glance at European social, intellectual, and legal history would show.[52] There, too, women are defined by their physical attributes, and the inequality of men and women is described, as in Rousseau, as "not a

[45] Mawdudi, *Human Rights in Islam*, 18.

[46] Corresponding examples can be found in Abou el Fadl, *Speaking in God's Name*, 209–263.

[47] Riffat Hassan, "On Human Rights and the Qur'anic Perspective," *Journal of Ecumenical Studies* 19 (1982): 63.

[48] Mayer, *Islam and Human Rights*, 141.

[49] For a Muslim feminist critique, see Kecia Ali, *Sexual Ethics and Islam: Feminist Reflections of Qur'an, Hadith and Jurisprudence* (Oxford: Oneworld, 2006).

[50] In Max Henning's German translation, this verse reads, "Men are superior to women." Max Henning, *Der Koran* (Stuttgart: Reclam, 1989), 93.

[51] Zineb Miadi, "Gleiche Rechte für Mann und Frau im Koran," in *Menschenbilder Menschenrechte. Islam und Okzident: Kulturen im Konflikt*, ed. Stefan Batzli, Fridolin Kissling, and Rudolf Zihlmann (Zürich: Unionsverlag, 1994), 97.

[52] See Krämer, *Gottes Staat als Republik*, 159.

human institution—or, at least, it is the work not of prejudice but of reason."[53] Likewise, John Locke assumes with astonishing matter-of-factness that the "last determination" or "the rule" in a marital relationship "naturally falls to the Man's share as the abler and the stronger."[54]

But this is not my primary concern here. Rather, I want to draw attention to a paradox in the Muslim argument of appropriation with regard to the issue of gender relations. As Rotraud Wielandt points out, almost all Muslim authors agree that slavery violates human dignity.[55] The Qur'an, it is argued, presupposes slavery as an existing social reality but does not declare it obligatory. On the contrary, scholars emphasize that important statements in the Qur'an seem to be aimed at the abolition of slavery.[56] It is striking, Wielandt continues, that this hermeneutically fruitful distinction between presupposed social conditions and permanently valid norms of social life, which is now the consensus with regard to slavery, does not even occur to the more conservative theologians with regard to the status of women: "They recognize that the Qur'an also shows a tendency to improve the situation of women. But instead of concluding that the Qur'anic regulations regarding women should be partially suspended for the sake of human dignity, they give them a global justification by appealing to considerations of supposedly timeless higher justice."[57] The differences in the treatment of slavery as opposed to gender relations certainly cannot be attributed to argumentative consistency. Thus, Baderin rightly criticizes, "[I]t is hypocritical if men on the one hand acquire and enjoy many rights and liberties of today's world, often through constructive and evolutionary interpretations of the *Shari'ah*, but on the other hand consider the rights and liberties of women to be stagnated upon the juristic views of the classical schools of Islamic law."[58]

On closer inspection, the inconsistency between the respective patterns of argumentation can be traced back to the reactive context and political opportunism of the appropriation argument, which aims to defend a supposed Islamic authenticity against the West. As Kecia Ali notes, "Those who have

[53] Jean-Jacques Rousseau, *Emile or On Education*, trans. Allan Bloom (New York: Basic Books, 1979), 361.
[54] John Locke, *Two Treatises of Government* (Cambridge: Cambridge University Press, 1988), 321.
[55] Wielandt, "Menschenwürde und Freiheit in der Reflexion zeitgenössischer muslimischer Denker," 192.
[56] See, for example, Abdul Rahman al-Sheha, *Misconceptions on Human Rights in Islam* (Riyadh: n.p., 2001), 133–144.
[57] Wielandt, "Menschenwürde und Freiheit in der Reflexion zeitgenössischer muslimischer Denker," 192.
[58] Baderin, *International Human Rights and Islamic Law*, 65.

appointed themselves the guardians of communal orthodoxy are particularly vigilant on matters concerned with women and gender—in part, because it is in these realms that the construction of Muslim identity in self-conscious opposition to a decadent West takes place."[59] Krämer draws a similar conclusion: "The defensive struggle against superior Western influences is waged in the name of defending 'authentic values,' and these values are largely equated with inherited moral notions."[60]

As I already emphasized, the central motivation of the argument seems to be to find a modern identity without "losing face." The authors in question attempt to defend the Islamic tradition against "the West" by propagating its compatibility with, and even its superiority over, Western ideas and institutions, since all modern ideas and institutions known to the West were established long before by Islam. These claims are not the product of a critical engagement with the Islamic tradition, nor do they reflect an understanding of the ideas and institutions propagated, both of which are alien to the appropriation argument. They serve merely as a defense against external criticism and as a means of cultural self-assertion. The idea of appropriation is thus torn between the determination to remain faithful to the past and the desire to integrate the modern concept of human rights. The conceptions of human rights that emerge from this tension exhibit an inconsistency that, as Mayer notes, can be attributed to the lack of a methodological foundation: "[T]he authors lack any clear theory of what rights should mean in an Islamic context or how to derive their context from the Islamic sources in a consistent and principled fashion. Instead, they merely assemble pastiches of ideas and terminology drawn from two very different cultures without determining a rationale for these combinations or a way to reconcile the conflicting premises underlying them. That is, the deficiencies in the substantive human rights principles are the inevitable by-products of methodological confusion and weaknesses."[61]

Accordingly, "Islamic human rights" are not defined from within Islam, since the philosophical premises on which an Islamic approach to human rights would have to be based do not exist and an adequate method for developing coherent interpretations of Islamic sources is lacking. Instead, according to the appropriation argument, human rights acquire the attribute of "Islamic" by being "filtered" through the traditional conception of Islamic

[59] Ali, *Sexual Ethics and Islam*, xiii.
[60] Krämer, *Gottes Staat als Republik*, 158.
[61] Mayer, *Islam and Human Rights*, 53–54.

law. As we have seen, however, the validity of human rights remains precarious given the theoretical primacy of traditional Islamic law, understood as divine and essentially immutable law. The impression is that the Islamic declarations of human rights can be used to justify authoritarian restrictions on rights, especially in the area of women's rights. Ironically, it is the very people who claim to have respected human rights for 1,400 years who are now restricting them.

6
Assimilation

> The Enlightenment did not bring light into the darkness of the Islamic tradition—the Qur'an and the Sunnah; rather, a light emanates from these norms that is refracted by the prism of modernity.[1]

As the above account of the appropriation position has shown, the Muslim arguments examined so far concerning the compatibility of Islam and human rights seem to have been caught in a dilemma. Either they ran the risk of doing violence to the Islamic tradition in order to reconcile it at all costs with the modern conception of human rights—especially with regard to the status of women, the prohibition of apostasy, and corporal punishment—or they gave precedence to the formal provisions of scripture in order to ensure the triumph of tradition at the cost of potentially doing violence to the modern conception of human rights.

That this dilemma is based on a misunderstanding of the Islamic tradition is the core idea of the position we will now consider, the argument of assimilation. The problem, it is argued, is not the tradition itself but the way in which it has traditionally been interpreted. The assimilation argument is characterized by the claim that the norms of Islamic law always depend on particular circumstances. Therefore, it is argued, Islamic revelation contains nothing that contradicts human rights; at most, it contains some detailed provisions that can be explained by particular historical circumstances.[2] In contrast to an ahistorical emphasis on a homogeneous *sharīʿa*, the proponents of this argument recognize the historically conditioned character of legal traditions and consider it essential to exercise the utmost caution

[1] Hofmann, *Religion on the Rise*, 152.

[2] Charfi, "Die Menschenrechte im Bezugsfeld von Religion, Recht und Staat in den islamischen Ländern," 100.

Human Rights Between Universality and Islamic Legitimacy. Mahmoud Bassiouni, Oxford University Press.
 DOI: 10.1093/oso/9780197753897.003.0007

in separating the religious from the historical. What is incompatible with human rights, they argue, is not the Islamic religion but classical Islamic law in its form derived from the early Islamic period. Instead of an anachronistic and essentialist appropriation of human rights, proponents of assimilation seek to identify alternative reference points for a modern understanding of human rights. They try to determine whether Islamic legal sources can guarantee human rights or at least do not constitute an obstacle to their acceptance. Five methodological approaches can be identified, which will be discussed and distinguished on the basis of their respective solutions to the above-mentioned problems: a textual, an evolutionary, an intentional, a hermeneutical, and a pragmatic approach. This division should not be taken to imply that these approaches are in competition with one another or that they are mutually exclusive. For the sake of clarity, however, they are treated separately here. The aim is to examine the respective methodological approaches to the problem areas and the conclusions that are drawn in each case. Finally, we will ask what implications they have for the relationship between Islam and human rights.

Textual Approach

A characteristic methodological feature of the textual approach is that it bases its understanding of religion solely on the Islamic source texts, the Qur'an and the Sunnah. Among other things, it seeks to reinterpret the Islamic sources on the basis of literary analysis. In particular, it subjects the wording of crucial verses regarding the status of women, such as the above-mentioned verse 4:34, to linguistic criticism.[3] It claims that the Qur'an must be read through a specifically masculine lens in order to find a basis for the superiority of men over women in verse 4:34. The Arabic wording of the verse—*al-rijāl qawamūna 'ala al-nisā'*—is instead translated as "Men take responsibility for women."[4] According to Molay Rachid Abderrezak, "It is well known that the Arabic word *qawamūn* cannot be translated as 'to have authority.' The expressions corresponding to the word 'authority' are *sultan, wufūd, satwa or sulta*. The words that can be equated with the term 'superiority' are also different: *a'lā, mutafawiq, rāki*. . . . By rejecting the patriarchal

[3] See Ali, *Sexual Ethics and Islam*, 117–126.
[4] Hofmann, *Religion on the Rise*, 112.

postulate, we advocate the following interpretation: 'Men take responsibility for women in accordance with the gifts with which God has favored them over others (other men) and on account of what they spend (for the benefit of women) from their property.' "[5] Accordingly, men are obligated to take full care of their wives and take responsibility for their upkeep.[6] As Azizah al-Hibri points out, any other interpretation of the verse that considers men to be superior to women would contradict other verses, in which the Qur'an emphasizes the equality of the sexes and describes men and women as each other's protectors (*awliyā'*).[7]

Likewise, the textual approach invalidates the common interpretation of the rules of legal testimony, which state that two female witnesses are required to counterbalance one male witness in testimony in cases involving debts (2:282). Hofmann points out that the Qur'an deals with women's testimony only in financial loan disputes, although it contains a total of eight passages on testimony and the administration of oaths:[8] "Evidently, the Qur'an correctly assumed that women at the time of revelation usually were ignorant in matters of finance. For that reason then, Verse (2:282) ensured the best legal protection available, while not ruling out that improved education of women and their integration into the economic process would enable them to acquire expertise (and full testimonial competence) in this field as well."[9] Similarly, the claim that Islam promotes polygamy, "a point that has occupied the imagination and thought of Europe since time immemorial and is considered a characteristic of Islam,"[10] misses the mark according to the textual approach.[11] For in Sura 4:3, the Qur'an makes marriage with up to four wives conditional on equal treatment: "But if you have reason to fear

[5] Quoted in Samia Osman, "Die Stellung der Frau im Islam und im Okzident," in Batzli, Kissling, and Zihlmann, *Menschenbilder Menschenrechte*, 98.

[6] For a different feminist reading that emphasizes the nonmaterial responsibilities of men, see Amina Wadud, *Qur'an and Woman: Rereading the Sacred Text from a Woman's Perspective* (Oxford: Oxford University Press, 1999), 70–74.

[7] Azizah al-Hibri, "A Study of Islamic Herstory: Or How Did We Ever Get into This Mess?," *Women's Study International Forum* 5, no. 2 (1982): 218.

[8] Hofman, *Religion on the Rise*, 120. The same argument is made by Asma Barlas, *"Believing Women" in Islam: Unreading Patriarchal Interpretations of the Qur'an* (Austin: University of Texas Press, 2002), 190. A detailed discussion of this verse can be found in al-Alwani, *Issues in Contemporary Islamic Thought*, 161–186. See also Mohammad Fadel, "Two Women, One Man: Knowledge, Power, and Gender in Medieval Sunni Legal Thought," *International Journal of Middle East Studies* 29, no. 2 (1997): 185–204.

[9] Hofman, *Religion on the Rise*, 120–121. See also Mohammad Hashim Kamali, *Freedom, Equality and Justice in Islam* (Cambridge, UK: Islamic Texts Society, 2002), 68–69.

[10] Osman, *Die Stellung der Frau im Islam und im Okzident*, 57.

[11] See Aziza al-Hibri, "A Study of Islamic Herstory," 216–217; Wadud, *Qur'an and Woman*, 82–85; Barlas, *"Believing Women" in Islam*, 190–192.

that you might not be able to treat them with equal fairness, then marry only one." Meanwhile, in the same Sura (4:129), the Qur'an asserts that this condition cannot be met: "And it will not be within your power to treat your wives with equal fairness, however much you may desire it," while Sura 33:4 states, "Never has God endowed any man with two hearts in one body."

In the case of apostasy (*ridda*), the textual approach simply points out that the Qur'an and the Sunnah do not prescribe any punishment for mere apostasy from Islam.[12] Although the Qur'an condemns apostasy and refers to consequences in the hereafter, there is no mention of a secular punishment.[13] Even the Prophet, of whom the Qur'an says "He is only a plain warner" (7:184), is not responsible for keeping people in their faith.[14] Thus, the Qur'an addresses the Prophet with the words "And had thy Sustainer so willed, all those who live on earth would surely have attained to faith, all of them: dost thou, then think, that thou couldst compel people to believe... ?" (10:99). The view that apostasy should be punished by death, according to this argument, is rather bound up with the memory of the apostasy of the Arab tribes after the death of Mohammad: "Those apostates who were killed during the Prophet's lifetime or shortly after his death were invariably individuals who, as a result of their 'apostasy,' turned their weapons against the Muslims, who at that time were still a small and vulnerable community. Under these circumstances, capital punishment appears to be an act of self-defense in war."[15]

Apostasy from Islam was thus equated mainly with a political act. Conversion based solely on religious conviction and without any aggressive intent toward the Muslim community, on the other hand, was hardly considered.[16] This was undoubtedly the reason why the death penalty did not apply to female apostates, "since women, unlike men, are not created for

[12] The issue of apostasy is discussed in detail in Abdullah Saeed and Hassan Saeed, *Freedom of Religion, Apostasy and Islam* (London: Routledge, 2016). For a Shīʿi perspective, see Mohsen Kadivar, *Blasphemy and Apostasy in Islam: Debates in Shiʿa Jurisprudence* (Edinburgh: Edinburgh University Press, 2021). On freedom of religion in general, see the excellent essay by Mohsen Kadivar, "Freedom of Religion and Belief in Islam," in Kamrava, *The New Voices of Islam*, 65–97; also Mohammad Talbi, "Religionsfreiheit—Recht des Menschen oder Berufung des Menschen?," in Schwartländer, *Freiheit der Religion*, 242–260.

[13] Compare Suras 2:217, 3:86–91, 3:106, 4:115, 5:21, 9:74, 16:106–107, 47:25–26, 47:34.

[14] Compare Suras 3:20, 5:92, 5:99, 6:66, 6:107, 7:184, 11:12, 13:7, 13:40, 16:64, 16:125, 17:54, 22:49, 24:54, 25:43, 25:56, 27:92, 29:18, 39:41, 42:48, 50:45, 88:21–22.

[15] Talbi, "Religionsfreiheit," 65–66. For a similar argument, see Mohammad Hashim Kamali, *Shariʿah Law: An Introduction* (Oxford: Oneworld, 2008), 220–1.

[16] Krämer, *Gottes Staat als Republik*, 154.

war."[17] Regarding the treatment of apostates, it is emphasized that the Qur'an argues, warns, or recommends justice, depending on the circumstances, but never resorts to the argument of the sword.[18] On the contrary, the Qur'an emphasizes, "There shall be no coercion in matters of faith" (*lā ikrāha fī al-dīn*; 2:256) and points out that it is up to the individual to make his or her own choice.[19] "In other words," Khan comments, "apostasy as such, however reprehensible it may be, is a spiritual offense and does not entail any secular punishment. This is the essence of the freedom to change one's faith. The Qur'an is clear on this issue."[20]

Although one of the merits of the textual approach is that it uses the Qur'an and the Sunnah as the standard for what should be considered sacred or religious, it is subject to the constraint that its reinterpretations, however ambitious, cannot provide a comprehensive and conclusive understanding of religion. Although the textual approach has great potential for a modern and enlightened interpretation of the Qur'an, it is forced to remain silent on passages whose wording is clear and explicit. For example, it has little to offer in dealing with *ḥudūd* (corporal punishment). It is also open to the charge that it is rather eclectic in the way it cites Qur'anic passages to support a modern understanding of human rights.[21] Thus, as we have seen, the issues of legal testimony and polygamy can be resolved, but the issue of inheritance remains untouched because it is based on a categorical text. Thus further potential attempts at mediation face the dilemma of having to draw on religious textual sources while at the same time having to deal with perceived inconsistencies.

[17] ʿAbd al-Raḥmān al-Jazīri, *Kitāb al-Fiqh ʿAlā al-Madāhib al-Arbaʿa* (Beirut: Dār Iḥyāʾ al-Turāth al-ʿArabī, 1972, 426. For a discussion of classical views on apostasy and punishment, see Mohammad Hashim Kamali, *Freedom of Expression in Islam* (Cambridge, UK: Islamic Texts Society, 1997), 93–105.

[18] Talbi, "Religionsfreiheit," 66, 70.

[19] Compare Suras 2:62, 5:48, 6:35, 10:108, 16:93, 18:29, 11:118, 42:8, 74:55, 76:3, 76:29, 80:12, 109:1–6.

[20] Muhammad Zafrullah Khan, *Islam und Menschenrechte* (Frankfurt: Verlag der Islam, 2004), 133.

[21] As argued by Bielefeld, *Philosophie der Menschenrechte*, 142. Özsoy goes one step further and criticizes the fact that the Qur'an can be made to say anything on the basis of a textual approach: "Thus, a secular, democratic, pluralistic or even a liberal concept of state and society can be read into the Qur'an; but also a theocratic and a totalitarian system, a scientistic as well as an anti-scientific conception. Indeed, you can then read how the Qur'an praises the oligarchy of your own society, how it speaks of the great technical achievements of the twentieth century and what it has to say about contemporary religious or political leaders." Ömer Özsoy, "Erneuerungsprobleme zeitgenössischer Muslime und der Qur'an," in *Alter Text—Neuer Kontext: Qur'anhermeneutik in der Türkei heute*, ed. Felix Körner (Freiburg: Herder, 2006), 23.

Evolutionary Approach

In an attempt to resolve this dilemma, Abdullahi an-Naʿim advocates an approach based on the development of the Qur'an.[22] The basic idea of this approach is to reconsider the legally binding status of certain Qur'anic verses. Following Mahmoud Mohammad Taha,[23] an-Naʿim proposes a reading of the Qur'an that distinguishes between the Meccan and Medinan Suras within the text, which, according to an-Naʿim, constitute two different revelations that are substantively independent of each other. While the Suras revealed in Mecca contain the timeless message of the Qur'an, those revealed later in Medina were tailored to the specific circumstances of the community in Medina and are therefore not of timeless validity: "The basic premise . . . is that a close examination of the content of the Qur'an and Sunnah reveals two levels or stages of the message of Islam, one of the earlier Mecca period and the other of the subsequent Medina stage. . . . [T]he earlier message of Mecca is in fact the eternal and fundamental message of Islam, emphasizing the inherent dignity of all human beings, regardless of gender, religious belief, race and so forth. That message was characterized by equality between men and women and complete freedom of choice in matters of religion and faith."[24] However, because society was not ready to accept this eternal and fundamental message that God had revealed to His messenger in Mecca, the implementation of the universal Meccan message was replaced by the Medina revelation, which was more realistic under the circumstances: "When that superior level of the message was violently and irrationally rejected and it was practically demonstrated that society at large was not yet ready for its implementation, the more realistic message at the Medina stage was provided and implemented. In this way, aspects of the message of the Mecca period which were inappropriate for practical implementation within the historical

[22] An-Naʿim is one of the leading scholars on the subject of Islam and human rights and has made substantial contributions to the theory and practice of human rights in general. In what follows I will limit myself to an analysis of his proposal for an internal reformation of Islamic law as advanced in Abdullahi A. An-Naʿim, *Toward an Islamic Reformation: Civil Liberties, Human Rights, and International Law* (Syracuse, NY: Syracuse University Press, 1990). An overview of his other writings on the topic can be found in Abdullahi an-Naʿim and Mashood A. Baderin, eds., *Islam and Human Rights. Selected Essays of Abdullahi An-Naʿim* (London: Routledge, 2010). The topic of human rights also figures prominently in Abdullahi an-Naʿim, *Islam and the Secular State: Negotiating the Future of Shariʿa* (Cambridge, MA: Harvard University Press, 2008). See also Abdullahi an-Naʿim, *Decolonizing Human Rights* (Cambridge: Cambridge University Press, 2021).

[23] Mahmoud M. Taha, *The Second Message of Islam* (Syracuse, NY: Syracuse University Press, 1989).

[24] An-Naʿim, *Toward an Islamic Reformation*, 52.

context of the seventh century were suspended and replaced by the more practical principles revealed and implemented during the Medina stage."[25]

According to an-Naʿim, those provisions of the Qur'an that are problematic from a human rights perspective can be attributed to the Medinan phase. This applies, for example, to the prohibition of polygamy (4:3), the rules of inheritance (4:7–14), and the superiority of men over women (4:34), as well as to the *ḥudūd* (24:2, 24:4, 5:38) and the verses condemning apostasy. However, in view of the lack of maturity of its addressees, the implementation of the Meccan message was not annulled but only temporarily suspended, so that it could be applied again in the future under appropriate circumstances: "T]he suspended aspects of the Mecca message were not lost forever as a source of law. Rather, they were postponed for implementation under appropriate circumstances in the future. Otherwise . . . the superior and eternal aspects of Islam would have been irredeemably lost."[26] The legal norms of the Qur'an that originated in the Medina period must therefore be understood and relativized in the light of the original Meccan message, since only the latter has timeless validity. An-Naʿim here invokes the principle of abrogation (*naskh*), which was used by early Muslim scholars to resolve inconsistencies in the religious sources by interpreting later verses as revoking or canceling earlier verses. He proposes that this earlier process of abrogation be reversed in order to declare the verses of the Qur'an from the Meccan revelation to be binding, with the aim of developing a modern version of the *sharīʿa* whose content is largely compatible with international human rights norms.

At first glance, the evolutionary approach offers a plausible solution to the problem of inconsistency, but on closer inspection it raises several theoretical and practical problems. The hermeneutically productive observation that the Medinan verses were addressed to a specific historical society by no means justifies their outright rejection or abrogation. More fruitful, it seems to me, is the attempt to question the general validity of *individual* norms by demonstrating their socially conditioned and particular character. Such an approach leads to the same result, but without having to reject a third of the Qur'an, which seems unacceptable since Muslims consider the Qur'an to be a unified discourse. An-Naʿim is also aware of this problem and writes, "However coherent and effective this approach may be, it still has to face the

[25] Ibid., 52–53.
[26] Ibid., 53.

question of practical acceptability. . . . In this regard, it may appear that the prospect of wide acceptance and implementation of [the] evolutionary principle by the majority of Muslims in the near future does not seem to be promising."[27] Ultimately, the rejection of the Medinan Qur'an proves problematic, especially since it deals with fundamental religious matters such as prayer, *zakāt*, fasting, and pilgrimage. In any case, as Lorenz Müller points out, the distinction between Meccan and Medinan verses cannot "be made seamlessly, if we want to avoid throwing the baby out with the bathwater." Thus, for example, verse 2:256 ("There shall be no coercion in matters of faith"), which is used to justify religious freedom under Islamic law, is considered Medinan.[28]

The goal of the evolutionary approach is to eliminate as many of the norms of Islamic law as possible that are incompatible with human rights; however, as Abdulaziz Sachedina notes, this leaves a central question unanswered, namely, according to which concrete method human rights–conforming norms can be extracted from the Islamic legal system.[29] Finally, it should be noted that many of the areas identified by an-Naʿim as incompatible with human rights, such as apostasy and the preferential position of men, have already been refuted by the textual approach.

Intentional Approach

The aim of the intentional approach is to identify the *spirit* of the Qur'anic instructions. It seeks to determine the *normative direction* of the revelation within the mass of historical contingencies in order to give it a contemporary interpretation.[30] This direction is identified by comparing the conditions that prevailed in the pre-Islamic period with the normative aspirations of the Qur'anic revelation. It is not the literal meaning but the underlying normative spirit of the Qur'an that is considered relevant. For example, while in pre-Islamic times women had no right to inherit, with the advent of Islam they acquired the right to inherit half as much as men. According to

27 Ibid., 97.

28 Müller, *Islam und Menschenrechte*, 251.

29 Abdulaziz Sachedina, "Review of Abdullahi An-Naʿim, *Toward an Islamic Reformation: Civil Liberties, Human Rights and International Law*," *International Journal of Middle East Studies* 25, no. 1 (1993): 156.

30 Merad, "Die Sharīʿa—Weg zur Quelle des Lebens," 393. See also Nasr Hamid Abu Zayd, *Critique of Religious Discourse* (New Haven: Yale University Press, 2018), 263–272.

this argument, the intent of the statement that "a woman inherits half of the man's share" is not that women should receive *only* half. Rather, it means that women *also* have the right to inherit. The spirit of the Qur'anic regulation of inheritance, it is argued, is to initiate a gradual and progressive change in the status of women. "What counts is the quality, not the quantity."[31] God's intention was to improve the situation of women. Accordingly, Abu Zayd calls for equal inheritance rights for men and women, interpreting the dynamic of the text as a quest for gender equality.[32] Similarly, Wadud argues, "The Qur'ān establishes a radical momentum towards continual reforms in gender relations. Even where it appears to fall short of explicit articulations these might be inferred by following the directions of the textual linguistic and moral momentum."[33]

Fundamental to the argument of the intentional approach is the observation that the Qur'an introduced social reforms gradually in order to ensure their acceptance under the sociocultural conditions prevailing at the time.[34] This gradualism (*tadarruj*) is evident, for example, in the Qur'an's treatment of alcohol consumption. At first, it only points out the harmful effects of alcohol consumption: "They will ask thee about intoxicants and games of chance. Say: 'In both there is great evil as well as some benefit for man; but the evil which they cause is greater than the benefit which they bring'" (2:219). Subsequently, a verse was revealed that forbade the consumption of alcohol only at the time of prayer: "O you who have attained to faith! Do not attempt to pray while you are in a state of drunkenness" (4:43). Finally, an absolute prohibition followed: "O you who have attained to faith! Intoxicants, and games of chance, and idolatrous practices, and the divining of the future are but a loathsome evil of Satan's doing: shun it, then, so that you might attain to a happy state!" (5:90).

The gradual approach of the Qur'an in dealing with social and cultural practices thus points to a qualitative direction of meaning that must be taken into account in the interpretation of the law. In the case of polygamy,

[31] Ibid.

[32] Abu Zayd, *Critique of Religious Discourse*, 269–270.

[33] Amina Wadud, "Qur'an, Gender and Interpretive Possibilities," in *Hawwa—Journal of Women of the Middle East and the Islamic World* 2:3 (2004), 334.

[34] See for instance Azizah al-Hibri, "Muslim Women's Rights in the Global Village. Challenges and Opportunities," in *Journal of Law and Religion* 15:1–2 (2000), 55–56: "The Qur'anic philosophy of gradualism is predicated upon the fact that fundamental changes in human consciousness usually do not occur overnight. Instead, they require a period of individual or even social gestation. For this reason, the Qur'an uses a gradual approach to change entrenched customs, beliefs, and practices, except in fundamental matters . . . "

the qualitative meaning of the revelation points to monogamy. While there were no restrictions on polygamy in pre-Islamic times, the revelation placed restrictions on it before abolishing it altogether: "Qur'anic law concerning marriage, rather than intending to ratify the widely prevalent practice of polygamy, sought to reform it as far as was possible at the time. The ultimate intent . . . was to transform marriage from a polygamous to a monogamous relationship. The ultimate objective of Qur'anic marriage law, then, was to legitimize monogamy, rather than to endorse polygamy."[35] The intentional approach also appeals to a higher meaning in the case of corporal punishment. The real problem that Islam sought to address when it introduced the penal code under the existing historical circumstances was not the punishment of theft per se, but "establishing the 'penal code' in the context of a just social order structured in such a way that there is no place for theft and hence no further reason for punishment."[36] Garaudy cites the example of a slave who stole wheat from a field, whereupon the owner of the field demanded that he be punished. The Prophet replied to the slave's master, "This man was hungry and you give him nothing to eat. It is you who I will punish."[37] According to this approach, social justice is a higher moral value than the protection of property. Therefore, the application of punishment is contrary to the spirit of the Qur'an until social justice is achieved.

More far-reaching but less productive proposals of the intentional approach amount to a total or partial rejection of the legal character of the *sharīʿa*. Referring to the etymological meaning of the term *sharīʿa* ("the path that leads to the well"), some commentators point out that *sharīʿa* does not actually mean "law" but rather "guidance."[38] Proponents of this view, such as Ali Merad, argue that the *sharīʿa* is essentially not an all-encompassing legal system, but rather contains general religious and ethical principles: "From a few pliant, light, ethereal and spiritual lines of the Qur'an iron and bombs were forged, which were then established as the law of God. But in truth, it is not a law at all but a path!"[39] A contradiction is thus seen in the "discrepancy between the Shari'ah as a guide for people to spiritualize their lives and its

[35] C. G. Weeramantry, *Islamic Jurisprudence: An International Perspective* (Kuala Lumpur: The Other Press, 2001), 69.
[36] Garaudy, "Die Menschenrechte und der Islam: Begründung, Überlieferung, Verletzung," 123.
[37] Ibid.
[38] Bielefeldt, *Philosophie der Menschenrechte*, 141.
[39] Merad, "Die Sharīʿa," 392.

situation in a legal system as an imposed will, as a legal order constructed in the name of alleged divine legitimation."[40]

Hermeneutical Approach

While the intentional approach moves away from the letter of the Qur'an and concentrates on its "spirit," the hermeneutical approach is concerned with the understanding of scripture. The emphasis here is on understanding, since it is not the literal wording of the scripture that is considered decisive but the *understanding* of the religious norms. The hermeneutical approach seeks to distinguish between religious and cultural norms, that is, between what belongs to the sacred and what belongs to the historical realm: "A deep understanding requires a knowledge of the dichotomies in Islamic discourse, namely the absolute and the relative, the general and the specific, the continuous and the temporary, and the local and the global in the Qur'anic teachings. In the absence of this discourse, we cannot understand the sacred text."[41]

In order to separate the religious from the historical, the approach, as its name suggests, proceeds hermeneutically by attempting to uncover the social and historical conditionality of various norms in order to justify corresponding limits to their normative validity. A fundamental observation is that the Qur'an was revealed in the context of a specific sociohistorical background.[42] It was not revealed in a single act or as a whole text, but over a period of twenty-three years, in the course of which it refers to specific events and responds to concrete historical situations. Therefore, according to Fazlur Rahman, the interpretation of a Qur'anic or prophetic norm must proceed in three methodological steps. First, it must ask what exactly a particular Qur'anic or prophetic statement meant in its historical situation or to what specific problem it responded at that time. For it is not always possible to determine beyond doubt whether the Prophet was spontaneously commenting on a very specific problem of his time and his social environment, or whether he intended to commit Muslims to a certain way of behaving for all time.

[40] Ibid., 393.
[41] Al-Alwani, *Issues in Contemporary Islamic Thought*, 135–136.
[42] Mumisa notes accordingly, "Although we believe in the supra-historicity of the Qur'an, we need to understand that the revelation of the Qur'an is an event that took place within human history." Mumisa, *Islamic Law*, 38.

Second, it must "extract" and articulate the general religious or ethical principle that this particular response entails. Finally, it must show how this general principle can be given concrete substance with respect to the present situation; that is, it must specify as precisely as possible what it means today or how it should be implemented in the contemporary world.[43] For Rahman, *ijtihād* means "the effort to understand the meaning of a relevant text or precedent in the past, containing a rule, and to alter that rule by extending or restricting or otherwise modifying it in such a manner that a new situation can be subsumed under it by a new solution."[44] Understanding religious norms therefore requires rediscovering the raison d'être behind each rule of the Qur'an or the Sunnah, the principle that inspired it, and the historical circumstances in which it was applied. If we read the Qur'an as if it had been revealed yesterday, we would not even be able to understand it. Simply pointing out that the Qur'an deals with this or that issue in this or that way is not very informative, because it makes little sense to read the Qur'an without knowing its contextual background (*asbāb al-nuzūl*): "In order that the texts be understood and applied properly, it is essential that lexical and historical studies be undertaken to place each one in its respective context. Only in this way will the student or researcher fully understand the texts' higher purposes, underlying principles, and basic concepts. A proper interpretation of the texts is impossible without first clearing away the influence of circumstances existing at the time and place of their revelation or, in case of Sunnah texts, articulation."[45]

In the debate on Islam and human rights, the hermeneutic approach is prominently used by Mohsen Kadivar, who distinguishes between what he calls "traditional" and "reformist" Islam.[46] The former is characterized by a fundamental belief in the constant, unchanging, and timeless nature of all the commandments contained in the religious source texts and the inability of human reason to understand their higher objectives, making it virtually impossible to overcome the conflict between Islam and human rights.[47]

[43] Rahman, *Islam and Modernity*, 5–8. For other hermeneutic approaches, see Wielandt, "Menschenwürde und Freiheit in der Reflexion zeitgenössischer muslimischer Denker," 205–206, and the essays in Körner, *Alter Text*.

[44] Rahman, *Islam and Modernity*, 8.

[45] Abū Sulaymān, *Crisis in the Muslim Mind*, 106–107.

[46] Mohsen Kadivar, *Human Rights and Reformist Islam* (Edinburgh: Edinburgh University Press, 2021).

[47] Kadivar identifies six fundamental conflicts: the inequality between (1) Muslims and non-Muslims, (2) men and women, (3) slaves and freemen, and (4) commoners and jurists, (5) freedom of religion and the punishment for apostasy, and (6) the issue of arbitrary and severe punishment. See ibid., 92–123.

In contrast, reformist Islam is based on the belief that religious commandments, especially those dealing with human interactions (i.e., the *muʿāmalāt*), are open to questioning and intellectual debate. More specifically, Kadivar distinguishes two categories of legal rules. The first includes general norms that remain permanently valid regardless of time and place, such as the need to be fair and to keep one's promise, or the prohibition of lying and treachery. The second category includes norms whose validity depends on the presence of certain temporal and locational circumstances, making them subject to change and reform. According to Kadivar, most of the legal norms of the *sharīʿa* dealing with human interactions belong to the second category, and it is here that all the conflicts between Islam and human rights arise.[48] To resolve them, Kadivar argues, we must cleanse the religious source texts of their temporal "sediments"[49] and extract and preserve their eternal rationale. In the same vein, Khaled Abou El Fadl advocates a paradigm shift in the way Muslims view the existing positive legal injunctions of the *sharīʿa*: "It is reasonable to deal with the ethical and moral values of the Shari`ah as immutable, eternal and absolute, but any positive and context-based laws are temporal and changeable."[50]

The hermeneutical approach is particularly useful for interpreting Qur'anic verses that refer to women and gender.[51] For example, the Qur'anic provisions on inheritance must be understood in the context of the social conditions that prevailed at the time of revelation. According to this argument, the Qur'an grants a male heir twice as much as a female heir because it is the man's duty to provide for the needs of the family, while the woman has the right to dispose of her property as she sees fit. Women may work, but unlike men, they are not required to provide for the family.[52] On this reading,

[48] Ibid., 154.

[49] Ibid., 152, 179.

[50] Khaled Abou El Fadl, "Shari'ah and Human Rights," in Chase, *Routledge Handbook on Human Rights and the Middle East and North Africa*, 275. See also Khaled Abou El Fadl, "Cultivating Human Rights: Islamic Law and the Humanist Imperative," in *Law and Tradition in Classical Islamic Thought*, ed. Michael Cook, Najam Haider, Intisar Rabb, and Asma Sayeed (New York: Palgrave Macmillan, 2013), 167–183; Khaled Abou El Fadl, "The Human Rights Commitment in Modern Islam," in *Human Rights and Responsibilities in the World Religions*, ed. Joseph Runzo, Nancy M. Martin, and Arvind Sharma (Oxford: Oneworld, 2003), 301–364.

[51] It is used extensively by Khaled Abou el-Fadl in his *Speaking in God's Name*. See also Mohsen Kadivar, "Revisiting Women's Rights in Islam: 'Egalitarian Justice' in Lieu of 'Desert-Based Justice,'" in *Gender and Equality in Muslim Family Law: Justice and Ethics in the Islamic Legal Tradition*, ed. Ziba Mir-Hosseini, Kari Vogt, Lena Larsen, and Christian Moe (London: I. B. Tauris, 2013), 213–234.

[52] Lise J. Abid, "Die Debatte um Gender und Menschenrechte im Islam," in Rumpf, Gerhard, and Jansen, *Facetten islamischer Welten*, 154.

the regulation of inheritance would not be a form of discrimination against women but a logical compensation for the burden borne by men. Taken to its logical conclusion, this would mean that a woman would inherit only half as much as a man if the circumstances that conditioned this rule prevailed. If the circumstances were different—for example, if both the husband and the wife worked, but both had to contribute to the maintenance of the household—then this rule would no longer be valid. Thus the validity of a norm depends on the existence of certain circumstances. If these change, then the validity of the norm must be reconsidered. In this sense, Mumisa asks, "[W]hat was the cause and reason for deciding to grant women less than the share of men in the inheritance laws of Islam mentioned in the *Qur'an*? Does the cause and reason [*illah*] still exist? If it does, we will have to continue giving them less, and if it has ceased to exist, we will have to re-interpret the verses of inheritance laws."[53] In response to these questions, Kalisch comments, "Ideas about the role of women and the social situation have changed considerably in this regard, and under these changed conditions the unequal treatment of women in matters of inheritance is no longer fair."[54]

With regard to Qur'anic criminal law, the hermeneutical argument first notes that the corporal punishments contained in the Qur'an are not an invention of the Qur'an, but were largely taken over from the pre-Islamic tribal laws of the Arabs.[55] Despite the critical attitude of the Qur'an toward the social and moral environment of the Arabs, the local customs and peculiarities of the Arab tribal society, to which the revelation was directly addressed, were taken into account. Using the example of hand amputation for theft, Kamali shows that this punishment made sense given the social circumstances of the time:

> Bedouin Arab society consisted largely of nomads who traveled with their camels and tents in search of pastures, and it was not feasible under the circumstances to penalize the thief with imprisonment. Imprisonment necessitates durable structures and guards, feeding and care of inmates and so forth; hence the physical punishment was the only reasonable option.

[53] Mumisa, *Islamic Law*, 104–105.

[54] Muhammad Kalisch, "Muslime als religiöse Minderheit: Ein Beitrag zur Notwendigkeit eines neuen *ijtihād*," in *Muslime im Rechtsstaat*, ed. Thorsten G. Schneiders and Lamya Kaddor (Münster: Lit, 2005), 57.

[55] On this, see Walter Young, "Stoning and Hand Amputation: The Pre-Islamic Origins of the Ḥadd Penalties for Zinā and Sariqa" (PhD diss., McGill University, 2005).

> Since there were no protective barriers to safeguard the property of people, society could not afford to tolerate proliferation of theft. Mutilation of the hand of the thief also provided the kind of punishment that disabled the thief from persisting in his wrongdoing, just as it also left a visible mark on the offender to warn people against his menace. Mutilation was thus an eminently rational punishment for theft.[56]

The second observation, then, is that the Qur'anic penal codes must be understood in their social context. In the Qur'an, the *principle* of punishment is only contextualized or "accentuated" in the light of the prevailing social reality, without, however, prescribing a specific *form* of punishment for all time. This observation, however, is open to the literalist objection that both the principle and the form of punishment must be regarded as willed by God: "In sum, it is impossible to isolate the divine intent from the methods laid out in the revealed text. Moreover, the intents are embodied in the methods in the sense that they are actualized only by those stated methods. As some methods are definitely prescribed, any manipulation of the text's meaning leads to an avoidance of the intents."[57]

The hermeneutical approach counters this objection by pointing out that social practices do not acquire a normative religious character simply because they are mentioned in the Qur'an. This would imply a religious imperative to restore the historical circumstances of seventh-century Arabia, which would be tantamount to a sacralization of history. In Rahman's words: "To insist on a *literal* implementation of the rules of the Qur'ān, shutting one's eyes to the social change that has occurred and that is so palpably occurring before our eyes, is tantamount to deliberately defeating its moral-social purposes and objectives. It is just as though, in view of the Qur'ānic emphasis on freeing slaves, one were to insist on preserving the institution of slavery so that one could 'earn merit in the sight of God' by freeing slaves. Surely, the whole tenor of the teaching of the Qur'ān is that there should be no slavery at all."[58]

[56] Kamali, *Shari'ah Law*, 130–131. See also Mohammed Abed el-Jabri, *Democracy, Human Rights and Law in Islamic Thought* (London: I. B. Tauris, 2009), 84–85.

[57] Abd al Majid an-Najjar, *The Vicegerency of Man between Revelation and Reason: A Critique of the Dialectic of the Text, Reason and Reality* (Herndon, VA: International Institute of Islamic Thought, 2000), 62.

[58] Rahman, *Islam and Modernity*, 19.

Pragmatic Approach

Specifically with regard to corporal punishment, a final approach can be identified that seeks to establish procedural limitations on the use of corporal punishment without questioning its normative validity.[59] Baderin notes, "Questioning the *ḥudūd* punishments is considered as questioning the divine wisdom underlying them and impugning the divinity of the Qur'an and the theocentric nature of Islamic law."[60] In the face of increasingly loud calls for the implementation of Islamic law, he argues, it is therefore more practical "to seek for reconciliation between the *ḥudūd* punishments and the prohibition of cruel, inhuman, and degrading punishments under international human rights law indirectly through legal procedural shields available within Islamic law."[61] To this end, the pragmatic approach relies on various legal maneuvers developed by Islamic jurisprudence.[62] For example, according to the principle of causality in Islamic jurisprudence, (1) there must be a necessary connection between causes (*asbāb*) and effects (*musabbibāt*), (2) certain circumstances must prevail (*shurūt*), and (3) there must be a lack of obstacles (*mawāniʿ*).[63] So, to take the example of theft: (1) If theft (cause), then punishment (effect). (2) However, this is true only if the object exceeds a certain minimum value (condition a), if the object was kept in a secure and enclosed place (condition b), and if there is sufficient evidence (condition c). In addition, (3) the intention and the social circumstances of the accused (obstacle a) as well as the social framework conditions (obstacle b) must be taken into account. Therefore, the punishment can be imposed only if the theft took place under all these conditions and the personal and social circumstances of the accused have been taken into consideration. It is also necessary, for example, to define at what point an object has exceeded a certain threshold value, and what social framework conditions must exist for a punishment to be imposed. Krämer notes that a widely accepted position is that it is only in a society that is truly permeated by Islam that theft can be punished with

[59] For a detailed analysis, see Mohamed S. el-Awa, *Punishment in Islamic Law* (Plainfield, IL: American Trust Publications, 2000).

[60] Baderin, *International Human Rights and Islamic Law*, 84.

[61] Ibid., 85.

[62] For a discussion of the various evidentiary requirements, technical preconditions, and mitigating factors for the enforcement of *ḥudūd* penalties, see Intisar A. Rabb, *Doubt in Islamic Law. A History of Legal Maxims, Interpretation and Islamic Criminal Law* (Cambridge: Cambridge University Press, 2015).

[63] On this, see Kamali, *Principles of Islamic Jurisprudence*, 431–436.

the canonical punishment of amputation of the hand.[64] The same principle applies to the rule governing the punishment of adultery, which can be applied only "when all basic requirements and conditions for such a verdict are fulfilled."[65] Although the basic if-then validity of these punishments remains unaffected, their practical applicability is often doubted or disputed, because it is almost impossible to meet the requirements. Bielefeldt comments, "According to the classical sharia, stoning for adultery (which is not based on the Quran) cannot be imposed unless four male Muslim eyewitnesses with a good reputation give a detailed account of the act of penetration. The question that naturally arises in that case is whether it is conceivable that people could observe such an act of sexual intercourse without thereby jeopardizing their requisite good reputation. . . . The only conceivable possibility is that the act of adultery is committed publicly, leading to the presumption that the people involved are insane and, consequently, cannot be punished."[66] As an aside, Hofmann notes somewhat sarcastically that former U.S. president Bill Clinton would have fared better under Islamic rules of evidence for adultery than under American rules.[67]

One objection that arises here, however, is that the pragmatic approach may limit the practical applicability of a disputed norm but not its theoretical claim to validity. As a result, the problem is only postponed rather than resolved. Accordingly, Ramadan is critical: "Anyone who reads the books of the ulamā', listens to their lectures and sermons, travels inside the Islamic world or interacts with the Muslim communities of the West will inevitably and invariably hear the following pronouncement from religious authorities: 'almost never applicable.' Such pronouncements give the majority of the ulamā' and Muslim masses a way out of dealing with the fundamental issues and question without risking appearing to have betrayed the Islamic scriptural sources."[68] Ramadan, who criticizes the instrumentalization of the *sharī'a* for the purposes of political power and its reduction to the punitive aspect

[64] Krämer, *Gottes Staat als Republik*, 63.
[65] Nassir el-Din el-Assad, "Politik auf der Grundlage göttlicher Autorität," in Batzli, Kissling, and Zihlmann, *Menschenbilder Menschenrechte*, 214.
[66] Bielefeldt, "Muslim Voices in the Human Rights Debate," 613.
[67] Hofmann, *Religion on the Rise*, 81.
[68] Tariq Ramadan, "An International Call for Moratorium on Corporal Punishment, Stoning and the Death Penalty in the Islamic World," April 5, 2005 https://tariqramadan.com/an-international-call-for-moratorium-on-corporal-punishment-stoning-and-the-death-penalty-in-the-islamic-world/. For the debate this triggered, see Tariq Ramadan, "A Call for a Moratorium on Corporal Punishment—The Debate in Review," in *New Directions in Islamic Thought: Exploring Reform and Muslim Tradition*, ed. Kari Vogt, Lena Larsen, and Christian Moe (London: I. B. Tauris, 2009), 163–174.

of *ḥudūd*, calls instead for the immediate abolition of corporal punishment: "[I]t is our moral obligation and religious responsibility to demand for the immediate suspension of the application of the *hudūd* which is inaccurately accepted as an application of 'Islamic sharīʿa.'"[69]

A different argument against the application of the *ḥudūd* is presented by Mohammad Fadel, who, in contrast to Ramadan, is concerned to keep the normative validity of the *ḥudūd* intact in order to prevent the potential alienation of traditionalist Muslims.[70] Rather than calling for their procedural limitation, he suggests shifting the focus to their distinctively religious nature, that is, the fact that they function as a means for sinners to expiate their sins. In Fadel's reading, the primary function of the *ḥudūd* is to purify the individual defendant from disobedience to God's command and thus to further his or her salvific interests. For this reason, some classical jurists exempted non-Muslims from *ḥudūd* punishments, on the grounds that they did not constitute acts of penance for those outside the faith. The same argument, according to Fadel, could be extended to dissenting Muslims. For a *ḥadd* punishment can achieve its salvific benefit only if the defendant in question voluntarily submits to it. Accordingly, it can be applied only when an individual explicitly requests to be subjected to the punishment as an act of atonement. Otherwise, the punishment would lose its religious function and serve purely secular purposes, in which case "it should be subject to all applicable limitations on lawful secular punishments, including those of international human rights laws."[71] But there are at least two objections to this argument. One, which Fadel himself points out, is that the classical justification for *ḥudūd* punishments is by no means limited to their religious function.[72] Instead, at least some of the punishments derive their coercive nature from the secular interests they are intended to promote. The extent to which Fadel's proposal can effectively convince a traditionalist Muslim audience therefore remains highly questionable. But even if his proposal is accepted and *ḥudūd* penalties are imposed only on those who voluntarily agree to them, a second difficulty arises with regard to the mechanisms by which the

[69] Ibid.

[70] Mohammad H. Fadel, "Public Reason as a Strategy for Principled Reconciliation: The Case of Islamic Law and International Human Rights Law," *Chicago Journal of International Law* 8, no. 1 (2007): 1–20. See also Mohammad H. Fadel, "The Challenge of Human Rights," *Seasons* 5, no. 1 (2008): 59–80.

[71] Fadel, "Public Reason as a Strategy for Principled Reconciliation," 18.

[72] Mohammad H. Fadel, "The True, the Good, the Reasonable: The Theological and Ethical Roots of Public Reasons in Islamic Law," *Canadian Journal of Law and Jurisprudence* 21, no. 1 (2008): 62n251.

voluntary nature of such a decision could be ascertained. Given the social and political pressures that surround the application of *ḥudūd* in practice, it seems unlikely that a definitive and exclusively *religious* motivation can be established from the outside, leaving aside the question of whether it should be the role of the modern nation-state to ensure the salvation of its citizens at all.

7
Summary and Outlook

The preceding analysis of the Muslim discourse on human rights has shown that Muslims hold a wide variety of views on the question of the compatibility of Islam and human rights. Thus the often asserted notion of a uniform, homogeneous Islamic position on human rights is unfounded. The question of whether Islam is compatible with human rights requires a more nuanced response. The greatest obstacles to the adaptation of human rights are what Bielefeldt calls "defensive and embracive attitudes toward human rights."[1] "Defensive attitudes," which we have termed the position of rejection, reject human rights as a culturally alien concept, whereas "embracive attitudes" assert an uncritical claim to exclusive ownership of the concept of human rights. While human rights are not categorically rejected, they are not unconditionally embraced either. The position of assimilation, with its attempt to overcome the discrepancies between Islam and human rights, undoubtedly comes closest to the idea of human rights. The positions examined here differ in their treatment and understanding of Islamic law. Conflicting assessments of human rights are a function of divergent understandings of the Islamic tradition and of legal reasoning. Thus it is not Islam per se that prevents the recognition of human rights but rather a particular interpretation of Islam based on a particular conception of Islamic law. What matters, then, is how Islamic law is approached. It can be interpreted in a way that is sympathetic to human rights—as the position of assimilation attempts to do—so that the sources of Islamic law do not necessarily pose an obstacle to the adoption of human rights.[2]

The last sentence, however, already illustrates the problematic situation of contemporary Muslim human rights discourse and the scholarly debate on the compatibility of Islam and human rights in general. Even at its best, this discourse has the sole purpose of proving that Muslims are *not incapable* of coming to terms with human rights. What Muslims often fail to

[1] Bielefeldt, "Muslim Voices in the Human Rights Debate," 602.
[2] Müller, *Islam und Menschenrechte*, 322.

Human Rights Between Universality and Islamic Legitimacy. Mahmoud Bassiouni, Oxford University Press.
 DOI: 10.1093/oso/9780197753897.003.0008

realize is that, in this way, they do not develop an independent conception of human rights but merely engage in patchwork. From a Muslim perspective, this raises the question of how useful the compatibility paradigm is as a framework for dealing with the issue of human rights. For it automatically implies a scheme of evaluation that examines only whether and to what extent Muslims have succeeded in copying or adopting "Western values." From the outset, this binds every line of argumentation into a discursive structure in which the dependent variable "Islam" strives to conform to the independent variable "human rights," thereby entering into a master-servant relationship in which accusation leads to apologetics and the granting of legitimacy entails an obligation to account for oneself. In other words, there is a risk of getting caught up in a justificatory maelstrom that all too often leads to a strong tendency toward defensiveness and apologetics, and generally produces arguments that reflect external pressures to profess human rights rather than serious efforts to engage with them. Accordingly, contemporary Muslim human rights discourse is not in a position to advance or expand our general understanding of human rights, because it is primarily concerned with refuting the accusations leveled against it and ridding itself of the stigma of being the problem child of human rights. To be clear, my criticism is not that Muslim thinkers are incapable of demonstrating the compatibility of Islam and human rights—they are—or that they are incapable of guaranteeing equal rights for all. Rather, the criticism is that Muslim thinkers are so *preoccupied* with proving the compatibility of Islam that they are discursively inhibited from critically expanding or challenging our current understanding of human rights.[3] Since there is no reason to believe that our current understanding of human rights is either complete or infallible,[4] Muslim thinkers would do well to move beyond the discursive paradigm of compatibility and ask how our imperfect understanding might be improved

[3] A similar worry is expressed by Sherman A. Jackson, "Islam and the Promotion of Human Rights," *Telos* 203 (2023): 60–61: "Faced with the reality of having to speak from the minus side of this equation [of cultural and intellectual authority], even the proudest and most principled Muslims often find it useful if not necessary to speak in the voice of the dominant civilization, especially when trying to speak *to* that civilization or to a world that has been thoroughly saturated by its vision. This is what we find in the most common approaches to human rights among Muslims, which begins with the Western definition and philosophical underpinnings and tries to show how Islam can reconcile itself with these. My fear, however, is that this can habituate Muslims to overlooking aspects of their own civilization, simply because the dominant civilization is not calibrated to recognize these. At the same time, it can habituate the dominant civilization to thinking that its approach to human rights is the only approach, or shall we say the only relevant approach."

[4] See chapter 11.

or positively transformed by bringing the resources of the Islamic tradition to bear on it.

The inability to contribute to a deeper and broader understanding of human rights becomes particularly evident when we turn to the question of how human rights are justified in Muslim discourses. As Krämer points out, the basic assumption that "human rights derive not from human reason or a human sense of justice, let alone from a 'natural law,' but rather from God as the sole sovereign and legislator"[5] raises serious problems. Although the argument emphasizes "the pre-political character of human rights, which is also conveyed by the reference to natural law, it inextricably binds them to the fulfillment of one's duties to God, thus depriving them of their absolute character according to the modern Western understanding."[6] The fulfillment of human rights thus becomes a ritual act toward God,[7] while the resulting interpersonal duty remains secondary.

Contrary to Krämer, I do not think that the problem of the theocentric conception is that it prevents all human beings from being recognized as equal holders of human rights.[8] For the above-mentioned justification of human rights does not link them to faith in the sense that only those who believe in God are entitled to them. Rather, the real problem with the Muslim justification seems to be its inability to oblige everyone equally to respect human rights. By making respect for human rights dependent on belief in God, it establishes a foundation of values that raises the question of *validity* for those who do not believe in God. How, for example, would atheists and agnostics be bound by human rights? The reference to God in the justification of human rights does not cast doubt on the idea that human rights apply *to* every human being; rather, the problem is that the justification is not valid *for* every human being. The assumption that human rights are endowed by or through God is a *faith-based assumption.* Faith-based assumptions are products of a vertical relationship between individuals (x) and God (G), and thus are based on personal convictions that cannot claim to be binding or valid for people of other faiths or no faith at all (Figure 7.1).

[5] Krämer, *Gottes Staat als Republik*, 148.

[6] Ibid.

[7] See the Preamble of the Cairo Declaration on Human Rights in Islam, which states "that safeguarding those fundamental rights and freedoms is an act of worship whereas the neglect or violation thereof is an abominable sin."

[8] According to Krämer, the Muslim justification "leaves open the question whether the human rights of those who do not perform their duties toward God should also be respected and protected." Krämer, *Gottes Staat als Republik*, 149.

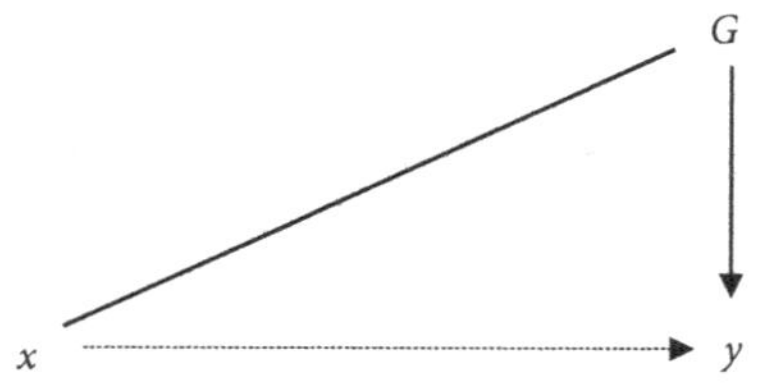

Figure 7.1 A theocentric model of justification.

The faith-based assumption that human rights are God-given, represented here as the connection of person *x* to *G*, would be plausible only if *x* actually sees herself as standing in such a vertical relationship, that is, if *x* shares the premise that human rights are granted by God. In this case, the connection of *x* to *G* is a plausible reason for *x* to respect the human rights of person *y*. As noted above, it is irrelevant whether *y* also believes in *G* or not. What matters is that *x* must make a faith-based assumption in order to fit into the scheme of human rights justification presented above. If *x* does not believe in *G*, then the above scheme seems irrelevant for *x*. For how can I convince *x*, as a person of no faith or of another faith, of an assumption that requires a particular faith? The obvious result would be that *x* would no longer have any binding reason to respect the rights of *y*.

What follows from these considerations for the Muslim justification of human rights is the simple fact that Muslims cannot and should not expect all people to share their assumption that human rights are granted by or through God. With this assumption, Muslims make a presupposition that cannot be shared by all people. The same, of course, applies to other faith-based assumptions. For example, suppose that person *x* sees human rights as grounded in the crucifixion and resurrection of Christ, or in the biblical justification that *y* was created in the image of God and, for that reason alone, must be respected as a subject of human rights. This justification may seem plausible to *x* and all those who share her view. But it is not an intelligible reason for action for someone who does not attach the same importance to the Bible as *x*. And since *x* cannot forcibly project her conviction onto others, the justification she advocates has no general validity. Therefore, *x*'s justification is based on a specific understanding of human rights, which in this case requires a hermeneutic adoption of the Christian perspective. As a result, it is not equally accessible to all people and therefore does not oblige all people to respect human rights. Thus the apparent paradox of theocentric justifications of human rights in general and Muslim justifications of human rights in particular is that they are based on a nonuniversal foundation of values while at the same time claiming to justify universal human rights. But as long as they are not based on a set of values shared by all human beings, so-called Islamic human rights cannot be considered universal human rights. Falaturi is therefore right when he says that a normative foundation must be created "that is valid for all people in the world, past and present, and that convincingly demonstrates the binding nature of these rights."[9] This foundation can be laid only if human rights are justified in a way that is, in principle, acceptable to all human beings.

Of course, one could interject and ask why an Islamic justification of human rights needs to be universally accessible at all. Would it not be sufficient for it to be convincing to adherents of the Islamic faith? The short answer to this question is that a justification whose validity is limited to the confines of the Muslim faith community would ultimately undermine the normative claims of the Islamic faith, which, after all, does not simply claim to regulate the life of a particular culture at a particular time, but rather claims to be valid for all times, places, and people. In other words, Islam itself makes a claim to universality, which has two important implications. First, proponents of an Islamic position cannot reject the idea of universality as such without also rejecting the Islamic claim to universality. Claims of cultural relativity are thus fundamentally self-defeating, which leads to the second implication, namely that proponents of an Islamic position must justify their claims in the name of the universal. It is not enough to provide a justification that merely manages to convince fellow Muslims. Rather, to live up to the universal claim of their religion, Muslims must find ways to make their claims about human rights accessible and acceptable to those who hold different beliefs.

What are the implications of these considerations for the relationship between Islam and human rights? Can an Islamic justification of human rights make a legitimate, general claim to validity, or must the religious claim to human rights ultimately be abandoned altogether? Halliday argues that only a secular justification of human rights can make a legitimate claim to validity: "[T]he long-term issue is not that of finding some more liberal, or compatible, interpretation of Islamic thinking, so much as that of removing the discussion of rights, as of other issues, from the claims of religion itself.

[9] Falaturi, *Westliche Menschenrechtsvorstellungen und Koran*, 8.

As long as this fails to be the case, the multiple levels of limitation identified here—text, culture, instrumentality and religious hegemony—will prevail."[10] However, in response to this argument, an-Na'im emphasizes that a secular conception of human rights is not an attractive solution for Muslims, because it is not sufficiently legitimized from an Islamic point of view and would therefore lead to negative consequences: "To seek secular answers is simply to abandon the field to the fundamentalists, who will succeed in carrying the vast majority of the population with them by citing religious authority for their policies and theories. Intelligent and enlightened Muslims are therefore best advised to remain within the religious framework and endeavour to achieve the reforms that would make Islam a viable modern ideology."[11] He continues, "In essence, by conceding religious authority to the proponents of Sharia, secularist intellectuals are conceding defeat without a fight. Consequently, the end result of opting for secularism in the Muslim world is the same as that of gravitating toward conservatism. Both, in the end, bolster the ascendance of the proponents of a Sharia state."[12] According to an-Na'im, if a justification of human rights is to gain acceptance among Muslims, then a conception of human rights that is legitimate in Islamic terms is required, "because secularism is not an Islamic response to the challenges facing Muslim societies."[13]

In the same vein, Abdulaziz Sachedina launches a blistering attack on the secularist worldview that he believes underlies the Universal Declaration of Human Rights.[14] According to him, the "ongoing Muslim criticism of the Declaration as being prejudicially antireligious and politically hegemonic are founded upon rejection of a universal claim of secular morality."[15] Sachedina therefore emphasizes the need to provide an alternative moral foundation, anchored in the Islamic tradition, in order to give human rights cultural legitimacy in the Muslim world and to garner the necessary support

[10] Halliday, "Relativism and Universalism in Human Rights," 165–166.

[11] An-Na'im, *Toward an Islamic Reformation*, xii.

[12] Ibid., 62.

[13] Ibid., 42. It should be noted that in this quotation an-Na'im equates the concept of secularism with the idea of relegating religion to the private sphere. He takes essentially the same position in his *Islam and the Secular State*, where he presents a more nuanced conception of secularism, advocating the separation of Islam from the state while maintaining the connection between Islam and politics. On the question of secularism and human rights in general, see Michael Freeman, "The Problem of Secularism in Human Rights Theory," *Human Rights Quarterly* 26, no. 2 (2004): 375–400.

[14] Abdulaziz Sachedina, *Islam and the Challenge of Human Rights* (Oxford: Oxford University Press, 2009), 9. For a thorough critique of Sachedina's assumptions, see T. Jeremy Gunn, "Do Human Rights Have a Secular, Individualistic and Anti-Islamic Bias?," *Daedalus* 149, no. 3 (2020): 148–169.

[15] Ibid., 9.

for their implementation: "Without engaging those Muslims scholars and intellectuals who deny these universal principles and their cross-cultural application, these important values—which underlie the protection of human dignity and human agency in the context of universal human rights—will lack the necessary legitimacy and enforcement in the Muslim world. As long as the moral and metaphysical foundations of human rights norms remain unarticulated, they will be easily dismissed as yet another ploy to dominate Muslim societies by undermining their religiously based culture and value system."[16]

Interestingly, this thesis is also supported by a study published by The Netherlands Scientific Council for Government Policy. It emphasizes that the chances of realizing human rights in predominantly Muslim countries will improve considerably "if they can be imbedded in the local tradition and culture,"[17] since "[human rights] can only go beyond the level of rights on paper when they can boast internal legitimacy, in other words, when they are viewed as 'one's own law.' . . . [I]n a number of countries . . . this 'own law' is based on Sharia, and it is precisely because of its highly symbolic value that it is not realistic to expect religiously based human rights soon to be replaced by secular human rights."[18] In light of this, the study argues, the human rights debate would be better conducted within rather than outside an Islamic framework, since the practical realization of human rights depends on the cultural acceptance it receives as a result: "Precisely because international law primarily acquires its force through national law, the EU must recognize that the legitimizing power of Sharia in Muslim countries can be used to realize international human rights."[19]

An-Na'im expresses exactly the same point when he writes, "If international norms of human rights are to be implemented in a manner consistent with their own rationale, the people (who are to implement these norms) must perceive the concept of human rights and its content as their own. To be committed to carrying out human rights norms, people must hold these norms as emanating from their worldview and values, not imposed on them

[16] Ibid., 5.

[17] Netherlands Scientific Council for Government Policy, *Dynamism in Islamic Activism Reference Points for Democratization and Human Rights* (Amsterdam: Amsterdam University Press, 2006), 10–11.

[18] Ibid., 169–170.

[19] Ibid., 170. Similar conclusions are drawn by Muriel Asseburg, ed., *Moderate Islamisten als Reformakteure?* (Bonn: Bundeszentrale für politische Bildung, 2008); Neil Hicks, "Does Islamist Human Rights Activism Offer a Remedy to the Crisis of Human Rights Implementation in the Middle East?," *Human Rights Quarterly* 24, no. 2 (2002): 361–381.

by outsiders."[20] It is therefore imperative to engage productively with Islamic law, especially when it comes to the practicalities of implementing human rights.[21] As Johnston observes, it would be "difficult to imagine a grassroots movement advocating the kind of human rights norms guaranteed by international law without doing so from within an Islamic framework."[22] The reason for this difficulty can be traced back to a phenomenon that Wilfred Blunt described as early as 1882 as the "vice of illegality."[23] This refers to the fact that for most Muslims, social norms and practices carry a stigma of illegitimacy unless they can be legitimized in Islamic terms. As Ali notes, this is true for the majority of Muslims: "For the vast majority of Muslims worldwide, not only extremists or conservatives, but also those who consider themselves moderate or progressive—determining whether a particular belief or practice is acceptable largely hinges on deciding whether or not it is legitimately 'Islamic.' Even many of those who do not base their personal conduct or ideals on normative Islam believe, as a matter of strategy, that in order for social changes to achieve wide acceptance among Muslims they must be convincingly presented as compatible with Islam."[24] Applied to human rights, this means that both the theoretical acceptance and the practical validity of human rights in the Islamic world depend on whether they can be justified in Islamic terms. As Baderin notes, "More than just establishing a religious or legal order, Islam is an institution of legitimacy in many states of the Muslim world. Many regimes in the Muslim world today seek their legitimacy through portraying an adherence to Islamic law and traditions. Thus, any attempt to enforce international or universal norms within Muslim societies in oblivion of established Islamic law and traditions creates tension and reaction against the secular nature of the international regime no matter how humane or lofty such international norms may be."[25] Since the lack of legitimacy is the greatest obstacle to the acceptance and realization of human rights, they require a cultural sounding board that underpins their

[20] Abdullahi A. an-Na'im, "Conclusion," in *Human Rights in Cross-Cultural Perspectives: A Quest for Consensus*, ed. Abdullahi A. an-Na'im (Philadelphia: University of Pennsylvania Press, 1991), 431. Similarly Makau Mutua, *Human Rights: A Political and Cultural Critique* (Philadelphia: University of Pennsylvania Press, 2002), 81.

[21] See the argument of Naz K. Modirzadeh, "Taking Islamic Law Seriously: INGOs and the Battle for Muslim Hearts and Minds," *Harvard Human Rights Journal* 19 (2006): 191–233.

[22] David L. Johnston, "Maqāṣid al-Sharīʿa: Epistemology and Hermeneutics of Muslim Theologies of Human Rights," *Die Welt des Islams* 47, no. 2 (2007): 155.

[23] Wilfred Blunt, *The Future of Islam* (Dublin: Nonsuch, 2007), 82.

[24] Ali, *Sexual Ethics and Islam*, xii

[25] Baderin, *International Human Rights and Islamic Law*, 30.

legitimacy in the Islamic context: "[T]he positive means to promote any concept within a particular culture is through evidential support from within its legitimizing principles. . . . Islamic principles and norms constitute a principal legitimizing factor for cultural-legal norms in most parts of the Muslim world."[26] In this sense, human rights depend on an Islamic reception that acts as a catalyst for their acceptance and realization.

As these observations show, the relationship between Islam and human rights and the related formation of Muslim understandings of human rights is caught between two different normative requirements: the requirement of universality and the requirement of Islamic legitimacy. On *the level of justification*, this entails the necessity of applying religiously independent criteria in order to guarantee the universal validity of human rights. Human rights are universally valid when they are accepted for reasons that every human being can in principle understand and accept. On *the level of legitimation*, however, human rights require an Islamic justification that allows Muslims to adopt a positive attitude toward them and to make use of the motivational resources of religion. Ali Merad captures the dilemma posed by this dual challenge to a Muslim conception of human rights as follows: "Is there an Islamic human rights doctrine that is homogeneous in itself and at the same time compatible with other ethical positions on human rights? Or rather, is it possible to develop an Islamic conception of human rights that is authentically Islamic, i.e. one that strictly adheres to the existing sources of Islam (such as faith, law, moral teachings) and at the same time can satisfy a modern mind that is not prepared to curtail the human and civil rights that are almost universally recognized today?"[27] This is the question I will try to answer in the third part of this book.

[26] Ibid., 6.
[27] Ali Merad, "Das islamische Bewusstsein vor dem Anruf der Menschenrechte," in Schwartländer, *Freiheit der Religion*, 347–348.

PART III

ISLAMIC FOUNDATIONS OF A UNIVERSAL CONCEPTION OF HUMAN RIGHTS

As we noted in the previous chapter, any viable Islamic conception of human rights is bound by the twin requirements of Islamicity and generalizability. Islamicity requires that any such conception be authentically Islamic in the sense that it is anchored in the edifice of Islamic law and thought, while the postulate of generalizability requires that it be able to command universal agreement. In what follows, I will attempt to formulate a conception of human rights that satisfies these two requirements. The goal, therefore, will be to establish an Islamic conception of human rights that is capable of commanding universal assent.

This raises the legitimate question of whether the attribute "Islamic" is necessary at all, since the conception is also supposed to be "universal." As the following explanations will show, the requirement that the conception be "Islamic" can indeed be dispensed with without affecting the content of the conception to be established here. For although its substantive values are *also* religious, they are not *essentially* so, since they could in principle also be based on nonreligious grounds. In this sense, religion has a legitimizing rather than a justifying function. This aspect is particularly central in the context of modern pluralistic societies, where different religious and nonreligious individuals and groups must coexist, and where a single religion cannot prescribe what is right for everyone.

The attribute "Islamic" is justified by the simple fact that the conception to be presented is based on a central aspect of Islamic jurisprudence and can be traced back to Muslim thinkers such as the Andalusian jurist al-Shāṭibī (d. 1388/790). He and other, more influential scholars, such as al-Juwaynī (d. 1085/478) and al-Ghazāli (d. 1111/505, undoubtedly the most seminal medieval Islamic thinker), sought to demonstrate that the common denominator of the norms of the *sharīʿa* regulating social relations is that they protect basic *human needs*. This legal objective and the related concept of *maqāṣid al-sharīʿa* (purposes of Islamic law) emerged from an inductive study of religious sources and was thus based on religious premises. However, it explicitly served to develop a generalizable legal concept that could be applied independently of Islamic law.

With regard to contemporary human rights discussions, the notion of human needs as the anthropological foundation of the *sharīʿa* provides a conceptual framework for an independent understanding of the human person and thus paves the way for a transcultural discussion of human rights. As Höffe emphasizes, we must "refrain from all group-, culture-, and time-specific conceptions of humanity . . . and develop a culturally independent, strictly universal concept of the human being [in order to] identify the rights that human beings possess as such."[1] Especially when it comes to the justification of human rights, the concept of human needs seems to be more appropriate than the usual concept of natural law. For the justification of rights by appeal to natural law, like the theological justification, merely serves to remove certain legal contents from the sphere of human influence and to give them a prepolitical character.[2] While the concept of natural law locates the higher normative authority that human beings must respect in nature, the theological justification of human rights identifies God as that authority. The sheer similarity between the two concepts becomes apparent when we consider the religious roots of the natural law–based justification of human rights. According to John Locke, human rights and the liberty they entail are the result of a God-given, natural freedom: "For Men being all the Workmanship of one Omnipotent, and infinitely wise Maker; All the Servants of one Sovereign Master, sent into the World by his order and about his business, they are his Property, whose Workmanship they are, made to last during his, not one another's Pleasure."[3]

[1] Otfried Höffe, "Transzendentaler Tausch: Eine Legitimationsfigur für Menschenrechte?," in *Philosophie der Menschenrechte*, ed. Stefan Gosepath and Georg Lohmann (Frankfurt: Suhrkamp, 1998), 32.

[2] See Gabriele Kuhn-Zuber, "Der Islam und die Universalität der Menschenrechte in der Kritik," in *Menschenrechte: Bilanz und Perspektiven*, ed. Jana Hasse, Erwin Müller, and Patricia Schneider (Baden-Baden: Nomos, 2002), 323–324.

[3] Locke, *Two Treatises of Government*, 271. On this, see Rainer Forst, *Toleration in Conflict: Past and Present* (Cambridge: Cambridge University Press, 2013), 171–172, 334–335 and Michael Freeman, "The Problem of Secularism in Human Rights Theory," who speaks of a "hidden God in human rights" (387).

Ultimately, then, the natural law conception of human rights remains as resistant to rational justification as the theological conception.

In what follows, I will argue that the concept of human needs can, under conditions to be defined, serve as a *universally consensual justificatory foundation* for human rights. Without excluding other approaches,[4] I believe that the needs approach has a number of advantages that are particularly useful with respect to the requirement that human rights be culturally neutral. The central idea of the argument is that recourse to human needs addresses a defining feature of the human condition that is independent of subjective attitudes and cultures and can therefore serve as an interculturally valid foundation for human rights that can command universal agreement. To elaborate on this core idea, I will first discuss its Islamic articulation within the concept of *maqāṣid al-sharīʿa*. The concept of *maqāṣid* originated in discussions of the methods of normative justification and related attempts to provide a rational justification for divine decrees. Chapter 8 will therefore first address the question of how and on what basis norms can be justified within the framework of Islamic legal methodology. I will then provide a detailed account of the resulting concept of *maqāṣid* with reference to the work of classical Muslim jurists. In chapter 9, I will address some points of criticism and some open questions that prove problematic when viewed through the lens of the classical *maqāṣid* conception. Chapter 10 then takes a closer look at the contemporary reception of the *maqāṣid* idea and examines some

[4] One notable approach that shares the twin concerns of universality and Islamic legitimacy is that of Abdulaziz Sachedina. In his book *Islam and the Challenge of Human Rights*, Sachedina seeks to unfold the universal content of key Islamic concepts in order to demonstrate "that modern notions of liberty, pluralism, and human rights have their antecedents in the authoritative theological and legal traditions of Islam" (44). To this end, he draws primarily on the ethical and theological resources of the Islamic tradition, arguing that a focus on the *sharīʿa* and juridical discourses holds less productive value (16, 87, 114). At the heart of his proposal is the Qurʾanic notion of *fiṭra*, which he claims denotes intuitive reason and an innate ability to know right from wrong. According to Sachedina, this notion provides a universal and authentically Islamic basis for affirming the fundamental ideas of dignity, equality, and, by extension, human rights. While I do not necessarily disagree with Sachedina, I believe that much more theoretical heavy lifting is needed to flesh out a coherent and methodologically sound conception of human rights. The vague appeal to the idea of a moral conscience, God's justice, or the duty to establish good and prevent evil may provide a suitable gateway through which the concept of human rights can be incorporated into the Islamic tradition, but it fails to address specific problems in human rights discourse and tells us little about the ways in which the specific content of human rights can be generated or justified. Given that the legitimacy of human rights in Islamic discourses is challenged primarily with reference to the *sharīʿa*, I also think it unwise to avoid a substantive engagement with it, especially if the objective is to address the suspicions and objections of traditionalist Muslim scholars. Since human rights derive their force primarily through law, I believe it is imperative to engage the subject within an Islamic legal framework, which naturally includes theological elements and, as the following discussion will show, provides valuable substantive insights and methodological tools that can be used to construct a coherent theory of human rights.

contributions to its reconceptualization. A comprehensive treatment of such a long-standing body of legal thought is beyond the scope of the present study. Accordingly, I will not be able to discuss the ideas covered here in the exhaustive detail that would be required for an in-depth treatment of the Islamic legal tradition. Nevertheless, I hope that my presentation will provide at least an intellectual foundation upon which a more fruitful discussion of human rights can be built.

8

The Purpose of Islamic Law (*maqāṣid al-sharīʿa*)

> In no other field can those who are not afraid to search and reflect be so certain of discovering the purpose as in the field of law—to search for it is the supreme task of jurisprudence.[1]

A central, though generally neglected feature of Islamic law is that it did not "fall from the sky" as a finished legal code. Islamic law is not contained in a document, paragraph, or catalogue. Rather, Islamic law is something that people had to and still have to carefully develop on the basis of certain source texts. These consist of the Qur'an as the first primary source and the recorded Sunnah (statements, deeds, approvals, and condemnations) of the Prophet as the second source. The term "source" here refers to a place from which legal norms can be drawn. However, since the legal norms contained in the Qur'an are only a small part of the entire text, it would be wrong to call it a legal document. Of its 6,236 verses, only about 245 have a legal character.[2] Moreover, these legal norms were not created in a vacuum but usually refer to specific cases and situations that occurred at the time of the revelation.[3] Although Muslim jurists assumed that the revealed text possessed timeless validity, they were aware that the Qur'an and the Sunnah regulated only a limited number of cases. Thus the question arose of how to deal with future legal questions, to which neither the Qur'an nor the Sunnah provided an answer, without neglecting the will of revelation, for the Qur'an (4:59) states, "[I]f you are at variance over any matter, refer it unto God and the Apostle." How, then, could the Qur'anic revelation, anchored in a specific historical

[1] Rudolf von Jhering, *Der Zweck im Recht* (Leipzig: Breitkopf & Härtel, 1884), 1:442.
[2] Mumisa, *Islamic Law*, 159. Strictly speaking, the legal norms are limited to the part of the Islamic normative system that deals with the regulation of interpersonal relations.
[3] Kamali, *Shari'ah Law*, 19.

Human Rights Between Universality and Islamic Legitimacy. Mahmoud Bassiouni, Oxford University Press.
 DOI: 10.1093/oso/9780197753897.003.0009

time (the seventh century) and place (the Arabian peninsula), be kept alive as a timeless source of inspiration and guidance in the face of ever-changing living conditions? With this question in mind, Muslim jurists were faced with the task of developing methods of deriving norms that would enable them to extrapolate legitimate answers from the Islamic source texts as new legal needs arose.

From Reason to Purpose

A suitable solution to this problem was first found in reasoning by analogy (*qiyās*).[4] *Qiyās* is a process by which the rule applied in a case that is regulated in the source texts is applied to a new case that is not regulated in the source texts, on the grounds that the reason underlying both cases is the same.[5] Accordingly, an analogy consists of four components: (1) an original case (*aṣl*) dealt with in the source texts, (2) a new case (*far*ʿ) for which a norm is sought, (3) the norm applied in the original case (*ḥukm*) that can be inferred from the textual sources, and (4) a feature that the original case and the new case have in common and that constitutes the reason (*ʿilla*) for the norm. For example, the Qur'an (5:90) explicitly prohibits the use of wine but is silent on the use of drugs. Since there is nothing explicit about the use of drugs in the Sunnah either, we must answer the question of whether the use of drugs is also prohibited by analogy. For this purpose, we first ask what is the reason for the prohibition of drinking wine and discover that it is the intoxicating property of wine. Since drugs have the same intoxicating property, we can conclude that the use of drugs is prohibited (Figure 8.1).[6]

The core of the analogy, then, is the identification of the *ʿilla*, the feature that justifies a norm. It makes a norm rationally intelligible, so that we are now able to understand the prohibition of wine consumption even without explicit reference to the Qur'an. Thus the reason for the prohibition is not because it is written in the Qur'an but because of the intoxicating effect of alcohol on the human mind. But how exactly can we justify the choice of this

[4] Islamic jurisprudence developed both linguistic and rational methods for deriving norms that cannot be discussed in detail here. For comprehensive treatment of the doctrine of the sources and methods of norm derivation (*uṣūl al-fiqh*), see Kamali, *Principles of Islamic Jurisprudence.*

[5] Ibid., 267; Nyazee, *Theories of Islamic Law*, 198.

[6] For an in-depth discussion of Muslim justifications of the ban on drugs, see Felicitas Opwis, "Schariarechtliche Stellungsnahmen zum Drogenverbot," *Die Welt des Islams* 39, no. 2 (1999): 159–182.

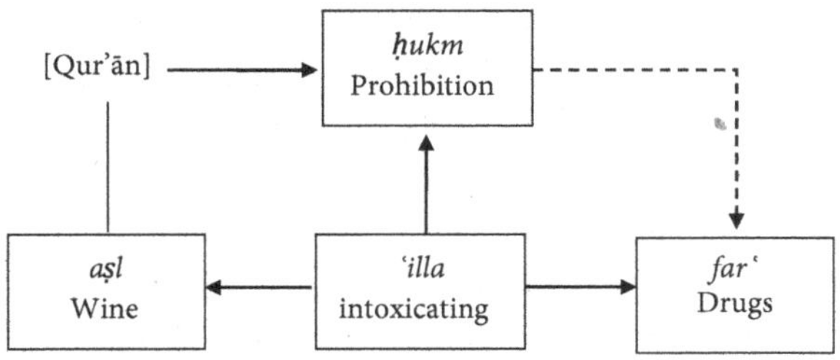

Figure 8.1 Method of analogy: example of the prohibition of wine.

reason? In some cases, the Qur'an itself provides the justification for a norm, for example, the directive to reserve a certain share for orphans and the poor when dividing the spoils of war, so that "it may not be [a benefit] going round and round among such of you as may [already] be rich" (59:7). In the case of wine, however, we know only that the Qur'an forbids its consumption without giving an explicit reason. So how do we methodologically arrive at a legitimate justification in this case?

Muslim jurists assume that every object and every state of affairs can be represented as a complex of properties. Wine, too, is a collection of different properties: it is, among other things, (a) made of grapes, (b) red or white, (c) liquid, (d) has a certain taste and (e) smell, and (f) is intoxicating. In order to identify the reason for the prohibition, the jurists established several criteria that a property must meet in order to qualify as a reason.[7] First, the property must be clear (*ẓāhir*)—in other words, it must be a property that can be perceived with the sense organs, that is, it must be empirically ascertainable. Furthermore, the property must be precise (*munḍabiṭ*) in the sense that it can be unambiguously defined and is independent of a person's subjective feeling or opinion. Finally, and crucially, we must be able to assume that the property is suitable for realizing the legislative purpose of the norm (*ḥikma tashrīʿiyya*), which in this case is to ensure the functioning of reason and to avert the harmful effects of consumption for the consumer and society. Only in this light does it make sense to prohibit the consumption of wine because of its intoxicating character, since only the property of being "intoxicating" is suitable for realizing the purpose of the norm. Prohibiting wine because of its color or taste would serve no particular purpose. By prohibiting the consumption of intoxicating substances, however, the legislator can achieve the

[7] See Khallāf, *ʿIlm Uṣūl al-Fiqh*, 66–67.

purpose identified above. The intoxicating property thus satisfies a criterion that Islamic jurisprudence calls "suitability" (*munāsaba*). Accordingly, the *ʿilla* is the property that serves to realize the purpose of the norm. It is a suitable means for realizing the purpose of the norm.

The criterion of suitability implies that the real motive for enacting a norm is not the *ʿilla* itself but the realization of its purpose (*riʿāyat al-maqāsid*).[8] In other words, what *ought* to be realized is the purpose. Thus, what is relevant is not the intoxicating property per se but its ability to realize the purpose of the norm. Taken in isolation, the *ʿilla* does not express an "ought" but merely describes an empirical fact (wine intoxicates). This fact contains no inherent value judgment and is therefore neither good nor bad in itself, but only true or false. It is its teleological relation to the purpose that gives the *ʿilla* an evaluative character, that is, makes it good or bad, and endows it with a normative meaning that also justifies its binding force. For example, one might ask why it is obligatory to stop at a traffic light. The simple answer would be: because the light is red. But how does the property "red" constitute the normative reason for the prohibition on running the light? Apart from the fact that it is stated in the Highway Code, the answer is that "red" as a traffic signal serves to regulate traffic and helps to prevent accidents that occur when traffic is not regulated. The obligation to stop at a red light makes sense only in relation to this purpose. The red light itself has no meaning in this context other than to serve that purpose. When it comes to the justification of norms, then, we must distinguish between a means of *realization* (*causa efficiens*) and an end *to be realized* (*causa finalis*), or, in Schopenhauer's words, between that *through which* something exists and that *on account of which* it exists.[9] Only when we know the latter can we understand the meaning of the norm or why it exists. This is why Rudolf von Jhering describes the purpose as "the creator of all law."[10]

Muslim jurists agree that Islamic legal norms, far from being arbitrary or meaningless, have specific purposes, motives, or intentions (*maqāsid*).[11]

[8] See Abū Ḥāmid al-Ghazāli, *Shifāʾ al-Ghalīl fī Bayān al-Shabah wʾal-Mukhīl wa Masāliku al-Taʿlīl* (Baghdad: Matbaʿat al-Irshād, 1971), 159; Ibrahīm Ibn Mūsa al-Shāṭibī, *al-Muwāfaqāt fī Uṣūl al-Aḥkām* (Beirut: Dār al-Maʿrifa, 1996), 1:216–217; Muḥammad Ibn ʿAlī al-Shawkāni, *Irshād al-Fuḥūl ilā Taḥqīq al-Ḥaqq min ʿIlm al-Uṣūl* (Riyadh: Dār al-Faḍīla, 2000), 1:896.

[9] Arthur Schopenhauer, *The World as Will and Representation* (New York: Dover, 1966), 2:331.

[10] Von Jhering, *Der Zweck im Recht*, 1:viii: "The basic idea is . . . that the purpose is the creator of all law, that there is no legal norm that does not owe its existence to a purpose, i.e., a practical motive."

[11] Yūsuf al-Qaraḍāwi, *Madkhal li Dirāsāt al-Sharʿiyya al-Islāmiyya* (Cairo: Maktabat Wahba, 2009), 73. Muḥammad Fatḥi al-Drīni, *al-Haqq wa Madā Ṣulṭān al-Dawla fī Taqyīdihi* (Beirut: Muʾassasat al-Risāla, 1984), 219–220.

Their premise is that the general purpose of Islamic law is to benefit human beings (*jalb al-maṣāliḥ*) and to protect them from harm (*dar' al-mafāsid*).[12] This assumption, which was "accepted without objection by the companions of the Prophet and their successors,"[13] claims a practical consensus within Islamic jurisprudence and is considered an "irrefutable premise that forms the foundation of Islamic thought and shapes the development of the theory of the creation of law in Islam to the present day."[14] This premise provides a rough synopsis of a complex legal idea that we will explore in more detail below.

The Search for the Purposes of Islamic Law

The attempt to rationally justify revealed Islamic norms and the related question of their purposes has preoccupied Muslims since the early Middle Ages. As early as the late ninth century, the philosopher and mystic al-Ḥakīm al-Tirmidhī (d. 908/206) attempted to analyze the purpose of individual revealed norms. He was also the first to use the term *maqāsid* in this context.[15] Other notable figures who attempted to justify norms in terms of their purposes were Abū Zayd al-Balkhī (d. 933/322), Abū Mansūr al-Maturīdi (d. 944/333), Abū Bakr al-Qaffāl al-Shāshī (d. 975/365), Abū Bakr al-Abharī (d. 985/375), Ibn Bābawayh al-Qummī (d. 991/381), Abū al-Ḥassan al-'Āmiri (d. 991/381), and al-Bāqillāni (d. 1012/403).[16]

This tradition reached a turning point in the fifth Islamic century with al-Juwayni (d. 1085/478).[17] In his work *al-Burhān*, he not only inquired into the purposes of individual norms but also categorized norms on the basis of their underlying purposes in an attempt to systematize the objectives of Islamic

[12] For a comprehensive treatment of this topic, see Felicitas Opwis, *Maṣlaḥa and the Purpose of the Law: Islamic Discourse on Legal Change from the 4th/10th to 8th/14th Century* (Leiden: Brill, 2010).

[13] Yūsuf Ḥāmid al-'Ālim, *al-Maqāsid al-'Āmmah lil Sharī'a al-Islamiyya* (Herndon, VA: International Institute of Islamic Thought, 1991), 182.

[14] Adel el-Baradie, *Gottes-Recht und Menschen-Recht* (Baden-Baden: Nomos, 1983), 168.

[15] al-Ḥakīm Abū 'Abdallāh al-Tirmidhī, *al-Ṣalāh wa Maqāṣiduha* (Cairo: Dār al-Kitāb al-'Arabī, 1965).

[16] For an overview, see Jasser Auda, *Maqāṣid al-Sharī'ah: A Beginner's Guide* (Herndon, VA: International Institute of Islamic Thought, 2008), 14–17; Ahmad al-Raysuni, *Imam al-Shatibi's Theory of Higher Objectives and Intents of Islamic Law* (Herndon, VA: International Institute of Islamic Thought, 2005), 4–11.

[17] Abū al-Ma'ālī 'Ālī Muḥammad 'Abdallah Ibn Yūsuf al-Juwayni, also known as Imam al-Ḥaramayn, was born in 1028/419 in a place called Juwayn near the city Nishapur in the northeastern part of present-day Iran.

law.[18] In this endeavor, al-Juwayni proceeded from the premise that every life situation (*wāqiʿa*) must be regulated in accordance with Islamic legal sources.[19] Since the Qur'an and the Sunnah do not provide an explicit rule for every life situation, it is imperative, according to al-Juwayni, to extend the law through rational inference (*istidlāl*) so that the regulation of human life does not become arbitrary. Otherwise, the law—and the divine legislator behind it—would be incapable of regulating human life. It would therefore be wrong to limit the framework of legal reasoning to the explicit wording of the norms of the Qur'an and the Sunnah (*al-manṣūṣāt*), for this would close the gates of *ijtihād*.[20] In fact, al-Juwayni argues, the *manṣūṣāt* constitute only a small part of the Islamic *sharīʿa*.[21] Moreover, it is not the norms themselves that are authoritative but the purposes they contain and convey.[22] The norms of the source texts are thus merely the epistemic medium through which the authoritative purpose of the norm is expressed. But this purpose does not emerge from the explicit wording; rather, it must be brought to light through rational analysis and interpretive effort (*al-naẓar w'al-ijtihād*).[23] Accordingly, al-Juwayni repeatedly emphasizes the need to understand the norms of revelation in the light of their purposes, for "those who are unable to recognize the purposes behind the precepts and prohibitions have also failed to recognize the basis on which the Shari'ah is justified."[24]

According to al-Juwayni, however, not all norms of the *sharīʿa* can be understood by examining their purposes. In order to clarify this point, he divides the norms into different categories, which on the one hand differ in their rational comprehensibility, and on the other hand pursue purposes of varying degrees of importance:[25]

1. The first category includes norms whose purposes are rationally comprehensible (*ma yuʿqal maʿnatu*). According to al-Juwayni, they deal with necessary and indispensable matters (*amr ḍarūri la bud minhu*) and serve to secure the universal, political, and general welfare (*al-iyāla al-kulliyya al-siyāsiyya al-ʿammiyya*). In other words, their purpose is

[18] ʿAbd al-Mālik Abū al-Maʿālī al-Juwayni, *al-Burhān fī Uṣūl al-Fiqh*, ed. ʿAbd al-ʿAẓīm al-Dīb (Doha: Jāmiʿat Qatar, 1979).
[19] Ibid., 2:1116.
[20] Ibid., 2:1116–1117.
[21] Ibid., 2:1117.
[22] Ibid., 2:1117–1118: *laysat al-uṣūl wa aḥkāmiha ḥujjajan, wa innama al-ḥujaj fī al-maʿna.*
[23] Ibid., 2:1118.
[24] Ibid., 1:295.
[25] Ibid., 2:923–926.

to protect essential necessities, an example of which is the norm of retaliation (*qisās*) (2:178), which is justified by the purpose of preventing innocent bloodshed (killing) and attacks on innocent people.[26]

2. The second category includes norms that relate to general but non-essential needs (*al-ḥāja al-ʿāmma*). These include norms that allow people to rent and lease housing so that they can live in a dwelling without having to own it.[27]
3. The norms of the third category relate neither to essential nor to general needs, but to things that are noble in themselves (*makrama*). Examples of these are commandments concerning ritual purity.[28]
4. The norms of the fourth category are similar in purpose to those of the third category, but they are subordinate to them and serve to supplement them. Unlike the third category, they are not explicit commandments, but merely supplementary recommendations (*mandūbāt*).[29]
5. The fifth category is the only one that contains norms whose purpose is either entirely unknowable or cannot be clearly known.[30] According to al-Juwayni, they are not concerned with essential (1), needs-based (2), or noble (3) matters. Rather, they are specific norms, such as those prescribing the forms of prayer or the times of fasting, which refer to the domain of ritual action and are not associated with any recognizable benefit.[31]

As the description of the last category shows, al-Juwayni combines the third and fourth categories so that we are left with four categories, resulting in the scheme illustrated in Figure 8.2:

With this categorization, al-Juwayni laid the foundation for a theory of Islamic legal purposes (*maqāsid al sharīʿa*) that was elaborated and continued by later jurists. At this point, we can already see that, according to al-Juwayni, the purpose of Islamic legal norms is to protect various human necessities and needs that differ in their importance for human life and stand in a hierarchical relationship.

The renowned scholar al-Ghazāli (d. 1111/505), a disciple of al-Juwayni, was the first to take up his teacher's ideas and develop them, in three separate

[26] Ibid., 2:923.
[27] Ibid., 2:924.
[28] Ibid., 2:924–925.
[29] Ibid., 2:925.
[30] Ibid., 2:926.
[31] Ibid., 2:958.

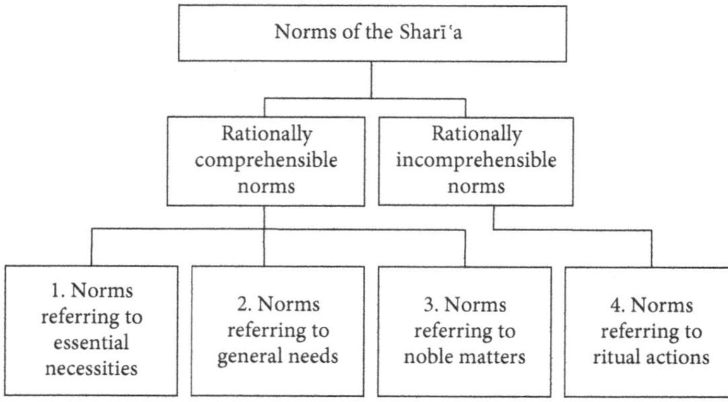

Figure 8.2 Categorization of norms according to al-Juwayni.

works. In his first work on legal theory, *al-Mankhūl*, he offers a detailed exposition and interpretation of his teacher's ideas.[32] In his second book, *Shifāʾ al-Ghalīl*, al-Ghazāli deals more intensively with the question of the justification of norms and formulates an independent legal theory that revises and develops some of al-Juwayni's ideas.[33] Al-Ghazāli seems to be aware of the originality of his legal theory, for at the beginning of his work he urges the reader to rid himself of outdated beliefs and habits of thought that would prevent a sound understanding of his theory. In addition, he requires the reader to have a thirst for knowledge in order to understand insights that have remained hidden from him in other works.[34]

In terms of content, al-Ghazāli, like al-Juwayni, starts from the premise that all norms of the Islamic *sharīʿa* have certain purposes. According to al-Ghazāli, however, we must distinguish between an otherworldly (*dīni*) and a worldly (*dunyawi*) purpose.[35] While the norms of ritual acts serve the otherworldly purpose of the *sharīʿa*, the norms of interpersonal relations realize its worldly purpose. The latter consists in the protection of life (*nafs*), reason (*ʿaql*), chastity (*budʿ*), and property (*māl*).[36] These are the basic needs whose protection is pursued by the norms of Islamic law (by which is meant now

[32] Abū Ḥāmid al-Ghazāli, al-*Mankhūl min Taʿliqāt al-Uṣūl*, ed. Muḥammad Ḥassan Hītu (Damascus: Dār al-Fikr, 1998).
[33] Abū Ḥāmid al-Ghazāli, *Shifāʾ al-Ghalīl fī Bayān al-Shabah wʾal-Mukhīl wa Masāliku al-Taʿlīl* (Baghdad: Matbaʿat al-Irshād, 1971).
[34] Ibid., 5–8.
[35] Ibid., 159.
[36] Ibid., 160.

exclusively the norms regulating interpersonal relations). In this sense, their protection is the purpose of Islamic legislation (*maqsūd al-sharʿ*).

But why does Islamic law have these specific purposes? Al-Ghazāli's answer is that they are basic goods that are indispensable for the existence of human creatures (*darūrāt al-khalq*).[37] In this regard, a consensus could be reached regardless of religion and regardless of "whether one ascribes to reason the ability to independently recognize good and evil."[38] Reason, according to al-Ghazāli, is thus capable of recognizing these basic goods as worthy of protection even without the guidance of revelation.[39] What is at stake is nothing less than the protection of the basic conditions of human existence. For without the protection of life, human beings' physical existence would be endangered, while the protection of property secures their material livelihood. The protection of reason serves to preserve human beings as responsible creatures, and the protection of chastity serves to establish clear relationships of kinship in order to ensure the proper care of the children associated with these relationships.[40] Accordingly, in one of his last works, *al-Mustaṣfa*,[41] al-Ghazāli replaces the "protection of chastity" with the "protection of offspring" (*ḥifẓ al-nasl*).[42] He also adds the protection of religion (*ḥifẓ al-dīn*) to the list of legal purposes, thus removing the strict distinction between worldly and religious purposes.[43] Following Hallaq, we can attribute this development to the fact that *Shifā al-Ghalīl*, the earlier work, was written when al-Ghazāli was at the height of his academic influence and was intensively engaged in jurisprudential and rational-philosophical issues, so that his thought was shaped by pragmatic concerns. *Al-Mustaṣfa*, on the other hand, was written at a time when al-Ghazāli was increasingly concerned with spiritual and Sufi issues as a result of a spiritual crisis. According to Hallaq, *al-Mustaṣfa*, which in al-Ghazāli's own words was intended to serve as a handbook for jurisprudence, reflects an attempt to formulate an uncontroversial "minimal doctrine" in order to

[37] Ibid., 162.

[38] Ibid. With this, al-Ghazāli is alluding to the Muʿtazili school of faith, which held the opinion that reason independent of divine revelation is able to distinguish between good and bad and between the useful and the harmful.

[39] Ibid., 162: *al-ʿuqūl mushīra ilayhi wa qāḍiya bihi laula wurūd al sharāʾiʿ*.

[40] Ibid., 160.

[41] On this, see George F. Hourani, "A Revised Chronology of al-Ghāzalī's Writings," *Journal of the American Oriental Society* 104, no. 2 (1984): 289–302.

[42] Abū Ḥāmid al-Ghazāli, *al-Mustaṣfa min ʿIlm al-Uṣūl*, ed. Ḥamza Ibn Zuhayr Ḥāfiẓ (Medina: al-Jāmiʿa al-Islāmiyya, n.d.), 2:482.

[43] Ibid.

forestall conservative objections as much as possible.[44] Nevertheless, al-Ghazāli emphasizes that the list of these (now) five basic needs can still claim to be capable of commanding consensus because "it would be inconceivable that any society or legal system whose aim is to achieve the human good [*iṣlāḥ al-khalq*] would not include measures to protect these five basic needs."[45]

To illustrate how Islamic law guarantees the protection of these basic needs, al-Ghazāli turns to a discussion of the term *maṣlaḥa*. *Maṣlaḥa* (pl. *maṣāliḥ*) is an ambiguous term that can be translated as "good," "benefit," "interest," "welfare," or "well-being."[46] Al-Ghazāli notes that it generally refers to anything that serves to benefit people (*jalb manfaʿa*) and prevent their being harmed (*dafʿ madarra*).[47] But this is not the context in which he himself uses the term. Rather, by *maṣlaḥa* he means only that which serves to protect the five basic needs mentioned above: "What we mean by *maṣlaḥa* is the protection of legal purpose [*maqsūd al-sharʿ*]. The purpose of the law is to protect the religion, life, reason, offspring, and property of humankind. Whatever involves the protection of these five basic needs is a *maṣlaḥa* [good], and whatever hinders [the protection of] these basic needs is a *mafsada* [evil], the elimination of which is also a *maṣlaḥa*."[48] The term *maṣlaḥa* thus refers to specific goods that serve to guarantee the purpose of Islamic law, that is, the protection of the five basic human needs mentioned above. Thus, it is important to distinguish between basic needs *to be protected* (*maqāsid*) on the one hand and *protective* goods (*maṣāliḥ*) on the other. Moreover, according to al-Ghazāli, we must distinguish three levels of *maṣāliḥ*, since not all goods contribute equally to the protection of basic needs, and thus to the protection of the conditions of human existence:

1. In the first place are the *necessary goods* (*ḍarūrāt*), the realization of which is an indispensable condition for the protection of the five basic needs. They serve to eliminate those evils (*mafāsid*) that pose a direct threat to the basic needs. For example, manslaughter is an evil that

[44] Wael Hallaq, "Uṣūl al-Fiqh: Beyond Tradition," *Journal of Islamic Studies* 3, no. 2 (1992): 189–190.
[45] al-Ghazāli, *al-Mustaṣfa*, 2:483.
[46] On the linguistic and jurisprudential meaning of *maṣlaḥa*, see Ihsan Abdul-Wajid Bagby, "Utility in Classical Islamic Law: The Concept of Maṣlaḥa in Uṣūl al-Fiqh" (PhD diss., University of Michigan, 1986), 19–34.
[47] al-Ghazāli, *al-Mustaṣfa*, 2:481.
[48] Ibid., 2:482.

threatens the "protection of life," so legal measures to prevent manslaughter are a necessary good.[49]

2. Second are those goods whose realization may not be necessary but is nevertheless required (*muḥtāj ilayh*) to guarantee people's existential well-being. Accordingly, al-Ghazāli refers to them as *required goods* (*ḥājāt*). If such goods were not realized, people's existence would not be endangered, but their ability to conduct their lives would be impaired.[50]
3. Finally, in the third place are those goods that are neither necessary nor required to protect basic needs; rather, they contribute to improving the conditions of human existence. These *ameliorative goods* (*taḥsīnāt*) help to shape the individual and social life of human beings in the best possible way (*ri'āyat aḥsan al-manāhij fi al-'ādāt wa'l-mu'āmalāt*).[51]

As these explanations make clear, the relationship between the various levels of goods and basic needs is a purely instrumental one in which the realization of the former contributes to the protection and preservation of the latter. The hierarchical arrangement of the various goods is based on the urgency they acquire in relation to the protection of the basic needs. We can compare this relationship with another that al-Ghazāli presents in his work *Iḥyā' 'Ulūm al-Dīn*, where he argues that certain human activities are required if social affairs are to be well ordered. However, he points out that not every activity contributes to this purpose to the same extent, so human activities can be divided into three hierarchical categories:

1. The first category includes necessary activities, without which human life would descend into chaos. Among these al-Ghazāli includes agriculture, which is necessary for the production of food; weaving, which is necessary for the production of clothing; architecture, which is necessary for the construction of houses; and politics, which is necessary for the establishment of human relations and the promotion of social cooperation.[52]
2. The second category includes the kinds of activities that, according to al-Ghazāli, play a supporting role for the above activities. For example,

[49] Ibid., 2:482–483.
[50] Ibid., 2:483–484.
[51] Ibid., 2:485.
[52] Abū Ḥāmid al-Ghazāli, *Iḥyā' 'Ulūm al-Dīn* (Beirut: Dār al-Ma'rifa, 1982), 1:12–13.

blacksmithing is a requisite activity because it provides the weavers with tools with which they can improve the processing of cotton.[53]

3. Finally, the third category includes those activities that supplement the first category of activities. For example, tailoring is a supplementary activity in that it transforms the textiles produced by the weavers into wearable clothing.[54]

The importance of these activities for the proper ordering of social affairs can also be compared to the importance of individual parts of the body for the maintenance of the human body as a whole. Again, we can distinguish three hierarchically ordered categories:

1. Necessary organs such as the heart, liver, and brain.
2. Supporting organs such as the stomach, veins, arteries, nerves, and tendons.
3. Supplementary organs such as nails, fingers, and eyebrows.[55]

As these examples illustrate, al-Ghazāli evaluates the relative importance of the respective objects according to their importance for the realization of the purpose in question. In the case of human activities, this purpose consists in the production of basic goods such as food, clothing, shelter, and social cooperation. These basic goods, in turn, constitute those elements without which a well-ordered society cannot be guaranteed. Similarly, in the case of law, the importance of the various goods depends on how necessary they are for the protection of the five basic needs. These, in turn, are the *universal* and *indispensable* conditions of human existence. This shows that al-Ghazāli's answer to the question of the purpose of Islamic law involves different levels of abstraction. In summary, the purpose is (a) to realize the necessary, required, and ameliorative goods (*maṣāliḥ*) and to eliminate their corresponding evils (*mafāsid*), in order to (b) ensure the protection of life, reason, offspring, property, and religion, which (c) represent the basic conditions of human existence (Figure 8.3).

[53] Ibid., 1:86.

[54] Ibid., 1:16. To these activities, al-Ghazāli later adds a list of essential sciences, including medicine, which is necessary to maintain the human body, and mathematics, which he considers necessary for conducting financial transactions. According to al-Ghazāli, these are "the sciences that no human society can do without."

[55] Ibid., 1:13.

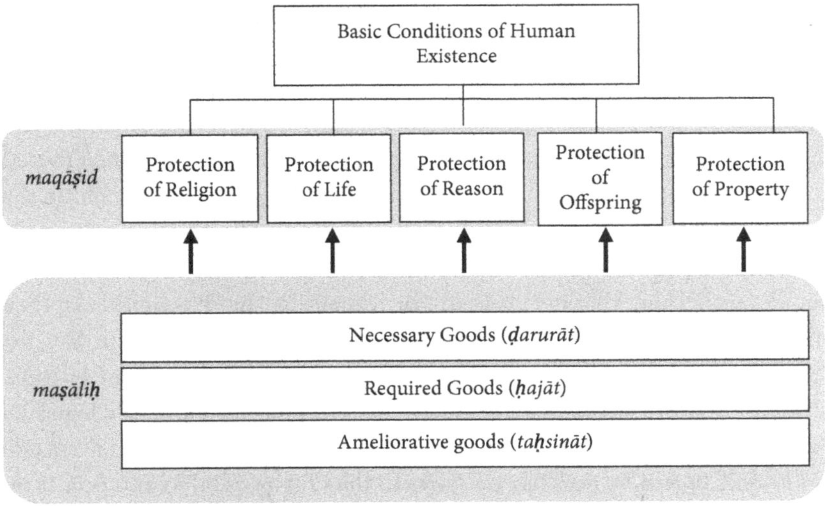

Figure 8.3 Classification of legal purposes according to al-Ghazāli.

With al-Ghazāli, the concept of *maqāsid al-sharīʿa* took the dominant form that it retains to this day. Subsequent treatments have focused less on developing the concept and more on evaluating its underlying premises and theological implications. As our presentation has shown, one of the basic premises of the concept of *maqāsid* is that every divine command and prohibition has a specific purpose. A second, related premise is that this purpose relates to the existential well-being of human beings.

To justify these premises, the prominent jurist and theologian Fakhr al-Dīn al-Rāzi (d. 1209/606) presents an interesting argument.[56] First, al-Rāzi postulates that the enactment of a particular norm regarding a particular life situation can be either meaningful (*murajjaḥ*) or meaningless. But he rejects the notion that God could legislate a norm without a specific meaning, since God describes both Himself and the Qur'an as wise (*ḥakīm*).[57] According to al-Rāzi, the attribute of wisdom implies that God's actions cannot be meaningless when He uses his creative power. The Qur'an points this out, for example when it asks, "Did you, then, think that We created you in mere idle play?" (23:115)[58] Moreover, those who act aimlessly are usually described

[56] See Fakhr al-Dīn al-Rāzi, *al-Maḥsūl fī ʿIlm ʿUṣūl al-Fiqh* (Beirut: Mu'assasat al-Risāla, 1997), 5:172–176.

[57] See also Qur'an 2:32, 9:71, 15:25, 36:2, 59:24.

[58] Qur'an 23:115. Al-Rāzi, *al-Maḥsūl fī ʿIlm ʿUṣūl al-Fiqh*, 5:173 also refers to verses 3:191 and 44:39.

as foolish (*ʿābiṯ*). God, however, cannot be foolish, for that would imply stupidity (*safah*), which is incompatible with the divine. Muslims are in agreement (*ijmaʿ*) on this point. Therefore, we must conclude that divine legislation is both meaningful and purposeful. It can be directed either to the needs of God or to the needs of human beings. However, since there is general agreement that God does not have needs, we must conclude that the purpose of legislation refers to human beings. The final question to be answered, then, is whether the legislator's goal is something that benefits people, something that harms them, or something that has neither of these effects. Al-Rāzi answers this question by pointing out that the last two options are unanimously rejected by all reasonable people (*bāṭil bi ittifāq al-ʿuqalāʾ*). Accordingly, he concludes "that God has undoubtedly legislated the norms for the good of humanity" (*innamā sharaʿa al-aḥkām li maṣāliḥ al-ʿibād*).[59] In support of this, he refers to the Qur'an (17:70) and points out that God created human beings with dignity and honor. From this we can conclude that God prescribes only what is beneficial for His creatures, since "honor" and "harm" contradict each other, and God cannot possibly contradict Himself.[60] Moreover, the Qur'an itself indicates that revelation is for the benefit of humanity when God says of the Prophet, "And [thus, O Prophet], We have sent thee as [an evidence of Our] grace towards all the worlds."[61] Furthermore, in the Qur'an (7:156), God describes Himself as merciful to human beings, so it is reasonable to assume that God legislated the norms of revelation for the benefit of humanity.[62]

Thus, while Muslims agree that God seeks the well-being of humanity, al-Rāzi maintains that they disagree about the *theological* implications of this premise. The question it raises, he argues, is whether the correlation between divine revelation and human well-being should be attributed to a personal motive (*gharaḍ*) of God, so that the divine will is based on a rationally discernible causality, or whether the correlation is due to a fortuitous coincidence between divine intention and human well-being. In contrast to the *muʿtazilī* school of thought, which holds that God is *obligated* to do good because of the causal relationship between revealed norms and human well-being, al-Rāzi emphasizes that God seeks to realize human well-being *by His*

[59] Al-Rāzi, *al-Maḥsūl fī ʿIlm ʿUṣūl al-Fiqh*, 5:173.
[60] Ibid., 5:174.
[61] Qur'an 21:107. Here al-Rāzi, *al-Maḥsūl fī ʿIlm ʿUṣūl al-Fiqh*, 5:173 refers to similar verses in the Qur'an, such as 2:29, 45:13, 2:185, and 22:78.
[62] Al-Rāzi, *al-Maḥsūl fī ʿIlm ʿUṣūl al-Fiqh*, 5:175.

grace, not because He is obligated to do so (*tafaḍḍalan minhu wa iḥsānan lā wujūban*).[63] According to al-Rāzi, divine action cannot be subject to causality, since this would imply that God's actions must conform to a specific logic. But the divine will cannot be grasped by human logic. With this argument, al-Rāzi does not deny that there is a correlation between divine revelation and human well-being but only questions the theological implications of this correlation.

With regard to the substantive content of the *maqāsid*, al-Rāzi largely agrees with al-Ghazāli. It is worth noting, however, that he replaces al-Ghazāli's term *nasl* (offspring) with *nasab* (lineage).[64] Nor does al-Rāzi observe any particular order of priority among the five basic needs. The first to comment explicitly on this issue was Sayf al-Dīn al-Āmidi (d. 1233/631), who listed the protection of religion first, followed by the protection of life, offspring, reason, and property.[65] However, as ʿAtiyya shows, the classical jurists do not agree on this.[66] Nor, as we shall see later, is there agreement on the number of basic needs. Al-Āmidi, who was the first to advocate limiting the basic needs to five, justifies this on the following grounds: "The limitation to these five [basic needs] is based on empirical observation [*naẓaran ila al-wāqiʿ*] and the [associated] realization that there are no necessities apart from these."[67] Al-Āmidi thus assumes that the five basic needs represent the universal foundations of human existence and fully encompass everything that human beings can experience as necessary. This insight comes from empirical observation of the human lifeworld without recourse to revelation. Weiss thus paraphrases al-Āmidi's argument as follows:

> As we reflect upon the human part of the created order, that is to say, upon human life, we discover patterns of need and aspiration that are as much a part of the divine custom as patterns visible in the nonhuman part of the created order, such as the daily rising and setting of the sun. We discover

63 Ibid., 5:176.

64 Ibid., 5:160.

65 Al-Āmidi justifies the privileged status of religion on the grounds that it serves human beings' eternal happiness (*al-saʿāda al-abadiyya*) in the hereafter, which is to be preferred over worldly welfare. See al-Āmidi, *al-Aḥkām fī ʿUṣūl al-Aḥkām*, 4:493–495. For an in-depth study of al-Āmidi's legal theory, see Bernard G. Weiss, *The Search for God's Law: Islamic Jurisprudence in the Writings of Sayf al-Din al-Amidi* (Salt Lake City: University of Uthah Press, 2010).

66 Gamal Eldin Attia, *Toward Realization of the Higher Intents of Islamic Law: Maqāṣid al-Shariʿah: A Functional Approach* (Herndon, VA: International Institute of Islamic Thought, 2007), 16–37.

67 al-Āmidi, *al-Aḥkām fī Uṣūl al-Aḥkām*, 3:240.

> that there are recurring human conditions that constitute well-being (*maslaha, manfa'a*) and that there are other such conditions that constitute affliction (*madarra*); and we also discover that certain things are conducive to well-being and certain other things to affliction. We discover, for example, that security of life, rationality, lineage, property, and even worship of God are constitutive of well-being and that certain concrete measures or social arrangements are conducive to their realization. These discoveries in no way depend upon revelation as mediated through prophets.[68]

If we interpret al-Āmidi correctly and take his arguments seriously, then all the necessities that, on the basis of empirical reflection and insight, constitute a necessary component of human existence would have to be included in the canon of basic needs. This touches on a critical point that plays a prominent role in contemporary discussion of the *maqāṣid*, which increasingly questions the dogmatic nature of the five basic needs and calls for the list to be expanded to include other essential necessities. But before turning to these and other issues, I would like to discuss the ideas of the Andalusian scholar al-Shāṭibi, whose treatise on the *maqāsid* marks the culmination of the theoretical development of the classical conception.[69]

Al-Shāṭibi's Theory of Legal Purposes

Al-Shāṭibi (d. 1388/790) is certainly one of the most interesting figures for modern Muslim legal thought, not only because of the content of his legal philosophy but also because of the historical context in which he developed his ideas on legal theory.[70] Al-Shāṭibi lived and taught in Granada, Andalusia, which was undergoing drastic political and socioeconomic changes during the fourteenth century.[71] Faced with the new social realities and the inability

[68] Weiss, *The Search for God's Law*, 613–614.

[69] This is not to suggest that no important contributions were made in the field of the *maqāsid* in the period between al-Āmidi and al-Shāṭibi. In this connection, we should mention Ibn al-Hājib (d. 1248/646), Izz al-Dīn Ibn 'abd al-Salām (d. 1261/660), al-Bayḍāwi (d. 1286/685), al-Isnāwi (d. 1370/772), Ibn al-Subki (d. 1369/771), Shihāb al-Dīn al-Qarāfi (d. 1285/684), al-Tūfi (d. 1316/716), Ibn Taimiyya (d. 1327/728), and Ibn Qayyim al-Jawziyya (d. 1350/751). We will return to some of these scholars below.

[70] Detailed examinations of al-Shāṭibi's legal philosophy can be found in al-Raysuni, *Imam al-Shatibi's Theory of the Higher Objectives and Intents of Islamic Law*; Muhammad Khalid Masud, *Shatibi's Philosophy of Islamic Law* (Kuala Lumpur: Islamic Book Trust, 2005); Wael B. Hallaq, *A History of Islamic Legal Theories: An Introduction to Sunnī Uṣūl al-Fiqh* (Cambridge: Cambridge University Press, 1997), 162–206.

[71] On this, see Masud, *Shatibi's Philosophy of Islamic Law*, 26–68.

of the law to meet the corresponding legal needs, al-Shāṭibi's main concern was to adapt Islamic legal thought to the new social conditions.[72] His legal philosophy can thus be read as a response to the challenge of social change. The fact that contemporary Muslims face a similar challenge, albeit on a much larger scale, gives al-Shāṭibi's legal theory special significance for contemporary Muslim thought. More important, al-Shāṭibi's thought not only illustrates the adaptability of law but also reflects an attempt to formulate a legal theory that can provide *methodologically sound* answers to new legal questions. In line with earlier scholars, he argues that the ability to understand the legal sources in the light of their purposes is a necessary condition for providing such answers. According to al-Shāṭibi, however, we cannot deduce the purpose of the law by considering legal norms in isolation, because they are merely fragments of a comprehensive legal system that must be understood as purposeful. But by analyzing the purposes underlying specific legal norms, we can assemble the individual pieces of the mosaic into a unified picture so that we can inductively conclude that the purpose of Islamic law is to realize the goods that are useful for human beings (*maṣāliḥ al-ʿibād*).[73] By these al-Shāṭibi means precisely those goods "that relate to the preservation of human life and the completion of human existence [*qiyām ḥayāt al-insān wa tamām ʿayshihi*] and serve to satisfy what the physical and intellectual characteristics of human beings require in an absolute sense so that they may enjoy a pleasant life."[74] As this definition suggests, al-Shāṭibi distinguishes between different levels of human existence. In line with al-Ghazāli, he divides the *maṣāliḥ* into the hierarchical categories of *ḍarūriyāt*, *ḥājiyāt*, and *taḥsīniyāt*.

In al-Shāṭibi's account, the category of necessary goods (*ḍarūriyāt*) includes goods whose necessity relates to human existence both in *this world* and in *the hereafter*. With regard to this world, the goods in question are the indispensable conditions of human life without which the very existence of the human species would be impossible. Any threat to these goods, he argues, would result in anarchy and the inability to conduct one's life in this world.[75] With regard to the hereafter, a threat to these goods would result in the loss

72 Bagby, *Utility in Classical Islamic Law*, 133.

73 al-Shāṭibi, *al-Muwāfaqāt*, 1:322, 362. On induction as a method for identifying purposes, see al-Raysuni, *Imam al-Shatibi's Theory*, 280–287 and Wael B. Hallaq, "On Inductive Corroboration, Probability and Certainty in Sunnī Legal Thought," in *Islamic Law and Jurisprudence: Studies in Honor of Farhat J. Ziadeh*, ed. Nicholas Heer (Seattle: University of Washington Press, 1990), 3–31.

74 al-Shāṭibi, *al-Muwāfaqāt*, 339.

75 Ibid., 324.

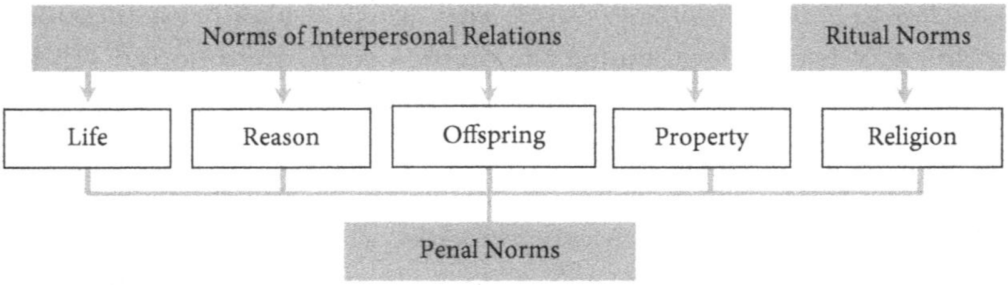

Figure 8.4 Protection of basic goods by the Islamic system of norms according to al-Shāṭibi.

of divine blessing and salvation.[76] In terms of content, they include the following five goods: religion, life, reason, offspring, and property.

These basic goods are both preserved and promoted by Islamic law and protected by preventive measures. At the level of preservation, the *'ibādāt* (ritual norms) aim to preserve religion, while the *'ādāt* (interpersonal norms) are concerned with the preservation of life, reason, offspring, and property.[77] At the level of prevention, the *jināyāt* (penal norms) serve to ensure the protection of all basic goods (Figure 8.4).[78]

Scholars, al-Shāṭibi continues, have observed that these essential goods are universal in nature and are considered necessary by all societies and legal systems.[79] The restriction of the necessary goods to the above five is based on empirical observation of reality (*ṯābit bi al-naẓar al-wāqi'*).[80] With this statement, al-Shāṭibi refers to the statements of scholars such as al-Ghazāli and al-Āmidi, among others, who, as we have seen, already emphasized the universal, necessary, and empirically verifiable character of the basic goods. But there is an important difference here: while al-Shāṭibi assumes that the above-mentioned basic goods are *included* in the category of *ḍarūriyāt*, al-Ghazāli's model assumes that the *ḍarūrāt* have a purely instrumental function in *protecting* these basic goods (see Figure 8.3). While this may seem like a minor difference, it leads to important discrepancies in the theoretical coherence of the *maqāsid*, which we will explore in chapter 9.

Al-Shāṭibi states that the category of required goods (*ḥājiyāt*) includes those things and conditions that make life bearable. They serve to make life

[76] Ibid.
[77] In al-Shāṭibi's terminology, the term *'ādāt* (customs) includes the notion of *mu'āmalāt* (human interactions) and refers in principle to all nonreligious actions.
[78] al-Shāṭibi, *al-Muwāfaqāt*, 324–325.
[79] Ibid., 326; see also 36, 339, 476, and 584.
[80] Ibid., 326.

easier and more pleasant and must be realized "in order to make life easier and remove the sufferings that cause people to overexert themselves."[81] If they remain unfulfilled, people will indeed overexert themselves, but not to the same extent as in the case of the necessary goods. Although individual and social life would not be out of control, it would be very difficult to bear. The purpose of these required goods is therefore to create the conditions required for a tolerable or decent life.

Finally, the category of ameliorative goods (*taḥsīniyāt*) includes those goods that ensure the smooth conduct of life; without them, life would be repulsive "according to sound reason."[82] Their purpose is to shape life in the best possible way, and they lead to the creation and observance of noble dispositions, good manners, and the preservation of good morals and character traits.[83]

According to al-Shāṭibi, each of these levels of goods must be viewed as part of a systematic structure in which the necessary goods form the basis of the required goods, which in turn form the basis of the ameliorative goods; conversely, the ameliorative goods supplement the required goods, which in turn supplement the necessary goods.[84] In light of this hierarchy, al-Shāṭibi introduces five principles that specify the structural relationships among the various levels of goods (Figure 8.5):[85]

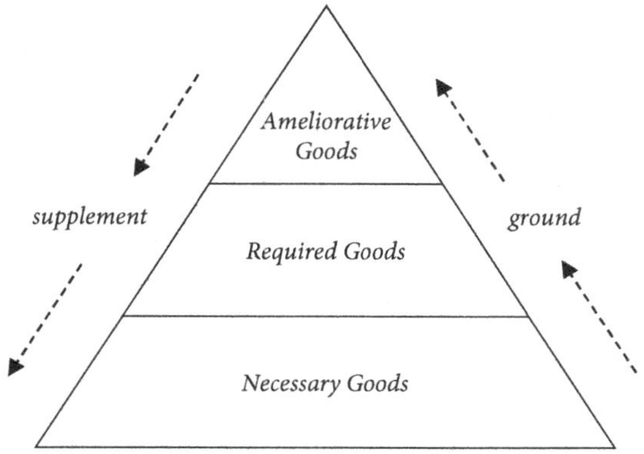

Figure 8.5 Hierarchical taxonomy of goods according to al-Shāṭibi.

[81] Ibid.
[82] Ibid., 327.
[83] Ibid.
[84] Ibid., 328–329.
[85] Ibid., 331.

1. Necessary goods are the foundation of all other goods.
2. The impairment of necessary goods inevitably leads to the impairment of all other goods.
3. The impairment of the required or ameliorative goods does not necessarily lead to the impairment of the necessary goods.
4. However, a complete impairment of the ameliorative or required goods could result in a partial impairment of the necessary goods.
5. Thus the realization of the required and ameliorative goods serves to protect the necessary goods.

These five principles represent al-Shāṭibi's attempt to explain that the primary purpose of law is to realize the essential goods and guarantee the individual rights associated with them. As a result, they take precedence over the higher-level goods because their realization is the necessary condition of human existence. In order to guarantee this legal purpose, however, we should strive to realize the required and ameliorative goods, which take on the function of protective zones (*ḥā'ima*) in relation to the necessary goods (Figure 8.6).[86]

Thus, the required and ameliorative goods combine with the essential goods to form an interdependent unit in which any impairment of one part simultaneously represents a potential impairment of the whole.[87] In this

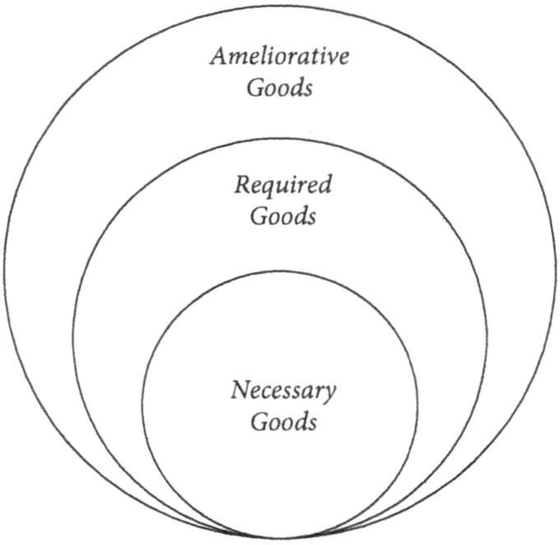

Figure 8.6 Higher-level goods as protective zones.

[86] Ibid., 332.
[87] Ibid., 336–338.

sense, the impairment of the outermost protective zone provides a gateway (*madkhal*) for threats that could lead to the impairment of the next protective zone, whose impairment in turn could lead to the impairment of the necessary goods. In this model, therefore, the necessary goods constitute the legal core whose impairment must be prevented by the realization of the required and ameliorative goods.

To give substance to the notion of goods, al-Shāṭibi introduces three criteria that a good must meet in order to be considered legally binding. According to these criteria, goods must be eternal (*abadī*), universal (*kullī*), and general (*ʿāmm*), so that all three criteria taken together amount to excluding the aspects of relativity and subjectivity from the notion of a good.[88] A good is relative when it is equated with personal preferences (*ahwā al-nufūs*), personal benefits (*manāfiʿ*), personal desires (*nayl al-shahawāt*), or individual wishes (*aghrāḍ*).[89] These aspects vary from person to person, place to place, and time to time, and therefore cannot serve as criteria for determining legal claims.[90] Moreover, taking subjective interests into account would lead not only to personal divergences but also to conflicts in which personal interests are asserted at the expense of other interests.[91] If the universality of a good is not to be impaired, it must be freed from all relativity. What distinguishes the concept of the good (*maṣlaḥa*), then, is its objectivity, which, as Kamali observes, makes it a rationally intelligible concept.[92]

To understand the aspect of rationality in al-Shāṭibi's concept of *maṣlaḥa*, it is important to note a distinction he makes between worldly and otherworldly goods. As we have seen, this distinction was already present in al-Ghazāli's early thought, although he revoked it in his later work. Nevertheless, it was taken up again by later scholars, most notably Ibn ʿAbd as-Salām (d. 1261/660), who distinguished between worldly and otherworldly goods on the grounds that the former can be known by reason (*ʿaql*), while the latter can be known only by revelation (*naql*).[93] Al-Shāṭibi addresses this point in his treatise on the observance of norms, where he argues that the duty to follow a norm follows primarily from its rationality. Norms are rational when

[88] Ibid., 350.
[89] Ibid., 351–352.
[90] Ibid., 352.
[91] Ibid., 353.
[92] Kamali, *Shariʿah Law*, 34.
[93] ʿIzz al-Dīn Ibn ʿAbd al-Salām, *Qawāʿid al-Aḥkām fī Maṣāliḥ al-Anām* (Damascus: Dār al-Qalam, n.d.), 1:7, 11.

they have a purpose that can be understood by rationally thinking people (*iḏā ʿurida ʿalā al-ʿuqūl talaqqathu bi-l-qubūl*).[94] However, this applies only to the norms regulating interpersonal relations (*muʿāmalāt* or *ʿādāt*). Norms governing ritual acts (*ʿibādāt*), on the other hand, must be followed even if their purpose cannot be understood. In fact, it would be pointless to try to analyze the purposes of ritual norms, since they remain largely hidden from human reason. For example, there is no obvious reason why Muslims should fast during Ramadan rather than in another month, or why fasting begins at dawn rather than at sunrise. There is also no explanation for why there are exactly five daily prayers or why some prayers have two segments and others three or four. These norms are not rationally comprehensible and must be accepted and followed obediently and unquestioningly, for which al-Shāṭibi uses the term *taʿabbud*.[95] He refers only to the formal and quantitative aspects of ritual acts and does not deny that the meaning of rituals can be grasped *as such*. In fact, their meaning is usually specified in the sources themselves. For example, regarding prayer, the Qur'an says, "Be constant in prayer: for, behold, prayer restrains [man] from loathsome deeds and from all that runs counter to reason" (29:45). And as for fasting, it says, "O you who have attained to faith! Fasting is ordained for you as it was ordained for those before you, so that you might remain conscious of God" (2:183). The general purpose of ritual acts, then, is to instill in believers a sense of reverence, to increase their humility, and to strengthen their awareness of God so that they may devote themselves to Him with body and soul.[96] In this sense, ritual acts pursue the otherworldly good of human beings (*maṣāliḥ ukhrawiyya*). However, the *observance* of ritual norms is not *based on* this fact; rather, they are to be observed simply because they have been established by the divine legislator.[97] On the other hand, the obligation to observe norms regulating interpersonal relations is not based on the letter of the law but on the purpose pursued by the legislator.[98] This purpose is rationally ascertainable and relates to the protection of worldly goods (*maṣāliḥ dunyawiyya*), which, as described above, are divided into necessary, required, and ameliorative goods. Legal norms must be justified in terms of this purpose, and if they fail to achieve it, they must be modified accordingly.

[94] al-Shāṭibi, *al-Muwāfaqāt*, 590–591.
[95] Ibid., 585–589.
[96] Ibid., 523.
[97] Ibid., 587.
[98] Ibid., 591.

The distinction between worldly and otherworldly goods also provides the theoretical framework for al-Shāṭibi's conception of rights, which he divides into the rights of God (*ḥaqq allāh*) and the rights of human beings (*ḥaqq al-ʿabd* or *ḥaqq al-ādamī*).[99] The rights of God refer to that part of the legislation which cannot be changed in any way by the addressees of the legislation and which they must comply with regardless of whether they understand its meaning or not. By this, al-Shāṭibi means the domain of *ʿibadāt*, which is inaccessible to human reason and aims at the otherworldly good of human beings. The rights of human beings, on the other hand, refer to their worldly interests, which are the objective of the rationally accessible domain of *muʿāmalāt/ʿādāt*.[100] The connection that al-Shāṭibi makes here between the rights (*ḥuqūq*) and interests or goods (*maṣāliḥ*) of human beings has a long tradition in Islamic legal thought, which may explain why he does not offer a more detailed account of how this connection should be understood.[101] But what exactly does it mean to say that the rights of human beings relate to their *maṣāliḥ*? And how is the concept of right to be understood in this context?

Regarding the second question, it is instructive to recall that, according to Islamic jurists, both rights and duties arise from the norms of Islamic law. Depending on how these norms are expressed, they demand either the performance or the omission of a particular action. The idea of individual right then comes into play with the question of who is entitled or has a claim to demand this action. "When we say that someone has a right [*ḥaqq lahu*]," writes al-Qāḍi ʿAbd al-Jabbār (d. 1024/415), "it means that he has a claim on the action of another [person]."[102] Therefore, the claim that God's rights refer to the realm of *ʿibadāt* means that God (and only God) is entitled to demand that human beings perform ritual acts. The right of human beings, on the other hand, is to demand from other human beings those acts that are prescribed by the norms that govern interpersonal relations. As we have seen, these norms serve human well-being in this world by striving to realize the necessary, required, and ameliorative goods and to avoid the corresponding

99 Ibid., 600.

100 Ibid.

101 See, e.g., al-Qāḍi ʿAbd al-Jabbār, *al-Mughni fī Abwāb al-Tawḥīd wa'l-ʿAdl* (Cairo: al-Mu'assasa al-Miṣriyya al-ʿĀmma li'l-Ta'līf w'al-Anbā', 1965), 14:334; Ibn ʿAbd al-Salām, *Qawāʿid al-Aḥkām*, 1:222; Shihāb al-Dīn al-Qarāfi, *Kitāb al-Furūq: Anwār al-Burūq fī Anwāʾ al-Furūq* (Beirut: Dār al-Kutub al-ʿIlmiyya, 1998), 1:256; Saʿd al-Dīn Masʿūd Ibn ʿUmar al-Taftazāni, *al-Talwīḥ ʿala al-Tawḍīḥ* (Beirut: Dār al-Kutub al-ʿIlmiyya, n.d.), 2:315, 323.

102 ʿAbd al-Jabbār, *al-Mughni fī Abwāb al-Tawḥīd wa'l-ʿAdl*, 6:32.

harms. Thus the right of human beings implies the authorization (*ikhtiṣāṣ*) to demand from other human beings precisely those actions (positive or negative) that serve the realization of a particular good, be it a necessary, a required, or an ameliorative good.[103]

Here, however, al-Shāṭibi draws attention to an important problem.[104] He points out that it makes sense to speak of a right only if the obligatory actions associated with it can actually be enforced. The enforceability of these actions, however, presupposes that they are both determinate in their content and addressed to identifiable persons. According to al-Shāṭibi, these conditions are met in the case of the rights of God, since the ritual duties associated with them are clearly addressed and spelled out in the textual sources. For example, every Muslim has an individual duty to pray or fast at certain times and in a certain manner. The content of these duties owed to the holder of the right—in this case, God—is specified in terms of both their quantity (*taḥdīd*) and their quality (*taqdīr*), so that those who fail to fulfill them can be held accountable before God. Similarly, individuals are accountable to other people, for example, if they fail to pay their debts or to pay the agreed price for something they have purchased. Here, too, we have duties whose content is determined (repayment of debts or purchase prices) and which are addressed to specific individuals (the debtor or the buyer) and which are owed to the people who hold the rights.

Al-Shāṭibi emphasizes, however, that the textual sources do not specify all the duties in the case of the rights of human beings. For example, the Qur'an commands believers to feed the needy and poor (22:36) or to clothe the destitute and to spend freely in the cause of God (2:195), but without specifying the exact content or addressees of these obligations. The duties in question cannot impose obligations on individuals for which they can be held individually accountable. According to al-Shāṭibi, it is understandable that the Qur'an left these duties unspecified, since the legislator's purpose is the complete satisfaction of human needs (*innamā maqaṣūd al-Shāriʿ sad al-khallāt ʿala al-jumla*).[105] This would be undermined by specifying and quantifying the content of the corresponding means, since both the manner and the necessary extent of fulfillment depend on temporal and local circumstances. Therefore, in order to make the duty effective, the extent and the necessary means of satisfying the needs must be specified concretely in light of the

[103] Al-Drīni, *al-Ḥaqq wa Madā Ṣultān al-Dawla fī Taqyīdihi*, 193.
[104] See al-Shāṭibi, *al-Muwafaqāt*, 135–139.
[105] Ibid., 138.

prevailing circumstances and not on the basis of textual sources. Thus, while the obligation to satisfy needs is derived from the Qur'an, its content must be determined empirically by human beings.

But even then, it remains open to whom this duty is addressed. Al-Shāṭibi emphasizes that this cannot be an individual duty (*fard 'aynī*), since not every individual is capable of performing the required actions and therefore cannot be held accountable in case of nonperformance. Therefore, the duty in question is addressed to the social collective (*ṭalab al-kifāyah*), and specifically to "those who are able to perform the required act."[106] But this does not mean that the rest of society is exempt from responsibility. Rather, according to al-Shāṭibi, we must assume an asymmetrical distribution of social responsibility, in which those who are able to perform the required actions bear a direct (*mubāshira*) responsibility, while those who are unable to perform them bear an indirect responsibility, which consists in enabling and supporting the agency of others.[107] In other words, al-Shāṭibi is concerned with the creation of social structures and institutions that enable a society to fulfill its collective obligation with regard to the needs and associated rights of human beings through a moral division of labor.

In a later part of the work, al-Shāṭibi makes clear that this is also and above all a *political* duty when he links the intentions of the legislator (God) with the intentions of the norm recipient (*mukallaf*).[108] He emphasizes that the original purpose of the legislator is the absolute and general protection of human well-being, which, as explained above, is achieved through the fulfillment of the necessary, required, and ameliorative goods. The protection of these goods symbolizes the raison d'être of Islamic law and represents the intention of God in the revelation of His decrees. This intention, according to al-Shāṭibi, must be reflected in the intentions of the recipient of the norms, that is, in the practical application of the law.[109] For human beings act as God's representatives (*khalīfat Allāh*) on earth and are therefore obligated to uphold and realize the divine intention of legislation.[110] Hallaq comments, "Thus, God's intentions behind promoting and maintaining the three universals—the *ḍarūriyyat*, *ḥājiyyāt*, and *taḥsīniyyāt*—must be identical to the individual's intentions in implementing the law as grounded in these

106 Ibid., 154.

107 Ibid., 156–157.

108 The norm recipient in this case is the one who is legally qualified and authorized to guarantee and satisfy the requirements of the law.

109 Al-Shāṭibi, *al-Muwafaqāt*, 613.

110 Ibid., 614.

universals. The individual is then God's representative on earth in that he represents, or ought to represent, God in promoting social welfare through adopting the same intentions that God had adopted when He decreed the law."[111] The law thus acquires the function of an institution that protects the foundations of human existence and, building on them, seeks the legal protection of higher goods. This implies, on the one hand, the assignment of rights based on such goods and, on the other hand, the assignment of duties to protect these goods. As a result, the state, as the holder of legal authority, acquires a new reason of state, and its legitimacy depends on the extent to which it realizes this legal purpose: "According to the classical theory, an equitable and just society would treat the necessities as sacrosanct and not subject to compromise. A society that could protect the needs of people in addition to the necessities would be considered even more just and equitable. Finally, a society that could provide people with the luxuries of life, in addition to protecting the necessities and needs, would be the most just and equitable of all."[112]

Implications of *maqāṣid* for Islamic Legal Reasoning

Apart from its implications for the practical application of law and the granting of rights, the most important implication of considering the *maqāṣid* is a paradigm shift in the methods of legal reasoning. In what follows, I would like to draw some conclusions from the premises and considerations reconstructed above. The first, general conclusion to be drawn from the *maqāṣid* idea is that the norms of Islamic law—and by this I mean only the norms of interpersonal relations—were not enacted for their own sake, nor for the sake of mere obedience. Rather, their aim is to realize certain purposes that the legislator intends to achieve by enacting them.[113] In this sense, the purpose symbolizes the will of the legislator, what he intended, and is thus the central point of orientation. At the same time, it provides an answer to the question of why a particular norm exists. It symbolizes its *ratio legis*, the reason for its existence. Accordingly, both the interpretation and the application of a norm are based on its purpose. For Islamic jurists, this means that they must base

[111] Hallaq, *A History of Islamic Legal Theories*, 185.

[112] Abou el Fadl, *The Great Theft*, 189–190. Here Abou el Fadl uses the terms "necessities," "needs," and "luxuries" for what I have called "necessary," "required," and "ameliorative" goods, respectively.

[113] Kamali, *Shari'ah Law*, 55.

their interpretations on the immutable purpose of the norm and ensure that it is realized in the context of the prevailing circumstances. Thus their primary concern is not to adhere to the literal wording of the norm, but to understand it in the light of its underlying intention. In other words, this means that a norm is legitimate and normatively valid only as long as it fulfills its intended purpose. When it no longer does so, it must be modified in the light of its underlying purpose. To do otherwise would be to neglect the intention of the legislator.[114] The goal, according to Ibn Qayyim al-Jawziyya (d. 1350/751), is to fulfill the legislator's intention as fully as possible, if not with the original norm, then with another, more effective one.[115]

Since the legislator's intention is to protect the existential well-being of human beings, it is imperative that the *maṣlaḥa* intended by a norm be realized even under changed conditions. A prominent proponent of this view, in addition to those already mentioned, is the Ḥanbali jurist Najm al-Dīn al-Ṭūfi (d. 1316/716). According to al-Ṭūfi, the protection of human welfare is both the starting point and the goal of legal reasoning and embodies the essential principle of Islamic law in the concept of *maṣlaḥa*.[116] Legal norms are always legitimized by the purpose they achieve or are intended to achieve. If they fail to do so, then whatever leads to the fulfillment of the purpose is legitimate. Legal norms that no longer achieve the originally intended benefit must therefore be changed so that their benefit can be realized. "Due to ignorance of these matters," says Ibn Qayyim, "serious mistakes were made regarding the Shari'ah, which led to hardship and severity. Obligations were imposed that are not prescribed when one follows the great Shari'ah, which seeks the highest level of well-being."[117] In the light of this problem, jurists have formulated two principles that legitimize the modifiability of norms:[118]

1. A law enacted on the basis of a *maṣlaḥa* ceases to exist with the disappearance of the *maṣlaḥa*.
2. A law enacted to achieve a benefit or *maṣlaḥa* is void if it subsequently produces the opposite of that benefit or *maṣlaḥa*.

[114] Ibid.
[115] Ibn Qayyim al-Jawziyya, *A'lām al-Muwaqqi'īn 'an Rabb al-'Ālamīn*, 3:19.
[116] Najm al-Dīn al-Ṭūfi, *Sharḥ al-Arba'īn*, appendix, in Muṣṭafa Zayd, *al-Maslaḥa fī al-Tashrī' al-Islāmi* (Cairo: Dār al-Fikr al-'Arabī, 1954), 18. On al-Ṭūfi, see also Hallaq, *A History of Islamic Legal Theories*, 148–153.
[117] Ibn Qayyim al-Jawziyya, *A'lām al-Muwaqqi'īn 'an Rabb al-'Ālamīn*, 3:11.
[118] See Kalish, *Vernunft und Flexibilität in der islamischen Rechtsmotehodik*, 115.

To illustrate these principles, let us consider a norm from the Sunnah that forbids a woman to undertake a long journey unless she is accompanied by a *maḥram*. A *maḥram* is a close relative who cannot enter into a marital relationship with the woman because of their kinship with her (i.e., father, brother, uncle, etc.). According to Abū Bakr Ibn al-ʿArabi (d. 1148/543), the purpose of this norm is clearly to protect the woman from sexual harassment (hence the requirement of kinship) and to ensure her safety from assault (hence the requirement of a male traveling companion). In light of these purposes, according to Ibn al-ʿArabi, some scholars also considered it permissible for a woman to travel with a group of trustworthy and virtuous men who would not molest her and could ensure her safety.[119] As further proof that women are allowed to travel without a *maḥram*, Ibn al-ʿArabi quotes a saying of the Prophet that a time will come when Muslims will be so secure that women will be able to travel to Mecca without fear from al-Ḥīra (Iraq). According to Ibn al-ʿArabi, this confirms that the above norm should be understood in terms of its security aspect, which must be guaranteed in an appropriate manner depending on the prevailing conditions. For, as a general rule, "[e]verything that the Prophet did was based on a purpose, a need and a reason. It follows that if the need and the reason cease to exist, the norm must also cease to apply. However, if the need arises again, then the norm comes back into effect."[120] In other words, the primary concern is to situate a norm in its historical and social context and to understand what function it served under those conditions. Once that function has been identified, we must analyze whether the norm continues to perform that function in the contemporary context. If so, it retains its normative validity; if not, the norm must be either suspended or adapted to the new context.

In our example, therefore, we must be aware that the norm refers to a historical and social context in which travel was conducted through the arid desert of the Arabian Peninsula where travelers, especially women, were subject to harassment and assault. The scope of the norm thus refers, in the abstract, to systemically insecure conditions in which measures must be taken to ensure the safety of women. This requirement should not be understood solely in the restrictive sense that women may travel only when their safety is guaranteed; rather, it calls for the creation of conditions and the adoption

[119] Abū Bakr Ibn al-ʿArabi, *ʿĀriḍat al-Aḥwāḏi fī Sharḥ Ṣaḥiḥ al-Tirmiḏi*, 5:118–119, quoted in al-Raisūni, *Nazariyyat al-Maqāṣid*, 369.

[120] Abū Bakr Ibn al-ʿArabi, *ʿĀriḍat al-Aḥwāḏi fī Sharḥ Ṣaḥiḥ al-Tirmiḏi*, 3:172, quoted in al-Raisūni, *Naẓariyyat al-Maqāṣid*, 368.

of measures that will allow a woman to travel without fear for her safety. Given the sociohistorical conditions prevailing at the time of the revelation, the accompaniment of a *maḥram* was an appropriate way to meet this requirement. Under contemporary travel conditions, however, it is reasonable to assume that women traveling alone no longer face a systemic risk to their safety. In the age of regulated road and rail travel, of local public transport and international air travel, and the associated regulatory and security mechanisms, women as well as men can travel longer distances in safety and without hindrance. Under these conditions, the norm prohibiting women from traveling without the accompaniment of a *maḥram* would no longer serve its original function.[121] On the contrary, its application would potentially cause harm by restricting women's freedom of movement and violating their dignity as independent and responsible persons. It must therefore be repealed, as the above principle postulates. In summary, if we say that a norm has a purpose, the realization of which logically depends on the existence of certain circumstances and conditions, then it follows that if these conditions change, the norm must also change, since it no longer serves its purpose and could lead to harm. The latter, as Ibn Qayyim observes, would be unacceptable because "[Islamic law] is full of justice, mercy, wisdom, and benefit. Therefore, any matter that leads from justice to injustice, from mercy to its opposite, from benefit to harm, and from wisdom to nonsense, is incompatible with the law, even if it is asserted as a matter of interpretation."[122] In the same vein, Khaled Abou el Fadl comments, "The ultimate objective of the law is to achieve goodness, which includes justice, mercy, and compassion, and the technicalities of the law cannot be allowed to subvert the objectives of the law. Therefore, if the application of the law produces injustice, suffering, and misery, this means that the law is not serving its purposes. In this situation, the law is corrupting the earth instead of civilizing it. In short, if the application of the law results in injustice, suffering, or misery, then the law must be reinterpreted, suspended, or reconstructed, depending on the law in question."[123] These considerations suggest that a literalist or static conception of Islamic law, which denies that norms are changeable, is untenable. As Ramadan observes, the approach based on purposes "sheds fresh light on rules, rulings or laws per se: literal implementation is actually impossible

121 See Yusuf al-Qaradawi, *Approaching the Sunnah: Comprehension and Controversy* (Herndon, VA: International Institute of Islamic Thought, 2006), 129.
122 Ibn al-Qayyim al-Jawziyya, *Aʿlām al-Muwaqqiʿīn ʿan Rabb al-ʿĀlamīn*, 3:11.
123 Abou el Fadl, *The Great Theft*, 131.

(apart from most worship-related rulings) and they must constantly be placed in perspective from the standpoint of the Way's higher objectives that must at all times determine the modalities of their possible implementation (even for the most explicit texts)."[124]

A static conception of Islamic legal norms is untenable, as Ibn 'Ashūr (d. 1973) explains, not least because it would amount to denying the universal (*kullī*) and timeless (*abadī*) character of Islamic law. For the claim that Islamic legal norms are immutable in the face of the obvious fact of social change would imply that Islamic law is only temporarily valid, since its application would be limited to a particular social and historical condition. If this condition were to change, God would have to address a new revelation to humanity to replace the earlier norms.[125] But this is untenable from an Islamic perspective, since Muslims assume that Islam is the final revelation of God to human beings: "Therefore, it follows from this that the meaning of the suitability of the Islamic Shari'ah for every time and place must be understood in a different manner as follows. Its commands and injunctions (*aḥkām*) consist of universal principles and meanings comprising wisdom and benefits (*maṣāliḥ*), which can be projected into various rulings that are diverse in form but unified in purpose."[126] Thus, the norms of Islamic law are based on timeless and constant purposes, which, however, must always be given new substance under existing conditions, so that there is a necessary correlation between law and social change.[127]

The fact that social change is endless, while the sources of law provide only a limited number of norms, means that the legal system must be based on a rational foundation, in terms of both content and methodology, so that it can be understood and expanded by human reason.[128] The legal purposes derived by induction from the revealed norms become a source of law *in their own right*, providing the *benchmark for legal interpretation and reasoning* independent of factors of time and place. Existing legal norms must therefore be evaluated, interpreted, and, if necessary, modified in their spatial and

[124] Tariq Ramadan, *Radical Reform: Islamic Ethics and Liberation* (Oxford: Oxford University Press, 2009), 75.
[125] Muhammad al-Tahir Ibn Ashur, *Treatise on Maqāṣid al-Sharī'ah* (Herndon, VA: International Institute of Islamic Thought, 2006), 213.
[126] Ibid., 143.
[127] See Mumisa, *Islamic Law*, 23. Islamic jurisprudence expresses the correlation between law and social change in the following maxim: *lā yunkar tajayyur al-aḥkām bi tajayyur al-zamān* ("It cannot be denied that norms change with social change or altered conditions").
[128] Masud, *Shatibi's Philosophy of Islamic Law*, 223–224.

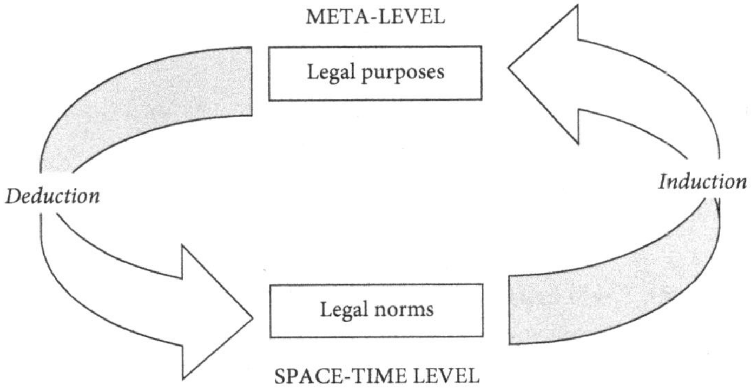

Figure 8.7 The cycle of legal reasoning.

temporal contexts in light of these purposes, while new legal norms must be derived from the purposes.

The result is a *cycle of legal reasoning* (Figure 8.7) that leads inductively from the legal norms to their purposes and deductively from the purposes back to the norms. The purposes are considered constant, "for no amount of interpretation or textual manipulation can affect or diminish their pervasive presence in the Sharīʿa. But the specific and individual rules that bring about the realization of these [purposes] in society are mutable according to changing circumstances, locales and times."[129] In this sense, ʿAllāl al-Fāsi (d. 1974) comments, "The objectives of the Islamic Shari'ah are the only point of reference for the extension of the law. They are not outside the Shari'ah, but are part of its essence . . . and, if necessary, even influence what the source texts prescribe."[130] The purposes of the law thus become the most important instrument for understanding legal norms, translating them into reality, and obtaining new norms that are not laid down in the source texts.[131] A comprehensive understanding of the legal purposes and the ability to derive law from them (*istinbāṭ*) thus becomes a necessary condition of independent legal reasoning (*ijtihād*).[132]

[129] Hallaq, *A History of Islamic Legal Theories*, 224.

[130] ʿAllāl al-Fāsi, *Maqāṣid al-Sharīʿa al-Islāmiyya wa Makārimihā* (Beirut: Dār al-Gharb al-Islāmi, 1993), 51–52. On ʿAllāl al-Fāsi, see David L. Johnston, "ʿAllāl al-Fāsi: Shari'a as a Blueprint for Righteous Global Citizenship?," in *Shari'a: Islamic Law in the Contemporary Context*, ed. Abbas Amanat and Frank Griffel (Stanford, CA: Stanford University Press, 2007), 83–103.

[131] Khallāf, *ʿIlm Uṣūl al-Fiqh*, 197.

[132] For a detailed discussion, see al-Raysuni, *Imam al-Shatibi's Theory*, 326–336.

9
A Critical Review

In this chapter, I will critically review the classical conception of *maqāṣid* reconstructed in the previous chapter. My aim will be to arrive at a coherent understanding of *maqāṣid* theory through a closer examination of some aspects that have been mentioned but remain unclear. Let us begin by asking what exactly is the purpose of Islamic law. As my earlier reconstruction has made clear, the underlying idea of the classical *maqāṣid* conception is that the norms of Islamic law pursue a common purpose, namely the realization of the existential well-being of human beings. This is a premise on which the classical jurists agree. However, we have also seen that the concretization of this basic idea shows some variations on which we must now shed some light.

Let us first return to al-Shāṭibi. In order to specify the purpose of Islamic law concretely, he identifies three hierarchical categories of goods that must be fulfilled successively in order to realize different levels of human existence. Within this framework, the necessary goods (*ḍarūriyāt*) serve to ensure the *mere existence* of human beings, while the required goods (*ḥājiyāt*) build on this to enable a *decent life*. Finally, the ameliorative goods (*taḥsīniyāt*) serve to make a *good life* possible.[1] Al-Shāṭibi makes this tripartite division in order to clarify the respective normative dimensions and related priorities of the law. Accordingly, the first and most fundamental legal purpose is to guarantee the existence of human beings. According to al-Shāṭibi, this requires five basic goods that are included in the necessary goods, namely religion (*dīn*), life (*nafs*), offspring (*nasl*), reason (*ʿaql*), and property (*māl*). In this context, therefore, the primary legal purpose is to protect these basic goods.

However, before we examine these basic goods in detail, we must first answer an obvious question: Why does al-Shāṭibi specify only the content of the necessary goods, while leaving the other two categories of goods largely undefined? What about these secondary and tertiary legal purposes? Why does he neglect such a fundamental component of the Islamic doctrine of legal purposes? Upon closer examination, this question turns out to be based

[1] Al-Shāṭibi, *al-Muwāfaqāt*, 1:324–327.

Human Rights Between Universality and Islamic Legitimacy. Mahmoud Bassiouni, Oxford University Press.
 DOI: 10.1093/oso/9780197753897.003.0010

on an ambiguity that, according to ʿAtiyya, stems from the fact that al-Shāṭibi did not make a clear enough distinction between purposes (*maqāṣid*) and the means required for their fulfillment (*wasāʾil*).[2] As the presentation of al-Ghazāli's concept of *maqāṣid* showed, the five basic goods do not constitute the *content* of the necessary goods but rather the higher purposes that are to be protected *through* the realization of the necessary goods (see Figure 8.3). In fact, al-Shāṭibi himself points this out when he says that goods such as food, clothing, and shelter are the necessary conditions for the protection of life.[3] However, these goods provide only minimum protection for the basic good of "life," which is why Islamic law also seeks to realize the required goods and the ameliorative goods. Thus both the necessary goods and the required and ameliorative goods refer to the protection of the basic goods, but at different levels of necessity.

In order to systematize the classical conception of the *maqāṣid*, I propose to distinguish two distinct but interrelated dimensions of purposes that together provide the normative frame of reference for the *maqāṣid*. We can think of these as a vertical and a horizontal dimension of purpose. The vertical dimension refers to the various *levels of human existence* that are to be realized through the fulfillment of the respective categories of goods. In other words, the vertical purpose of the law is to facilitate a bare, a decent, and a good human existence. These are not distinct normative claims that the law seeks to satisfy, but rather claims that build upon one another. The law seeks to satisfy these levels within the framework of a horizontal dimension of purpose that refers to the substantive *conditions of human existence*. These are the familiar five basic needs: religion, life, offspring, reason, and property. According to the classical jurists, this selection is based on the assumption that these are (a) the necessary conditions without which no human existence is possible, (b) the universal conditions that affect the existence of all human beings, and (c) the empirically ascertainable conditions of human existence. At the same time, these components represent the spheres to which Islamic law refers. In other words, they symbolize the basic needs that the entire system of Islamic legal norms seeks to protect and preserve. However, not all of these norms relate to the protection of basic needs to the same extent, so in a further step they are divided into three categories according to their degree of urgency.

[2] See Attia, *Towards Realization of the Higher Intents of Islamic Law*, 38–41.
[3] Al-Shāṭibi, *al-Muwāfaqāt*, 1:325 or 2:409.

Within this framework, the goal of the first category, the *ḍarūriyāt*, is to realize the goods necessary for the protection and preservation of the five basic needs. At the same time, they serve to eliminate the evils (*mafāsid*) that pose an immediate threat to the protection of the basic needs. Necessary goods, then, are those whose nonfulfillment would make the protection of the basic needs impossible in practice, and this would threaten the very existence of human beings. Food, clothing, and shelter are examples of life-sustaining necessities. "The minimum level of these things," according to Ibn 'Abd al-Salām (d. 1261/660), "is assigned to the category of necessary goods."[4] The category of *ḥājiyāt* concerns less urgent goods. Its purpose is to realize those goods that are required, but not indispensable, for the protection of basic needs. If a required good is not realized or a corresponding evil is not eliminated, this does not mean that a basic need cannot be protected, but it will be severely impaired.

Remaining with the basic need "life," while the aim of the necessary goods is to ensure mere "survival," the required goods serve to facilitate a life beyond mere subsistence. In other words, they serve to create decent living conditions, for example, by providing adequate food or comfortable accommodation. Finally, the *taḥsīniyāt* represent a category of goods that serve to optimize or supplement the protection of basic needs in order to contribute to an improved or good life (Figure 9.1). However, as Khaled Abou el Fadl

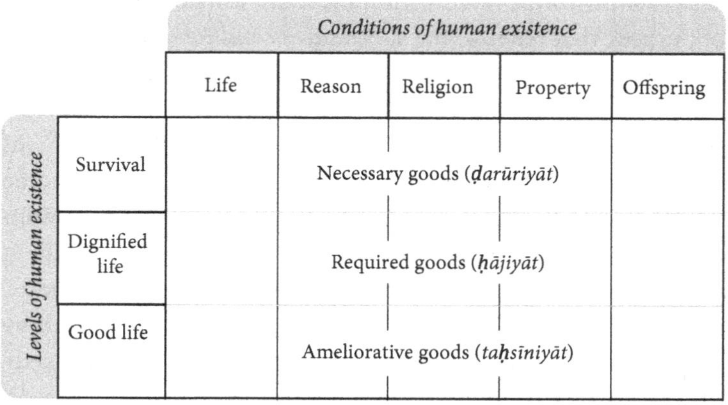
Conditions of human existence
Life
Reason
Religion
Property
Offspring
Levels of human existence
Survival
Dignified life
Good life
Necessary goods (ḍarūriyāt)
Required goods (ḥājiyāt)
Ameliorative goods (taḥsīniyāt)

Figure 9.1 Dimensions of the purposes of Islamic law.

4 Ibn 'Abd al-Salām, *Qawā'id al-Aḥkām fī Maṣaliḥ al-Anām*, 2:71, quoted in Attia, *Toward Realization of the Higher Intents of Islamic Law*, 39.

notes, Islamic scholars did not specify which goods in particular were to be classified as necessary, required, or ameliorative, since this could vary from time to time and place to place: "The classical scholars contended that it falls upon each generation of Muslims to explore and define *in accordance with the shifting demands of the circumstances and changing times* what ought to be defined as the necessities, needs, and luxuries. Therefore, it was considered unwise to set out a specific list of inflexible necessities, needs, and luxuries that are constant and unchanging."[5]

We will revisit these considerations in a later part of the book and attempt to elaborate on them in the context of the discussion of human rights. At this point, it should be noted that the realization of human goods in the vertical dimension of purposes serves to enable different levels of human existence, while in the horizontal dimension it is intended to contribute to the protection and preservation of the five basic needs, which I will now to examine in more detail.

As just noted, Muslim scholars consider the five basic needs to be the necessary, universal, and empirically verifiable conditions of human existence. They are therefore often referred to simply as the "five necessities" (*al-ḍarūrāt al-ḫamsa*). Al-Ghazāli (d. 1111/505) was the first to emphasize the necessary and universal character of the basic needs, stressing that it would be inconceivable "that any society or legal system whose goal is the achievement of the human good (*iṣlāḥ al-khalq*) would not include measures to protect these five basic needs."[6] Al-Āmidi (d. 1233/631) also spoke of the "five legal purposes that every society and legal system seeks to protect"[7] and was confirmed in this assertion by Ibn al-Ḥājib (d. 1248/646).[8] Al-Qarāfi (d. 1285/684) speaks of a "consensus of societies" (*ijmāʿ al-milal*) in this context and was the first to replace the term "five necessities" with the term "five universals" (*al-kulliyāt al-ḫamsa*).[9] Often, the statements of the scholars even give the impression that these universal goods were first discovered independently of Islamic law and only later confirmed by it. Thus, according to al-Āmidi, the recognition of these five basic needs is guided by a purely empirical reflection on reality (*naẓaran ila al-wāqiʿ*), which leads us to conclude that these are the fundamental and necessary components of human

[5] Abou el Fadl, *The Great Theft*, 189, emphasis in original.
[6] Al-Ghazāli, *al-Mustaṣfa min ʿIlm al-Uṣūl*, 2:483.
[7] Al-Āmidi, *al-Aḥkām fī Uṣūl al-Aḥkām*, 3:343.
[8] Ibn al-Ḥājib, *Muntaha al-Wuṣūl wʾal-Amal fī ʿIlmay al-Uṣūl wʾal Jadal* (Beirut: Dār al-Kutub al-ʿIlmiyya, 1985), 182.
[9] Shihāb al-Dīn al-Qarāfi, *Sharḥ Tanqīḥ al-Fuṣūl* (Beirut: Dār al-Fikr, 2004), 304.

life. Moreover, he argues that an examination of the legal sources leads us to conclude a posteriori that the purpose of Islamic law is to protect these very elements.[10] Al-Shāṭibi also assumes that the law in every human society seeks to protect these necessities.[11] They are also recognized by Islamic law because they can be inductively derived from the legal sources. This induction, al-Shāṭibi argues, is not based on a particular piece of evidence (*dalīl*) or a particular source, but on the cumulative force of countless pieces of evidence.[12]

It should be noted, however, that these and similar claims can be easily dismantled once we take a look at the evidence actually cited by Muslim jurists to justify basic needs. The identification of the needs and their restriction to exactly five was evidently based on a positivist reading of the penalties contained in the Qur'an (*ḥudūd*).[13] Accordingly, al-Ghazāli qualifies his statement about the universality of the basic needs by claiming that "there is no disagreement between the various legislations regarding the prohibition of unbelief, homicide, licentiousness, theft, and the consumption of alcohol."[14] The relevance of the five basic needs can thus be explained, as al-Shāṭibi later emphasizes, in terms of the punishments that are threatened in the event of their impairment.[15] According to the classical view:

- The protection of life is derived from the principle of retribution (*qiṣāṣ*) in the case of murder (2:178).
- The protection of religion from the punishment of apostasy (*irtidād*).
- The protection of reason from the punishment of drinking alcohol (*shurb*).
- The protection of offspring from the punishment of adultery or licentiousness (*zinā*) (24:2).
- The protection of property from the punishment of theft (*sariqa*).[16]

[10] Al-Āmidi, *al-Aḥkām fī Uṣūl al-Aḥkām*, 3:240.
[11] Al-Shāṭibi, *al-Muwāfaqāt*, 1:36, 326, 339, 476.
[12] Ibid., 1:36–37.
[13] "The list of five essential values was evidently based on a reading of the relevant parts of the Quran on prescribed penalties (*ḥudūd*). The value that each of these penalties sought to vindicate and defend was consequently identified as an essential value." Kamali, *Shari'ah Law*, 126. See also al-Qaraḍāwi, *Madḫal li Dirāsat al-Sharīʿa al-Islāmiyya*, 73.
[14] Al-Ghazāli, *al-Mustaṣfa*, 2:483.
[15] Al-Shāṭibi, *al-Muwāfaqāt*, 1:584.
[16] See al-Juwayni, *al-Burhān*, 2:1151; al-Ghazāli, *Shifāʾ al-Ghalīl*, 160, 164, 288; Nāṣir al-Dīn ʿAbd Allāh Ibn ʿUmar al-Bayḍāwi, *Minhaj al-Wuṣūl ila ʿIlm al-Uṣūl* (Khartoum: Dār al-Fikr, 1980), 4:75; al-Rāzi, *al-Maḥṣūl*, 5:160; al-Āmidi, *al-Aḥkām fī Uṣūl al-Aḥkām*, 3:240; al-Shāṭibi, *al-Muwāfaqāt*, 1:326. Al-Shāṭibi argues in a later passage that the imperative to protect the five basic needs follows from the (chronologically earlier revealed) Meccan norms of the Qur'an. See *al-Muwāfaqāt*, 2:42–43.

This justificatory approach can be traced back to al-ʿĀmiri (d. 991/381).[17] It is most pronounced in al-Ṭūfi, who does not speak in this context of abstract necessities or universal goods, but of the "five necessary universal norms" (*al-aḥkām al-ḫamsa al-kulliya al-ḍarūriya*), which consist in "executing the murderer and the apostate, amputating the hand of the thief, [and] imposing the punishments for defamation and alcohol consumption."[18] In the light of these sanctions, and by reflecting on their respective purposes, the scholars were able to determine the objects worthy of protection, which were—retrospectively— declared to be the higher purposes of the law. This also explains why jurists such as Ibn ʿAbd al-Salām (d. 1261/660), al-Qarāfi, al-Ṭūfi, Ibn al-Subki (d. 1369/771), and al-Shawkāni (d. 1834/1250) included the protection of honor (*al-ʿirḍ*) among the basic needs.[19] They justified this addition on the grounds that the Qur'an[20] provides a separate punishment for slander and libel (*qaḏf*).[21]

Even if we ignore the dubiousness of this sanctions-based methodology for the moment, it should be noted that there does not seem to be complete agreement among classical scholars as to what each punishment is supposed to accomplish. For example, what exactly is the purpose of the prohibition of sexual license (*zinạ*)? According to al-Juwayni, its purpose is to protect chastity, for which he uses the term *furūj* (literally: genitals). Al-Ghazāli initially agreed, but used the alternative term *buḍʿ* (literally: vulva). Later, however, al-Ghazāli changed this determination of purpose to the protection of offspring (*nasl*), which was adopted by scholars such as al-Āmidi and al-Shāṭibi. In contrast, al-Rāzi interprets the prohibition of sexual license to mean that its purpose is to protect lineage (*nasab*), a position again adopted by such scholars as Ibn al-Subki, al-Isnāwi, and al-Badaḫshi.[22]

The terms *nasl* and *nasab* refer to two completely different things. While *nasl* (from the verbal root *na-sa-la*, meaning "to procreate," "to reproduce") refers to something in the future, namely the offspring to be produced, *nasab* (from the verbal root *na-sa-ba*, meaning "to relate," "to trace back") refers

[17] See Jasser Auda, *Maqasid al-Shariah as Philosophy of Islamic Law* (Herndon, VA: International Institute of Islamic Thought, 2008), 21–22.

[18] Al-Ṭūfi, *Sharḥ al-Arbaʿīn*, 238.

[19] See Kamali, *Shari'ah Law*, 126.

[20] See Qur'an 24:4–5.

[21] According to al-Shāṭibi, the protection of honor falls under the protection of life. Al-Shāṭibi, *al-Muwāfaqāt*, 2:42. By contrast, al-Mawardi (d. 1058/450) emphasizes that honor is an independent value which, like physical integrity and property, is among the essential components of human life. Abu al-Ḥasan al-Mawardi, *al-Ḥāwi al-Kabīr* (Beirut: Dār al-Kutub al-ʿIlmiyya, 1994), 11:10.

[22] See Attia, *Towards Realization of the Intents of Islamic Law*, 16–20.

to human lineage, descent, or genealogy, namely something in the past. Regardless, the obvious question in both cases is what exactly is meant by the protection of offspring or lineage. As Ibn ʿAshūr notes, the terms in question are used by classical scholars without any explanation.[23]

If we assume that the protection of offspring is about protecting the process of human reproduction, then it is indeed a necessary legal purpose, since the cessation of reproduction would lead to the disappearance of the human species.[24] On this reading, however, the protection of offspring can be subsumed under the protection of life (*ḥifẓ al-nafs*).[25] In the case of protecting lineage, on the other hand, it is not entirely clear why this should be considered a fundamental legal purpose, since there is no compelling reason why one must know that X is the descendant of Y.[26] It is well known that Arabs attach great importance to their lineage, as evidenced by the long names in which the relationship of descent is usually indicated by the particles *Ibn* (son of) and *Abū* (father of). But this is more a reflection of classical Arab tribal culture than a universal need that must be satisfied out of necessity.[27]

An alternative interpretation of the protection of lineage, however, is that it is not so much a matter of lineage per se as of the consequences of an unclear lineage. As we have seen, this line of argument must be understood against the background of the prohibition of sexual license, which is its starting point. In this context, al-Rāzi, for example, argues that the protection of lineage is relevant because the care of the child would be jeopardized by the inability to identify the father (as a result of sexual license), which brings us back to the protection of offspring.[28] A social order in which men and women had sexual intercourse at will would lead to chaos and confusion in the determination of parentage, which in turn would make it impossible to assign the (primarily male) responsibility for the protection and support of children and to guarantee their inheritance rights. Accordingly, the purpose

[23] Ibn Ashur, *Treatise on Maqāṣid al-Shariah*, 117–118. Nyazee also observes that "this is a field that has not been fully developed by lawyers, so there is room for interpretation and reinterpretation." Nyazee, *Theories of Islamic Law*, 247.

[24] As argued, for example, by al-Shāṭibi, *al-Muwāfaqāt*, 1:332.

[25] Al-Shāṭibi, *al-Muwāfaqāt*, 2:410, also reaches this conclusion.

[26] Ibn Ashur, *Treatise on Maqāṣid al-Shariah*, 118.

[27] Shibli Numani (d. 1914) describes this phenomenon as follows: "The Arabs had precedence over other nations in the possession of certain characteristics which tended to contribute towards the solidarity of the chain of History. Thus genealogy was their passion. Even a child learnt by rote the genealogical table of his house and forefathers up to the tenth or twelfth degree, and his relish for preserving their lineage was so intense that they took to keeping the pedigrees even of their horses and camels." Shibli Numani, *Al-Farooq: The Life of Omar the Great* (Delhi: Adam, 1996), 2.

[28] See al-Rāzi, *al-Maḥṣūl*, 5:160.

of the prohibition of sexual license is to regulate human sexual activity in order to avoid the birth of illegitimate children and thus ambiguous kinship relationships. Within this framework, marriage functions as an institution for regulating human reproduction. On the one hand, it ensures that family relationships can be clearly identified and hence that responsibility for the care of children can be allocated; on the other hand, it promotes the natural affection of parents for their children.[29] This shows that, strictly speaking, the protection of the lineage or offspring is a matter of satisfying the needs of the next generation for security and sustenance, as well as the emotional needs that must be satisfied within the framework of orderly family relationships.

The difficulty in specifying the concrete meaning of the protection of offspring or lineage is certainly related to the ambiguity of the terms used and the failure to explain their precise meaning. Significantly, however, Muslim jurists do not specify how offspring or lineage is to be protected, other than to refer to the prohibition of sexual license. The same problem arises with respect to the protection of reason (*ḥifẓ al-ʿaql*), which Muslim jurists typically justify on the grounds that the legal sources prohibit and punish the use of intoxicating substances. This, of course, immediately raises the question of whether the prohibition of the use of intoxicating substances does not serve some other, perhaps even several purposes besides the mere protection of reason. Perhaps the purpose of the prohibition is to ensure the legal or moral responsibility of people, or to prevent damage to health. Or it may be to increase people's social productivity, or it may simply be to preserve the ability to concentrate on prayer.[30] But even if we agree that its purpose is to protect reason, one cannot help but ask what exactly is meant by reason in this context. Is it the basic ability to understand or the ability to think critically or the ability to abstract a priori? Is it common sense or simply mental health? The horizon of meaning remains open. If we look to the classical jurists for answers to the question of how reason should be protected—that is, what measures are necessary to protect it—all they have to say is that reason is protected by the prohibition of intoxicating substances.[31] Even the twentieth-century scholar Ibn ʿAshūr sees the protection of reason as ensured by "[preventing] people from consuming alcohol and becoming drunk . . . as well as the spread

[29] See Ibn Ashur, *Treatise on Maqāṣid al-Shariah*, 118; Weiss, *The Spirit of Islamic Law*, 155.

[30] See Khaled Abou el Fadl, *And God Knows the Soldiers: The Authoritative and Authoritarian in Islamic Discourses* (Lanham, MD: University Press of America, 2001), 53, 63.

[31] Al-Ghazāli, *Shifāʾ al-Ghalīl*, 160, 164, 288; al-Bayḍāwi, *Minhaj al-Wuṣūl ila ʿIlm al-Uṣūl*, 4:75; al-Rāzi, *al-Maḥṣūl*, 5:160; al-Āmidi, *al-Aḥkām fī Uṣūl al-Aḥkām*, 3:240.

of all kinds of intoxicating substances corrupting the minds, such as hashish, opium, morphine, cocaine, heroin and all such drugs, the consumption of which has increased markedly during the nineteenth century."[32]

There are several problems with this explanatory model that call into question the fundamental character of *maqāṣid*. Recall that the claim associated with the *maqāṣid* is that they are the legal purposes extrapolated on the basis of a holistic reading of the legal sources. In this context, it seems questionable whether a conception of reason derived from a sanction-based reading of the sources can be reconciled with an understanding of reason derived from a comprehensive analysis of the sources. The discourse on reason in the Qur'an alone opens up a broad horizon of meaning in that it repeatedly speaks of those who observe (*yanẓurūn*), think (*yatafakkarūn*), reflect (*yatadabbarūn*), make reasonable judgments (*ya'qilūn*), understand (*yatafaqqahūn*), and know (*ya'lamūn*).[33] In addition, there is a much more fundamental problem that Sherman Jackson points out.[34] For even if we assume that the protection of reason is derived only from the norms prohibiting the use of intoxicants, and further that the protection of reason is not just a specific normative purpose but a comprehensive legal purpose, it is still very strange that the sole function of this legal purpose is supposed to be to reaffirm the prohibition of intoxicants. In order to achieve this purpose, it would theoretically be sufficient to enumerate the various verses and prophetic sayings on the prohibition of intoxicants. Nor is it necessary to resort to induction to establish that other nonalcoholic substances such as hashish and opium are forbidden. An argument by analogy is sufficient. The whole point of inductive reasoning is to reach conclusions that cannot be reached by reasoning from individual norms or by reasoning by analogy.

This can be illustrated with the following example. Suppose my doctor, who has been treating me for years and is very familiar with my dietary preferences, instructs me to avoid eating chocolate, cake, jelly beans, and cola. Since I have complete confidence in my doctor and am convinced that she has my best interests at heart, I am determined to follow her instructions to the letter. So on my next trip to the grocery store, I deliberately avoid the

[32] Ibn Ashur, *Treatise on Maqāṣid al-Shariah*, 121.

[33] See Kamali, *Freedom, Equality and Justice in Islam*, 22. For a detailed discussion of the Qur'anic concept of reason, see Fatima M. Isma'īl, *al-Qur'ān wa'l-Naẓar al-'Aqli* (Herndon, VA: International Institute of Islamic Thought, 1993).

[34] See Sherman Abdelhakim Jackson, "Literalism, Empiricism, and Induction: Apprehending and Concretizing Islamic Law's *Maqāsid al Sharī'ah* in the Modern World," *Michigan State Law Review* (2006), 1469–1486.

shelves where I usually buy chocolate, cake, jelly beans, and cola, and instead concentrate on the adjacent shelves of candy, donuts, licorice, and Fanta. Since my doctor has not forbidden me to consume any of these items, I put them in my cart and am happy to have found suitable alternatives. But as I walk to the checkout counter, I begin to wonder what my doctor would say. Would she approve of my choices? I begin to think about what she had in mind when she advised me against my original preferences. After pondering this question for a while, I conclude that the old products had exactly one thing in common: their high sugar content. Much to my disappointment, I find that my new products also have high sugar content. I can therefore assume with a high degree of confidence that my doctor would also forbid me to consume these products, although she did not mention them explicitly, and I put them back on the shelves.

However, I'm a little irritated because I can't get the question out of my head: Why high-sugar products in particular? What motivated my doctor to ban them? I'm sure she's not trying to annoy me for no reason but is interested in my well-being. But how does banning sugary products contribute to my well-being? Since my doctor is currently on vacation, I go to a nutritionist. After explaining the situation, he tells me that high-sugar consumption often leads to diabetes. In all likelihood, my doctor was trying to protect me from diabetes. When she specifically told me not to eat chocolate, cake, jelly beans, or cola, she did not mean that I should avoid only these products. Rather, she mentioned them because she knew they were among my specific preferences. Therefore, my decision to avoid similarly sugary products at the grocery store was correct. But to fulfill my doctor's intent, the nutritionist continues, it is not enough to simply avoid eating "sugar bombs," as this is only one measure to prevent diabetes. Research has shown that people who are overweight are more susceptible to diabetes than those who lead a healthy lifestyle, so comprehensive protection against diabetes also requires a balanced and calorie-conscious diet, which means eating less fatty foods and more fruits and vegetables. It is also important to exercise regularly so that the body has the opportunity to break down fat. Finally, it is strongly recommended not to smoke, as this significantly increases the risk of diabetes. My doctor did not prescribe any of these measures. But they are necessary if I am to fulfill her intention to protect me from diabetes.

To explain the connection with the protection of reason, let us draw the following parallels. (a) Just as I could learn from my doctor's explicit instructions that I should not consume chocolate, cake, jelly beans, or cola, so I can learn from the explicit norms of the Qur'an and the Sunnah that I should not consume alcoholic beverages. (b) Just as the analogy I drew in the supermarket led me to put other products with similar sugar content back on the shelves, an analogy in the case of alcohol leads me to conclude that other substances with similar intoxicating properties are also prohibited. (c) Although my doctor did not explicitly say so, the nutritionist could infer that her intention was to protect me from diabetes. Similarly, the suggestive power of a large number of norms has led jurists to conclude that the legislator's intention is to protect reason, even though He did not explicitly say so. (d) The recognition of the doctor's intention leads the nutritionist to prescribe measures to protect against diabetes in addition to the "sugar ban." These measures do not follow from the doctor's statements or from an argument by analogy but are based solely on the doctor's will, which must be fulfilled. In the same way, the knowledge of the divine will should lead to the adoption of measures that go beyond the "prohibition of intoxicants" and aim at the protection of reason. For "[h]ow many a person's mind has been lost without his or her ever having touched a drop of liquor?"[35]

Understood in this way, the protection of reason would have to refer to both material and sociocultural influences that have a negative effect on the use of reason. This would also imply taking positive measures to enable a proactive development of reason (e.g., through education). But this is precisely what is missing from the protection of reason in the classical sense. It is not a norm-generating purpose capable of formulating normative implications that go beyond the prohibition of narcotics. Rather, it is a construct that serves primarily to confirm the legal status quo—in Jackson's words, "a mere paper tiger, invoked primarily to insulate existing doctrine."[36] The result is a legal purpose that ultimately proves useless in its theoretical function and practical application. This seems to confirm the suspicion that the classical conception of the *maqāṣid* is "empty rhetoric,"[37] a conclusion that, as Khaled Abou el Fadl points out, applies not only to the protection of reason but to all derived legal goods:

> Muslim jurists did not develop the five basic values as broad categories and then explore the theoretical implications of each value. Rather, in a

[35] Al-Raysuni, *Imam al-Shatibi's Theory*, 265.
[36] Jackson, "Literalism, Empiricism, and Induction," 1471.
[37] Abdullah Saeed, *Interpreting the Qur'an: Towards a Contemporary Approach* (London: Routledge, 2006), 127.

> positivistic spirit, they examined existing legal injunctions that could be said to serve each of the values and concluded that by codifying each of these specific injunctions, the five values would be sufficiently served. So, for example, Muslim jurists contended that the law of apostasy protected religion, the prohibition of murder served the basic value of life, the prohibition of intoxicants protected the intellect, the prohibition of fornication and adultery protected lineage, and the right of compensation protected the right of property. But limiting the protection of the intellect to the prohibition of alcohol or the protection of life to the prohibition of murder is hardly thorough. Unfortunately, it appears that the juristic tradition reduced these five values to technical objectives.[38]

A final example that serves to illustrate the problems with the methodological approach of the classical scholars is the injunction to protect religion (*ḥifẓ al-dīn*). Here, too, it is at first glance rather unclear what the concept of religion refers to, and thus what exactly is implied by the "protection" of religion. If we assume on the conceptual level that the operative notion of religion is a subjective one, referring to individual religiosity, then we must ask in what sense religion qua religiosity is a universal and necessary basic need. Again, we should recall that according to scholars, the *criterion of universality* implies a supratemporal relevance for all people, places, and times.[39] It seems questionable to what extent religion satisfies the criterion of universality thus understood, since it is obviously not relevant to *every* person.

Regarding the *criterion of necessity,* it also seems questionable whether religion is really a basic condition of human existence. To answer this question, I would like to refer to an argument about the necessity of government that al-Ghazāli cites in one of his later works.[40] There he develops a two-step thesis according to which (1) religion cannot be well ordered (*niẓām al-dīn*) unless worldly affairs are well ordered (*niẓām al-dunya*), while experience shows that (2) worldly affairs cannot be well ordered without government. The task of government, then, is to create a well-ordered society in which "the needs of this world" are guaranteed "in their entirety."[41] This, al-Ghazāli argues, is the necessary condition (*sharṭ*) for the proper ordering of religion,

[38] Khaled Abou el Fadl, *Islam and the Challenge of Democracy* (Princeton, NJ: Princeton University Press, 2004), 24.

[39] Al-Shāṭibi, *al-Muwāfaqāt*, 1:536; Ibn Ashur, *Treatise on Maqāṣid al-Shariah*, 130.

[40] Abū Ḥāmid al-Ghazāli, *al-Iqtiṣād fī al-I'tiqād* (Ankara: Nur Matbaasi, 1962), 235.

[41] Ibid.: *jamī' mā hua muḥtāj ilayh qabl al maut*, literally: "all that is needed [by human beings] before death."

which is achieved through the pursuit of spiritual knowledge (*ma'rifa*) and the worship of God (*'ibāda*). However, this quest would be impossible without physical health (*ṣiḥḥat al-badan*) and security (*amn*), as well as adequate clothing, shelter, and food. For it is inconceivable that "one who spends all his time defending himself against the sword of the oppressor and seeking his daily bread from tyrants will have the opportunity to devote himself to learning and worship, although these are the means of well-being in the hereafter."[42] Thus, according to al-Ghazāli, religion not only has a great interest in human well-being in this world, but also depends on it; otherwise it cannot function properly. Only the existence of a just and well-ordered society makes it possible to devote oneself to the religious, and only the religious opens the door to well-being in the hereafter.[43]

This line of argument opens up a new way of judging the necessity of religion, if we distinguish between a *worldly* and an *otherworldly* necessity. In this sense, one can argue that religion is a necessary condition for ensuring human well-being in the hereafter.[44] And indeed, Muslim jurists argue that the purpose of the Islamic *sharī'a* is to protect the well-being of people in this life (*fi al-'ājil*) and in the next life (*wa'l-ājil*).[45] Within this framework, well-being in this world is protected by the norms that govern interpersonal relations, while well-being in the hereafter (*maṣāliḥ uḫrawiyya*) is protected by the norms that govern beliefs and rituals (*'ibadāt*). The latter can also contribute to the welfare of human beings in this world, for example, by freeing

[42] Ibid., 236. This idea is widely echoed in the writings of contemporary Muslim thinkers. A very eloquent formulation is found in Soroush, *Reason, Freedom, and Democracy in Islam*, 44: "The distress of acquiring one's daily bread, shelter, and clothing would hardly allow for engagement in arts and the pursuit of worldly knowledge and mystical gnosis. But once mankind is liberated from the arduous and worrisome tasks of the mundane world, it can take wing and fly in the sphere of the higher concerns. Once the needs of the body are met, the hunger of the soul may be more apparent."

[43] Ibid. Al-Ghazāli does not elaborate on what form of state or government is necessary to ensure a just and well-ordered society. However, contemporary thinkers such as Khaled Abou el Fadl echo al-Ghazāli's central idea to make a religiously grounded reference to justice, democracy, and human rights: "If injustice is prevalent within a society . . . this leads to the spread of traits and characteristics that are inconsistent with the ability of submission to God. Those traits include fear, apprehension, and lack of tranquility as people live in fear of injury; dishonesty and hypocrisy as people have to lie and dissimulate their true beliefs and convictions in order to survive; insecurity and opportunism as people learn that there is no correlation between acts and results; and suffering as people are ultimately robbed of their rights. In essence, the existence of injustice means the absence of Godliness, while justice means the presence of Godliness. And although only God is capable of perfect justice, humans must work hard and strive to achieve as much justice as possible. . . . Furthermore, the pursuit of justice obligates Muslims to find a system in which people must have access to powers and institutions within society that can redress injustices and protect people from oppression." Abou el Fadl, *The Great Theft*, 186–187.

[44] Thus al-Shāṭibi, *al-Muwāfaqāt*, 1:332.

[45] Ibid., 1:322.

them from inner constraints and earthly worries. But the necessity of religious norms is derived exclusively from the welfare of human beings in the hereafter. Therefore, if people want to earn God's favor, religion in the sense of worship becomes a necessity for them.

However, since Muslim jurists derive the protection of religion from *'ibadāt*, the question of whether religion is a universal basic need also arises from an internal Islamic perspective. For the norms of faith and ritual, in contrast to the interpersonal norms, refer only to the community of Muslim believers, so that the claim to universality of religion is limited to the believers. Moreover, these norms are not legally enforceable, but must be followed out of religious insight and conviction. From this perspective, we must ask whether religion can be described as a legal good at all.

The classical terminology refers to the protection of religion or the observance of ritual norms as a "right of God" (*ḥaqq Allah*).[46] This expression is misleading, however, because God is not a vulnerable being in need of rights. Rights are needed to assert one's interests against someone else, who in turn is obligated to respect those rights. My right to life is meaningful only if my counterpart respects his duty not to kill me. In this sense the realization of my interests depends on others. But God is not dependent on human beings. Unlike human beings, He is not harmed if His "rights" are not fulfilled. He is *al-Ghanī*, the one who is self-sufficient and is free from all needs: "O men! It is you who stand in need of God, whereas He alone is self-sufficient, the One to whom all praise is due" (Qur'an 35:15).[47] The Qur'an repeatedly emphasizes that the observance of religious rules does not serve God, but only human interests.[48] Likewise, diregarding religious rules does not harm God, but only human beings: "SAY [O Prophet]: 'O mankind! The truth from your Sustainer has now come unto you. Whoever, therefore, chooses to

[46] See al-Shāṭibi, *al-Muwāfaqāt*, 1:135, 600.

[47] See also Qur'an 10:68: "Limitless is He in His glory! Self-sufficient is He"; 2:263: "God is self-sufficient, forbearing"; 31:26: "Unto God belongs all that is in the heavens and on earth. Verily, God alone is self-sufficient, the One to whom all praise is due!"; 2:267: "And know that God is self-sufficient, ever to be praised"; 6:133: "And thy Sustainer alone is self-sufficient, limitless in His grace."

[48] See Qur'an 2:232: "This is an admonition unto every one of you who believes in God and the Last Day; it is the most virtuous [way] for you, and the cleanest"; 27:40: "he who is grateful [to God] is but grateful for his own good; whereas he who chooses to be ungrateful [should know that], verily, my Sustainer is self-sufficient, most generous in giving!"; 31:12: "for he who is grateful [unto Him] is but grateful for the good of his own self; whereas he who chooses to be ungrateful [ought to know that], verily, God is self-sufficient, ever to be praised!"; 29:6: "whoever strives hard [in God's cause] does so only for his own good: for, verily, God does not stand in need of anything in all the worlds!" 35:18: "whoever grows in purity, attains to purity but for the good of his own self"; 47:38: "And yet, he who acts niggardly [in God's cause] is but niggardly towards his own self: for God is indeed self-sufficient, whereas you stand in need [of Him]."

follow the right path, follows it but for his own good; and whoever chooses to go astray, goes but astray to his own hurt. And I am not responsible for your conduct'" (10:108).[49]

The notion of a "right of God" is therefore not an enforceable, divine legal claim against human beings. Rather, it is intended to emphasize human beings' *moral* obligation and responsibility to God. People are morally, but not legally, obligated to observe the ritual norms. If they neglect prayer or fasting, they will not have to answer for it in a court of law but only before God, who will judge them in the hereafter.[50] This is because the legal evaluation of prayer in this world is limited to its external or visible dimension.[51] However, the validity of prayer (and all ritual acts) depends not only on the visible act but also on the inner conviction and underlying intention (*niyya*).[52] It is no coincidence that the Qur'an criticizes those who line up to pray only to be seen by others,[53] or who give the appearance of religiosity

[49] See also Qur'an 6:104: "Means of insight have now come unto you from your Sustainer [through this divine writ]. Whoever, therefore, chooses to see, does so for his own good; and whoever chooses to remain blind, does so to his own hurt. And [say unto the blind of heart]: 'I am not your keeper'"; 2:57: "And [by all their sinning] they did no harm unto Us—but [only] against their own selves did they sin"; 7:160: "And [by all their sinning] they did no harm unto Us—but [only] against their own selves did they sin"; 3:176–177: "And be not grieved by those who vie with one another in denying the truth: verily, they can in no wise harm God. It is God's will that they shall have no share in the [blessings of the] life to come; and tremendous suffering awaits them. Verily, they who have bought a denial of the truth at the price of faith can in no wise harm God, whereas grievous suffering awaits them"; 47:32: "Verily, they who are bent on denying the truth and on barring [others] from the path of God, and [who thus] cut themselves off from the Apostle after guidance has been vouchsafed to them, can in no wise harm God; but He will cause all their deeds to come to nought"; 57:23–24: "And he who turns his back [on this truth ought to know that], verily, God alone is self sufficient, the One to whom all praise is due!"; 64:5–6: "And so they denied the truth and turned away. But God was not in need [of them]: for God is self-sufficient, ever to be praised"; 3:97: "And as for those who deny the truth—verily, God does not stand in need of anything in all the worlds"; 4:131: "And if you deny Him—behold, unto God belongs all that is in the heavens and all that is on earth, and God is indeed self-sufficient, ever to be praised"; 14:8: "If you should [ever] deny the truth—you and whoever else lives on earth, all of you—[know that,] verily, God is indeed self-sufficient, ever to be praised!"; 39:7: "If you are [an] ingrate—behold, God has no need of you; none the less, He does not approve of ingratitude in His servants: whereas, if you show gratitude, He approves it in you"; 60:6: "And if any turns away, [let him know that] God is truly self-sufficient, the One to whom all praise is due."

[50] See Qur'an 10:109.

[51] On this, see Johannes C. Wichard, *Zwischen Markt und Moschee: Wirtschaftliche Bedürfnisse und religiöse Anforderungen im frühen islamischen Vertragsrecht* (Paderborn: Schöningh, 1995), 69–79 and Johannes Christian Wichard, "Recht und Religion im islamischen Recht," *Verfassung und Recht in Übersee* 30, no. 4 (1997): 533–544.

[52] On the concept of *niyya*, see the comprehensive study by Paul R. Powers, *Intent in Islamic Law: Motive and Meaning in Medieval Sunni Fiqh* (Leiden: Brill, 2005). A more accessible and less legal treatment is provided by al-Ghazāli in book 37 of his magnum opus, *Iḥyā' 'Ulūm al-Dīn* (*Kitāb al-Niyya wa'l-Ikhlāṣ wa'l-Ṣidq*), translated into English by Asaad F. Shaker, *Al-Ghazali on Intention, Sincerity and Truthfulness: Book XXXVII of the Revival of the Religious Sciences* (Cambridge, UK: Islamic Texts Society, 2018).

[53] See Qur'an 4:142, 107:4–6.

while in their hearts they are unbelievers.[54] While legal judgment in these matters is limited to the *forum externum*, religious judgment by God in the hereafter includes those motives and intentions that are not accessible to human judgment and therefore escape legal judgment. This is what al-Ghazāli has in mind when he states that "the hearts of men do not belong to the domain [of the jurist]."[55] The task of jurists, whom al-Ghazāli calls "scientists of this world" (*'ulamā' al-dunya*),[56] is rather to regulate interpersonal relations and to promote justice among people.[57] Only God knows what is in people's hearts,[58] and He alone can punish or reward them accordingly. In light of this fact, a legal duty to protect religion derived from *'ibadāt* only implies the protection of an empty ritualism that does not serve the welfare of human beings in this world or the next. Ibn Taimiyya (d. 1328/728) appropriately uses the term "external religion" (*al-dīn al-ẓāhir*) in this context.[59] Within the Islamic system of norms, therefore, we must distinguish between norms that are enforceable in this world and those that are sanctioned only in the hereafter.

In this context, we must also refute another argument used to justify the protection of religion. As we have seen, classical Islamic jurisprudence identified the purposes of law on the basis of a positivist reading of the penal norms elaborated in the Qur'an (*ḥudūd*). Following this approach, scholars derive the protection of religion not only from *'ibadāt* but also from the punishment of apostasy. Leaving aside the question of the extent to which the prohibition of apostasy actually contributes to the protection of religion, let us instead ask which religion the prohibition of apostasy is supposed to protect. The fact that the protection of religion is derived from a norm that punishes apostasy from Islam with death suggests that the protection of religion here applies exclusively to Islam. It is unlikely, to say the least, that

[54] See Qur'an 2:14, 63:1.

[55] Al-Ghazāli, *Iḥyā' 'Ulūm al-Dīn*, 1:18: *wa am al-qalb fa ḥārij 'an wilāyatu.*

[56] Ibid., 1:17.

[57] Ibid., 1:19: "The jurisprudent does not, and should not, express an opinion regarding the things which allure and perplex the heart (*ḥazāzāt al-qulūb*), or how to deal with them but confines his opinion to those things which militate against justice. Hence the entire scope of the jurisprudent's domain is limited to the affairs of this world which pave the road to the hereafter. Should he then touch upon the attributes of the heart and the rules of the hereafter, he does so as an intruder just as he would be whenever anything relative to medicine, arithmetic, astronomy and theology confront him." Abū Ḥāmid al-Ghazāli, *The Book of Knowledge*, trans. Nabih Amin Faris (New Dehli: Islamic Book Service, n.d.), 38.

[58] See Qur'an 13:9, 11:5, 100:8–11.

[59] Aḥmad Ibn 'Abd al-Ḥalīm Ibn Taimiyya, *Majmū' al-Fatāwa li Shaykh al-Islām Ibn Taimiyya* (Mansura: Dār al-Wafā', 2005), 32:146.

Islamic scholars would agree that apostasy from Christianity should be punishable by death in order to help protect Christianity. But it is obvious that restricting the protection of religion to Islam in this way faces an objection arising from the criterion of universality. For clearly not "every legal system or society" will have a legal purpose whose sole aim is to protect the Islamic religion.

But there is another, much more fundamental objection to deriving the protection of religion from the punishment of apostasy: there is no such sanction in the Qur'an. None of the Qur'anic passages dealing with apostasy speaks of imposing a secular punishment on those who renounce the Islamic faith.[60] Accordingly, apostasy is not a secular *crime* to be atoned for in this world, but a *sin* for which the apostate will be punished in the hereafter.[61] Since the Qur'an does not specify any punishment for apostasy, the justification offered by scholars for the protection of religion loses its foundation. Coincidentally, the same is true for the protection of reason, which the scholars justify by appealing to the punishment for drinking wine (*shurb al-ḫamr*). This is also a case of a punishment that is not specified in the Qur'an. Therefore, it cannot be counted among the *ḥudud*, which by definition must be derived from the text of the Qur'an.[62] In this context, it should be noted that the Qur'an lists five crimes that are subject to sanctions, namely, murder,[63] highway robbery,[64] theft,[65] licentiousness,[66] and slander.[67] Thus, according to the sanctions-based methodology of the classical *maqāṣid* conception, the purposes of Islamic law should be as follows: (1) protection of life (murder), (2) protection of public safety (highway robbery), (3) protection of property (theft), (4) protection of offspring (licentiousness), and (5) protection of honor (defamation). Consequently, both the protection of religion and the protection of reason would have to be removed from the list of legal purposes because they are not based on Qur'anic sanctions.

[60] See Qur'an 2:217, 3:86–91, 3:106, 4:115, 4:137, 5:12, 5:54, 9:74, 16:106–107, 47:25–26, 47:34.

[61] This issue is discussed in detail in Abdullah Saeed and Hassan Saeed, *Freedom of Religion, Apostasy and Islam* (London: Routledge, 2016); see also el-Awa, *Punishment in Islamic Law*, 49–64.

[62] Kamali, *Shari'ah Law*, 191.

[63] Qur'an 2:178.

[64] Qur'an 5:33.

[65] Qur'an 5:38.

[66] Qur'an 24:2.

[67] Qur'an 24:4.

10

New Conceptions of the *maqāṣid*

In the previous chapter, I tried to show that the classical conception of the *maqāṣid* is beset with some profound problems, both in substance and in function, especially in the horizontal dimension. I have been able to establish the following:

- Neither the quality nor the quantity of basic needs is derived from a holistic reading of the Islamic sources, but rather from a narrow interpretation of the penal norms (*ḥudūd*).
- Different basic needs can be developed from the same penal norm, since there is disagreement about the precise purpose of each particular penal norm.
- The basic needs identified are conceptually indeterminate, so that it is not always clear *what* exactly the protection of a particular basic need entails and *how* exactly it is to be protected.
- The basic idea of the *maqāṣid* is endangered by restricting its norm-generating function to the normative status quo.
- The postulated criteria of necessity, universality, and empirical demonstrability are not met by all basic needs.
- The classical list of basic needs must be modified even if the sanctions-based method is applied consistently.

With these criticisms, I have attempted to show that the classical conception of the *maqāṣid* needs to be revised if it is to live up to its own claims.

Before offering my own reflections on this, in this chapter I would first like to address the modern reception of the *maqāṣid* and assess some of the proposed reevaluations of the concept. The idea of the *maqāṣid* has undoubtedly gained prominence in contemporary Muslim discourse and is increasingly seen as a ray of hope that can rescue Islamic thought from its deep crisis.[1] A positive feature of this development is that, far from hailing the

[1] See, for example, the volumes edited by Adis Duderija, ed., *Maqāṣid al-Sharīʿa and Contemporary*

Human Rights Between Universality and Islamic Legitimacy. Mahmoud Bassiouni, Oxford University Press.
 DOI: 10.1093/oso/9780197753897.003.0011

classical *maqāṣid* conception as a panacea, Muslim authors are quite willing to criticize various aspects of the theory and to add new ones. Their criticism is primarily directed at the classical catalogue of basic needs and not at the idea of *maqāṣid* as such. For example, the Moroccan scholar Aḥmad al-Raisūni argues for a reconsideration of the classical list of legal purposes because "there are other vital interests . . . which may well be no less significant and inclusive than some of the five presently recognized essentials."[2] According to al-Raisūni, they are merely a product of human thought, so it is legitimate to modify or expand them through new intellectual efforts.[3] This is confirmed by Gamal Eldin Attia, who states that "limiting [the legal purposes] to five is nothing more than a personal interpretation put forth by Abū Ḥāmid al-Ghazāli, who based his enumeration on the prescribed punishments in Islam."[4] Syed Nawab Haider Naqvi expresses his discomfort even more clearly when he criticizes some authors for continuing to treat the classical legal purposes as the ultimate frame of reference: "True, these *maqāṣid* . . . must have made an interesting list of objectives, in the time these were formulated, to address legal and metaphysical issues; yet they need to be refocused, expanded and amended to become useful guides for public policy in modern times. Leaping between totally different eras and time zones to cull nuggets of traditional wisdom is, at best, an exercise in futility."[5]

The contemporary debate on reforming the *maqāṣid* is dominated by two trends, *reinterpretation* and *expansion*. The first approach is simply to give the classical legal purposes a new horizon of meaning, with the obvious aim of adapting them to the spirit of the times. Thus, Khaled Abou el Fadl proposes "that the protection of religion should be developed to mean protecting the freedom of religious belief; the protection of life should mean that the taking of life must be for a just cause and the result of a just process; the protection of the intellect should mean the right to free thinking, expression and belief; the protection of honor should mean the protecting of the dignity of a human being; and the protection of property should mean the

Muslim Thought: An Examination (New York: Palgrave Macmillan, 2014) and Idris Nassery, Rumee Ahmed, and Muna Tatari, eds., *The Objectives of Islamic Law: The Promises and Challenges of the Maqāsid al-Sharīʿa* (Lanham, MD: Lexington Books, 2018).

2 Al-Raysuni, *Imam al-Shatibi's Theory*, 364.

3 Ibid., 364–365.

4 Attia, *Towards Realization of the Higher Intents of Islamic Law*, 83.

5 Syed Nawab Haider Naqvi, *Perspectives on Morality and Human Well-Being: A Contribution to Islamic Economics* (Leicester: Islamic Foundation, 2003), 129.

right to compensation for the taking of property."[6] Mohamed Ibrahim argues that the protection of religion should be reinterpreted in the more secular form of "protection of the social order."[7] With respect to the protection of offspring, Imran Nyazee suggests that we speak of "protection of the family unit."[8] Meanwhile, other commentators interpret the protection of property as an imperative to promote economic development.[9]

The reinterpretation approach is often accompanied by a proposal to expand the classical catalogue of legal purposes. The first criticism of the classical legal purposes in this sense was probably formulated as early as the fourteenth century by the Ḥanbali scholar Ibn Taimiyya (d. 1328/728). He criticized the sanctions-based method of his contemporaries and the associated limitation of Islamic legal purposes on the grounds that they did not do justice to Islamic law. He argued that attributing the purposes of the law solely to the penal norms deserves the accusation of negligence.[10] According to Ibn Taimiyya, the list of the five legal purposes neglects "other aspects about which God has issued commandments and prohibitions in order to maintain the best possible living conditions [*al-aḥwāl al-saniyya*] and the cultivation of morality (*tahḏīb al-aḫlāq*)."[11] These include, for example, "norms that God has ordained regarding contractual fidelity *(wafā' bil-'uhūd)*, the maintenance of family relationships (*ṣilat al-arḥām*), the rights of slaves (*ḥuqūq al-mamalīk*) and neighbors (*al-jirān*), and the rights of Muslims among themselves."[12] However, these are only "some of the many" concerns (*juz' min ajzā'*) that Islamic law pursues.[13] This illustrates that Ibn Taimiyya opens up the horizontal framework of the *maqāṣid* without limiting it to a specific number of legal purposes.

Ibn Taimiyya's call to expand the classical legal purposes has found a wide echo in modern times. The theme of *maqāṣid* received its first modern

[6] Abou el Fadl, *Islam and the Challenge of Democracy*, 41.

[7] Mohamed Ibrahim, *Islamische Scharia versus Menschenrechte?* (Darmstadt: Averroes Institut für wissenschaftliche Islamforschung, 2007), 6: "The word 'religion' in the European sense does not really exist in Islam. Religion is referred to as 'din,' by which is generally understood 'way of life.' Therefore, the first need, 'protection of religion,' can be reformulated as 'protection of the social order' via 'protection of the way of life.' This reformulation is so general that any society can affirm this objective. And it urges us to ask: Which social orders are worthy of protection? The attempt to answer this question forces us to reflect on the political and social order that we are prepared to defend."

[8] Nyazee, *Theories of Islamic Law*, 247–248.

[9] See Auda, *Maqasid al-Shariah as Philosophy of Islamic Law*, 24.

[10] Ibn Taimiyya, *Majmū' al-Fatāwa li Shaykh al-Islām Ibn Taimiyya*, 11:343.

[11] Ibid., 32:234.

[12] Ibid.

[13] Ibid.

impulse in the thought of the Egyptian reformer Muḥammad ʿAbdūh (d. 1905). Although ʿAbdūh himself did not write a detailed work on legal theory, the idea of the *maqāṣid* undoubtedly figures prominently in his writings.[14] Moreover, he often speaks of the "spirit" (*rūḥ*) of revelation or of higher wisdom (*ḥikam*), inner "truths" (*ḥaqīqa*), and underlying "secrets" (*asrār*). But unlike his medieval predecessors, ʿAbdūh does not use these terms in an exclusively legal sense, referring to the purposes of the law, but also to the ethical and theological content of religion as a whole. In this context, ʿAbdūh also speaks of the purposes of revelation (*maqāṣid al-tanzīl* or *maqāṣid al-waḥy*) or religion (*maqāṣid al-dīn*). For him, the most important medium for understanding these purposes is the Qur'an. This is why he speaks of the *maqāṣid al-qur'ān* as the general framework for determining the theological, ethical, and legal content of religion.[15]

Muḥammad Rashīd Riḍa (d. 1935), who took up and developed the ideas of his teacher ʿAbdūh, identified ten purposes of the Qur'an that are spiritual, ethical, and legal in nature. The first purpose of the Qur'an, as identified by Riḍa, is to establish the three pillars of religion, namely belief in God, belief in the Last Day, and righteous action.[16] Its second purpose, he says, is to prove the mission and miracles of the Prophet.[17] The third purpose is to purify and perfect the human character.[18] The fourth purpose of the Qur'an is social and political reform leading to the unity and equality of human beings.[19] As its fifth purpose, Riḍa identifies "general characteristics of Islam," such as promoting worldly and otherworldly blessedness, establishing good relationships, and avoiding overwork.[20] The sixth purpose he identifies is the political principle of *shūra*, a deliberative form of decision-making, and the "general principles of legislation" (*qawāʿid al-ʿāma lil-tashrīʿ*). Among the latter, Riḍa includes establishing rights (*ḥaqq*) and justice (*ʿadl*), equality (*musāwa*), creating benefit and averting harm, respecting customs (*ʿurf*), and preventing injustice (*taḥrīm al-ẓulm*).[21] In another passage, he says, "An inductive examination of the legal norms contained in the Qur'an and Sunnah

[14] On this, see the article by Yasir S. Ibrahim, "Muḥammad ʿAbduh and Maqāṣid al-Sharīʿa," *Maghreb Review* 32, no. 1 (2007): 2–30.
[15] Ibid., 11–12.
[16] See Muḥammad Rashīd Riḍa, *al-Waḥy al-Muḥammadi* (Beirut: Mu'assasat ʿIzz al-Dīn, 1985), 193–219.
[17] Ibid., 221–225.
[18] Ibid., 257–274.
[19] Ibid., 275–282.
[20] Ibid., 283–286.
[21] Ibid., 287–297.

regarding private, civil, political, or military matters shows that all norms have the purpose of realizing values such as truth (*ḥaqq*), justice (*ʿadl*), sincerity (*ṣidq*), trust (*amāna*), fidelity (*wafāʾ*), mercy (*raḥma*), love (*maḥabba*), gentleness (*muwāsa*), righteousness (*birr*), and purity of heart (*iḥsān*), as well as the avoidance of vices such as injustice, betrayal, mistrust, insincerity, disloyalty, aggressiveness, fraud, swindling, usury, and bribery."[22]

It is noteworthy that Riḍa links his enumeration of the "general principles of legislation" with a discussion of *ḥudūd*, in which he also refers to the classical legal purposes. Riḍa states that the punishment of manslaughter is for the protection of life, the punishment of adultery is for the protection of honor and offspring, the punishment of theft is for the protection of property, the punishment of highway robbery is for the protection of safety, and the punishment of alcohol consumption is for the protection of reason.[23] Some striking features are of interest here. First, Riḍa omits the protection of religion, certainly because the Qur'an does not define a corresponding punishment. With regard to the protection of reason, he also adds that some jurists do not include the punishment of drinking alcohol among the *ḥudūd*, since neither the Qur'an nor the Sunnah specifies such a punishment.[24] It is also noteworthy that Riḍa adds the protection of security and derives it from the punishment for highway robbery (*ḥirāba*), whereas he derives both the protection of honor and the protection of offspring from the punishment for adultery.[25] However, the fact that Riḍa treats the purpose of the penal norms separately from the general purposes of the law suggests that he does not count the classical protected goods among the general purposes of the law, but at most among those of the criminal law.

As for the other purposes of the Qur'an, Riḍa emphasizes that they serve to remedy four social injustices. The first of these injustices is the "tyranny of wealth," to which the seventh purpose of the Qur'an refers. Riḍa calls this the "way of financial reform" (*al-irshād ila al-iṣlāḥ al-māli*); it includes, among other things, financial support for the poor, the protection of property, and the duty to provide for one's wife and family.[26] The eighth purpose of the Qur'an relates to the injustice of war and thus consists of "reforming warfare and avoiding the harm it causes for the benefit of humanity" (*iṣlāḥ niẓām*

[22] Ibid., 296.
[23] Ibid.
[24] Ibid.
[25] Ibid., 296–297. Riḍa remarks in this connection that the classical jurists conceive the application of the punishment for adultery in such a way as to render it all but inapplicable.
[26] Ibid., 299–317.

al-ḥarb wa dafʿ mafāsidihā wa qasrahā ʿala mafīhi al-ẖayr lil-bashar).[27] To address injustices against women, the ninth purpose of the Qur'an, according to Riḍa, is to grant women "all human, religious, and civil rights" (*iʿtāʾ al-nisāʾ jamīʿ al-ḥuqūq al-insāniyya wʾal-dīniyya wʾal-madaniyya*).[28] The tenth and final purpose of the Qur'an is to eliminate the injustice against slaves and to contribute to their liberation (*taḥrīr al-raqīb*).[29]

The ideas propagated by ʿAbdūh and elaborated by Riḍa regarding the purposes of the Qur'an represent the first modern attempt to develop the concept of the *maqāṣid*, whose function was now increasingly to bring about a renewal of Islamic thought. This is precisely what the Indian poet and philosopher Muhammad Iqbal (d. 1938) sought to do in his "Reconstruction of Religious Thought in Islam." Iqbal called upon the Muslim of his time to "reconstruct his social life in the light of ultimate principles, and evolve, out of the hitherto *partially revealed purpose* of Islam, that spiritual democracy which is the ultimate aim of Islam."[30] The fact that Iqbal considered the development of a spiritual democracy to be the ultimate goal of Islam must be attributed to the historical context in which the political future of Indian Muslims was at stake. In a 1937 letter to the future founder of the state of Pakistan, Muhammad Ali Jinnah (d. 1948),[31] Iqbal calls for the establishment of a social-democratic Muslim state to solve the problem of poverty afflicting Indian Muslims. Iqbal writes:

> [O]ur political institutions have never thought of improving the lot of Muslims generally. The problem of bread is becoming more and more acute. The Muslim has begun to feel that he has been going down and down during the last 200 years. . . . The question therefore is: how is it possible to solve the problem of Muslim poverty? . . . Happily there is a solution in the enforcement of the Law of Islam and its further development in the light of modern ideas. After a long and careful study of Islamic Law I have come to the conclusion that if this system of Law is properly understood and applied, at last the right to subsistence is secured to every body. But the enforcement and development of the Shari'aht of Islam is impossible in this country without a free Muslim state or states. . . . But it is clear to my mind

27 Ibid., 319–329.
28 Ibid., 331–338.
29 Ibid., 339–348.
30 Iqbal, *The Revival of Religious Thought in Islam*, 142, emphasis added.
31 The state of Pakistan was founded in 1947.

> that if Hinduism accepts social democracy it must necessarily cease to be Hinduism. For Islam the acceptance of social democracy in some suitable form and consistent with the legal principles of Islam is not a revolution but a return to the original purity of Islam.[32]

The Tunisian scholar Muḥammad al-Ṭāhir Ibn ʿAshūr (d. 1973) was less concerned with founding a new state than with establishing a new scientific discipline. In his work on *maqāṣid al-sharīʿa* published in 1946, Ibn ʿAshūr argues that the classical science of the sources and methods of legal reasoning (*uṣūl al-fiqh*) should be replaced by an independent "discipline dealing with the higher objectives of the Shari'ah" (*ʿilm maqāṣid al-sharīʿa*).[33] He is particularly critical of the literalist bent of classical jurisprudence, arguing that it focuses only on the external aspects of law and contributes little to clarifying its inner wisdom and purpose. According to Ibn ʿAshūr, Islamic jurisprudence must resemble a rational science whose philosophical reasoning is based on comprehensible, categorical evidence, so "that the obstinate is forced to yield and the confused is guided."[34] Fundamental to this rationalization, according to Ibn ʿAshūr, is the Qur'anic assertion that Islam is a religion of human *fiṭra*.[35] The term *fiṭra* refers to "the natural disposition (*ḫilqa*) and order (*niẓām*) that God has instilled in every created being."[36] It means "the inward and outward condition in which human beings have been created, that is, in both intellect and body."[37] For example, walking on one's feet is an aspect of the human physical disposition (*fiṭra jasadiyya*), whereas attempting to grasp objects with one's feet would contradict this disposition. Similarly, relating effects to their causes is part of the human intellectual and mental disposition (*fiṭra ʿaqliyya*), whereas attempting to draw conclusions from untrue premises contradicts this disposition.[38] Accordingly, the thesis that Islam is a religion of *fiṭra* has two important implications. On the one hand, it implies that the divine norms are in harmony with the natural disposition of human beings, in the sense that they can be recognized and

32 Mohamed Iqbal, *Letters of Iqbal to Jinnah: A Collection of Iqbal's Letters to the Qaid-l-Azam Conveying His Views on the Political Future of Muslim India*, ed. Sh. M. Ashraf (Lahore: n.p., 1974), 16–18.

33 Ibn Ashur, *Treatise on Maqāṣid al-Shari'ah*, xix.

34 Ibid., xvii.

35 Qur'an 30:30: "And so, set thy face steadfastly towards the [one ever-true] faith . . . in accordance with the natural disposition [*fiṭra*] which God has instilled into man."

36 Ibn ʿAshūr, *Maqāṣid al-Sharīʿa al-Islamiyya* (Tunis: Dār al-Salām, 2009), 81.

37 Ibid.

38 Ibid.

confirmed by human reason.[39] To clarify this aspect, Ibn ʿAshūr refers to an extensive passage by Abū ʿAli Ibn Sīna (lat. Avicenna, d. 1037/428), who wrote, among other things, that true *fiṭra* consists of insights and views whose acceptance necessarily follows from the fact that everyone can agree with them (*shahādat al-kull*).[40] To achieve this universal acceptance, Ibn ʿAshūr argues, God based the norms of the law on inner wisdoms (*ḥikam*) and underlying causes (*ʿilal*) that are rationally comprehensible (*mudrakāt al-ʿuqūl*) and exist independently of time and space.[41] If we examine these underlying reasons carefully, he continues, we will find that they serve exclusively to preserve human *fiṭra*—which brings us to the second implication of the above thesis:[42] Islamic law is in complete harmony with the universal and empirically ascertainable needs and interests of human beings and takes them into account in the administration of justice. The Moroccan scholar and contemporary of Ibn ʿAshūr, ʿAllāl al-Fāsi (d. 1974), agrees with this and emphasizes that "Islam came to guarantee the satisfaction of the needs that human beings as human beings require in order to establish civilization. For this reason, one cannot find anything in Islamic law that contradicts human *fiṭra*."[43]

By tracing Islamic law back to the concept of human *fiṭra*, Ibn ʿAshūr succeeded in paving the way for a theory of *maqāṣid* that transcends the epistemological and methodological reductionism of the classical conception. He criticizes the sanctions-based methodology of his medieval predecessors with the simple assertion that he cannot see any necessary correlation between the penal norms and the objectives of Islamic law.[44] Although this insight does not lead him to undertake a comprehensive revision of the classical conception, it does enable him to expand the classical framework and integrate new legal purposes into the theory of *maqāṣid*, among which equality (*musāwa*) and freedom (*ḥurriyya*) merit special attention. According to Ibn ʿAshūr, both of these legal purposes follow from human *fiṭra*, since all human beings are born equal[45] and freedom is part of the natural disposition of human beings.[46]

39 Ibid. 81, 134–135.
40 Ibn Sīna, *Kitāb al-Najāt fī al-Ḥikma al-Mantiqiyya wa'l-Ṭabīʿiyya wa'l-Ilāhiyya*, 99, quoted in Ibn Ashur, *Treatise on Maqāṣid al-Shariʿah*, 81–82.
41 Ibn Ashur, *Treatise on Maqāṣid al-Shariʿah*, 136.
42 Ibid., 85.
43 Al-Fāsi, *Maqāṣid al-Sharīʿa al-Islāmiyya wa Makārimihā*, 71.
44 Ibn Ashur, *Treatise on Maqāṣid al-Shariʿah*, 123.
45 Ibid., 146–147.
46 Ibid., 155.

Unfortunately, Ibn ʿAshūr did not elaborate on the theoretical connection between human *fiṭra* and *maqāṣid* as the basis for a systematic and coherent account of Islamic legal purposes. This may be due to the caution he expresses in the first part of his book about reforming the *maqāṣid*. There he says that "scholars ought to think carefully and take their time before venturing to affirm a Shariʿah objective. They must avoid partiality and hastiness, for the determination of a Shariʿah objective . . . can have many ramifications in the legal proofs and rulings ensuing from it during juristic deduction. Errors, therefore, have very grave consequences. Scholars should never determine any Shariʿah objective before undertaking a comprehensive thematic study . . . and before consulting the works of the scholars of Islamic jurisprudence, to gain enlightenment and understanding from their profound experience of the subject."[47] Despite the wide reception of Ibn ʿAshūr's work in contemporary discussions, appeals such as this have not led to the caution that he urged in expanding the *maqāṣid*. On the contrary, there has been a virtual explosion of new legal purposes, with different authors offering different justifications. A more political justification emphasizes the need to include purposes related to public and social life in the *maqāṣid* construct. For example, the Egyptian scholar Muḥammad al-Ghazāli (d. 1996) justifies the expansion of the *maqāṣid* on the grounds that the classical five basic needs have lost their relevance because they can no longer regulate the public issues facing people today. He argues that we must learn from the accumulated experience of the past fourteen centuries, in which corrupt regimes in Islamic countries led to oppression and injustice. Therefore, in order to regulate the authority of the state, he proposes to add freedom (*ḥurriya*) and justice (*ʿadāla*) to the five basic needs, "especially in view of the fact that the Qur'an says 'We send forth Our apostles with all evidence of truth; and through them We bestowed revelation from on high, and [thus gave you] a balance [wherewith to weigh right and wrong], so that men might behave with equity'" (57:25).[48] Similar views are expressed by the Moroccan intellectual Aḥmad al-Khamlīshi (b. 1935), who also denies that the classical *maqāṣid* have the potential to regulate contemporary interpersonal relations. According to al-Khamlīshi, justice, equality, and freedom, as well as social, economic, and political rights, belong to the higher *maqāṣid*. Their inclusion

[47] Ibid., 50–51.

[48] Quoted in Jamāl al-Dīn ʿAṭiyya, *Naḥw Tafʿīl Maqāṣid al-Sharīʿa* (Damascus, Dār al-Fikr, 2003), 98.

could serve as an authoritative point of reference in today's world and enable Islamic thought to shape the public life from which it has hitherto kept its distance.[49] Yūsuf al-Qaraḍāwi (b. 1926) adds his voice to this criticism, stressing the need to include not only those *maqāṣid* that refer to the individual, but also those that refer to society as a whole. According to al-Qaraḍāwi, these include especially justice (*ʿadl*) or fairness (*qisṭ*), brotherhood (*iḫāʾ*), social solidarity (*takāful*), freedom (*ḥurriyya*), and dignity (*karāma*).[50]

In order to take into account both social and individual legal purposes, Jamāl al-Dīn ʿAṭiyya proposes a categorization that distinguishes between different addressees. ʿAṭiyya identifies a total of twenty-four *maqāṣid*, which he divides into four categories. The first category includes those *maqāṣid* that refer to the *individual* alone. Following the classical concept, ʿAṭiyya lists the protection of (1) life, (2) reason, (3) religiosity, (4) honor, and (5) property.[51] It is noteworthy that he no longer speaks of the protection of religion (*dīn*) but of the protection of personal religiosity (*tadayyun*). ʿAṭiyya moves the protection of offspring (6) to the second category, whose purposes are related to the *family*. These include (7) the "ordering of relations between the sexes," (8) the "production of harmony, affection, and compassion," (9) the "protection of lineage," (10) the "protection of religiosity within the family," (11) the "ordering of the institutional," and (12) "the financial aspects of the family."[52] In the third category of *maqāṣid* he includes purposes related to the *Islamic community*: (13) "institutional organization of the community," (14) "protection of security," (15) "establishment of justice," (16) "protection of religion and morality," (17) "cooperation, solidarity, and shared responsibility," (18) "dissemination of knowledge and protection of reason in the community," and (19) "civilization of the earth and protection of communal property."[53] Finally, the fourth category of *maqāṣid* includes purposes that concern *humanity* as a whole. Among these ʿAṭiyya includes (20) "mutual understanding, cooperation, and integration," (21) the "realization of human governance on earth," (22) the "establishment of world peace and global justice," (23) the "international protection of human rights," and (24) the "dissemination of the message of Islam."[54]

[49] Aḥmad al-Khamlīshi, *Wujhat Naẓar*, 2:162, quoted in ibid.
[50] Al-Qaraḍāwi, *Madkhal li Dirāsat al-Sharīʿa al-Islāmiyya*, 74.
[51] ʿAṭiyya, *Naḥw Tafʿīl Maqāṣid al-Sharīʿa*, 142–147.
[52] Ibid., 148–154.
[53] Ibid., 154–164.
[54] Ibid., 164–172.

When it comes to the expansion of the *maqāṣid*, another, though related, justification can be identified that emphasizes the historical and social conditionality of the *maqāṣid*. For example, Isma'īl al-Ḥasani, who wrote his doctoral dissertation on the "theory of the *maqāṣid* in Ibn 'Ashūr," argues that the *maqāṣid* should be determined in light of the relevant social and historical circumstances. It is not enough to simply refer to the norms of the law in order to identify its objectives. Rather, one must be aware of social changes and developments and formulate the legal purposes accordingly. Thus, al-Ḥasani implies, on the one hand, that the classical *maqāṣid* are conditioned by history and, on the other hand, that we must give priority to other interests that are more in need of protection in contemporary Islamic societies. Among the latter are "freedom of expression and assembly, the right to choose and change rulers, the right to work, the right to adequate food, shelter, and clothing, the right to health care, and a long list of other rights that, like those mentioned here, are necessary for human existence in a modern society."[55] Mohammad Hashim Kamali makes a similar proposal: "I propose to add protection of the fundamental rights and liberties, economic development, and R & D in technology and sciences as well as peaceful coexistence among nations to the structure of *maqāṣid*, as they are crucially important and can find support for the most part in the Qur'ān and Sunnah."[56] Kamali adds that this list of legal purposes is open-ended, since further expansions as a result of new social developments cannot be ruled out: "It would appear from this analysis that the *maqāṣid* remains open to further enhancement which will depend, to some extent, on the priorities of every age."[57]

Another attempt to determine the *maqāṣid* in accordance with new social developments has been made recently by Tariq Ramadan. While in his earlier books Ramadan confined himself to the traditional formulations of *maqāṣid* by scholars such as al-Ghazāli and al-Shāṭibi,[58] in a more recent

[55] Isma'īl al-Ḥasani, *Naẓariyyat al-Maqāṣid 'ind Imām Muḥammad al-Ṭāhir Ibn 'Ashūr* (Herndon, VA: International Institute of Islamic Thought, 1995), 298. Mohammad Abed al-Jabri argues along the same lines in *Democracy, Human Rights and Law in Islamic Thought* (London: I. B. Tauris, 2008), 92–93.

[56] Kamali, *Shari'ah Law*, 127.

[57] Ibid. See also Kamali, *Principles of Islamic Jurisprudence*, 517.

[58] The first question addressed by Tariq Ramadan (notably in the books *To Be a European Muslim* (Leicester: Islamic Foundation, 1999) and *Islam, the West and the Challenges of Modernity* (Leicester: Islamic Foundation, 2001)) is essentially this: As a Muslim in Europe, can I be both Muslim and European, or is there a discrepancy between these two identities? The answer Ramadan tries to give to this question is that Muslims not only can be European citizens, but must be. They are not Muslims in Europe, he argues, but European Muslims who can live in their respective societies without renouncing their Muslim identity. In fact, it is precisely the Muslim identity that entails a

book, *Radical Reform: The Message of Islam for Modern Society*, he goes a "radical" step further. Not only must the limitation of the universal principles and objectives of Islamic law to five be reevaluated, Ramadan argues, but the sources and origins of Islamic law must also be reconsidered and reformulated.[59] Thus it is not enough to consider the Qur'an and the Sunnah as the only sources of legal justification. Rather, the universe, nature, the life-world "context," and the related empirical and social sciences must also be included in the process of formulating the purposes of Islamic law.[60] God revealed "two books" of equal normative and epistemic status: the Qur'an and the universe.[61] The universe, the social and human context, is thus not merely an aspect that serves to *interpret* the sources of law, Ramadan argues, but must be considered as an *independent source* for elaboration of the law.[62] Therefore, according to Ramadan, "the Universe and the sciences related to it must imperatively be considered as objective, indispensable sources of Islamic law and jurisprudence."[63] As a result, normative authority in the Islamic context now belongs not only to legal and religious scholars ("text scholars"), but also to physicians, economists, jurists, sociologists, and other

duty of loyalty to society: "Loyalty to one's faith and conscience requires firm and honest loyalty to one's country: the Sharīa requires honest citizenship within the frame of reference constituted by the positive law of the European country concerned" (*To Be a European Muslim*, 171–172). In addition, Ramadan wants to enable European Muslims to respond to the problems and challenges of life in secularized societies by developing an understanding of Islam that can be applied in twenty-first-century Europe. His aim is "to understand the universality of the message of Islam and to highlight the means we are given to help us live in our own time, in the West, with respect for ourselves and for others" (*Western Muslims and the Future of Islam*, 3). The peculiarity of Ramadan's project is the attempt to formulate a modern Islamic "universal ethics" solely on the basis of the sources and concepts of the classical Islamic legal tradition: "The approach I propose is anchored in the Islamic tradition and amplified from within it: in this sense it is both deeply classical and radically new. Beginning with the Quran and the Sunna and the methodologies set down by the ulama throughout the history of the Islamic sciences, I have tried to immerse myself again in reading these sources in the light of our new Western context; even though the methodology I have adopted is classical, I have not hesitated sometimes to question certain definitions and categorizations and to suggest others. . . . My conviction is that . . . the movement toward reform . . . can take place effectively only from within, in and through a rigorous faithfulness to the sources and the norms of reading them" (*Western Muslims and the Future of Islam*, 3–4). The concept of *maqāṣid* plays a central role in Ramadan's project. Following the classical conception, he argues that the *sharīʿa* contains a fixed set of general values and principles that must be implemented in accordance with changing circumstances. How and in what form this is to be done should remain open. Particularly important in this context, he argues, are the five basic goods—life, property, religion, offspring, and reason—to which specific provisions of the Shari'ah must be subordinated in cases of doubt.

[59] Ramadan, *Radical Reform*, 136.
[60] Ibid., 5.
[61] Ibid., 87.
[62] Ibid., 82–83.
[63] Ibid., 112.

social scientists, whom Ramadan calls "context scholars" (*'ulamā' al-wāqi'*).[64] This "shifting the center of gravity of religious and legal authority"[65] should make it possible to identify a list of legal purposes that takes into account "what we know of the Universe and what the diversity and evolution of human societies have taught us."[66] On the basis of the two normative sources (revelation and the lifeworld context) and taking into account the knowledge of both fields of research (the "text sciences" and the "sciences of the Universe"), it therefore seems necessary, according to Ramadan, to "set on inferring, identifying, and categorizing the higher objectives and aims of the Way (*maqāṣid al-sharī'a*) and thereby determining the theoretical and practical outline of an applied contemporary ethics."[67]

In light of these considerations, Ramadan now develops a multilevel and multidimensional concept of the *maqāṣid*, at the top of which he places the protection of religion (*dīn*), "in the sense of an understanding of life and death stemming from recognition of the One and of the Way [of the *sharī'a*]," and the protection of human well-being (*maṣlaḥa*), "in the sense of the common good and interest of humankind and of the Universe."[68] The protection and promotion of these two primary goals depend in turn on the protection of three other fundamental pillars, namely the respect and protection of life (*ḥayāh*), nature (*ḫalq*, *ṭabī'a*), and peace (*salām*). According to Ramadan, "The whole of the Islamic message, through verses, the Prophet's (or the Prophets') practices and the recognition of the Universe as a sign and a gift, refers to those three essential, *a priori* goals."[69] Although the list of verses and prophetic traditions that could be cited to justify these three goals is too long to quote in full, Ramadan points to the verse that equates the killing of one human being with the killing of all humanity,[70] the Qur'anic admonition not to destroy God's creation,[71] and the root of the word *islām*, in which the call for peace is anchored.[72]

[64] Ibid., 130.
[65] Ibid., 122.
[66] Ibid., 134.
[67] Ibid., 136.
[68] Ibid., 138.
[69] Ibid., 138–139.
[70] Qur'an (5:32): "Because of this did We ordain unto the children of Israel that if anyone slays a human being unless it be [in punishment] for murder or for spreading corruption on earth—it shall be as though he had slain all mankind; whereas, if anyone saves a life, it shall be as though he had saved the lives of all mankind."
[71] Qur'an (4:119): "And I shall lead them astray, and fill them with vain desires; and I shall command them—and they will cut off the ears of cattle [in idolatrous sacrifice]; and I shall command them—and they will corrupt God's creation!"
[72] Ramadan, *Radical Reform*, 139.

On a third level, Ramadan now identifies thirteen further objectives "that are more directly linked to humankind's being and action, both as an individual and as a member of society,"[73] namely the promoting and protection of dignity (of human beings, living species, and nature), well-being, knowledge, creativity, autonomy, development, equality, freedom, justice, fraternity, love, solidarity, and diversity.[74] These are "higher objectives stipulated by the texts, sometimes either more or less explicitly, but whose essential and primary character is made clear by history and the evolution of societies."[75] They are, moreover, purposes whose presence and necessity are felt in all areas of human activity.[76] They therefore "trace the path along which a contemporary ethical elaboration that is both normative and practical must be developed."[77]

This path, however, seems to be traced rather roughly, for Ramadan thinks that the *maqāṣid* still need of a clearer and more systematic categorization. In fact, according to Ramadan, we need to distinguish whether these purposes relate to inner, individual, or collective life, and draw up a specific list of higher purposes for each of these categories. With regard to the *inner*, spiritual dimension of life, he refers to the promotion of "Education (of the heart and mind), Conscience (of being and responsibility), Sincerity, Contemplation, Balance (intimate and personal stability), and Humility."[78] Regarding the *individual* dimension, he identifies the promotion and protection of "Physical Integrity, Health, Subsistence, Intelligence, Progeny, Work, Belongings, Contracts, and our Neighborhoods."[79] Finally, the *social* purposes include the promotion and protection of "the Rule of law, Independence (self-determination), Deliberation, Pluralism, Evolution, Cultures, Religions, and Memories (heritage)" (Figure 10.1).[80]

Despite his introductory remarks on the sources of justification and the new methodological foundation of *maqāṣid*, it is not entirely clear how Ramadan actually arrives at this catalogue of forty-one *maqāṣid*. He notes that contemporary conditions compel us "to return to the texts and extract objectives that may have appeared secondary in the past."[81] But the criteria

73 Ibid.
74 Ibid.
75 Ibid.
76 Ibid., 139–140.
77 Ibid., 140.
78 Ibid., 141.
79 Ibid., 142.
80 Ibid.
81 Ibid., 140.

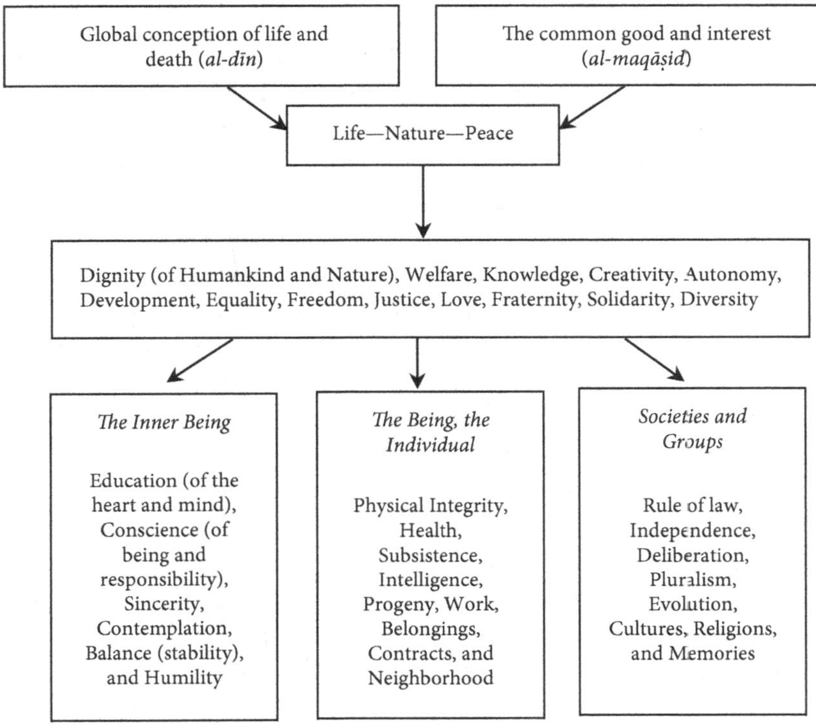

Figure 10.1 Conception of the *maqāṣid* according to Tariq Ramadan.

by which these purposes were derived and distributed among the various levels remain unclear. Ramadan emphasizes that his aim is to "present higher objectives in an original—and always open—way, involving, most importantly, a new, more specialized, and more pragmatic relationship to reality."[82] This pragmatic reference to reality also implies that his conception of Islamic legal purposes always has a provisional and conditional character, he adds, because "[n]ew scientific knowledge, shaping a new outlook on human beings or Nature, might lead us to extend that list, since this must always remain a dialectical elaboration."[83] Therefore, these are not timeless purposes, but ones that have acquired importance in the face of the "historical context, but also the risks and dangers of our own time."[84] But here in particular,

[82] Ibid., 136.
[83] Ibid., 139.
[84] Ibid.

Ramadan's conception faces the question of how to avoid the problem of arbitrariness in determining the *maqāṣid*. In other words, how can we prevent the process of determining new *maqāṣid* from becoming merely a matter of our own discretion? This question arises in relation not only to Ramadan's conception but also to the entire contemporary discourse surrounding the reconceptualization of *maqāṣid*.[85] For, as the above considerations have made clear, every author seems to have his or her own notion of how and why the list of Islamic legal purposes should be modified or supplemented.[86] It cannot be overlooked that many authors include in the canon of *maqāṣid* those goods that they consider desirable independently of more precise criteria. However desirable the goods in question may be, this tendency clearly makes Islamic law a plaything of individual authors' wishful thinking, with the consequent danger of reducing the role of *maqāṣid* to giving a religious stamp of approval to arbitrary subjective choices.[87]

It is also surprising that most authors fail to base their criticism of the classical *maqāṣid* conception on a sufficiently thorough examination of its underlying logic. For as the arguments of the classical jurists show (see chapter 8), the goods they identify are not mere intellectual speculations or the result of arbitrary theological prescriptions. Nor are they the product of a specific historical or social necessity. Rather, according to the classical jurists, these goods are rooted in human nature and therefore represent the *empirically ascertainable*, *necessary*, and *universal* basic conditions of human existence.[88] It is precisely from this fact that they derive their relevance in Islamic law, whose purpose, according to the jurists, is to guarantee the protection of these basic needs. Unfortunately, this crucial aspect seems to have escaped the attention of contemporary discourse. At the same time, this should not be taken to mean that the classical conception of Islamic legal purposes is not

[85] This is also noted by Kamali, *Shari'ah Law*, 136: "[T]here still remains the residual question of how arbitrariness can be avoided in the identification of *maqasid*. For the *maqasid* . . . are open-ended and still in need of a more accurate methodology to ensure unwarranted indulgence through personal or partisan bias in their identification."

[86] On the basis of a survey of modern proposals concerning the *maqāṣid*, Auda therefore draws the following conclusion: "The above twentieth-century views also show that *maqasid al-shariah* are, actually, representations of each scholar's own viewpoint for reform and development of the Islamic law, despite the fact that all these *maqasid* were induced from the scripts." Auda, *Maqasid al-Shariah as Philosophy of Islamic Law*, 8.

[87] For a discussion of how a modernist understanding of the *maqāṣid* is instrumentalized for authoritarian purposes, see Yomna Helmy, "From Islamic Modernism to Theorizing Authoritarianism: Bin Bayyah and the Politicization of the *Maqāṣid* Discourse," *American Journal of Islam and Society* 38, nos. 3–4 (2021): 36–70.

[88] Fahmi Muḥammad ʿAlwān, *al-Qiyam al-Ḍarūriyya wa Maqāṣid al-Tashrīʿ al-Islāmi* (Cairo: al-Hayʾa al-Miṣriyya al-ʿĀmma li'l-Kitāb, 1989), 95.

in need of revision. For, as shown in chapter 9, the five basic needs ultimately identified by the jurists do not correlate with the criteria they postulated.

I would like to emphasize that the premises of the classical conception must be understood in such a way that the revision of *maqāṣid* is based on a coherent methodological foundation and not on individual wishful thinking or arbitrary determinations. To avoid the latter, we need to develop a conception of *maqāṣid* that satisfies the criteria of necessity, universality, and empirical verifiability. The primary goal should not be to try to read a new meaning into the classical *maqāṣid* (reinterpretation approach) or to multiply them in number (extension approach). Rather, the goal should be to rethink and, if necessary, modify the classical conception *on the basis of its inherent logic*. Thus if we accept the classical premise that Islamic law protects basic needs that represent the empirically ascertainable necessary conditions for the existence of *all* human beings, then the primary task is to ascertain which goods are capable of satisfying these criteria. In this context, the call by Ramadan and others to incorporate the findings of the empirical and social sciences into the systematics of Islamic law in general and into the conception of the *maqāṣid* in particular is to be welcomed.[89] This can facilitate scientifically justified statements about the necessary, universal, and empirically ascertainable conditions of human existence and thus serve the development of empirically grounded and theoretically well-thought-out science of Islamic legal purposes.

Moreover, since the purpose of Islamic law is to protect universal human needs, it would provide a basis for legal reasoning concerning human rights that satisfies the requirements of universality and Islamic legitimacy identified at the outset. This basis would enjoy Islamic legitimacy because it represents the purpose of Islamic law as derived from an inductive study of Islamic legal norms. On the other hand, it can command universal agreement because it is based on human needs, which form a universal canon of values independent of religious considerations and thus provide a universally understandable basis for legal argumentation. Thus, in this context, religion functions more as a legitimation than as a justification of values, since human needs can in principle also be justified nonreligiously. In this sense,

[89] See Mohammad Omar Farooq, *Toward Our Reformation: From Legalism to Value-Oriented Islamic Law and Jurisprudence* (Herndon, VA: International Institute of Islamic Thought, 2011), 221–259; Auda, *Maqasid al-Shariah as Philosophy of Islamic Law*, 205; Kamali, *Principles of Islamic Jurisprudence*, 503, 519; ʿAbdul-Ḥamīd Abū Sulaymān, *Towards an Islamic Theory of International Relations: New Directions for Methodology and Thought* (Herndon, VA: International Institute of Islamic Thought, 1993), 87–92.

the value basis of legal reasoning is *also* religious, but it is not *essentially* religious. The concept of human needs provides a corresponding legal basis that is independent of both attitudes and culture and can therefore function as a universally understandable and interculturally valid foundation of human rights. In order to elaborate this core idea, the next part of the book will attempt to conceptualize human rights as institutions for the protection of human needs.

PART IV
HUMAN RIGHTS AND HUMAN NEEDS

Historically, the attempt to take human needs as the starting point for determining human beings' legal claims is not exclusive to the Islamic legal tradition. Human needs also play a prominent role in the historical context of European debates on the rights of man. Thomas Hobbes's (d. 1679) *Leviathan*, which was originally published in 1651, already mentions rights to which human beings are entitled because they are inseparable from the conditions of existence without which it would not be possible to live a human life. Hobbes writes, "As it is necessary for all men that seek peace, to lay down certain Rights of Nature; that is to say, not to have libertie to do all they list: so is it necessarie for mans life, to retaine some; as right to governe their owne bodies; enjoy aire, water, motion, waies to go from place to place; and *all things else, without which a man cannot live, or not live well*."[1] Similarly, John Locke (d. 1704) argues in his *Two Treatises of Government* that human beings have a fundamental right to the satisfaction of their needs, since "Men, being once born, have a right to their Preservation, and consequently to Meat and Drink, and such other things, as Nature affords for their Subsistence."[2] This right is so fundamental, he argues, that it is a "sin" to deny it to a person, because "God the Lord and Father of all, has given no one of his Children such a Property, in his peculiar Portion of the things of this World, but that he has given his needy Brother a Right to the Surplusage of his Goods; so that it cannot justly be denyed him, when his pressing Wants call for it."[3]

[1] Thomas Hobbes, *Leviathan*, ed. R. Tuck (Cambridge: Cambridge University Press, 1996), 107; emphasis added.
[2] John Locke, *Two Treatises of Government*, ed. Peter Laslett (Cambridge: Cambridge University Press, 1989), 285.
[3] Ibid., 170.

The assertion that human beings have a right to life, and thus a legal right to the satisfaction of their vital needs, can also be found in William Blackstone's *Commentaries on the Laws of England*, published in 1765. Since life is a "direct gift of God"[4] and is thus the right of every human being, it follows that all human beings have not only a right to life but also a right to everything necessary for life.[5] In his 1790 *Reflections on the Revolution in France*, Edmund Burke goes a step further, arguing that the raison d'être of government is to secure human needs. "Government," he writes, "is a contrivance of human wisdom to provide for human wants. Men have a right that these wants be provided for by this wisdom."[6] Finally, almost one hundred years after Burke, Rudolf von Jhering, in his treatise *Law as a Means to an End*, concludes that the primary purpose of law is to secure the living conditions of society.[7]

As these examples illustrate, the idea of human needs is far from being a modern element in the conceptualization of human legal claims. Nevertheless, the attempt undertaken in this book to formulate a conception of human rights based on human needs faces three fundamental tasks. The first is to address the basic question of what we mean when we speak of human rights in the first place. In chapter 11, therefore, I will discuss different conceptions of human rights and examine how they can contribute to a concrete understanding of human rights. I will argue that human rights can most plausibly be understood as institutions for the protection of objective, necessary, and universal human needs. I will begin by offering a more precise specification of the concept of need and by distinguishing it from similar concepts. Building on this, I will attempt to answer the question of what needs human beings have by drawing on interdisciplinary research on human needs (chapter 12). Finally—based on the idea of the *maqāṣid*—I will try to bring the notion of human rights into a coherent relation to human needs (chapter 13).

4 William Blackstone, *Commentaries on the Laws of England* (Chicago: University of Chicago Press, 1979), 1:125.

5 "The law not only regards life and member, and protects every man in the enjoyment of them, but also furnishes him with everything necessary for their support. For there is no man so indigent or wretched, but he may demand a supply sufficient for all the necessities of life from the more opulent part of the community." Ibid., 127.

6 Edmund Burke, *Reflections on the Revolution in France* (New Haven, CT: Yale University Press, 2003), 51.

7 Von Jhering, *Der Zweck im Recht*, 1:443.

11

Conceptions of Human Rights

Human rights are often understood as rights to which people are entitled simply by virtue of being human.[1] This definition is usually quoted without elaborating on the precise meaning of "being human." In my view, this has to do with the fact that the above statement is less an attempt to clarify what human rights are than in the first instance to describe what they are *not*. Thus it is asserted that human rights are not rights that people have by virtue of some distinguishing characteristic, such as gender or skin color. Nor are they rights that people have because of certain affiliations, such as to a religion or a state; nor are they rights that people are entitled to because of certain achievements, such as their economic productivity. Rather, the claim is that human beings have these rights because they are human. In other words, they are "born" with these rights as a "natural" endowment, which is why no state can take them away. Accordingly, they are "prepolitical" or "moral" rights that define the normative frame of reference from which legislative institutions must take their orientation. The reference to "being human" is thus intended to emphasize that these are rights to which a person is entitled in all times and places, whether or not they are actually enshrined in a particular piece of legislation.

Does this statement already tell us what human rights are? Until now we have only assumed that human rights exist even if they are not recognized by legislative institutions. But we are talking about rights whose existence we assume without knowing why they exist or what they entail. So far, it remains unclear *why* human beings have certain rights and precisely *which* rights these are supposed to be. Thus the assertion that human beings have certain rights by virtue of being human tells us very little about how human

[1] See Alan Gewirth, *Human Rights: Essays on Justification and Applications* (Chicago: University of Chicago Press, 1982), 41: "We may assume, as true by definition, that human rights are rights that all persons have simply insofar as they are human." James Griffin, *On Human Rights* (Oxford: Oxford University Press, 2008), 16: "[A] human right is a right that we have simply in virtue of being human." Alan John Simmons, *Justification and Legitimacy: Essay on Rights and Obligations* (Cambridge: Cambridge University Press, 2001), 185: "[H]uman rights are rights possessed by all human beings (at all times and in all places), simply in virtue of their humanity."

Human Rights Between Universality and Islamic Legitimacy. Mahmoud Bassiouni, Oxford University Press.
 DOI: 10.1093/oso/9780197753897.003.0012

rights should be understood in concrete terms. One might therefore be inclined to follow MacIntyre in comparing the existence of human rights to that of witches and unicorns[2] and to dismiss them as mere "moral fictions."[3] But one need not be a nihilist about human rights to recognize that they represent an idea about which there is very little clarity. For example, in the opening sentence of his study on human rights, James Griffin observes "that we do not yet have a clear enough idea of what human rights are."[4] Griffin even goes so far as to emphasize that the notion of human rights is "nearly criterionless."[5] Charles Beitz makes the same point when he says, "The problem is that, although the idea and language of human rights have become increasingly prominent in public discourse, it has not become any more clear what kinds of objects human rights are supposed to be, why we should believe that people have them, or what follows from this belief for political practice."[6]

There is a lively debate in contemporary political philosophy about the meaning of the concept of human rights and exactly what claims it should entail. In what follows, I would like to delve deeper into this debate and discuss some proposals for conceptualizing human rights. The aim will be to examine the extent to which the various approaches succeed in satisfying three basic criteria that I believe are necessary to formulate a plausible conception of human rights. The first is the ability to explain the *moral relevance* of human rights. In other words, a conception should be able to explain why and in what way it is important for human beings to have certain rights. Second, it should be able to explain the *content* of those rights, and third, it should do so in a way that is in principle understandable and acceptable to all human beings. In other words, a conception of human rights should be able to command *universal agreement*.

The thesis that I want to put forward following this discussion is, to repeat, that human rights can most plausibly be understood as institutions for the protection of human needs. Without excluding other approaches, I will

[2] Alasdair MacIntyre, *After Virtue: A Study in Moral Theory* (Notre Dame, IN: University of Notre Dame Press, 1981), 69.

[3] Ibid., 70.

[4] Griffin, *On Human Rights*, 1.

[5] Ibid., 14–15. "The term 'human right' is nearly criterionless. There are unusually few criteria for determining when the term is used correctly and when incorrectly—and not just among politicians, but among philosophers, political theorists, and jurisprudents as well. The language of human rights has, in this way, become debased. . . . [I]t needs more explanation before its use will have the rationality it should have."

[6] Charles Beitz, *The Idea of Human Rights* (Oxford: Oxford University Press, 2009), xi.

draw on the notion of the *maqāṣid al-sharīʿa* to argue that the concept of needs has a number of advantages when it comes to the moral relevance of human rights, the determination of their content, and the requirement that they should be culturally neutral. The idea at the heart of the argument is that the recourse to human needs addresses defining features of the human condition that are independent of attitudes, time, and place, and can therefore serve as an interculturally valid basis for the justification of human rights.

Human Rights and Consensus

The need for a universally consensual justification of human rights follows from their claim to being transcultural, that is, valid for every human being in every place. This claim to validity implies, on the one hand, that these rights belong to every human being everywhere and, on the other hand, that they should be respected by every human being everywhere. In this sense, human rights are normative claims that grant human beings a certain scope for action but also prescribe a certain way of acting. Human rights thus encroach on moral terrain to which various religious and cultural orders simultaneously lay claim. In order to do justice to their transcultural claim to validity, human rights must therefore rest on a foundation with which people can agree on the basis of rational insight, regardless of their cultural affiliation or religious convictions. In other words, human rights must be justified in such a way that everyone can accept their binding force from a first-person perspective. This is the only way to counter the objection that human rights are "merely" the product of a particular culture.

One could, of course, object here and claim that human rights are in fact already accepted. In recent decades, international declarations and treaties have produced a seemingly authoritative list of human rights that enjoys broad international recognition and also seems to be essentially complete, at least in the context of international law. It could be argued that this shows that the acceptance of human rights can also be achieved if we do not question them further. So why reinvent the wheel? In fact, this might even be counterproductive, since the pragmatic acceptance of human rights that has been achieved might be shaken precisely by examining them too closely. In this context, Jacques Maritain refers to a (now often quoted) statement made during a UNESCO session on drafting the Universal Declaration of Human Rights: "[W]e agree on these rights, *providing we are not asked why.* With the why, the dispute begins."[7] Maritain himself describes the search for a common rational justification of human rights as "futile," since we are faced with completely contradictory approaches to justification, all of which claim to be the only correct one.[8] Nevertheless, he thinks that it is possible to build a *practical* consensus on human rights, since these are normative claims that are shared by different moral conceptions in the world.[9] So although, in the words of Stefan Gosepath, "we argue about the *correct* moral justification, this can be bracketed because we agree on the matter morally, independently of the justification."[10] In this sense, human rights represent "an overlapping consensus among the different moral conceptions of this world."[11] Different culture-specific justifications can thus coexist without detracting from the cross-cultural validity of human rights,[12] since each moral conception leads to the same result in its own way in any case.

In my view, it does not require detailed argumentation to recognize that this is a highly questionable assumption. At least if we take the content of international human rights documents seriously, the claim that a transcultural consensus on human rights exists is untenable. For not every understanding of a moral order in fact contains the right to democratic participation, freedom of religion, or equal treatment. Of course, this does not preclude that the attempt to superimpose different moral conceptions like templates might yield a moral overlap. As Michael Walzer points out, however, this would probably be limited to negative prescriptions against serious human rights violations such as murder, fraud, torture, oppression, and tyranny.[13] Accordingly, Michael Ignatieff proposes a conception of human rights that is limited to the "minimal conditions for any life at all."[14] But even this may not be minimalist enough to secure general approval, according to Ignatieff.[15] The assumption that human rights can be determined on the basis of an

[7] Jacques Maritain, *Man and the State* (Chicago: University of Chicago Press, 1998), 77, emphasis in original.

[8] Ibid., 76.

[9] Ibid., 77.

[10] Stefan Gosepath, "Sinn der Menschenrechte," in *Die Menschenrechte: unteilbar und gleichgewichtig?*, ed. Georg Lohman et al. (Potsdam: Universität Potsdam, 2005), 25.

[11] Ibid.

[12] Ibid., 26.

[13] Michael Walzer, *Thick and Thin: Moral Argument at Home and Abroad* (Notre Dame, IN: University of Notre Dame Press, 1994), 10.

[14] Michael Ignatieff, *Human Rights as Politics and as Idolatry* (Princeton, NJ: Princeton University Press, 2001), 56: "Human rights can command universal assent only as a decidedly 'thin' theory of what is right, a definition of the minimal conditions for any life at all."

[15] Ibid.

actually existing, overlapping consensus would thus force us to reject a large portion of currently recognized human rights.

If one is not prepared to do that, one can pursue an alternative strategy and claim that human rights are not based on an actual, but instead on a *possible* transcultural consensus of moral orders. According to this view, human rights would not be the intersection of all factually existing systems of values, but a normative goal that can be reached by following different paths. Human rights would accordingly represent an interculturally *accessible* idea.[16] Contrary to the assumption that human rights can in fact be found in all moral conceptions, here the argument is that each moral conception contains its own cultural resources that enable it to establish an internal cultural reference to human rights. Everyone who belongs to these moral orders would thus in theory be able to find points of connection within their own moral order that could lead them to accept human rights. For example, if we want to persuade a Muslim to recognize the right to religious freedom, we could point out that according to his own religion there is "no compulsion in faith."[17] The right to democratic participation could also be made more "palatable" to a Muslim by referring to the notion of *shūra*, which dictates a deliberative decision-making process and is a fundamental principle of Islamic rule.[18] A Muslim, it could be argued, is thus able to regard the right to democratic participation as binding on the basis of his religious belief.

Things become problematic, of course, when we encounter a Muslim who thinks that his faith is endangered by the possibility of democratic participation, since, according to him, not the people but God alone can lay claim to sovereignty, and thus must be regarded as the sole and supreme source of legitimate law. It is therefore quite possible that a Muslim can also dispute the right to democratic participation on the basis of his religious beliefs. This is because cultures, like religions, are rarely uniform, self-enclosed systems, but rather contain a variety of manifestations and currents that interpret the normative content of their moral order in extremely diverse ways.[19] So while it is perfectly possible to establish a cultural link to human rights, it may be equally possible to question them within the culture. The attempt

[16] In this sense, the preamble of the Universal Declaration of Human Rights also emphasizes that human rights are "a common standard *of achievement* for all peoples and all nations" (emphasis added), that is, something *to be achieved* by all nations and peoples.

[17] Qur'an 2:256.

[18] On this, see Abou el Fadl, *Islam and the Challenge of Democracy*, 16–18.

[19] This was illustrated in the second part of this book by the example of the Muslim discourse on human rights.

to demonstrate the acceptance or the acceptability of human rights exclusively with reference to possibilities of access within the culture is therefore based on a selective interpretation of the culture in question that deliberately emphasizes certain components while ignoring others.[20] While this can be a politically effective procedure that serves to mobilize the *motivational* resources of a culture to respect, promote, or protect human rights, it by no means guarantees that human rights will necessarily gain inner-cultural acceptance as a result or will be regarded as binding by all members of a moral order.

In order to substantiate the universal validity claim of human rights, therefore, we have to do more than merely examine the extent to which the different cultures are able to integrate a list of human rights declared to be universal into their respective moral orders. In the absence of a universally intelligible justification, the cultures in question would in fact have good reasons for asking why they should do so at all. Human rights are, as Regina Kreide emphasizes, "the object of an ongoing international dispute, in which one is sooner or later compelled to provide reasons for the validity of human rights in general, and for a specific interpretation in particular. Therefore, a theory of human rights cannot evade the discourse of justification, and if it does, then only at the cost of having to adopt a theoretically and politically weak position from the outset."[21] Nor is the fact that human rights have been adopted within the framework of international declarations and treaties in itself a sufficient reason for their acceptance. James Nickel correctly observes in this connection, "[E]ven when the human rights in question are national or international legal rights, existence in law alone will not ensure us that they are powerful and compelling. If a human rights declaration or treaty tells us that a right is important enough to be a human right we will not believe it unless we think that suitably strong supporting reasons for that right are likely to be available."[22] Nickel emphasizes that the acceptance

[20] David Miller, *National Responsibility and Global Justice* (Oxford: Oxford University Press, 2007), 175.

[21] Regina Kreide, *Globale Politik und Menschenrechte: Macht und Ohnmacht eines politischen Instruments* (Frankfurt: Campus, 2007), 37.

[22] James Nickel, *Making Sense of Human Rights* (Malden, MA: Blackwell, 2007), 53. Griffin remarks along similar lines, "No matter who we are we cannot establish a human right just by declaring it to be one. Not even the Universal Declaration of Human Rights by the United Nations in solemn assembly is enough. We—whoever we are—can get it wrong, and we owe attention, therefore, to the criteria for right and wrong here." James Griffin, "Human Rights and the Autonomy of International Law," in *The Philosophy of International Law*, ed. Samatha Besson and John Tasioulas (Oxford: Oxford University Press, 2010), 340.

of human rights is not an automatic consequence of their anchoring in international agreements, but instead depends on the existence of intelligible reasons. Specifically with regard to the international catalogues of human rights, one could argue that these are merely the result of political decision-making processes "that could very well have taken a different course if, for example, different power relations or ideological constellations had prevailed in the relevant UN bodies."[23] Thus Nickel further notes, "Writing human rights documents in the UN and elsewhere was a heavily political process with plenty of imperfections. There is little reason to take international diplomats as the most authoritative guides to which human rights are justifiable."[24]

As these assertions illustrate, therefore, we have no compelling reason to assume that the human rights enshrined in international law are the only correct or even the only possible ones.[25] In other words, there may very well be human rights that have not been taken into account in the existing agreements. For example, one need only think of the calls for a right to a clean and safe environment.[26] Yet we cannot exclude the possibility that the existing treaties contain provisions whose status as human rights is unclear. For some philosophers it seems questionable, for example, how the right to periodic holidays with pay (Universal Declaration, Art. 24) is something to which people have a claim in the same sense as the right not to be enslaved (Art. 4) or tortured (Art. 5).[27] Therefore, to speak here of a human right may amount to an inflationary use of the concept.[28]

But how do we know which rights can be legitimately counted among the human rights and which cannot? Are human rights merely an arbitrary

[23] Arnd Pollmann, "Von der philosophischen Begründung zur demokratischen Konkretisierung: Wie lassen sich Inhalt und Umfang der Menschenrechte bestimmen?" *Zeitschrift für Menschenrechte* 1 (2008): 9. Lohmann and Gosepath even go so far as to claim that the Universal Declaration of Human Rights "represents a lucky compromise between the different interests of the political powers . . . which . . . a little later, during the entrenched phase of the 'Cold War,' might not have been possible in this form." Gosepath and Lohmann, *Philosophie der Menschenrechte*, 7.

[24] Nickel, *Making Sense of Human Rights*, 95.

[25] Robert Alexy expresses this point when he writes, "Enshrining in positive law is never a final answer. It represents an attempt to give an institutional form backed by positive law to what is valid solely in virtue of its correctness. Like all attempts, such an attempt can be more or less successful." Robert Alexy, "Menschenrechte ohne Metaphysik?," *Deutsche Zeitschrift für Philosophie* 52, no. 1 (2004): 16.

[26] See, for example, UN, *Draft Declaration of HR and the Environment*, 1994, http://www1.umn.edu/humanrts/instree/1994-dec.htm.

[27] For example, Griffin, *On Human Rights*, 5.

[28] For a general discussion, see Carl Wellman, *The Proliferation of Rights: Moral Progress or Empty Rhetoric?* (Boulder, CO: Westview Press, 1999).

collection of norms, or can we identify a criterion for determining their content and scope?

Human Rights and Sovereignty

According to a relatively recent tradition of thought, the most plausible way to answer these questions is to consider that human rights have a specific role to play within the framework of international law. This is a specifically political function, which, according to Rawls, consists in providing "a suitable definition of, and limits on, a government's internal sovereignty."[29] Human rights are thus a class of rights that "set a necessary, though not sufficient, standard for the decency of domestic political and social institutions."[30] Guaranteeing human rights, Rawls argues, is a necessary condition for being tolerated and accepted by other states as a member in good standing in a reasonably just Society of Peoples.[31] In this sense, human rights function as a standard of international legitimacy. According to Rawls, they are especially necessary "to exclude justified and forceful intervention by other peoples, for example, by diplomatic and economic sanctions, or in grave cases by military force."[32] A state that violates human rights is to be condemned accordingly "and in grave cases may be subjected to forceful sanctions and even to intervention."[33] The crucial function of human rights for Rawls is thus to determine when it is permissible or justified to intervene by force in a country.[34]

Once we are aware of this function, he argues, we know exactly when we can speak of a human right: a right can be deemed a human right only if its violation by a state represents a trigger for a coercive intervention. Since not every violation of a right serves to justify such an intervention, human rights merely "express a special class of urgent rights."[35] They include "the right to life (to means of subsistence and security); to liberty (to freedom

[29] John Rawls, *The Law of Peoples* (Cambridge, MA: Harvard University Press, 1999), 27.
[30] Ibid., 80.
[31] Ibid.
[32] Ibid.
[33] Ibid., 81.
[34] Although Rawls also speaks of diplomatic and economic coercive measures in this connection, one cannot help thinking that human rights as Rawls conceives them serve primarily to justify *military* interventions. This becomes clear, for example, when Rawls states that human rights "restrict the justifying reasons for war and its conduct, and they specify limits to a regime's internal autonomy." Ibid., 79.
[35] Ibid.

from slavery, serfdom, and forced occupation, and to a sufficient measure of liberty of conscience to ensure freedom of religion and thought; to property (personal property); and to formal equality as expressed by the rules of natural justice (that is, that similar cases be treated similarly)."[36]

It is striking that some prominent rights that we know from international human rights documents are absent from Rawls's list. Examples from the Universal Declaration of Human Rights include the right to nondiscrimination (Art. 2), the right to freedom of opinion and expression (Art. 19), the right to freedom of assembly (Art. 20), political participation rights (Art. 21), and the right to social security (Art. 22), as well as the rights to work (Art. 23), education (Art. 26), and an adequate standard of living (Art. 25). According to Rawls, these are not "human rights proper" but are "more aptly described as stating liberal aspirations."[37] Since human rights should not "be rejected as peculiarly liberal or special to the Western tradition,"[38] it would be wiser to limit the content of human rights to a "hard core."[39] The crucial factor, however, is not the assumption that human rights should be determined only on the basis of an overlapping consensus, but the thesis that the failure to respect human rights provides a justifying reason for coercive interventions, which, as Rawls correctly assumes, should be restricted to cases of grave human rights violations.

At this point, those who are sympathetic to a Rawlsian approach are faced with two alternatives. The first is to accept the Rawlsian conception of human rights and conclude that a large portion of the human rights recognized today must be rejected. Since this is likely to conflict with the liberal aspirations of most Rawlsians, however, the more attractive alternative is to extend the approach advocated by Rawls. This involves upholding the basic Rawlsian idea that human rights are precisely those rights whose violation justifies international intervention, but with the caveat that "intervention" here is not restricted, as in Rawls, to *coercive* intervention. According to Joseph Raz, this can involve any form of intervention that would normally—that is, in the absence of a violation of human rights by a state—be considered a violation of

[36] Ibid., 65.

[37] Ibid., 80n23. According to Rawls, only Articles 3–18 of the Universal Declaration of Human Rights represent human rights in the narrower sense.

[38] Ibid., 65.

[39] It remains unclear, however, why this should consist of the specific rights that Rawls includes in his list. Although Rawls stresses that these are "urgent" rights, it is not clear in what sense the rights he identifies (e.g., the right to personal property) are more urgent than the so-called liberal aspirations (such as the right to nondiscrimination).

state sovereignty.[40] But Raz does not specify when and by what forms of intervention exactly the sovereignty of a state can be violated. On a sufficiently broad interpretation, a formal criticism in an international forum could be interpreted as an intervention that restricts sovereignty.[41] Thus, although the assertion that human rights exist when their violation justifies a not further qualified restriction of state sovereignty opens up a theoretically broader spectrum of human rights, because of its vagueness it cannot contribute very much to identifying them in tangible terms.

In order to identify human rights in more concrete terms, Charles Beitz proposes an approach consisting of three propositions. The first refers to the purpose of human rights which, according to Beitz, is to protect "urgent individual interests" against "certain predictable dangers" or "standard threats."[42] It is not clear, however, what Beitz understands here by "urgent interests," because he does not specify to which interests this refers or how exactly such interests can be identified. Beitz's assertions in this connection are very vague, noting that an interest should be described as "urgent" if it can be considered important in a wide range of typical contemporary lives.[43] Examples would be interests in personal security and liberty, adequate food, and a certain level of protection against the arbitrary use of state power.[44] With his second proposition, Beitz identifies the addressees of human rights, among whom he primarily counts the political institutions of a state. They have a duty (a) to respect the interests just mentioned in the conduct of the state's official business, (b) to protect them against threats from nonstate agents who are nevertheless subject to the state's jurisdiction and control,

[40] See Joseph Raz, "Human Rights without Foundations," in Besson and Tasioulas, *The Philosophy of International Law*, 328n21: "Unlike Rawls who took rights to be human rights only if their serious violation could justify armed intervention, I take them to be rights whose violation can justify any international action against violators, provided that they are actions which normally would be impermissible being violations of state sovereignty."

[41] John Tasioulas, "Are Human Rights Essentially Triggers for Intervention?," *Philosophy Compass* 4, no. 6 (2009): 944.

[42] Beitz, *The Idea of Human Rights*, 109.

[43] Ibid., 110: "An 'urgent' interest is one that would be recognizable as important in a wide range of typical lives that occur in contemporary societies." Here Beitz seems to use the adjectives "urgent" and "important" synonymously, without recognizing that something can be urgent without necessarily being important, just as something can be important without necessarily being urgent.

[44] Ibid. Beitz stresses that the interests in question do not have to be those shared by all people, so that one must distinguish between "urgent" and "universal" interests. According to Beitz, in order to recognize an interest as urgent, we need only to be able to understand why it could make sense to regard its satisfaction as important in a range of normal lives: "[T]o recognize an interest as urgent, we must be able to understand why it would be reasonable to regard its satisfaction as important within some range of normal lives" (incorrectly printed in the book as "some range normal of lives").

and (c) to help those who become victims of deprivation.[45] If a state fails in one of these three respects, one can speak of a violation of human rights, according to Beitz, but only—and here the third and crucial proposition comes into play—if it can be shown at the same time that this violation can also give rise to "international concern":[46] "[I]t must be shown that any candidate human right is a suitable object of international concern. Whatever its importance regarded from the perspective of potential beneficiaries and however appropriate it would be as a requirement for domestic institutions, a protection cannot count as a human right if it fails to satisfy a requirement of this kind."[47] With this thesis, Beitz, in line with Rawls and Raz, expresses the idea that it is part of the function of human rights to provoke an international reaction when they are violated. While Rawls restricts this reaction to military interventions and Raz tries to extend it to interventions that restrict sovereignty, Beitz introduces the broader notion of "matters of international concern." This is broader because it presupposes neither a specific form of intervention nor a restriction of state sovereignty. Although Beitz does not exclude the latter, "matters of international concern" also include a variety of noninterventionist reactions, such as creating diverse incentives to improve the protection of human rights, corresponding offers of assistance, or even adapting nonstate or global structures to enable the protection of human rights within states.[48] Insofar as the conceptual and substantive determination of human rights depends on the nature and breadth of these possible reactions, Beitz's conception, in contrast to Rawls's and more clearly than that of Raz, makes it possible to recognize the majority of currently acknowledged human rights as such.

In the context of our discussion, it should be noted, however, that the crucial question is not so much whether and how this or that supposed human right can be confirmed as such by asking whether its violation warrants a specific form of international reaction. More fundamentally, we must

[45] Ibid., 109. Beitz is following the tripartite division of Henry Shue, *Basic Rights: Subsistence, Affluence, and U.S. Foreign Policy* (Princeton, NJ: Princeton University Press, 1996), 52–53.

[46] Beitz, *The Idea of Human Rights*, 109.

[47] Ibid., 140. Similarly: "[A]ny value counted as a human right should be such that a government's failure to respect it could give rise to reasons for external agents to act in its defense" (127); "[H]uman rights are standards for the governments of states whose breach is a matter of international concern" (31); "A government's failure to adhere to human rights standards should be a matter of international concern" (23).

[48] In total, Beitz identifies six forms of international concerns: (1) accountability, (2) inducement, (3) assistance, (4) domestic contestation and engagement, (5) compulsion, and (6) external adaptation. See ibid., 33–40.

question whether we are even justified in declaring the fact that their violation provokes an international response, however conceived, to be the essential characteristic of human rights. Beitz stresses that he is trying to develop a conception of human rights that takes its orientation from their role in current international practice. His aim is therefore to understand the concept of human rights as it exists within the framework of an already existing and functioning international practice.[49] Observation of this practice, he argues, leads to the conclusion that the primary role of human rights is to justify interventions by nonstate actors, "in the sense that a society's failure to respect its people's human rights on a sufficiently large scale may provide a reason for outside agents to do something."[50] Similarly, Raz argues that "the dominant trend in human rights practice is to take the fact that a right is a human right as a defeasibly sufficient ground for taking action against violators in the international arena, that is to take its violation as a reason for such action."[51] Thus both authors assume that human rights play an empirically observable and established role within the framework of international law, which consists precisely and exclusively in making domestic violations into external or international reasons for action.

But with this argument Beitz and Raz fail to recognize that human rights in contemporary practice also have a purely *intra*national function, for example by setting the standard by which domestic populations measure, criticize, and possibly reform the behavior of their governments. Human rights can also motivate the formation of solidarity movements within society to protest against social discrimination against minorities. From a purely factual perspective, therefore, we have no compelling reason to assume that the role of human rights is limited to that formulated by Beitz and Raz. Of course, this is not to deny that the failure to respect human rights can be a very serious reason for international intervention. We can also agree with Beitz when he emphasizes that these reactions can take more or less drastic forms. However, it would be misleading to make the existence of human rights dependent on the existence of interventionist reasons for action, since, as Rainer Forst observes, this would be putting the cart before the horse:

> We first need to construct (or find) a justifiable set of human rights that a legitimate political authority has to respect and guarantee, and then we can

[49] Ibid., 102–103.
[50] Ibid., 105–106.
[51] Raz, "Human Rights without Foundations," 328.

ask what kinds of legal structures are required at the international level to oversee this and help to ensure that political authority is exercised in that way. Only after we have taken this step will it become necessary to think about and set up legitimate institutions of possible intervention (as measures of last resort). The first question of human rights is not how to limit sovereignty from the outside; it is about the essential conditions of the possibility of establishing legitimate political authority. International law and a politics of intervention have to follow a particular logic of human rights, not the converse.[52]

Human Rights and Justification

As can be seen from the above quote, Forst also starts from the basic assumption that human rights have a specifically political character. According to him, however, it would be a mistake to assume that human rights can be conceived from the perspective of an external observer who judges the legitimacy of a political order and looks for reasons for intervention.[53] This would not only be a failure to recognize that demands for human rights come from within society. It would also, and above all, be to fail to recognize their purpose, which, according to Forst, is not to judge the legitimacy of a political order from the *outside* but to establish its *internal* legitimacy. In other words, human rights are the normative yardstick by which a political order must be measured if it is to enjoy legitimacy in the eyes of its subjects. According to Forst, a cursory look at history shows that the demand for human rights was articulated in social conflicts in which people were defending themselves against political and social oppression and were striving to be "no longer ignored, no longer subordinated as the mere means to the preservation of certain institutions and power relations."[54] Thus human rights have their origins in a discourse that is critical of domination and, according to Forst, are, now as in the past, a language of social emancipation that is spoken whenever people are treated by a ruling order in a way that violates

[52] Rainer Forst, "The Justification of Human Rights and the Basic Right to Justification: A Reflexive Approach," in Forst, *Justification and Critique: Towards a Critical Theory of Politics*, trans. Ciaran Cronin (Cambridge, UK: Polity, 2014), 54.

[53] Ibid., 55.

[54] Rainer Forst, *The Right to Justification: Elements of a Constructivist Theory of Justice*, trans. Jeffrey Flynn (New York: Columbia University Press, 2012), 211.

their dignity as human beings.[55] A violation of dignity occurs whenever a person is denied the claim "to be respected as someone who deserves to be given justifying reasons for the actions, rules, or structures to which he or she is subject."[56] A human being, according to Forst, is "a being who uses and 'needs' justifications in order to lead a life 'fit for human beings' among his or her fellows."[57] This means that every human being must be regarded as a being endowed with a fundamental "right to justification," that is, "the right to be respected as a moral person who is autonomous at least in the sense that he or she must not be treated in any manner for which adequate reasons cannot be provided."[58] This is not already a specific human right, but a *foundational* moral right on which all other human rights are based and by reference to which concrete rights must be justified.[59]

The right to justification is comparable to what Hegel once called the "supreme right of the subject," namely "[t]he right not to recognize anything that I do not regard as reasonable."[60] Forst himself speaks of a "veto right"[61] that people can make use of when they are faced with standards or practices that in their view are not adequately justified. One can speak of an adequate justification, according to Forst, only when the standards or practices in question meet the criteria of reciprocity and generality. The criterion of reciprocity requires that no one may make a normative claim that he denies others (reciprocity of content), and that no one may impute his own values, convictions, or interests to others while claiming to be speaking in their "real" interest or in the name of an undeniable truth (reciprocity of reasons). The postulate of generality further requires that a claim can be shared by all those affected or that none of them has good reasons for rejecting it.[62] Only when all those concerned can accept a claim in accordance with these criteria can it be considered justified and therefore also legitimate. It follows

[55] Forst, "The Justification of Human Rights and the Basic Right to Justification," 38.

[56] Forst, *The Right to Justification*, 209. See also "The Justification of Human Rights and the Basic Right to Justification," 63: "[D]ignity means that a person is to be respected as someone who is worthy of being given adequate reasons for actions or norms that affect him or her in a relevant way."

[57] Rainer Forst, "The Ground of Critique: On the Concept of Human Dignity in Social Orders of Justification," *Philosophy & Social Criticism* 37, no. 9 (2011): 966. Forst describes persons elsewhere as "reason-giving and reason-deserving beings." Forst, "The Justification of Human Rights and the Basic Right to Justification," 49.

[58] Forst, *The Right to Justification*, 209–210.

[59] Ibid., 210.

[60] Georg Wilhelm Friedrich Hegel, *Elements of the Philosophy of Right*, ed. Allen Wood, trans. H. B. Nisbet (Cambridge: Cambridge University Press, 1991), 159 (§ 132).

[61] Forst, *The Right to Justification*, 250.

[62] Forst, "The Justification of Human Rights and the Basic Right to Justification," 46–47.

that any political order that raises a claim to legitimacy must be based on precisely those norms and institutions that it can justify in a reciprocal and general way it to its subjects.[63] Therefore, political subjects are not just passive recipients of norms but also moral authorities to whom the exercise of political power must be adequately justified.[64] Anyone who is nevertheless able to make reciprocal and general objections against it can make use of his veto right, his right of justification. This ensures that no one is simply passed over in morally relevant matters and also that no one is subjected to a political order that he or she cannot authorize, criticize, or shape as an equal and autonomous member.[65] Herein resides the specific meaning of human rights for Forst. They are directed against political despotism and oppression and serve to protect and express the status of human beings as free and equal[66] by empowering them to participate in determining the conditions of their social and political environment as legislators.[67]

According to Forst, this right of codetermination also and especially applies to the question of which rights people should guarantee each other. Thus it is primarily a matter of participating in the process of determining the content of human rights. As to the content itself, Forst merely states that these are rights that cannot reasonably be denied to a person without violating her right to justification.[68] According to Forst, these include the rights to political participation, to physical and mental integrity, personal freedoms, and the right against social discrimination.[69] It is not entirely clear why Forst cites these human rights in particular and not others, since he says no more about them than that they are "basic standards of respect" that must be secured in the form of basic rights and given concrete substance in further steps.[70] Nevertheless, we should not assume that Forst wants to reduce the canon of human rights to the above-mentioned rights, since his main concern does not seem to be to identify a specific catalogue of human rights but rather to provide "a starting point, which is both universal and yet relatively open in terms of its content,"[71] for the moral *construction of* human rights. According to this account, human rights are best explained by assuming that

[63] Ibid., 63.
[64] Ibid., 48.
[65] Ibid., 64.
[66] Ibid., 46.
[67] Ibid., 70.
[68] Forst, *The Right to Justification*, 217.
[69] Forst, "The Justification of Human Rights and the Basic Right to Justification," 64.
[70] Ibid.
[71] Forst, *The Right to Justification*, 215.

they are the result of a discursive process in which only those claims that pass the test of reciprocity and universality are granted the status of human rights.[72] According to Forst, we do not need to "resort to a metaphysical or anthropological foundation for these rights" in order to establish a human right as such, since they are instead to be viewed "as constructions . . . that have an intersubjectively nonrejectable 'ground.' Moral persons, who see that they have no good reason to deny them, owe one another respect for these justified constructs."[73] For example, if one wanted to establish a human right to food, it would not be necessary, according to Forst, for this purpose to fall back on the anthropological observation that food is one of the essential conditions of human life. Rather, one would have to be able to show that the right to food is a claim that no one can reasonably deny, that is, that no one can deny it on reciprocal and general grounds.

But this very point leaves open a crucial question that Forst fails to address: Why can a right to food not be reasonably rejected? This question necessarily points to an anthropological argument that Forst goes out of his way to avoid, for the right to food cannot be rejected precisely because people cannot live without food. This is the specific reason that the actors in Forst's justification scenario must understand and that first leads them to the insight that a human right to food cannot be reasonably rejected. So although this is indeed a human right that one cannot reasonably reject, we do not speak of a human right here *because* it cannot be reasonably rejected. This fact must itself be traced back to a reason that arises only in view of the anthropological fact that human beings are beings who cannot survive without food. Since Forst rejects any reference to such anthropological aspects, he fails to explain *why* human beings should be accorded certain rights. This is also why the "moral construction" undertaken by Forst "can only lead to a very general list of rights for which we can *assume* that no normatively acceptable reasons count against their validity."[74] However, Forst cannot explain why no normatively acceptable reasons speak against them. This means in turn that Forst cannot explain *which* rights human beings should be accorded solely on the basis of his right to justification. As Ernst Tugendhat stresses, only the notion of need or interest can be fundamental for this question.[75] Forst seems to be aware of this fact when, toward the end of his remarks, he emphasizes that

[72] Forst, "The Justification of Human Rights and the Basic Right to Justification," 53.
[73] Forst, *The Right to Justification*, 214.
[74] Ibid., 218, emphasis added.
[75] Ernst Tugendhat, *Vorlesungen über Ethik* (Frankfurt: Suhrkamp, 1993), 358.

people who accord each other a right to justification recognize each other not only as autonomous beings who demand and are able to offer justifications but "at the same time as *vulnerable* and *needy* social beings."[76] He is therefore forced to admit that, in order to define the content of human rights, those aspects of human life must be taken into consideration that are supposed to be protected or enabled by human rights. Forst rightly emphasizes that the goods or interests in question are not arbitrary but must be ones that are shared by all people and cannot be rejected by anybody with good reason.[77] But he leaves open which goods or interests belong to this category.

Human Rights and Normative Agency

In this context, James Griffin proposes to trace the idea of human rights back to the uniquely human capacity to develop and pursue ideas about the good life. According to Griffin, what distinguishes human beings from other living creatures is their ability to reflect on their lives and to *decide* what they consider to be a worthwhile life. Humans choose, evaluate, and plan their lives, and they also try to *realize* their ideas of the good life through their actions.[78] According to Griffin, this is what constitutes our specifically human and therefore dignified existence: the ability to choose and pursue our own conception of the good life.[79] He uses the term "normative agency" to describe this capacity, and he divides normative agency into three components. In order to be a person who is capable of normative agency, one must first be able to choose one's life path without being oppressed or controlled by anything or anyone. This is the "autonomy" component. Furthermore, one must be endowed with sufficient intellectual and material resources if one is to be able to form and pursue one's conception of the good life at all. Griffin calls this "minimum provision" or "welfare."[80] The third component, "liberty," is the ability to pursue one's conception of the good life without being forcibly prevented from doing so by others.[81]

[76] Forst, "The Justification of Human Rights and the Basic Right to Justification," 65, emphasis added.
[77] Ibid.
[78] Griffin, *On Human Rights*, 32.
[79] Ibid., 44.
[80] Ibid., 149.
[81] Ibid., 33.

Griffin emphasizes that people have a fundamental interest in being protected and fostered in these three respects, since these are particularly important interests to which we, as "self-deciders,"[82] ascribe an especially high value. And precisely because we attach such an especially high value to them, we should declare their protection to be a human right.[83] Only in this way does the concept of human rights become intelligible—after all, these are rights to which human beings are entitled solely by virtue of their humanity. This humanity can be best explained with reference to human beings' normative agency, that is, the ability to form and pursue a conception of the good life: "Anyone who has the capacity to identify the good, whatever the extent of the capacity and whatever its source, has what I mean by 'a conception of a worthwhile life.' ... And it is the mere possession of this common capacity to identify the good that guarantees persons the protection of human rights."[84] Human rights, thus conceived, are not something to which all members of the species *Homo sapiens* are entitled, but only those human beings who are persons with normative agency.[85] This means, however, that neither newborn infants nor severely mentally handicapped or senile human beings can be regarded as holders of human rights,[86] so that, for example, it would not be a violation of human rights to torture newborn infants or people with serious mental disabilities. But this, according to Griffin, is a necessary theoretical sacrifice in order to make the concept of human rights more "user-friendly."[87] The only reason why we speak of a human right here, he argues, is that the act of torture "renders us unable to decide for ourselves or to stick to our decision" and is therefore "an attack on normative agency."[88] Since this aspect of torture does not occur in the case of the torture of infants, the severely mentally handicapped, or animals—all of whom belong to the same category of beings who are incapable of agency, according to Griffin—one could speak here of a violation of moral rights but not of a violation of human rights.[89] The reference to normative agency thus serves to specify

[82] Ibid., 46.
[83] Ibid., 35.
[84] Ibid., 46.
[85] Ibid., 50.
[86] Ibid., 83.
[87] Ibid., 91.
[88] Ibid., 52.
[89] At least in the case of infants, however, Griffin must face the question of the point at which in the course of its life it should be regarded as a person capable of normative agency, and thus as a subject of human rights. Griffin thinks he has answered this question when he says that children achieve agency in stages and therefore can be regarded as bearers of human rights only in stages (ibid., 95). However, he fails to explain which stages are involved and how these stages can be defined in greater

the notion of human rights and to distinguish it from the broader category of moral rights.[90] Declaring the normative agency to be what human rights protect, Griffin argues, also enables us to avoid the oft-lamented inflation of human rights claims, since the content of human rights can now be confined to those rights that enable normative agency.[91] According to the above subdivision, we can identify three metarights (to autonomy, freedom, and welfare) from which all other human rights can be derived in a further step.[92]

Strictly speaking, however, Griffin actually assumes only two metarights, since the right to welfare, as he conceives it, just like the right to security, for example, is relevant only insofar as it relates to the exercise of autonomy and the enjoyment of liberty.[93] Thus the interests in autonomy and liberty alone represent the basis of human rights in Griffin's theory, so that he now faces the arduous task of subsuming all human rights under these two concepts in order to justify their status as such. The example of torture has already made it clear that this is possible only at the expense of certain moral intuitions. Although Griffin rightly emphasizes here that the act of torture prevents us from abiding by our decision, and thus restricts our autonomy, this is not why we ascribe human beings a right to protection against torture. The worst thing about torture is not that it restricts human beings in their autonomy, but that it inflicts unnecessary and possibly unbearable pain and puts them in a state of fear that can inflict permanent psychological damage on them. Likewise, we do not speak of a right to food because without food human beings are unable to think or act freely and autonomously, but because without food they starve, their bodies degenerate, and they eventually die.[94] The thesis that human rights only serve to protect autonomy and freedom thus faces the objection that it is not even able to plausibly justify undeniable human rights.

detail. Therefore, in the case of an infant or a young child, it seems to be largely arbitrary when an act of torture should be regarded as a violation of human rights.

[90] Ibid., 92.

[91] Ibid., 34.

[92] Ibid., 149. According to Griffin, this derivation is made in the light of "practicalities," by which he means "empirical information about . . . human nature and human societies" and "about the limits of human understanding and motivation" (38). The relevant notion is defined only very vaguely, and it is ironic that it is supposed to serve to specify the content of individual human rights (192): "Personhood initially generates the rights; practicalities give them, where needed, a sufficiently determinate shape."

[93] See also ibid., 243, where Griffin merely speaks of "two abstract rights at the centre of normative agency: autonomy and liberty."

[94] For a detailed critique of the autonomy approach, see Barbara Schmitz, "Bedürfnisse und Gerechtigkeit" (Habil., University of Basel, 2008), 53.

Another powerful objection to Griffin's thesis is that it cannot take into account the aspect of equal treatment or nondiscrimination that has featured prominently in both the historical and the contemporary discussion of human rights.[95] Griffin tries to avoid this objection initially by emphasizing that the phenomenon of equal treatment is not a question of human rights but one of justice. Although these domains overlap, he argues, they are not congruent.[96] To illustrate this, Griffin cites the example of two executives who are equally competent and responsible but are paid differently because one of them is a relative of the managing director. According to Griffin, it would be absurd to speak of a violation of human rights here, since this is rather an injustice that must be criticized as such.[97] "It is a great, but now common, mistake to think that, because we see rights as especially important in morality, we must make everything especially important in morality into a right."[98] Nonetheless, Griffin concedes that there are "objectionable forms of discrimination," such as racist and sexist discrimination, that can be assumed to be violations of human rights.[99] According to Griffin, however, this is only the case because they could indirectly lead to a restriction of normative agency, for example when people are subjected to physical mistreatment or social oppression on account of their ethnic origin. According to Griffin, even membership in a despised or discriminated group can lead people to lose self-confidence and therefore be restricted in their normative agency: "A member of a hated minority would be inhibited from speaking out on unpopular issues, and from acting in a way that would attract the majority's attention. And members of a hated group living in a community with police given to physical abuse would be all the more constrained."[100] In order to integrate the phenomenon of discrimination into his conception of human rights, Griffin is therefore forced to cite theoretically possible extreme cases (loss of normative agency as a result of mistreatment due to discrimination) or to make questionable psychological assumptions (loss of normative agency as a result of lack of self-confidence due to discrimination). In all cases, however, it is not the act of discrimination as such that

[95] For a detailed statement of this criticism, see Allen Buchanan, "The Egalitarianism of Human Rights," *Ethics* 120, no. 4 (2010): 679–710.

[96] See Griffin, *On Human Rights*, 41.

[97] Ibid., 42.

[98] Ibid., 43.

[99] Ibid., 42.

[100] Ibid..

constitutes a human rights violation, but only the restriction of normative agency that Griffin anticipates.

However, he seems to have overlooked the fact that it is quite possible to be the victim of racial or sexist discrimination without that in any way impairing one's normative agency. A female manager who is paid less than her male colleague for the same work because of her gender or the color of her skin does not thereby already lose her ability to autonomously arrive at a conception of the good life and to pursue it freely. Although this is an impermissible form of discrimination, according to Griffin's thesis we cannot speak of a violation of human rights in this case because normative agency is not impaired. But why should we not also speak of a violation of human rights when interests other than normative agency are at stake? What are the reasons for restricting the purpose of human rights solely to the protection of autonomy and freedom, if this obviously means that fundamental human rights cannot be plausibly justified or even taken into account? Griffin's argument is as follows: "I single out functioning human agents via notions such as their autonomy and liberty, and I choose those features precisely because they are especially important human interests. *It is only because they are especially important interests that rights can be derived from them*; rights are strong protections, and so require something especially valuable to attract protection."[101] The reason why we can derive human rights only from the interests in autonomy and liberty supposedly has to do with the fact that they are especially important interests. But what makes the interests in autonomy and liberty so especially important, and why are we justified in regarding other interests as less important?

Griffin pursues two strategies in response to these questions. The first is to argue that autonomy and liberty are the essential components of human dignity.[102] Griffin emphasizes that he is merely trying to formulate a concept of human rights on the basis of the relevant declarations and their recognition that "these rights derive from the inherent dignity of the human person."[103] According to Griffin, the concept of dignity can be made intelligible only by tracing it back to human beings' normative agency, since it is precisely this capacity that endows our lives with dignity and sets human beings apart as

[101] Ibid., 35, emphasis added.

[102] See ibid., 44–45, 151, 192, 200–201, 205, 243.

[103] This is the wording in the Preamble of the International Covenant on Civil and Political Rights. The same wording can be found in the International Covenant on Economic, Social and Cultural Rights.

such.[104] As Allen Buchanan points out, however, we have no good reason for assuming that this is the only possible or even the only plausible explication of human dignity. In fact, here Griffin is open to the reproach that he does not take the notion of dignity seriously enough and fails to appreciate its complexity by merely equating it with the idea of normative agency, since

> dignity—or some conceptions of dignity—can plausibly be understood to include a comparative dimension that cannot be captured by the notion of protecting normative agency. To put the same point in a different way, being treated as if one were by virtue of one's nature inferior is to be denied the dignity accorded to others. Being relegated to an inferior status under the rigors of a caste system based on skin color, ethnicity, or gender, or being in a condition of extreme dependency compared to other persons, can be an affront to one's dignity, even if one has considerable scope for exercising normative agency.[105]

However, Griffin has a second strategy he can fall back on to justify the special significance of autonomy and liberty and to uphold the associated limits on the interests of relevance for human rights. This strategy is to argue that autonomy and liberty represent the components of our normative agency whose exercise improves the quality of our lives.[106] The importance of these interests, according to Griffin, is thus a function of the fact that they contribute to a good life. But he is aware that there are other interests that can also contribute to a good life. Although autonomy and liberty are "highly important . . . features," they are "none the less *not, in principle, immune to trade-off with other elements of a good life*, such as accomplishment, certain kinds of understanding, deep personal relations, enjoyment, and so on."[107] In light of this observation, Griffin now feels compelled to relativize his statement about the special importance of autonomy and liberty: "It is because of the special importance, *though by no means necessarily uniquely*

[104] Griffin, *On Human Rights*, 44: "What we attach value to, what we regard as giving dignity to human life, is our capacity to choose and to pursue our conception of a worthwhile life." Similarly: "We all need to understand why persons are regarded as especially valuable. Since the late Middle Ages many writers have explained it by pointing to the special feature of humanity that I have been stressing: our capacity for normative agency. We can easily understand why the term 'dignity' was attached to our status as normative agents, and why other forms of animal life were thought to lack that dignity" (66).

[105] Buchanan, "The Egalitarianism of Human Rights," 703.

[106] Griffin, *On Human Rights*, 36.

[107] Ibid., emphasis added.

great importance, of these particular human interests that, on this understanding, we ring-fence them with the notion of human rights."[108] It is not altogether clear how we should understand this statement. Griffin seems to be suggesting that, among the many important interests that belong to the elements of a good life, the interests in autonomy and liberty are especially important. This seems paradoxical, however, in view of his earlier assertion that they do not in principle take precedence over the other interests identified. Moreover, Griffin does not say anything about whether and in what way these interests contribute more than the others to improving the quality of life. Things become even more paradoxical, however, when Griffin emphasizes in a subsequent passage that the interests in autonomy and liberty are not especially important. Human rights, he writes, "are not even the most important of rights. Autonomy—or, more generally, personhood—is not necessarily the most important human interest."[109] With this, Griffin turns his own argument on its head, since in view of his above statement, he would now be logically compelled to conclude that no human rights can be derived from the interests in autonomy and liberty. But even if we assumed that these were important interests, there would still not be any good reason to restrict the moral basis of human rights to them.

Human Rights and Interests

Some authors therefore think it reasonable to pursue a pluralistic approach to justifying human rights. According to John Tasioulas, this has the advantage that individual human rights, which could be justified only indirectly on Griffin's conception, can now be justified more directly and thus more plausibly.[110] On the pluralistic approach, the right not to be tortured, for example, can be traced back to people's interest in avoiding pain, and rights to education, work, and leisure can be traced back to the interests in knowledge, accomplishment, and play.[111] Although, according to Tasioulas, autonomy and liberty are still among the interests in terms of which human rights can be justified, they are no longer the sole point of reference in this regard. This has the advantage, first, that the circle of human rights bearers

108 Ibid., emphasis added.
109 Ibid., 135.
110 See John Tasioulas, "Taking Rights out of Human Rights," *Ethics* 120, no. 4 (2010): 663.
111 Ibid.

is no longer restricted to the circle of persons who possess normative agency, but also includes those who do not have normative agency, do not have it yet, or do not have it any longer.[112] Second, it is easier to justify human rights in cultures that do not accord the same status to autonomy and liberty as Western culture, because now it is possible to refer to interests that enjoy a higher standing in those cultures.[113] But Tasioulas does not seem to be sure which interests these are supposed to be, because he does not make this clear anywhere in his remarks. On the basis of isolated references, however, we can conclude that accomplishment (desert), knowledge, friendship, avoidance of pain,[114] play[115] (alternatively, pleasure),[116] health,[117] and religion[118] are among the interests that can be considered relevant for human rights, according to Tasioulas.

Like Griffin, however, Tasioulas faces the question of what justifies one in making these interests in particular the basis of human rights. In response, he maintains that interests serve to justify human rights precisely when they are so important that they can justify imposing corresponding duties.[119] In other words, whether an interest can justify a human right depends on its ability to oblige others to protect, respect, or promote that interest.[120] Thus, Tasioulas's thesis can be reformulated as follows: A has an interest in X, but this interest can justify the claim that A has a corresponding human right only if it obliges B to respect, protect, or promote X. Thus X is the reason for a human right of A on the condition that it can provide B with a reason for action.

But in what sense must X (A's interest) represent a reason for B to act? Not everything that is in A's interest also seems to be in B's interest. Let us assume that A has an interest in smoking in public buildings, whereas B is a confirmed nonsmoker. Why in this case should B feel obligated to respect, protect, or promote A's interest? On the contrary, B would probably be keen to prevent A from smoking in public. It might be different if B were also a

112 Ibid., 667.

113 Ibid., 663. See also John Tasioulas, "Human Rights, Universality and the Values of Personhood: Retracing Griffin's Steps," *European Journal of Philosophy* 10, no. 1 (2002): 88, 94, where he speaks in terms of the enhanced "exportability" of human rights to non-Western cultures.

114 Tasioulas mentions these four interests in "Taking Rights out of Human Rights," 662.

115 Ibid., 663.

116 So described in Tasioulas, "Human Rights, Universality and the Values of Personhood," 94.

117 Ibid., 93.

118 Ibid.

119 Ibid., 96.

120 Tasioulas, "Taking Rights out of Human Rights," 662.

smoker. In that case, B could put himself in A's position and reason that it would be advantageous for him if his interest were respected, protected, or promoted by others. A's interest is thus a reason for B to act, because B shares the interest of A. But for A to claim a right that is supposed to be valid for and be respected by every human being, X must provide a reason to act not only for B but for any human being. This means that a necessary property of X must be that the interest in it can be universally shared.

It is questionable however, whether this property alone is sufficient to oblige others to perform certain actions. Indeed, it is perfectly conceivable that all people share A's interest in eating ice cream, but without thereby feeling obligated to protect or promote A in this interest. Not every shared interest is thus suited to justifying a human rights–based obligation and to explaining the moral relevance of human rights. For this purpose, a certain urgency or necessity of the interest seems to be required in addition to the fact that it can be universally shared, which is obviously not given in the case of ice cream consumption. But some of the interests on Tasioulas's list do not possess these qualifications either. For example, it seems incongruous to include games or pleasure in the list of interests of relevance for human rights, since these are rather trivial examples of goods in need of protection. Furthermore, not everyone necessarily has an interest in demonstrating academic, professional, or sporting accomplishment. And although religion plays an important role in many people's lives, it is not important for everyone. The key question to be answered in this context, therefore, is not *whether* an interest is important but *for whom*. Not everything that is important for me is necessarily important for someone else, and vice versa. However, only those goods that are *necessarily* important *for every* human being can be of relevance for human rights. To explain these ideas, I will argue in what follows that human rights can be most plausibly conceived as institutions for the protection of universal, objective, and vital human needs. For this purpose, I will first clarify what it means to speak of human needs; building on this, I will draw on interdisciplinary research to explore which needs human beings have (chapter 12). The third task will be to bring the idea of human rights into a coherent relation to human needs (chapter 13).

12
Human Needs

The concept of need has been the subject of scholarly discussion for many years, with researchers from a variety of disciplines attempting to define it. The marked differences in the meaning of the term in different disciplines are exacerbated by the fact that the term is not used consistently within each individual discipline. Contributing to this conceptual vagueness is the fact that "need" belongs to a family of concepts ranging from instincts, drives, motives, and motivations to desires, wants, purposes, tasks, and goals to interests, norms, and values.[1] In order to avoid misunderstandings and to make a clear distinction between different definitions, we must first clarify some facets of the concept.

What Are Needs?

When we speak of a need in everyday language, we are referring to the pursuit of what one needs or wants in order to achieve one's goals.[2] The verbs used in this context suggest that we speak of needs when we want, desire, or prefer something or when we need or require something. Thus an ambiguity in the notion of need is already apparent. While in the first case we can equate needs with higher mental states such as desires, longings, or cravings, in the second case the notion of need refers to basic things that we need regardless of our subjective state of mind.

Similar conceptual facets emerge when we turn to the use of the concept of need in scientific contexts. According to an older but still current definition from economics, a need is "the feeling of a deficiency coupled with

[1] Günter Ropohl, "Bedürfnisforschung und soziotechnische Praxis: Ein vorläufiges Resümee," in *Die "wahren" Bedürfnisse oder: Wissen wir was wir brauchen?*, ed. Simon Moser, Günter Ropohl, and Walther Zimmerli (Basel: Schwabe, 1978), 127. The English language, in which the distinction between *needs* and *wants* is semantically more clearly anchored, has an advantage over German in this regard.

[2] Karl Otto Hondrich, ed., *Bedürfnisse im Wandel: Theorie, Zeitdiagnose, Forschungsergebnisse* (Opladen: Westdeutscher Verlag, 1983), 28.

Human Rights Between Universality and Islamic Legitimacy. Mahmoud Bassiouni, Oxford University Press.
 DOI: 10.1093/oso/9780197753897.003.0013

the striving to eliminate it."[3] The effort to eliminate the deficiency is nothing more than the desire to satisfy one's need. According to this view, a need can also be seen as a state of tension or conflict in which there is a discrepancy between a perceived actual state and a desired state—as well as the attempt to overcome it.[4] However, as Ropohl notes, some aspects of this definitional framework prove problematic on closer inspection.[5] If a need is characterized as a "feeling" of deficiency or as a "perception" of a discrepancy between the actual and the desired state, then all those deficiencies that may objectively exist but are not directly felt by the individual, such as a vitamin deficiency, fall outside the scope of the concept of need. At the same time, according to the above definition, all those deficiencies that can be felt purely subjectively by an individual, such as a lack of nicotine, must be included. While in the former case it seems legitimate to speak of a human need for vitamins, it seems quite contradictory to speak of a basic human need for nicotine simply because it is felt by some people. As John Stuart Mill observes, "Mankind are always predisposed to believe that any subjective feeling, not otherwise accounted for, is a revelation of some objective reality."[6] Thus at the root of all differences concerning the concept of need is the question of whether a need is a subjective sense of lack or an objectively attributable requirement. This observation is important and worthy of attention, because this conceptual indeterminacy does indeed lead to interpretative discrepancies that result in substantive misunderstandings.

Interpretations of the concept of need can generally be divided into two groups.[7] An *objective-universal* interpretation understands needs as those that all human beings have and that remain constant regardless of time or culture, whereas a *subjective-historical* interpretation postulates that needs vary from individual to individual and from culture to culture, depending on the environment. The latter notion of needs implicitly covers the semantic space of desire, craving, longing, interest, and so on. In this context, one can fall back on K. O. Hondrich's distinction between (objective-universal)

[3] F. B. W. Hermann, *Staatswirtschaftliche Untersuchungen* (Munich: Weber, 1874), 5, quoted in Wilhelm Bernsdorf, *Wörterbuch der Soziologie* (Stuttgart: Enke, 1969), 81.

[4] See Karl Otto Hondrich, *Menschliche Bedürfnisse und soziale Steuerung: Eine Einführung in die Sozialwissenschaften* (Reinbek: Rohwolt, 1975), 27–28.

[5] Ropohl, "Bedürfnisforschung und soziotechnische Praxis," 115.

[6] John Stuart Mill, *Utilitarianism*, in Mill, *Utilitarianism and On Liberty: Including Mill's "Essay on Bentham" and Selections from the Writings of Jeremy Bentham and John Austin*, ed. Mary Warnock (Malden, MA: Blackwell, 2003), 216.

[7] See Katrin Lederer, ed., *Human Needs: A Contribution to the Current Debate* (Cambridge, MA: Oelgeschlager, Gunn & Hain, 1980), 3–9.

needs and (subjective-historical) need orientations.[8] A need orientation is a subjectively experienced sense of deficiency that is shaped in the broadest sense by cultural influences and is directed toward those objects that have meaning for a particular individual in a particular situation. Thus, by definition, a need orientation is always related to objects that, depending on the challenges and offers of the environment, constitute *a means to eliminate a subjectively experienced deficiency.* According to this interpretation, the assertion that needs are common to all human beings must of course be qualified. For example, an Inuit's need orientation for raw fish does not correspond to the need orientation of an inhabitant of the Central African Republic who would not touch raw fish. And logically, a shelter that the Inuit needs to protect herself from the cold would also be strange and uncanny to the African.[9] According to the subjective-historical interpretation, need orientations would also include those that constitute an individual craving for any good, such as a child's craving for candy or an adult's craving for coffee.

The objective-universal concept of need, by contrast, makes a sharp distinction between needs on the one hand, and demands or desires on the other, and emphasizes that it is not needs but only need orientations that depend on epochs and social environments. It understands human needs as *universal, objective, and indispensable conditions of human existence.* In this context, "universal" expresses the fact that the existence of needs is independent of historical and cultural differences. Thus, although the Inuit and the African may have different desires and interests, they share a basic need for physiological self-preservation (for food and shelter). Furthermore, human needs are *objective* in the sense that their existence can be studied empirically.[10] This means that a need does not arise from the perception of an experienced lack but can be based on unconscious processes.[11] "Indispensable" further qualifies the notion of need by limiting it to the conditions for a successful human life. The latter should not be understood in a strictly biological sense, "since human beings—with rare exceptions—always lead a life that is not merely biological."[12] Galtung describes a need "as

[8] Hondrich, *Bedürfnisse im Wandel*, 81.

[9] The example is taken from Erhard Eppler, *Was braucht der Mensch? Vision: Politik im Dienst der Grundbedürfnis* (Frankfurt: Campus, 2000), 127, who assumes a subjective-historical notion of need.

[10] Seev Gasiet, *Menschliche Bedürfnisse: Eine theoretische Synthese* (Frankfurt: Campus, 1981), 239.

[11] See Hondrich, *Bedürfnisse im Wandel*, 27. See also Schmitz, *Bedürfnisse und Gerechtigkeit*, 21.

[12] Hondrich, *Bedürfnisse im Wandel*, 27.

a necessary condition, as something that must be satisfied at least to some extent in order for the need-subject to function as a human being."[13] According to this usage, a need does not denote a specific object, but refers to indispensable, central, and fundamental conditions of human existence. With Barbara Schmitz we can therefore also speak of "necessities of the human form of life."[14] These are universal in the sense that they can be determined in an anthropologically objective and ethically neutral way.

The term "need" will thus be understood in what follows as a predicate that refers to the universal, objective, and indispensable conditions of individual and communal human existence. Accordingly, one can speak of a need for X only if those who lack X are threatened in the conduct of their lives as a result.

What Needs Do Human Beings Have?

Now that we have clarified the conceptual framework of the concept of needs, let us turn to the classification of needs in terms of their content. Taking our lead from a variety of authors, each of whom deals with human needs in the context of a different scientific discipline, we will ask what needs human beings have.

Needs from the Perspective of Motivational Psychology

One of the most influential attempts to identify and classify human needs is the holistic-dynamic theory of Abraham Maslow.[15] According to Maslow, when we talk about human needs, we are talking about the essentials of life.[16] Needs "are not only wanted and desired by all human beings, but also needed in the sense that they are necessary to avoid illness and psychopathology."[17] Approaching needs from a psychological perspective, Maslow suggests that human behavior is driven by hierarchically structured needs. He distinguishes between physiological needs, safety needs, and needs for belonging and love, respect, and finally self-actualization. These can be

[13] Johan Galtung, "The Basic Needs Approach," in Lederer, *Human Needs*, 60.
[14] See Schmitz, *Bedürfnisse und Gerechtigkeit*, 75–80.
[15] Abraham H. Maslow, *Motivation and Personality* (New York: Harper & Row, 1954).
[16] Ibid. xii.
[17] Ibid. xiii.

represented as a pyramid, with physiological needs at the base and self-actualization at the apex. According to Maslow, the higher needs emerge only after the lower ones have been satisfied to some degree.[18] By "emerge" Maslow does not mean that a new need is created "but that the *latent* higher-order needs that are inherent in the structure of the person, gradually become *manifest* through the satisfaction of the urgent needs."[19] In other words, the relative satisfaction of lower needs sets the stage for the emergence of higher needs: "Wanting anything in itself implies already existing satisfactions of other wants. We should never have the desire to compose music or create mathematical systems, or to adorn our homes, or to be well dressed if our stomachs were empty most of the time, or if we were continually dying of thirst, or if we were continually threatened by an always impending catastrophe, or if everyone hated us."[20] According to Maslow, as long as one need is dominant, all of an individual's activities are directed toward satisfying that dominant need. The starting point is physiological needs. People are initially dominated by these needs, while the other needs are suppressed.

Physiological Needs

Physiological needs include somatically localizable needs, such as sexual or nutritional needs. They are relatively independent of each other and of other types of needs and are largely "determined by the tendency of the body to establish and maintain a constant normal state or balance."[21] According to Maslow, physiological needs are "the most prepotent of all":[22]

> If all the needs are unsatisfied, and the organism is then dominated by the physiological needs, all other needs may become simply nonexistent or be pushed into the background.... The urge to write poetry, the desire to acquire an automobile, the interest in American history, the desire for a new pair of shoes are, in the extreme case, forgotten or become of secondary importance. For the man who is extremely and dangerously hungry, no other interests exist except food. He dreams food, he remembers food, he

[18] This limitation is important because Maslow concedes that needs can never be fully satiated and that "the human being is never satisfied except in a relative or one-step-along-the-path fashion" (ibid. 25).
[19] Hondrich, *Menschliche Bedürfnisse und soziale Steuerung*, 30.
[20] Maslow, *Motivation and Personality*, 24.
[21] Hondrich, *Menschliche Bedürfnisse und soziale Steuerung*, 30.
[22] Maslow, *Motivation and Personality*, 36.

> thinks about food, he emotes only about food, he perceives only food, and he wants only food.[23]

In fact, according to Maslow, a person's entire philosophy of the future changes when he is dominated by a particular need: "For our chronically and extremely hungry man, Utopia can be defined simply as a place where there is plenty of food. . . . Life itself tends to be defined in terms of eating. Anything else will be defined as unimportant. Freedom, love, community feeling, respect, philosophy, may all be waved aside as fripperies that are useless, since they fail to fill the stomach."[24] When physiological needs are satisfied, they cease to exist as active determinants of behavior: "They now exist only in a potential fashion in the sense that they may emerge again to dominate the organism if they are thwarted. . . . The organism is dominated and its behavior organized only by unsatisfied needs."[25]

Safety Needs

Once physiological needs are relatively well met, a new set of needs emerges that can be collectively characterized as safety needs. Provided that physiological needs are sufficiently satisfied, "we may then fairly describe the whole organism as a safety-seeking mechanism."[26] Safety needs include the need for protection from threats and for a predictable, orderly world in which all other needs can be met. According to Maslow, safety needs include needs such as "structure, order, law, limits; strength in the protector; and so on."[27] With reference to this, Seev Gasiet makes the critical observation that this catalogue contains extremely diverse needs. He rightly points out that the need for safety, for example in the case of a child, is quite different from the need for boundaries, laws, and order: "While security . . . belongs to the emotional interpersonal relationships, order and law . . . relate to a completely different domain not just of social life but also of psychological attitude. Moreover, structure and order together with stability have a meaning that does not necessarily correspond to emotional security or to more or less rational law abindingness; it may conflict with either or with both of them together."[28]

[23] Ibid., 37.
[24] Ibid.
[25] Ibid., 38.
[26] Ibid., 39.
[27] Ibid.
[28] Gasiet, *Menschliche Bedürfnisse*, 225–226.

Needs for Belongingness and Love

Emotional needs for love, affection, and belonging arise when both the physiological and safety needs are met:

> Now the person will feel keenly, as never before, the absence of friends, or a sweetheart, or a wife, or children. He will hunger for affectionate relations with people in general, namely for a place in his group or family, and he will strive with great intensity to achieve this goal. He will want to attain such a place more than anything else in the world and may even forget that once, when he was hungry, he sneered at love as unreal or unnecessary or unimportant. Now he will feel sharply the pangs of loneliness, of ostracism, of rejection, of friendlessness, of rootlessness.[29]

Against this, Gasiet argues:

> The strange developmental history according to which one once "sneered at love" because one "was hungry" is wrong on both the phylogenetic and the ontogenetic level. We can leave [to] one side for the moment what might be meant by "love." On the other hand, as regards emotional affection and belonging—which is presumably what is mainly meant by the basic need discussed here—everything points to the fact that they are more pronounced at a relatively early stage of development than at any later time. This is true both of infants, who personify all relations to the environment and are almost completely dominated by feelings of affection and aversion or of belongingness or rejection, and of "primitive" forms of society and their conceptions of the world.[30]

Esteem Needs

By "esteem needs" Maslow means both self-esteem and the esteem of others. Self-esteem includes "the desire for strength, for achievement, for adequacy, for mastery and competence, for confidence in the face of the world, and for independence and freedom."[31] The esteem of others includes "what we may call the desire for reputation or prestige (defining it as respect or esteem from other people), status, fame and glory, dominance, recognition, attention,

[29] Maslow, *Motivation and Personality*, 43.
[30] Gasiet, *Menschliche Bedürfnisse*, 227.
[31] Maslow, *Motivation and Personality*, 45.

importance, dignity, or appreciation."[32] At this point Gasiet again complains that the casual vagueness of the terms overlooks "how fundamentally different, for example, competence is from strength or trust from freedom—apart from the fact that there are no generally accepted meanings of all these terms."[33] Gasiet remains dissatisfied with Maslow's following reflection on self-esteem: "The most stable and therefore most healthy self-esteem is based on *deserved* respect from others rather than on external fame or celebrity and unwarranted adulation."[34] Gasiet argues, "Maslow seems to be equally oblivious to the fact that the need for esteem, especially if it is an inescapable basic need, is necessarily highly problematic because it is based on an unequal, antagonistic relationship between human beings. Dominance necessarily entails an opposition between the dominant and the dominated. And recognition is, as Hegel demonstrates in an exemplary way in the *Phenomenology of the Spirit*, the result of a life and death struggle that continues today in modified form."[35]

The Need for Self-Actualization

The need for self-actualization refers to "the tendency for [man] to become actualized in what he is potentially."[36] According to Hondrich, the needs in question constitute a kind of residual category with an unmistakable normative undertone: "What a man *can* be, he *must* be."[37] Maslow cites athletic, creative, and artistic aspirations as examples. It should be noted, however, that in his later writings, Maslow suggests that people are driven by two types of needs: growth needs and deficits or deficiency needs.[38] The need for self-actualization is one of the growth needs, that is, those based on abundance and basic need satisfaction. The clear emergence of self-actualization needs is based on the prior satisfaction of deficiency needs, that is, physiological needs and needs for safety, love, and esteem. Gasiet finds the term "self-actualization" an unfortunate choice to express what Maslow means by it, "namely a particular basic need; even if one concedes that it presupposes the satisfaction of all other basic needs for it to take precedence."[39] However,

32 Ibid.
33 Gasiet, *Menschliche Bedürfnisse*, 230.
34 Maslow, *Motivation and Personality*, 46, emphasis in original.
35 Gasiet, *Menschliche Bedürfnisse*, 231.
36 Maslow, *Motivation and Personality*, 46.
37 Hondrich, *Menschliche Bedürfnisse und soziale Steuerung*, 31, quoted in Maslow, *Motivation and Personality*, 46, emphasis in original.
38 Abraham H. Maslow, *Toward a Psychology of Being*, 3rd ed. (New York: Wiley, 1999), 28.
39 Gasiet, *Menschliche Bedürfnisse*, 232.

Maslow himself admits in this context that the specific form these needs will take "will of course vary greatly from person to person"[40] and describes the concept of self-actualization in the same context not as a need in the objective sense, but as a human desire.[41]

Needs from a Sociohistorical Perspective

Maslow's analysis of human needs in terms of a theory of stages is still one of the most influential attempts to explain human motivation.[42] However, the hypothesis that needs form a hierarchically structured pyramid must be confronted with the question, especially from the perspective of the social sciences, whether human behavior can really be described in such monomotivational terms as Maslow's pyramid of needs suggests. In fact, the automatism and primacy of certain needs in driving human behavior assumed by Maslow does not seem to stand up to empirical examination of human behavior. For example, it is clear that the need for love and affection is present even before a person's physiological needs are satisfied.[43] Gasiet emphasizes that the various human needs never occur in "pure" form in a normal human life, but are always interwoven in various ways: "This is the case, for example, when diplomats or eminent political, economic, religious-institutional or scientific-academic personalities hold a banquet at which food is also consumed, but all participants understand that they have not come together to satisfy their physiological needs, but for a very different purpose."[44] According to Gasiet, such "constellations of needs" are a product of four classes of needs, which can be summarized as follows: (a) physiological needs, (b) needs for interpersonal relationships, (c) needs for recognition, and (d) needs for meaning. The classification of human needs proposed by Gasiet, who approaches the subject from a sociohistorical perspective, has similarities with Maslow's classification but does not start from the notion of hierarchically ordered and strictly separated needs. As with Maslow, the physiological needs are those for food, breathable air, sleep, and so on, and therefore do not require further explanation in the present context. What

40 Maslow, *Motivation and Personality*, 46.
41 Ibid.
42 A comparison with other theories of motivation can be found in Philip G. Zimbardo, Robert L. Johnson, and Vivian McCann, *Psychology: Core Concepts* (Boston: Pearson, 2012), 369–374.
43 Schmitz, *Bedürfnisse und Gerechtigkeit*, 22.
44 Gasiet, *Menschliche Bedürfnisse*, 285.

is of interest for our purposes is Gasiet's characterization of the next three classes of needs, which I will discuss briefly here.

The need for interpersonal relationships, according to Gasiet, implies emotional belonging to a real or imaginary human group. Without emotional affiliation, "human beings are incapable of leading a bearable life, quite apart from the fact that the process of socialization and education would be impossible without this precondition."[45] The satisfaction of this need "consists in the current emotional relationship with other people, which is normally reciprocal and is expressed in a variety of emotional modes of behavior."[46] While the physiological needs, according to Gasiet, are the first to emerge in the development of a human being, and indeed must be assumed to be the only needs that exist in infancy and early childhood,[47] the ability to develop the emotional need for interpersonal relationships represents the crucial "leap" to actually becoming human.[48] As Mary Clark points out, however, the need for interpersonal relationships does not first emerge ontogenetically in infancy, as Gasiet assumes, but already in the first phase of human development: "Human beings have an absolute need for social intercourse from the first moments of life. Without social contact, babies fail to become people. They may not die, but they do not become fully human; their pre-programmed brains fail to develop normally."[49] Notwithstanding that the physiological needs of humans in general and children in particular cannot be met without interpersonal relationships, Clark emphasizes that the failure to satisfy the need for interpersonal relationships can lead to both physiological and psychological damage:

> [T]here is . . . true physiological depression that occurs following the breaking of long-established bonds. This can occur when isolated

[45] Ibid., 259.

[46] Ibid.

[47] Ibid., 257.

[48] Ibid., 260.

[49] Mary E. Clark, "Meaningful Social Bonding as a Universal Human Need," in *Conflict: Human Needs Theory*, ed. John Burton (New York: Palgrave Macmillan, 1990), 44. Clark provides the following example: "Genie, a girl who had been locked away by her parents all her life, was discovered at age thirteen by Los Angeles authorities, some years ago; she was mute and incontinent, crawled on all fours, and understood nothing that was said to her, a primitive creature without any evidence of mind. But it was not because of gross brain defectiveness; within four years, in foster care, she had developed some language ability, many social skills, and the mental capacity of an eight-year old." Quoted in Morton Hunt, *The Universe Within: A New Science Explores the Human Mind* (New York: Simon & Schuster, 1982), 228. For details on the Genie case, see Russ Rymer, *Genie: A Scientific Tragedy* (New York: Harper Collins, 1993). A related documentary is *The Secret of the Wild Child*, Internet Archive, 1994, https://archive.org/details/the-secret-of-the-wild-child-1994.

> immigrants are immersed in a new culture, or more notably, when a person loses a parent or spouse. This is not only a matter of "psychological" grieving. The entire body suffers, and particularly the immune system. The incidence of death among surviving spouses is significantly higher during the months immediately following the loss. Even the seemingly non-traumatic act of retirement—with its attendant social deprivation—can be accompanied by measurable physiological symptoms.[50]

Clark goes on to emphasize—and here she agrees with Gasiet—that the need for interpersonal relationships is not just a need for community. A person can be isolated even when she is among other people. What is meant is the phenomenon of "meaningful" belonging, which includes shared feelings, values, language, traditions, goals, and so on: "All of these things provide what I call 'sacred meaning' to human life. Without such meaning, life, despite one's being surrounded by multitudes of people, becomes lonely, and all too often leads to physiological deterioration, psychological depression or frequently to both."[51]

The human need that, according to Gasiet, is the third to emerge in phylogenetic and ontogenetic terms, "but has become an indispensable and necessary need in the case of contemporary adult human beings, one involved in all situations of life and in the satisfaction of all needs, is the need for social recognition."[52] A minimum satisfaction of this need, he argues, is "as indispensable for every human being individually and socially as is a minimum of nutrition for her physiological existence."[53] Gasiet suggests that the need for social recognition is expressed especially in the context of asymmetrically structured or antagonistic social relationships, which is why it gives rise to most conflict situations in individual and social life.[54] To recognize a person or to grant him or her a social status means "firstly, according him or her the right of autonomous decision (responsibility and authorization) in a certain area, and secondly, conceding that I, as the one who recognizes, do not claim

[50] Ibid., 45. Hans Selye, *Stress in Health and Disease* (Boston: Buttersworths, 1976), 241 makes the following observation about this: "Separation of infants from their mothers, and all types of relocation of people into strange environments which leave few possibilities for interpersonal contacts, are very common forms of sensory deprivation; they may become major factors in psychosomatic disease."

[51] Clark, "Meaningful Social Bonding as a Universal Human Need," 47.

[52] Gasiet, *Menschliche Bedürfnisse*, 264.

[53] Ibid., 265.

[54] Ibid., 264. However, Gasiet does not rule out the possibility that the need for recognition also finds expression in nonhierarchical relationships.

this right in the same area."[55] According to Gasiet, this is obvious in the case of recognizing a superior or a commander but not in the case of recognizing a subordinate: "Although human beings can survive temporarily (as slaves, infants, people with serious physical or mental illnesses, etc.) below the minimum level of a dignified existence, a humanly bearable life, even among the lowest strata of society, must satisfy the condition that it allows a minimum degree of autonomy, at least in certain 'private' areas."[56]

It is striking that Gasiet uses a very narrow concept of recognition here, which seems to be limited to the component of respect or esteem. He is referring to one of three forms of recognition that Axel Honneth distinguishes following Hegel and Mead.[57] Honneth assumes that human ego formation depends on the internalization of socially reactive behavior that has the character of intersubjective recognition. Through various forms of recognition, he argues, human beings learn to develop a core of personality consisting of various "levels" of a positive self-relation each of which corresponds to an increased capacity for autonomy. Among the most ontologically basic forms of recognition, Honneth considers emotional affection, the stable internalization of which enables the growing child to develop existential self-confidence. By this is meant not so much confidence in one's personal capabilities as the ability to understand the needs and desires experienced internally as an articulable part of one's self. The second form of recognition, to which Gasiet also refers in this context, is respect. According to Honneth, the relation to self of the person who is sufficiently respected by others takes the form of self-respect, which can be violated or even destroyed by discrimination or deprivation of rights. While emotional affection emphasizes the uniqueness of the person and respect seeks to emphasize the aspect of human equality or equal rights, the third form of recognition, esteem, is a matter of emphasizing the specificity of the person, that is, his or her qualities, capabilities, or achievements. Through the experience of social esteem, people learn to recognize themselves as valuable members of their community and, as a result, develop a sense of self-worth that can be undermined by acts of humiliation and stigmatization. "Within these perspectives," Charles Taylor writes, "misrecognition shows not just a lack of due respect. It can

[55] Ibid.
[56] Ibid.
[57] See Axel Honneth, *The Struggle for Recognition: The Moral Grammar of Social Conflicts*, trans. Joel Anderson (Cambridge, MA: MIT Press, 1996), ch. 5.

inflict a grievous wound, saddling its victims with crippling self-hatred. Due recognition is not just a courtesy we owe people. It is a vital human need."[58]

This brief description of Honneth's notion of recognition already reveals an important difference from Gasiet's classification of needs. In contrast to Honneth, who subsumes the phenomenon of love or emotional affection under the notion of recognition, Gasiet's classification assumes that emotional affection should be subsumed under the need for emotional interpersonal relationships, while the phenomenon of social recognition or respect represents a category of needs. According to Gasiet, this is due to the fact that the two phenomena are based on different spheres of social interaction. Whereas emotional affection occurs in the context of primary or close social relationships (family, friendship, and romantic relationships) and should be seen as one of their "products,"[59] social respect occurs in the context of a "fundamentally antagonistic relationship."[60]

Notwithstanding the fact that social respect, too, is nothing other than a product of interpersonal relations,[61] it seems questionable whether the categorical separation of emotional affection and social respect can be justified solely by attributing their production or reproduction to different spheres of human interaction. For Honneth is also aware that the different forms of recognition are based on different spheres of social interaction. In my view, therefore, it would make more sense to follow Honneth and assume that emotional affection, respect, and esteem are different forms of the same practice, each reproduced in a separate sphere of social interaction.

At the same time, this observation allows us to give substance to the need for interpersonal relations cited by Gasiet. For Gasiet describes this category in one place as the need for "humanity, affection, and love"[62] and in another as a need for "belonging to a real or imaginary human group,"[63] without realizing that these are two very different phenomena. Thus, to the extent that we consider affection or love to be one of the integral components of the need for recognition, the need for interpersonal relationships can be limited to the need for (group) membership, the nonsatisfaction of which, as Gasiet

[58] Charles Taylor, *Multiculturalism: Examining the Politics of Recognition*, ed. Amy Gutmann (Princeton, NJ: Princeton University Press, 1994), 26.
[59] Gasiet, *Menschliche Bedürfnisse*, 262.
[60] Ibid., 46.
[61] Gasiet confirms this himself: "For [social] recognition is the result—or the expression—of an interpersonal relationship; it is bestowed on a human being by others who recognize her" (ibid., 69).
[62] Ibid., 327.
[63] Ibid., 259.

points out, can lead to identity crises or alienation, among other problems.[64] In this context, it is interesting to note Honneth's thesis that the human need to belong is directly related to the human need for recognition.[65] The individual's dependence on experiences of recognition, Honneth argues, explains why subjects seek membership or belonging in different kinds of social groupings. Each form of recognition (love, respect, or esteem) on which a person depends in the course of his or her development corresponds to a different form of group membership that he or she seeks. Within this framework, the group performs the function of giving new concrete substance to intersubjective recognition and, accordingly, can be understood "as a social mechanism that serves the interests or needs of the individual by helping him or her to achieve personal stability and growth."[66] Thus, according to Honneth, we are justified in assuming "that subjects have a very normal and even natural need to be recognized as members in social groups in which they can receive constant affirmation of their needs, judgments and various skills in direct interactions with others."[67] According to Honneth, this is also how Adorno should be understood when he says, "The obvious precondition for all humanity is the intimate closeness to other persons, and therefore membership in groups that enable immediate human contact."[68]

Let us now return to Gasiet's classification of needs and examine the last need included in it, the need for meaning. According to Gasiet, this implies the need to give "meaning" to the renunciation of need satisfaction (which refers to all forms of hardship, suffering, and deprivation), which is expressed, among other ways, in the fact that "the impossibility of satisfying the need for meaning becomes an almost unbearable torment, whether as a result of an objectively absurd situation or simply because of the subjective inability to invest a normal (and thus meaning-enabling) situation with meaning."[69] Although this need appears to emerge phylogenetically and ontogenetically later than other needs, it is expressed as an overriding need

[64] The same need is implied when Clark speaks of "meaningful social bonding" or a "physiologically-based need for identity within a social group." Clark, "Meaningful Social Bonding as a Universal Human Need," 54.

[65] See Axel Honneth, "The I in We: Recognition as a Driving Force of Group Formation," in Honneth, *The I in We: Studies in the Theory of Recognition*, trans. Joseph Ganahl (Cambridge, UK: Polity, 2012), 201–216.

[66] Ibid., 203.

[67] Ibid., 206.

[68] Institut für Sozialforschung, ed., *Soziologische Exkurse: Nach Vorträgen und Diskussionen* (Frankfurt: Europäische Verlagsanstalt, 1956), 64, quoted in Honneth, *The I in We*, 212.

[69] Gasiet, *Menschliche Bedürfnisse*, 273.

especially in exceptional or crisis situations.[70] In other words, the basic need to give meaning is generated by borderline experiences such as suffering, illness, pain, separation, isolation, and victimization.[71]

It should be emphasized that conferring meaning should be understood not only in a causal sense ("Why?"), but also and especially in a purposive sense ("For what?").[72] The causal question "Why?" looks to the past for a cause that might explain suffering. For example, classical medicine asks the "why" of diseases by trying to determine how they came about. The knowledge gained from this question can then be used to prevent the recurrence of disease. The past-oriented determination of the causes of suffering reflects the attempt to gain a sense of control over the processes involved.[73] In contrast, the future-oriented question "For what?" seeks a teleological meaning, a purpose that makes it possible to justify the suffering experienced. In this framework, meaning is the answer to the question of why a person experiences a particular form of suffering and for what purpose he or she can live with and in spite of that suffering. In other words, meaning is the "wherefore" that enables the individual to transcend the specific situation.[74] Jan Hauser points out that especially in cases where causal investigations are not particularly productive or relevant (e.g., psychosomatic illnesses, chronic suffering, and fatal diseases), giving purposeful meaning is crucial to successfully coping with the illness.[75] It is, he argues, "an acknowledged fact that especially in situations that are considered hopeless from a medical point of view, finding meaning can initiate a process of coping that can sometimes extend to remission or even recovery."[76]

The neurologist and psychiatrist Viktor Frankl (1909–1997), who because of his Jewish origins was deported to several concentration camps and

[70] Ibid., 272.

[71] Empirical confirmation of this is provided by Paul T. Wong and Bernard Weiner, "When People Ask 'Why' Questions and the Heuristics of Attributional Search," *Journal of Personality and Social Psychology* 40, no. 4 (1981): 650–663.

[72] See Jan Hauser, *Vom Sinn des Leidens: Die Bedeutung systemtheoretischer, existenzphilosophischer und religiös-spiritueller Anschauungsweisen für die therapeutische Praxis* (Würzburg: Königshausen & Neumann, 2004), 151–155.

[73] Ibid., 153.

[74] Ibid.

[75] Ibid., 154.

[76] Ibid., 155. In this context, Hauser refers, among others, to the studies of Lawrence LeShan, *You Can Fight for Your Life: Emotional Factors in the Treatment of Cancer* (Lanham, MD: Rowman & Littlefield, 2014); Dieter Wyss, "Biographie als Sinngebung des Sinnlosen?," *Zeitschrift für klinische Psychologie, Psychopathologie und Psychotherapie* 32 (1984): 100–111; Herbert Csef and Annette Kube, "Sinnfindung als Modus der Krankheitsverarbeitung bei Krebskranken," in *Sinnverlust und Sinnfindung in Gesundheit und Krankheit: Gedenkschrift zu Ehren von D. Wyss*, ed. Herbert Csef (Würzburg: Königshausen & Neumann, 1998), 325–343.

witnessed the deaths of his parents and his wife, impressively described how crucial the need to confer meaning is to human life and survival. In the concentration camp, Frankl noticed that the chances of survival of those who were no longer able to give meaning to their lives decreased dramatically.[77] According to Frankl, people can survive only if they live for something.[78] Thus he ascribes to human beings an existential need for meaning, "that is, the deeply inherent human need to find meaning in one's life, or perhaps better expressed, to find meaning in every single situation of life—and to approach it and fulfill it. For the sake of such fulfillment of meaning, people are also ready to suffer, should this prove necessary. Conversely, if they are not aware of any meaning in their lives, then they could not care less about life, no matter how well they may be doing externally, and under certain circumstances even throw it away."[79] Under the pressure of circumstance, or by their own free choice, people seem to be able to endure extreme deprivation if they see a meaning in it.[80] On the other hand, when the need to give meaning is frustrated, it can lead to pathologies and, as the following quotation from Tolstoy shows, in the worst case, even to death:

> My question—that which at the age of fifty brought me to the verge of suicide—was the simplest of questions, lying in the soul of every man from the foolish child to the wisest elder: it was a question without an answer to which one cannot live, as I found by experience. It was: "What will come of what I am doing today or shall do tomorrow? What will come of my whole life?" Differently expressed, the question is: "Why should I live,

[77] See Viktor Frankl, *Man's Search for Meaning* (New York: Pocket Books, 1985), esp. 88–115. Similar conclusions are drawn by Etty Hillesum (1914–1943), a Dutch Jewish writer who recorded her experiences with people in concentration camps in a diary published posthumously as *An Interrupted Life: The Diaries 1941–1943 and Letters from Westerbork* (New York: Henry Holt, 1996). There Hillesum describes, among other things, how important it was for her to find meaning in order to deal with the suffering she experienced in herself and others: "Life and suffering had lost their meaning for me; I felt I was about to collapse under a tremendous weight. But once again I put up a fight and now I can face it all, stronger than before. I have tried to look that 'suffering' of mankind fairly and squarely in the face. I have fought it out, or rather something inside me has fought it out, and suddenly there were answers to many desperate questions, and the sense of emptiness made way for the feeling that there was order and meaning after all and I could get on with my life" (30–31). The importance of conferring meaning becomes especially evident when Hillesum describes how important it is for human survival: "People are dying here even now of a broken spirit, because they can no longer find any meaning in life, young people. The old ones are rooted in firmer soil and accept their fate with dignity and calm. You see so many different sorts of people here, and so many different attitudes to the hardest, ultimate questions" (295).

[78] Viktor E. Frankl, *Der Wille zum Sinn* (Bern: Hogrefe, 2005), 30.

[79] Ibid., 189.

[80] Gasiet, *Menschliche Bedürfnisse*, 274.

> why wish for anything, or do anything?" It can also be expressed thus: "Is there any meaning in my life that the inevitable death awaiting me does not destroy?"[81]

In order to avoid misunderstandings concerning the notion of giving meaning, another brief observation about how the need to give meaning can be satisfied should be mentioned. What is certain is that meaning does not arise and is not given from the outside, but must always be found in the sense that Frankl describes.[82] How and where this meaning is found, whether in religion, in certain worldviews, or in certain values, depends on the individual. In this respect, as Gasiet points out, the satisfaction of the need for meaning is no different from the satisfaction of other needs: "[I]n its true and definitive sense, it is always quite individual."[83]

Needs from the Perspective of Peace and Conflict Research

In the introduction, I alluded to the fact that human needs are the subject of research in a wide range of scientific disciplines. Another discipline whose findings I would like to consider briefly here is peace and conflict research. It is of particular interest for our purposes because it establishes a direct link between the issue of human needs and the phenomenon of violent conflict.

John Burton deserves special credit for giving prominence to the insight that the resolution of violent conflicts is to a considerable extent bound up with the fulfillment or nonfulfillment of human needs. Burton suggests that human beings have specific and universal needs that they seek to satisfy *in all circumstances*.[84] In addition to physiological needs, these include needs for identity, recognition, security, rationality, and control.[85] Conflicts arise, Burton argues, precisely when social institutions and structures systematically frustrate or suppress the fulfillment of these needs: "It is the politically realistic observation that, unless there is development and fulfillment of needs of individuals and groups, unless problems are solved and the need for

81 Leo Tolstoy, *A Confession* (Scotts Valley, CA: CreateSpace, 2017), 19–20.
82 Frankl, *Der Wille zum Sinn*, 27.
83 Gasiet, *Menschliche Bedürfnisse*, 215.
84 John Burton, *Deviance, Terrorism and War: The Process of Solving Unsolved Social and Political Problems* (Oxford: Martin Robertson, 1979), 76.
85 Ibid., 75. "These are the sociopsychological and sociobiological needs that finally underpin, modify or destroy institutions."

coercion avoided, a social and political order may not be stable and harmonious, no matter what the levels of coercion. Protest movements, violence at all social levels, terrorism, communal conflicts, dissident behavior, strikes, revolts, revolutions and wars are observable symptoms of unobservable motivations and needs."[86] Sustainable conflict resolution, Burton argues, requires reforming social institutions and structures in ways that enable people to meet their needs. In this sense, human needs are the primary navigational or reference point for conflict resolution, since they make it possible both to identify the causes of conflict and to determine the preconditions that enable the stable and harmonious existence of social systems: "Problem-solving at the social level—be it the small groups, the nation-state or interactions between states—is possible only by processes that take the needs of the individual as the basis for analyzing and planning. Any settlement of a conflict or attempt to order society that places the interests of institutions or even of the total society before those of its individual members, must fail."[87]

Like Burton, Coate and Rossi suggest that the stability of social structures depends on the extent to which they enable people to satisfy their needs: "[H]uman needs are a powerful source of explanation of human behavior and social interaction in international relations. . . . All individuals have needs that they strive to satisfy, either by using the system and working within the norms of mainstream society, or by socially deviant behavior in the form of withdrawal, acting on the fringes (e.g., criminal behavior), or acting as a reformist or revolutionary (e.g., mass movement behavior). Given this condition, social (including international) systems must be responsive to individual needs—or be subject to instability and forced change (possibly through violence or conflict)."[88]

In this quote, Coate and Rossi, like Burton, express that people have certain needs that they seek to satisfy under all circumstances. Based on this, they argue that people tend to engage in "socially deviant behavior" when their needs are violated by the ruling system. Burton agrees with this thesis with certain reservations. While it is true, he argues, that people strive to satisfy their needs even in times of structural oppression, and are thus forced to take extrastructural measures, this behavior should not be characterized

[86] John Burton, *Global Conflict: The Domestic Sources of International Crisis* (Brighton: Wheatsheaf, 1984), 12–13.

[87] Burton, *Deviance, Terrorism and War*, 79.

[88] Roger A. Coate and Jerel A. Rosati, eds., *The Power of Human Needs in World Society* (Boulder, CO: Lynne Rienner, 1988), ix.

as "socially deviant," because a person's needs-oriented nature leaves him with no other choice: "[H]e is needs-oriented, he is not capable of deviating from the pursuit of needs."[89] In other words, people cannot integrate themselves into a social system that forces them to renounce the satisfaction of their needs, because these are "non-negotiable interests."[90] Accordingly, the relevant question is "not which members of society fit social structures, but what social structures fit human needs."[91] According to Burton, therefore, institutions, structures, conventions, norms, laws, or administrative procedures that make it impossible for people to satisfy their needs should be described as "socially deviant."[92] In fact, he goes a step further and claims that a ruling order can be deemed *legitimate* only if it is capable of satisfying human needs. The concept of political legitimacy thus refers not only to the process by which a ruling order comes into being but also to the actual ability of that order to meet the needs of those who are ruled.[93] Note again that Burton is thinking not only of physiological needs but also of the needs for identity, recognition, security, rationality, and control.

This is not the place to explore the complexities that arise from the postulated link between these needs and the concept of political legitimacy. For our purposes, however, it is important to note that the needs identified by Burton are broadly consistent with the classifications discussed earlier. Nevertheless, a brief remark is in order to assess the need for control cited by Burton. As Sites points out, the notion of control here refers less to a need in itself than to the motive of ensuring the availability of the *means* that enable people to satisfy their needs. The fact that people must satisfy their needs and depend on relevant resources to do so thus motivates them to "control" the availability of these resources in order to ensure the satisfaction process.[94]

Before concluding this chapter, I would like to take a brief look at a classification of needs developed by Johann Galtung in the context of peace and conflict research. Galtung distinguishes between actor-dependent and structure-dependent needs.[95] Needs are actor-dependent when their satisfaction depends on the inclinations and actions of certain actors.[96] Actors in

89 Burton, *Deviance, Terrorism and War*, 183.
90 John Burton, *Conflict: Resolution and Provention* (New York: Macmillan, 1990), 36.
91 Burton, *Deviance, Terrorism and War*, 183.
92 Ibid.
93 Ibid., 130.
94 See Paul Sites, "Needs as Analogues of Emotions," in Burton, *Conflict*, 7 25–26.
95 See Johan Galtung, *Human Rights in Another Key* (Cambridge, UK: Polity, 1994), 56–58.
96 Ibid., 69.

this context include individuals, states, and other (national or international) groups and organizations.[97] Needs, in contrast, are structure-dependent when their frustration cannot be attributed to specific actions or identifiable actors but is conditioned by structures that are constituted in such a way that they lead to systematic violations of needs.[98] An example of this is the global economic order, which forces a large part of humanity to live in poverty and oppression so that even basic needs such as food remain unsatisfied.[99]

The reference to structural violations of needs raises an important point, the relevance of which is particularly evident in the field of human rights. Unlike state actors, who are the primary addressees of human rights in the classical human rights paradigm, structures cannot be prosecuted or brought to justice. In other words, structures cannot be held accountable, even when fundamental violations of needs are attributable to them. On the other hand, structures do not emerge and exist on their own, but are always maintained by certain actors. The conclusion to be drawn for human rights, which we will return to later, is therefore that human rights claims should not be limited to violations by the classical actor, the state, but must include in addition all those violations that result from a structure that violates needs. According to Galtung, how a need is violated also depends on whether its satisfaction depends on material or nonmaterial components. Taken together with the criterion of structural dependence, this results in a needs matrix in which four categories of needs can be identified: (a) survival needs to avoid violence, (b) well-being needs to avoid misery, (c) freedom needs to avoid oppression, and (d) identity needs to avoid alienation (Figure 12.1).[100]

Without going into the validity of the distinctions between material and nonmaterial and between actor-dependent and structure-dependent needs, we can state that the classification of needs developed by Galtung, despite conceptual differences, corresponds to the rough pattern of the classifications discussed so far. Like Burton, Galtung uses the concept of identity to describe the need to belong, the nonsatisfaction of which (as noted above) leads to identity crises or alienation. In doing so, Galtung subsumes the need for meaning under the concept of identity,[101] but this seems unjustified, since

[97] Ibid., 21–22.
[98] Ibid., 57.
[99] For a general discussion, see Thomas Pogge, *World Poverty and Human Rights* (Cambridge, UK: Polity, 2008).
[100] Galtung, *Human Rights in Another Key*, 57.
[101] Personal communication, Frankfurt am Main, May 9, 2011.

	Actor-dependent	*Structure-dependent*
Material	Survival (violence)	Well-being (misery)
Non-material	Freedom (oppression)	Identity (alienation)

Figure 12.1 Matrix of needs according to Galtung.

alienation and loss of meaning are distinct phenomena. Moreover, Galtung's choice of the notion of survival to describe the need for security seems to me unfortunate, since human survival is the result of the satisfaction of a variety of needs and does not depend exclusively on the existence of security. Furthermore, it seems to me more coherent to subsume the need for freedom cited by Galtung under the concept of recognition, since recognition of a person also implies—though it does not imply only—respect for him or her as an autonomous being. In line with this, Gasiet also notes that "recognition" means precisely "granting someone the 'freedom' to make decisions in a certain area as he sees fit, as if he were actually 'free' to do so."[102]

Summary

A review of the research literature discussed here reveals a remarkable congruence regarding the needs that must be attributed to human beings as such. This allows us to begin to answer our initial question about the nature and scope of human needs. On the basis of our evaluation, we can distill from the wealth of differently accentuated contributions from various scientific disciplines a total of five categories of needs, which can be summarized as follows:

1. The need for physiological health.
2. The need for security.
3. The need for belonging.

[102] Gasiet, *Menschliche Bedürfnisse*, 169.

4. The need for recognition.
5. The need for meaning.

We certainly cannot rule out the possibility of a different, perhaps even more plausible categorization of human needs. This is based on the fact that, as Gasiet emphasizes, human needs can be adequately assessed only from a "comprehensive anthropological" perspective in which "the entire knowledge of the human and social sciences and findings from biology and other natural sciences are used as far as possible in an interdisciplinary manner."[103] Such an analysis is not possible within the scope of the present study. Nevertheless, it does not seem to me too bold to assert that the above list of human needs can claim a reasonable degree of plausibility and scientific validity. Although the scientific validity of this list of needs can only be postulated in the Popperian sense, its plausibility is measured by the extent to which it can satisfy two necessary criteria.

The first criterion is that a list of needs can be deemed plausible only if the individual needs it contains are mutually exclusive, that is, if they cannot be subordinated to any other needs. For example, although the needs for food, clothing, and sleep are different, they can all be subsumed under the need for physiological health and, in this sense, represent partial aspects of it. This suggests that individual needs can always be further differentiated. For example, the need for food can be further subdivided into the need for certain nutrients or a certain number of calories, depending on the degree of specificity of the description. Such specifications, however, must be made in the context of concrete problems and questions, so that they are initially irrelevant for establishing a general list of human needs.

The second criterion that such a list of needs must meet if it is to claim plausibility is that the needs must collectively cover the totality of human needs. Again, it should be noted that human needs have been characterized here as universal, objective, and necessary conditions of individual and communal human existence. Accordingly, it must be shown to what extent these qualifications are met by a potential need candidate.[104] Based on

[103] Ibid., 244.

[104] For example, in his *Versuch einer Theorie der Bedürfnisse*, Lujo Brentano cites a list of needs that includes "care for death" and "provision for the future." It is doubtful, however, whether these are goods that can be regarded as human needs in the sense defended here. See Lujo Brentano, *Versuch einer Theorie der Bedürfnisse* (Munich: Verlag der Königlich Bayerischen Akademie der Wissenschaften, 1908), 12.

these criteria and the research literature discussed here, we can conclude that the needs for physiological health, security, belonging, recognition, and meaning are the basic constants that represent the universal, objective, and necessary conditions of human existence, regardless of cultural and historical differences.

13

Human Rights as Institutions for the Protection of Human Needs

Given the centrality of human needs to human existence, I will now argue that human rights can be most plausibly justified if they are understood as institutions for the protection of human needs.

As I emphasized at the beginning of the previous chapter, a justification of human rights should meet three criteria. First, it should be able to explain the *moral relevance* of human rights, since a justification should be able to show why and how it is important for people to have certain rights. Second, it should be able to explain *which rights* are involved, or at least show how the content of human rights can be specified. And third, it should do so in a way that everyone can in principle understand and accept—in other words, it should be able to command *universal agreement*.

I believe that these criteria can be met if we justify human rights in terms of human needs. The moral relevance of human rights can be explained by the fact that they serve to protect elementary and necessary needs without which human existence would be threatened. As we have seen, these needs are independent of subjective attitudes and are therefore ethically neutral and intersubjectively justifiable. In this sense, human needs provide a foundation for human rights that can command universal agreement, while at the same time defining the substantive frame of reference for human rights. Which rights in particular are to be regarded as human rights depends accordingly on whether and in what sense a right can contribute to the protection of human needs.

Recourse to the *maqāṣid al-sharīʿa*

In order to develop these ideas further, I would now like to propose an explanatory model whose basic features are based on the concept of *maqāṣid al-sharīʿa* presented in the second part of this book. Let us recall that the

Human Rights Between Universality and Islamic Legitimacy. Mahmoud Bassiouni, Oxford University Press.
 DOI: 10.1093/oso/9780197753897.003.0014

idea at the core of this concept is that the purpose of Islamic law is to protect basic human needs. The majority of classical jurists, including al-Ghazāli (d. 1111),[1] al-Rāzi (d. 1209),[2] al-Āmidi (d. 1233),[3] and al-Shātibi (d. 1388),[4] assume that these needs can be narrowed down to exactly five universal necessities of human existence, the "universal goods" (*kulliyāt*)—namely life, reason, offspring, property, and religion.[5] This follows from empirical observation of human reality and from an inductive analysis of Islamic legal sources, which, according to these jurists, shows that Islamic legal norms pursue the protection of precisely these needs. In this sense, therefore, they represent the purposes (*maqāṣid*) of Islamic law. This is not the place to reexamine the validity of this line of argument. However, our analysis of the various justifications showed[6] that the needs identified by the jurists do not satisfy the postulated premises of necessity, universality, and empirical demonstrability, so that in the previous chapter we tried to identify those goods that can satisfy these criteria.

For present purposes, it is relevant to recall the arguments of Muslim jurists concerning how Islamic law protects these needs. According to al-Ghazāli, (a) anything that leads to the protection of these needs constitutes a good (*maṣlaḥa*), while (b) anything that jeopardizes the protection of these needs constitutes an evil (*mafsada*), with (c) the elimination of an evil simultaneously constituting a good.[7] Since not all goods contribute equally to the protection of the above-mentioned needs, however, the classical jurists further distinguish three different levels of goods, which differ in their respective degrees of urgency:[8]

1. Necessary goods (*ḍarūriyāt*) counteract those evils that directly prevent the protection of a need and thus endanger human existence as such. For example, manslaughter is an evil that directly threatens human life, so that preventing manslaughter is a necessary good.
2. Required goods (*ḥājiyāt*) counteract those evils that severely impair the protection of a need and thus prevent a tolerable human existence.

[1] Al-Ghazāli, *al-Mustaṣfa min 'Ilm al-Uṣūl*, 2:482.
[2] Al-Rāzi, *al-Maḥṣūl fī 'Ilm Uṣūl al-Fiqh*, 5:160.
[3] Al-Āmidi, *al-Aḥkām fī Uṣūl al-Aḥkām*, 3:240.
[4] Al-Shāṭibi, *al-Muwāfaqāt*, 1:324.
[5] Other jurists, such as al-Qarāfi (d. 1285), al-Ṭūfi (d. 1316), Ibn al-Subki (d. 1370), and al-Shawkāni (d. 1834), add "honor" (*al-'irḍ*) to this list.
[6] See chapter 9.
[7] Al-Ghazāli, *al-Mustaṣfa*, 2:482.
[8] Ibid., 2:482–485.

For example, the evil of poverty does not directly make life impossible, but it severely impairs life. Measures to prevent poverty are therefore a required good.

3. Ameliorative goods (*taḥsīniyāt*) counteract those evils that prevent a decent level of existence and indirectly endanger the protection of a need. An unhealthy diet, for example, can lead to diseases that severely impair life. The creation of social conditions that facilitate a healthy diet is therefore an ameliorative good.

This classification is intended to clarify the priorities of Islamic law with respect to the protection of the aforementioned universal needs. Accordingly, the highest priority of Islamic law is the realization of the necessary goods, which derive their relevance from their indispensability for the protection of human needs. Their absence would constitute a threat to human existence as such. The next priority of Islamic law is to realize those goods that are required to enable human beings not only to survive but also to live a reasonably tolerable life. In addition, the law also seeks to enable human beings to live decently. The ameliorative goods serve this purpose by optimizing the protection of the human needs. In this sense, necessary, required, and ameliorative goods represent interdependent mechanisms of different degrees of importance that aim to protect human needs with different priorities. In this way, they enable successively higher levels of human existence, from survival to a tolerable life to a decent life.[9]

Human Rights between Needs and Threats

Let us now try to put these thoughts to work for our purposes, starting with the tentative thesis (following al-Ghazāli) that whatever serves to protect human needs is a human right, while whatever prevents their protection is a threat, the elimination of which simultaneously constitutes a human right. According to this thesis, then, we can speak of a human right when we can show that it can protect a human need from some threat. Which specific human rights exist depends on which need is endangered by which threat.

As explained in the previous chapter, people are needy in very different ways, which means that they can be threatened or injured in very different

[9] See al-Shāṭibi, *al-Muwāfaqāt*, 327.

ways. Physical violence, for example, is something that threatens people's need for security. According to our thesis, therefore, a human right to physical integrity can be asserted because this right serves to protect human security from physical violence. Of course, it can do so only if the right is addressed to someone who has a duty to refrain from physical violence. Thus the operative notion of a right necessarily implies the existence of an addressee who has an obligation to fulfill the right claim in question. As mentioned in the previous chapter, it should be kept in mind that human rights, unlike moral rights, are not directly addressed to individuals but are claims that are primarily addressed to the ruling political order.[10] Human rights treaties make this clear when they oblige "each State Party to the present Covenant"[11] or the "High Contracting Parties"[12] to protect the specified rights in respect of "everyone within their jurisdiction."[13] In this sense, human rights are *politically* oriented norms, since their primary aim is to obligate the collective political order, rather than individual moral subjects, to act in certain ways. But the political orientation of human rights is by no means incompatible with their moral character. Following Pollmann, we could also describe them as "morally justified claims to basic rights that are to be politically realized."[14] If we incorporate this aspect into our thesis, then human rights are all those claims that oblige a ruling political order to take actions that serve to protect human needs against threats. But what kind of actions are we talking about? How exactly can and should human needs be protected by a ruling political order? What does it mean to assert a human right to physical integrity?

First of all, it clearly means that a ruling political order must, in principle, refrain from using physical force against its subjects.[15] This *duty of*

[10] See Menke and Pollmann, *Philosophie der Menschenrechte*, 29–32; Nickel, *Making Sense of Human Rights*, 38–41, 147; Pogge, *World Poverty and Human Rights*, 63–73; Beitz, *The Idea of Human Rights*, 109; Christian Reus-Smit, "On Rights and Institutions," in *Global Basic Rights*, ed. Charles Beitz and Robert Goodin (Oxford: Oxford University Press, 2009), 25–48; Forst, "The Right to Justification," 733, 738–739.

[11] See Article 2 of the International Covenant on Civil and Political Rights and Article 2 of the International Covenant on Economic, Social and Cultural Rights.

[12] See Article 1 of the European Convention on Human Rights.

[13] Ibid.

[14] See Pollmann, "Von der philosophischen Begründung zur demokratischen Konkretisierung," 11. A detailed discussion of this topic can be found in Menke and Pollmann, *Philosophie der Menschenrechte*, 29–41.

[15] In what follows, I will use the term "state" as a synonym for a ruling political order without implying that such an order can only take the form of a state. Rebels who manage to seize effective power of government in a country can likewise constitute a ruling political order, although this usually leads to the establishment of new state structures. Furthermore, supranational orders could also be described as ruling insofar as they are in possession of the effective power of government in a country. Such cases cannot as yet be observed in our era, despite supranational influences on national structures.

forbearance applies to all state organs, authorities, and functionaries, as well as to all actors whose actions can be attributed to the state.[16] This includes private actors entrusted with public functions, such as employees of a private security firm who run a prison on behalf of the state. If they mistreat a prisoner, this constitutes a human rights violation attributable to the state. The actions of private individuals who are formally entrusted with the performance of public functions, but who act on behalf of or under the direction or control of the state, may also be imputed to the state. This is the case, for example, when organs of the state recruit thugs to commit acts of violence against opposition demonstrators. Purely private acts—that is, violent attacks by private individuals that are not committed at the behest or under the direction or control of the state—cannot be attributed to the state. Thus if a person is physically injured by another person or group in the course of private business, this may be a violation of a moral or legal right, but it is not a violation of a human right to physical integrity.[17]

This does not mean, however, that it is sufficient to satisfy a human rights claim to physical integrity for the state to refrain from physical violence itself. A human right to physical integrity also implies that it is the duty of the state to protect people from physical violence by nonstate actors.[18] Thus, in addition to the mere duty of forbearance, the state also has a positive *duty of prevention*, which must be fulfilled through appropriate legislation and active measures. Accordingly, we can also speak of a human rights violation when the state fails to legally criminalize violent attacks by private agents and fails to protect demonstrators from violent counterdemonstrators through

[16] The interrelated questions of who belongs to the "state" as an obligated party and which human rights violation can be imputed to the state are dealt with in the "Draft Articles on the Responsibility of States for Internationally Wrongful Acts," which were codified in 2001 by the International Law Commission of the UN: http://eydner.org. A helpful summary of these draft articles, on which I draw in what follows, can be found in Walter Kälin and Jörg Künzli, *Universeller Menschenrechtsschutz* (Basel: Helbing & Lichtenhahn, 2005), 87–90.

[17] Menke and Pollmann, *Philosophie der Menschenrechte*, 29.

[18] The UN Human Rights Committee, which is responsible for monitoring the International Covenant on Civil and Political Rights, notes in this context, "However the positive obligations on States Parties to ensure Covenant rights will only be fully discharged if individuals are protected by the State, not just against violations of Covenant rights by its agents, but also against acts committed by private persons or entities that would impair the enjoyment of Covenant rights.... There may be circumstances in which a failure to ensure Covenant rights ... would give rise to violations by State Parties of those rights, as a result of States Parties' permitting or failing to take appropriate measures or to exercise due diligence to prevent, punish, investigate or redress the harm caused by such acts by private persons or entities." See item 8 of the United Nations Human Rights Committee, *General Comment No. 31: The Nature of the General Legal Obligation Imposed on States Parties to the Covenant*, 2004, http://daccess-dds-ny.un.org/doc/UNDOC/GEN/G04/419/56/PDF/G0441956.pdf?OpenElement.

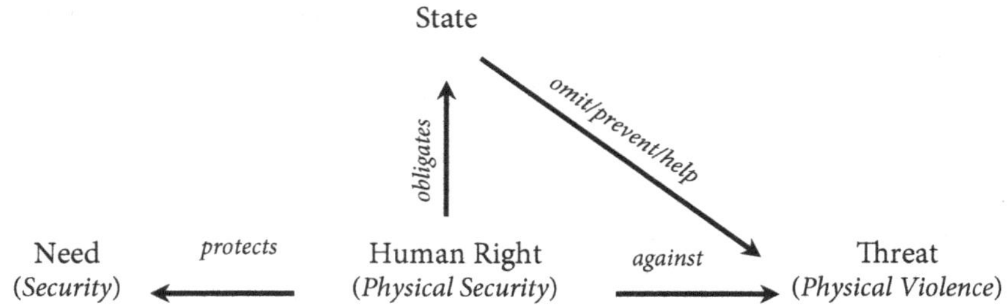

Figure 13.1 Human rights as institutions for the protection of human needs.

appropriate police action. Thus, although the right to physical integrity is addressed vertically to the state, it also has a horizontal effect on relations between individuals who have a duty, albeit only an indirect one, to refrain from physical violence.[19]

If people nevertheless become victims of physical violence involuntarily, although preventive measures have been taken, the state has an additional *duty of assistance*. In the case of injured demonstrators, government officials would have to ensure that emergency paramedical services and medical facilities are available and equipped with the necessary means to treat physical injuries as quickly and effectively as possible. When a state fails or refuses to provide the necessary institutions and infrastructure, we can also speak of a human rights violation. The human right to physical integrity thus implies a threefold obligation on the part of the state to refrain from using physical force, to prevent its use by third parties, and to assist those who are victims of it (see Figure 13.1).[20] In this sense, the human right to physical integrity serves to protect the human need for security.

In this context, one might wonder why we speak of the "protection" of human needs rather than, for example, of their "satisfaction" or "fulfillment." This is mainly because the role of the state within the tripartite division is largely limited to ensuring that human needs can be satisfied. Except in the case of persons who are not yet (e.g., infants), not fully (e.g., severely disabled persons), or no longer (e.g., persons suffering from old-age dementia) able to do so, people are largely responsible for satisfying their own needs. However, this does not mean that people are exclusively self-sufficient in this

[19] Robert Alexy, *Theorie der Grundrechte* (Frankfurt: Suhrkamp, 1985), 475, speaks of a "third-party effect" of rights in this context.

[20] For this tripartite division, see Shue, *Basic Rights*, 52–64.

respect. On the contrary, people usually depend on one another to satisfy their needs.[21] Although the measures that satisfy the need for health include those that people can take for themselves, such as a healthy diet and sufficient exercise, they also and especially depend on individuals and institutions that possess the necessary medical knowledge. In fact, the actions that individuals can take independently are only possible if certain framework conditions are in place that enable them to meet their needs independently in the first place. People can feed themselves only if they have access to a sustainable food supply. This presupposes the existence of a food supply infrastructure that can guarantee the production of and access to food. In addition, people depend on public goods such as clean air and water to meet their health needs. It would therefore be a mistake to assume that people are always capable of satisfying their needs independently, since they are always dependent on certain social framework conditions, the creation of which is the responsibility of the state.

Here, however, we must distinguish between independence and individuality in the satisfaction of needs. Although people have the same needs regardless of their cultural or historical differences, the satisfaction of these needs always depends on individual preferences, habits, and resources. People dress and eat differently, and they seek recognition or meaning in different ways. In many cases, therefore, it *should not* and *cannot* be the role of government to satisfy people's needs for these things. Quite apart from the fact that this would disregard human autonomy, it would drastically reduce the scope of human rights claims and the related duties of the state. If it were only a matter of satisfying human needs, a state would have already satisfied the human claim to food by ensuring that people were provided with a bare minimum of food. While this may well be one of the state's human rights obligations, it would be a mistake to assume that a human right to food consists solely of material entitlements. On the basis of the above thesis, the human right to food follows from the consideration that a lack of food constitutes a threat to the human need for health. At the first level, therefore, the human right to food obliges the state to *refrain* from contributing to food shortages by, for example, impeding or even destroying access to existing food or to the means necessary for its production. At the second level, the state is faced with the task of taking legislative and active measures to *prevent* food shortages as far as possible. This includes, for example, preventing

[21] See Schmitz, *Bedürfnisse und Gerechtigkeit*, 171–172.

economic agents from hoarding food and subsequently selling it at higher prices. Finally, at the third level, the state has a duty to *assist* those who are unable to feed themselves due to a lack of resources or the necessary skills.

The fact that in many cases human needs *cannot* be met by the state becomes particularly clear when we consider the human need for affection or emotional care. It would be absurd to infer from this need that people have the right to demand or even compel affection from other people, let alone from a political order. This is obviously related to the fact that affection is worthy of the name only when it is offered voluntarily, and that the need for affection can be satisfied only when it comes from someone to whom one feels personally attached. In other words, it is a need that can be satisfied only individually.

It does not follow, however, that one cannot derive any human rights from the need for emotional affection. To do so, according to our thesis above, we must first identify the threats that impair the need for affection. Since affection typically arises in close personal relationships, the absence of such relationships could be considered such a threat.[22] In a further step, we need to flesh out the human rights claims by identifying the duties of the state with respect to this threat that follow within the framework of the three levels of action outlined. For example, in the context of its duty of forbearance, the state could be required to refrain from impeding individuals in their efforts to establish close personal relationships. In this sense, Article 16 of the Universal Declaration of Human Rights emphasizes that "men and women of full age, without any limitation due to race, nationality or religion, have the right to marry and to found a family." At another level, it is the responsibility of the state to create the social framework conditions that enable people to form and maintain their own specific close relationships. This can be achieved, for example, through legislative measures that make it possible to reconcile work and family life. Finally, the state could be called upon to provide assistance when people are objectively prevented from having access to close personal relationships. In this sense, the Convention on the Rights of

[22] How painful the absence of close personal relationships can be is eloquently expressed by David Hume in his *Treatise on Human Nature*: "A perfect solitude is, perhaps, the greatest punishment we can suffer. Every pleasure languishes when enjoy'd a-part from company, and every pain becomes more cruel and intolerable. . . . Let all the powers and elements of nature conspire to serve and obey one man: Let the sun rise and set at his command: The sea and rivers roll as he pleases, and the earth furnish spontaneously whatever may be useful or agreeable to him: He will still be miserable, till you give him some one person at least, with whom he may share his happiness, and whose esteem and friendship he may enjoy." David Hume, *A Treatise on Human Nature* (Oxford: Clarendon Press, 1960), 2:363.

the Child calls on the state to provide assistance when a child is temporarily or permanently deprived of his or her family environment. In this case, the state would have a duty to provide other forms of care, such as placement in a suitable foster family or child care institution.[23]

To summarize these considerations, human rights refer to precisely those claims that are addressed to the state and obligate it to protect the needs of human beings from corresponding threats through omission, prevention, and assistance. Accordingly, we can speak of a violation of human rights whenever the state fails in one of these three respects. But when exactly does such a failure occur?

With respect to the duty of forbearance, this question is relatively easy to answer, since in most cases we can speak of a human rights violation when the state actively contributes to the violation of human needs and thus becomes a threat itself. Exceptions are violations that result from legally permissible sanctions, such as the imprisonment of criminals.

Things become more problematic in the case of the duty of prevention. Here we can principally speak of a violation of human rights when the state fails to prevent threats by third parties or certain threatening situations. It should be emphasized, however, that the notion of failure refers to passive behavior in a situation in which the state could become active. This presupposes, first, that the state recognizes or could have recognized an imminent threat and, second, that it is actually able to prevent that threat.[24] These two criteria would be met, for example, if the state authorities had information about a public demonstration, in which case they would be able to anticipate possible threats in the form of riots or violent confrontations and prevent them through an appropriate police operation. The situation is different, for example, when a woman is subjected to domestic violence. Here we are dealing with an act of violence that the state cannot directly influence due to a lack of information (no knowledge of private living conditions) and

[23] See Article 20 of the Convention on the Rights of the Child: "(1) A child temporarily or permanently deprived of his or her family environment, or in whose own best interests cannot be allowed to remain in that environment, shall be entitled to special protection and assistance provided by the State. (2) States Parties shall in accordance with their national laws ensure alternative care for such a child. (3) Such care could include, inter alia, foster placement, kafalah of Islamic law, adoption or if necessary placement in suitable institutions for the care of children. When considering solutions, due regard shall be paid to the desirability of continuity in a child's upbringing and to the child's ethnic, religious, cultural and linguistic background."

[24] For a detailed account from a legal perspective, see Jörg Künzli, *Zwischen Rigidität und Flexibilität: Der Verpflichtungsgrad internationaler Menschenrechte* (Berlin: Duncker & Humblot, 2001), 239–274.

factual limitations (no direct control over private living conditions), so that it cannot be held responsible for failing to prevent the actual act of violence. In such cases, however, it would be up to the state to recognize that domestic violence is a threat to human needs and to take measures that could, at least indirectly, contribute to the prevention of acts of domestic violence. Thus as part of its duty of prevention, a state would be required to legally sanction and prosecute acts of domestic violence. If it fails to do so, it could be held responsible for tolerating such acts and thus also be accused of a human rights violation. In other words, we can speak of a human rights violation under the duty of prevention when the state was aware of an existing or imminent threat or could have become aware by exercising due diligence but failed to take appropriate measures available to it and permitted by human rights[25] that could have contributed directly or indirectly to averting the threat in question.[26]

With respect to the state's duty of assistance, as in the case of the duty of prevention, a number of conditions must be formulated that must be met before the state can be accused of violating a human right. In principle, the state has a duty to provide assistance when people, through no fault of their own, become victims of a threat and thus find themselves in an emergency situation in which they are objectively prevented from satisfying their own needs. People voluntarily fall victim to a threat when they choose to forgo the satisfaction of their needs and thus accept the suffering that ensues. "Those who fast for religious reasons and voluntarily accept the associated health risks are therefore not in an emergency situation," Wilfried Hinsch observes, "unlike those who involuntarily suffer hunger because they have no way of obtaining food."[27] Withholding aid would therefore constitute a human rights violation only in the latter case, and even then only if—and this brings us to the second condition—the state is actually able to assist people in need. If a state were unable to assist those affected despite using all available resources—for example, in the case of famine—it could avoid the charge

[25] Preventive measures are in principle permissible under human rights law if they can be reconciled with the state's duties of forbearance. In the above case, this would exclude surveillance and intervention in the domestic private sphere. For relevant exceptions, for example in the case of combating terrorism, see the discussion in Künzli, *Zwischen Rigidität und Flexibilität*, 243–245, and Kälin and Künzli, *Universeller Menschenrechtsschutz*, 113–118.

[26] For a more detailed discussion, see Kälin and Künzli, *Universeller Menschenrechtsschutz*, 125–127.

[27] Wilfried Hinsch, *Gerechtfertigte Ungleichheiten: Grundsätze sozialer Gerechtigkeit* (Berlin: de Gruyter, 2002), 182.

of violating human rights.[28] However, it could not do so if the reason for its inability, or the cause of the famine itself, could be traced to an earlier act or omission by the state. As Amartya Sen has shown, this is generally true in the case of famine.[29]

Thus if a state itself has contributed to a threat or failed to take preventive measures to avert a threat, it can be held responsible for its occurrence and thus for the resulting damage. This can be illustrated by the example of the catastrophic oil spill in the Gulf of Mexico in 2010, which was not caused by the U.S. government but was largely attributable to inadequate regulatory measures by the U.S. government.[30] Accordingly, the health damage resulting from the oil spill should be considered a violation of human rights, so that those affected would have the right to hold the state accountable and would have the corresponding right to require it to remedy the damage suffered. This makes it clear that the state's duty to assist involuntary victims of a threat is not an act of charity but rather an act of justice, since the state, by its action or inaction, has contributed to a violation of needs and has incurred a debt that must be repaid. This also makes it clear that the state's duties of assistance and prevention are directly related, in the sense that the adequate fulfillment of the latter makes the fulfillment of the former less burdensome.[31] In other words, the most efficient way for the state to avoid capacity constraints in fulfilling its obligation to assist is by fulfilling its duties of forbearance and prevention. This places limits on the ability of the state to argue that it is unable to meet people's claims for assistance due to a lack of resources.

It is important to note, however, that a state's inability to provide assistance is not always due to a lack of resources. There are indeed cases in which the state, despite having the resources, is unable to assist people who are at risk through no fault of their own. For example, terminal illnesses pose a threat to people's need for health. But it would be absurd to conclude that human beings have a right to be cured of incurable diseases. Accordingly, a human rights claim can be made only if it relates to *foreseeable* and

[28] Here I cannot address the question of who should take responsibility for helping people in need when the state cannot do so. This question can be answered satisfactorily only within the broader framework of global justice.

[29] See Amartya Sen, *Poverty and Famines: An Essay on Entitlement and Deprivation* (Oxford: Clarendon Press, 1983).

[30] See the report of the Center for Progressive Reform, *Regulatory Blowout: How Regulatory Failures Made the BP Disaster Possible, and How the System Can Be Fixed to Avoid a Recurrence*, White Paper 1007, October 2010, https://escholarship.org/uc/item/06t9s399.

[31] On the interdependence of the three levels of duties, see Shue, *Basic Rights*, 60–64.

remediable threats and if it can be satisfied by *practicable* actions on the part of the state. In this sense, the state's duty to refrain and prevent would require it, for example, to ensure that people do not become infected with HIV through contaminated syringes or blood transfusions. In many developing countries, the number of infections could be further reduced by nonmedical measures, such as increasing literacy.[32] As David Miller notes, however, the state could also commit itself, as part of its duty of assistance, to taking practicable measures that might not lead directly to a cure for AIDS but could contribute indirectly to a cure. For example, the state could be required to invest a certain portion of its budget in institutions whose mission is to conduct research into medical cures for AIDS.[33] If such research leads to a cure, we could conclude that the human rights claim to the protection of human health has been extended to include a cure for AIDS. Whether or not a threat can be remedied may therefore change over time.[34]

The scope of human rights claims thus always depends on the practical possibilities for protecting a human need. In other words, human rights aspirations increase with technological and scientific progress because it provides us with ever greater opportunities to protect human needs against relevant threats.[35] At the same time, however, we can observe that technological, economic, social, and environmental change is accompanied by ever new threats that endanger human needs in new, previously unknown ways. This is relevant because, according to the thesis advanced here, the identification of the specific content of human rights depends on the existence of specific threats. It follows that the scope of human rights also increases with the emergence of new sources of threat, such as climate change.[36] The scope of human rights claims thus depends on two factors: the emergence of new threats and the emergence of new ways of protecting against threats. Nickel has these two factors in mind when he stresses the importance of being

[32] See Thorsten Sternkopf, *Bildung gegen Afrikas modernen Fluch: HIV-Prävention: Pädagogische Aufgabe in der Entwicklungszusammenarbeit* (Marburg: Tectum, 2007).

[33] Miller, *National Responsibility and Global Justice*, 186. Here Miller uses the example of incurable forms of cancer.

[34] Henry Shue also notes in this context, "What is . . . eradicable changes, of course, over time. Today, we have very little excuse for allowing so many poor people to die of malaria and more excuse probably for allowing people to die of cancer. Later perhaps we will have equally little excuse to allow deaths by many kinds of cancer, or perhaps not. In any case, the measure is a realistic, not a utopian, one, and what is realistic can change." Shue, *Basic Rights*, 33.

[35] See the article by Jeffrey H. Toney et al., "Science and Human Rights: A Bridge towards Benefiting Humanity," *Human Rights Quarterly* 32, no. 4 (2010): 1008–1017.

[36] See the article by Simon Caney, "Human Rights, Responsibilities, and Climate Change," in Beitz and Goodin, *Global Basic Rights*, 227–247.

"open-minded to new rights because justifiable lists of specific human rights depend on the problems, institutions, and resources of particular places and times. Increased productivity, stability, and democracy in many countries make it possible to take seriously claims of injustice that would once have been thought hopelessly utopian. [On the other hand], [t]he emergence of large human populations, dangerous technologies, and increased international interaction and trade can generate new problems and injustices."[37] These observations suggest that we must abandon the classical idea that human rights are the same at all times and in all places. Human rights, as Regina Kreide rightly observes, are not abstract demands that follow directly from considerations in moral philosophy. "They are a response to very specific threats and vulnerabilities that have arisen or may arise in a society" and are therefore subject to "constant change and *reiterated interpretation*."[38] This observation is important and deserves attention because it enables us not only to illustrate the constructivist and evolving nature of human rights but also to understand the emergence of existing human rights. For example, it would be impossible to understand large parts of the contemporary human rights canon without seeing it against the backdrop of the crimes of National Socialism. It is not without reason that the Preamble to the Universal Declaration speaks of "barbarous acts which have outraged the conscience of mankind."

It is the merit of Johannes Morsink to have explained the important role that the barbaric acts of the Holocaust played in the formulation of the Universal Declaration of Human Rights.[39] Morsink emphasizes that it would be a mistake to view the individual human rights as something that could simply have been derived from certain religious doctrines or transcendental moral principles:

> [T]he drafters of the Declaration did not deduce the articles of the Declaration from any abstract moral principles. . . . On the contrary, the delegates went for the justification of each article back to the experience of the war. Each human right has its own justification, one that is discovered when that right is violated in some gross way. This link with experience

[37] Nickel, *Making Sense of Human Rights*, 97.

[38] Kreide, *Globale Politik und Menschenrechte*, 30–31, emphasis in original.

[39] See Johannes Morsink, "World War Two and the Universal Declaration," *Human Rights Quarterly* 15, no. 2 (1993): 357–405; Johannes Morsink, *The Universal Declaration of Human Rights: Origins, Drafting and Intent* (Philadelphia: University of Pennsylvania Press, 1999), 36–91.

> explains why so many delegates from so many different social, political, cultural, and religious systems could nevertheless agree on a list of rights. They had witnessed the same horrors and therefore were able and willing to proclaim the same rights.[40]

Morsink draws on the records of the proceedings of the Human Rights Drafting Committee to show that each human right contained in the Declaration represents a specific normative response to particular practices and experiences to which people were subjected during the Nazi period. To illustrate this, consider Article 15 of the Universal Declaration, which declares the right of every human being to a nationality and emphasizes that no one may be arbitrarily deprived of his or her nationality. Why was this right included in the Declaration? It would be absurd to assume that it could somehow be deduced by the use of pure reason, or that it was bestowed on human beings by some higher authority. It would be equally absurd to call it "natural" in any sense, since it presupposes the existence of territorial nation-states, whereas people lived for millennia without being citizens of nation-states. And even in the centuries in which they lived as citizens of nation-states, they did so without ever demanding or proclaiming a universal right to a nationality.

To understand the right to a nationality, its existence must be seen against the background of the experiences that provided the essential impulse for its articulation. As Morsink shows, this impulse can be traced back to the Nazis' campaign to eliminate European Jews.[41] An important element of this campaign was to deprive the Jews of their citizenship in order to render them stateless and consequently without rights. As early as 1933, the Nazis initiated a process with the Law on the Revocation of Naturalization and the Annulment of German Citizenship[42] that enabled them to confiscate the property of German Jews with apparent legality. Conversely, the revocation of their citizenship made it legally impossible for German Jews to challenge these confiscations in German courts. By the time Adolf Eichmann took

[40] Morsink, "World War Two and the Universal Declaration," 399.

[41] See ibid., 391–393.

[42] According to this law, naturalizations concluded between November 9, 1918, and January 30, 1933, could be revoked "in case the naturalization is not considered desirable." Moreover, people residing abroad could "be deprived of their German citizenship, if they have harmed German interests through behavior that violates the obligation of loyalty towards Reich and people." Ingo Münch, *Die deutsche Staatsangehörigkeit: Vergangenheit—Gegenwart—Zukunft* (Berlin: de Gruyter, 2007), 68.

charge of the Reich Central Office for Jewish Emigration in 1940, the revocation of citizenship had become an instrument not only for the material dispossession of Jews but also for their total elimination. As part of the campaign to deport the Jews, the German Foreign Ministry reached an agreement with the governments of Germany's allies and the occupied territories, calling on the latter to deport the Jews in their territories back to Germany as stateless persons. As Hannah Arendt notes, the fact that the deported Jews were stateless was important for two reasons: "[I]t made it impossible for any country to inquire into their fate, and it enabled the state in which they were resident to confiscate their property."[43] The importance of having a nationality is illustrated by the fact that Jews who could prove that they were citizens of a country not occupied by or allied with the Nazis were spared deportation and thus certain death.[44] Therefore, as Morsink remarks, "To be without a nationality or without any citizenship is to stand naked in the world of international affairs. It is to be alone as a person, without protection against the aggression of states—an unequal battle in which the individual is bound to lose."[45]

The right to a nationality proclaimed in the Universal Declaration is a normative response to this state of affairs. Its function is to protect human security from the threats posed by statelessness, which can lead to acts such as or similar to those perpetrated during National Socialism. Human rights are the product of hundreds of such historical experiences of injustice. For example, the right to recognition as "a person before the law" proclaimed in Article 6 is a direct response to the Nazi practice of declaring Jews "legally dead" and thus depriving them of rights and legal capacity.[45] The right to asylum in Article 14 stems from the fact that Jews and other refugees were often denied refuge in a neutral country, forcing them to return to German-occupied territories, which was often tantamount to a death sentence.[47] Meanwhile, the right to marry and found a family "without any limitation

[43] Hannah Arendt, *Eichmann in Jerusalem* (New York: Viking Press, 1965), 157, cited in Morsink, "World War Two and the Universal Declaration," 392.

[44] "Often the possession of papers or passports to prove citizenship in neutral countries was for Jews a question of life over death. Some Dutch Jews had obtained citizenship in a neutral country. When the matter was brought to Eichmann's attention, he instructed his subordinate in the Hague that 'deportation in their cases must be waived . . . if their acquisition of the new nationality is legally valid, [but that those] in the process of acquiring . . . [must] be given priority for deportation to the East,' which meant certain death." Morsink, "World War Two and the Universal Declaration," 392.

[45] Ibid., 393.

[46] Ibid., 376–377.

[47] Ibid., 383–385.

due to race, nationality or religion," enshrined in Article 16, is a specific reaction to the Nuremberg Race Laws of 1935, which prohibited intermarriage between Jews and non-Jews in order to "keep German blood pure."[48]

As these examples show, the Universal Declaration of Human Rights must be understood as a document that contains normative responses to threats that occurred for the most part and in drastic forms during National Socialism. It would therefore be wrong to characterize the human rights it contains as "preexisting" in any sense. Rather, human rights must be understood as socially constructed mechanisms that emerged at different times and in response to particular practices and conditions that threatened and violated people's basic needs. Thus human rights do not emerge in a top-down fashion from some higher authority or transcendent principle that leads us to a particular canon of human rights independent of human experience. The process by which human rights emerge and are recognized proceeds in exactly the opposite direction. It begins with the observation or experience of certain practices or conditions that threaten or violate basic human needs and are therefore perceived as morally unacceptable. In response, certain norms are constructed and formulated to protect people from the real or perceived threats in question. Our contemporary understanding of human rights is a product of this process, which has occurred repeatedly throughout history and will continue to do so in the future. Accordingly, it would be a mistake to regard the current canon of human rights as definitive, since new, previously unknown or unperceived threats may lead to the articulation of new rights.[49]

At this point, one might legitimately ask in what sense human rights can be said to be universal if they are characterized as socially constructed mechanisms that were and are formulated in response to experienced threats. From a purely empirical point of view, it may well be the case that people in different societies face very different threats, which would imply that people in different societies could claim very different human rights. For example, people living in an industrial society face different threats than people living in an agrarian society. And those for whom the internet plays a central role in social life are exposed to different threats than people living in nomadic

[48] Morsink, *The Universal Declaration of Human Rights*, 88.

[49] It is important to note that new threats may arise not only from new developments in the social environment but also from changes in social practices. The reason why we do not speak of a right to go to the toilet, for example, is that in our daily practice we are not prevented from going to the toilet. Such a right could be articulated, however, if companies or schools, for example, decided to prevent employees or pupils from going to the toilet in order to save costs or avoid interruptions of work.

conditions. In these cases, therefore, it seems possible to assert a human rights claim in one society that would not necessarily extend to people in the other society, so that one might conclude that the validity of human rights is limited to certain societies.

This conclusion is plausible, but wrong. The fact that threats vary from place to place does not call into question the universality of human rights so much as it highlights an insight that is all too often overlooked in contemporary human rights thought—namely that the primary locus of human rights is not the international sphere but the social sphere. Human rights are demands addressed to the ruling public order of a society, and they refer to locally experienced and observable threats to basic human needs. This is also why, historically, human rights were first proclaimed and institutionalized in national rather than international declarations and constitutions. Human rights should therefore be understood as local in the sense that they refer to experiences and practices that may vary from place to place. At the same time, however, they are universal in the sense that the needs under threat to which they refer are common to all human beings. In this sense, human needs are universal spheres of vulnerability that can be threatened in very different ways, because the specific form that this threat takes depends on local, historical, and societal factors. However, in order to challenge the claim of universal validity of a human right, it is not enough to point out that the human right in question refers to a threat that a particular society does not actually face. It is true that people in a nomadic society would have little use for a right to protection of their data because they do not face the threat to which the right responds. That does not mean, however, that they would not be entitled to such a right if they faced such a threat as a result of increasing urbanization and social change. It would be equally wrong to claim that people in an agrarian society do not have the right to form trade unions because they are not currently exposed to the dangers of a capitalist market economy. Even when a human right is not directly applicable, its universal validity remains intact and functions as a hypothetical safeguard.

Thus while threats may indeed arise at different times and in different places, experience teaches us that certain threats can be generalized beyond specific contexts because they can be observed at all times in different societies. We know, for example, that in the absence of certain constraints and limitations, political institutions tend to mistreat their subjects by arbitrarily arresting, detaining, and even torturing them. The human rights not to be arbitrarily arrested and detained (Article 9) and not to be tortured

(Article 5) are therefore specific responses to historically recurring threats to the basic human needs for security, recognition, and meaning. The violation of the need for recognition in this case is linked to the fact that arbitrary arrest and torture are practices that, even if they do not cause physical pain, suggest to the persons concerned that they are not owed any respect as free and equal counterparts. Their purpose, among others, is to portray the persons concerned as powerless, and thus to degrade and humiliate them. At the same time, the objective senselessness of being deprived of one's liberty and the resulting borderline experience constitute an attack on one's need for meaning. Torture, in particular, seeks to destroy the ability to give meaning by placing its victim in a situation that he or she can neither comprehend nor control. The inevitability and unpredictability of torture leads to the loss of a sense of coherence and continuity and deprives its victims of any possibility of making sense of their situation, often resulting in a psychological breakdown.[50]

The example of torture is intended to illustrate the fact that individual threats typically do not affect just *one* need but often threaten multiple needs simultaneously. In the context of our thesis, therefore, we can conclude that individual human rights can also serve to protect multiple needs simultaneously. A right to close personal relationships can thus serve to protect the needs for belonging and recognition, since these two needs can be fulfilled only within the context of such relationships. A second observation, which probably does not need further elaboration but should be mentioned for the sake of completeness, is that individual needs are subject to a variety of threats. Accordingly, we can conclude that different human rights can simultaneously contribute to the protection of the same need.

However, another observation that can be made in this context, and which we will explore further in the next section, is that individual needs are also vulnerable to different threats *to different degrees*. Not every threat endangers a need to the same degree. A food shortage poses a more serious threat to human health than diabetes, which in turn poses a more serious health threat than an unhealthy diet. Meanwhile, torture poses a more serious threat to the need for recognition than, say, slavery, which in turn involves a more drastic denial of recognition than discrimination. In the context of our thesis, these observations lead to the analogous insight that different human rights may

[50] See Ursula Wirtz and Jürg Zöbeli, "Das Trauma der Gewalt," in *Hunger nach Sinn: Menschen in Grenzsituationen: Grenzen der Psychotherapie*, ed. Ursula Wirtz (Zürich: Kreuz, 1995), 114–169.

contribute more or less effectively to the protection of human needs, so that it is theoretically possible, and it may also make sense, to assume that there are different *levels of human rights* that differ in their relevance and urgency. In what follows, therefore, we will ask in what way and according to what criteria it makes sense to speak of a hierarchy of human rights.

Human Rights: Priorities and Interdependencies

The attempt to establish a hierarchy of human rights is immediately confronted with a thesis so deeply rooted in traditional human rights thinking that to question it seems almost blasphemous. According to this thesis, human rights as a whole should be considered *indivisible* and therefore *equally important*. Thus we are actually dealing with two theses, the second of which presupposes the first. Let us therefore first consider the indivisibility thesis, the core of which is the fundamental assertion that all human rights form a unified, inseparable structure in which the realization of one human right is directly linked to the fulfillment of all other human rights. Historically, this thesis can be traced back to the concern to emphasize the equivalence of economic, social, and cultural rights, on the one hand, and civil and political rights, on the other.[51] The first official expression of this concern can be found in the first UN World Conference on Human Rights, held in Tehran in 1968. The Proclamation of Tehran adopted at the conference emphasized, "Since human rights and fundamental freedoms are indivisible, the full realization of civil and political rights without the enjoyment of economic, social and cultural rights is impossible."[52] Similar language can be found in the Declaration on the Right to Development of 1986, which states "that all human rights and fundamental freedoms are indivisible and interdependent and that, in order to promote development, equal attention and urgent consideration should be given to the implementation, promotion and protection of civil, political, economic, social and cultural rights."[53] In line with these declarations, the Protocol of San Salvador of 1988 emphasizes "the close relationship that exists between economic, social and cultural rights, and civil and political rights" and further postulates that "the different

[51] On this debate, see Jack Donnelly, *Universal Human Rights in Theory and Practice* (Ithaca, NY: Cornell University Press, 2003), 27–31.

[52] §13 of the *Proclamation of Tehran*, adopted on May 13, 1968.

[53] § 6.2 of the *Declaration on the Right to Development*, December 4, 1986.

categories of rights constitute an indivisible whole . . . for which reason both require permanent protection and promotion if they are to be fully realized" so that "the violation of some rights in favour of the realization of others can never be justified."[54]

While these declarations do not go beyond emphasizing the indispensable importance of economic, social, and cultural rights for the possible realization of civil and political rights, the end of the Cold War witnessed an increasing formalization of the indivisibility thesis. This can be clearly seen in the Vienna Declaration of 1993 adopted at the second UN World Conference on Human Rights. It states, "All human rights are universal, indivisible and interdependent and interrelated. The international community must treat human rights globally in a fair and equal manner, on the same footing, and with the same emphasis."[55] Looking at the wording of this declaration, the first thing that strikes us is that, unlike its predecessors, it does not refer explicitly to the different types of human rights but speaks more generally of the indivisibility of all human rights.[56] It is also striking that the indivisibility thesis is described here with a set of adjectives (indivisible, interdependent, interrelated) that have become part of the official standard descriptions of human rights[57] and have even acquired the status of an "incontrovertible truth."[58] In this sense, the Maastricht Guidelines also emphasize that "it is now undisputed that all human rights are indivisible, interdependent, interrelated and of equal importance."[59]

[54] Preamble to the *Additional Protocol to the American Convention on Human Rights in the Area of Economic, Social and Cultural Rights*, adopted on November 17, 1988, also known as the "Protocol of San Salvador."

[55] Vienna Declaration and Program of Action, adopted on June 25, 1993.

[56] In addition to countering the neglect of economic, social, and cultural rights, the political purpose of this formulation was also to counter a tendency, which emerged especially in the context of the "Asian Values" debate, to make the acceptance of human rights dependent on their conformity with a country's cultural values. For a general discussion, see Oanne R. Bauer and Joanne R. Bauer, Daniel A. Bell, eds., *The East Asian Challenge for Human Rights* (Cambridge: Cambridge University Press, 1999).

[57] See the definition of the UN High Commission for Human Rights: "Human rights are rights inherent to all human beings, whatever our nationality, place of residence, sex, national or ethnic origin, colour, religion, language, or any other status. We are all equally entitled to our human rights without discrimination. These rights are all interrelated, interdependent and indivisible. . . . All human rights are indivisible, whether they are civil and political rights, such as the right to life, equality before the law and freedom of expression; economic, social and cultural rights, such as the rights to work, social security and education, or collective rights, such as the rights to development and self-determination, are indivisible, interrelated and interdependent. The improvement of one right facilitates advancement of the others. Likewise, the deprivation of one right adversely affects the others." http://unis.unvienna.org/unis/en/united_nations/un_human-rights.html.

[58] See United Nations, *Press Release GA/SHC/3501 39th Meeting (AM) 9 November 1998*, https://www.un.org/press/en/1998/19981109.gash3501.html.

[59] See §4 of "Maastricht Guidelines on Violations of Economic, Social and Cultural Rights," *Human Rights Quarterly* 20, no. 3 (1998): 691–704.

The point of this description is clearly to suggest that all human rights are so interconnected and so profoundly interdependent that it would be impossible to neglect one human right without compromising all the others. The image evoked here is that of a temple in danger of collapse if one of its supporting pillars begins to wobble. In this sense, human rights constitute an inseparable whole that depends on each of its components, so that each human right has equal value and cannot claim priority over any other. In other words, the indivisibility of the whole implies the equivalence of its components, and thus the equivalence of all the components makes it impossible to establish a hierarchy among them.

At this point, however, several reasons can be given for questioning the dogma of indivisibility and its corollary, the thesis of equivalence. The reasons for this are both conceptual and intuitive, but they also arise from the practice of human rights.

Conceptually, human rights can be interrelated without necessarily forming an indivisible whole. As James Nickel shows, human rights can be interrelated in quite different ways.[60] Nickel speaks of various "supporting relations." According to Nickel, a supporting relation can be said to exist between two rights when one right contributes to the stability or fulfillment of another right. The relation in question is a *strong supporting relation* if the existence of right R_1 is *indispensable* for the existence of right R_2. R_1 is indispensable whenever it is logically or practically inconsistent to support the realization of R_2 without also supporting the realization of R_1. In this sense, for example, a right to be protected from violent attacks (R_1) would be a necessary or indispensable condition for the right to freedom of assembly (R_2): "If people have no protection against violent attacks it will sometimes be risky to assemble for unpopular purposes. Thus, it is practically inconsistent to advocate implementing the right to freedom of assembly while rejecting all rights to protections against physical attack."[61] We can formally express such a strong supporting relationship as follows: $R_1 \rightarrow R_2$ (*R_1 is indispensable for R_2, or R_2 is dependent on R_1*).

In addition to a strong supporting relation, Nickel argues that we can also identify a weaker form of support. A *weak supporting relation* exists between two rights when R_1 is *useful* but not indispensable to R_2. In this case, R_2 would

[60] In what follows, I am drawing on James Nickel's remarks in "Rethinking Indivisibility: Towards a Theory of Supporting Relations between Human Rights," *Human Rights Quarterly* 30, no. 4 (2008): 984–1001.

[61] Ibid., 988.

benefit from R_1, without being dependent on R_1. Accordingly, it would not be logically or practically inconsistent to postulate the fulfillment of R_2 without postulating the simultaneous fulfillment of R_1. For example, the right to freedom of speech (R_1) would be useful but not indispensable for the fulfillment of the right to food (R_2). Such a weak supporting relationship can be formally represented by a thin arrow: $R_1 \rightarrow R_2$ (*R_1 is useful for R_2, or R_2 benefits from R_1*).

Nickel reminds us that a supporting relation between two rights can be not only unidirectional but also bidirectional. Thus we can identify three different patterns of relationships, each with a different form of interdependence.[62] We can speak of *weak interdependence* when two rights are useful for each other without being interdependent, such as when the functioning of the left hand is useful but not indispensable for the functioning of the right hand, and vice versa. For example, the right to freedom of expression is useful for the right to education, just as the right to education is useful for the right to freedom of expression. Formally expressed thus: $R_1 \leftarrow\rightarrow R_2$ (*R_1 and R_2 benefit from one another*).

Another pattern of relationship that two rights can exhibit is what Nickel calls *asymmetrical interdependence.* According to Nickel, this occurs when there is a strong supporting relation in one direction and a weak supporting relation in the other. The analogical biological relationship here would be between the heart and the hands. The function of the heart is indispensable to the function of the hands, whereas the function of the hands is useful but not indispensable to the function of the heart, for example, in helping to ingest food. Similarly, the right to freedom of movement is indispensable to the right to freedom of assembly, while only the latter is useful to the former. Formally expressed thus: $R_1 \leftarrow\rightarrow R_2$ (*R_1 is indispensable for and benefits from R_2. R_2 is dependent on and useful for R_1*).

The third pattern of relationship between two rights is what Nickel calls *strong interdependence.* This applies, of course, when two rights are indispensable to each other, as, for example, a functioning heart is indispensable to a functioning liver, and vice versa. In this sense, the right to free and periodic elections is indispensable for the fulfillment of the right to political participation, and vice versa. Formally expressed thus: $R_1 \leftarrow\rightarrow R_2$ (*R_1 and R_2 are indispensable for one another*).

[62] Ibid., 990.

Nickel cites these relations in support of a crucial conclusion, namely that we can speak of a condition of indivisibility only when two rights are indispensable to each other, that is, only when they exhibit a strong form of interdependence. If two rights are useful to each other (weak interdependence), there is still no condition of indivisibility, since a left hand could theoretically function without a right hand. Nor would a condition of indivisibility exist in the case of asymmetrical interdependence, since one could sacrifice a hand to save a heart, but not a heart to save a hand. Thus indivisibility applies only when one right is so dependent on another that its existence would be unthinkable without the other right. "Indivisibility is strong interdependence or indispensable bidirectional support. If two items are mutually indispensable, then they are bidirectionally indivisible. You cannot destroy either without destroying both."[63]

So far, we have confined ourselves to the case of two rights. But if we now follow the claim of the indivisibility thesis as expressed in the official doctrine, then "all human rights," not just two, would have to exhibit a form of interdependence so strong that each individual right is of indispensable importance for all other rights. Accordingly, we could speak of the collective indivisibility of human rights if the realization of one human right is a necessary condition for the realization of all others. Thus, in formal terms, this would mean:

$$R_1 \leftrightarrow R_2 \leftrightarrow R_3 \leftrightarrow R_4 \leftrightarrow \cdots \leftrightarrow R_x$$

However, one does not need to be a profound theorist to see that this is a very implausible claim. This is already suggested by the fact that different human rights may stand in a relation of weak or asymmetrical interdependence. For example, it is obviously possible to satisfy a right to food without presupposing a right to democratic participation. This does not preclude the possibility that a right to democratic participation may be quite useful or helpful in fulfilling the right to food, but only that it is a theoretical or practical precondition for its fulfillment.

Another reason for doubting the cogency of the indivisibility thesis follows from the already emphasized implication of attributing equal weight to all human rights. From a purely intuitive perspective, it seems implausible to assume that all human rights have the same value. For example, most of us

[63] Ibid.

would assume that the right not to be subjected to torture (UDHR, Article 5) outweighs the right to regular paid vacation (Article 24). This is not to say, of course, that the right to a regular paid vacation is worthless and could therefore be considered expendable.[64] As Pollman notes, "Just because homicide is fundamentally more serious than theft, no one would seriously consider removing the latter offense from the criminal code."[65] Thus to say that one human right weighs more heavily than another merely implies that its fulfillment is a higher priority.

The assumption that certain human rights weigh more heavily than others can be theoretically substantiated beyond a mere appeal to intuition if we consider a hypothetical scenario in which people have to purchase their rights with a limited amount of money. Suppose that each human right costs the same amount, but that there is only enough money to buy five human rights. Individuals who see no difference between the relevance of individual rights would be indifferent to which human rights they receive. They would buy "blindly," so to speak. It is more likely, however, that most people would adopt a purchasing behavior that would guarantee them at least those human rights that could protect them from life-threatening or extremely degrading threats.

From a practical legal perspective, the assumption that human rights do not have equal weight is confirmed by the fact that various human rights treaties contain "derogation clauses" that allow human rights guarantees to be suspended in the event of a public emergency,[66] but at the same time define an "emergency-proof" core of rights that must be upheld under all circumstances.[67] "In time of war or other public emergency threatening the life of the nation," according to the European Convention on Human Rights, "any High Contracting Party may take measures derogating from its obligations under this Convention to the extent strictly required by the

[64] This is the objection raised by of Claudia Mahler and Norman Weiß: "A fixed hierarchy of human rights, according to which a certain right always enjoys priority over another, cannot be derived from the 'value' of a right . . . for otherwise certain rights would always be subordinate and hence ultimately even . . . dispensable." Claudia Mahler and Norman Weiß, "Zur Unteilbarkeit der Menschenrechte—Anmerkungen aus juristischer, insbesondere völkerrechtlicher Sicht," in Lohman et al. (eds.), *Die Menschenrechte*, 41–42.

[65] Arnd Pollmann, "Die Menschenrechte: Teilbar und ungleichgewichtig!," in Lohman et al., *Die Menschenrechte*, 37.

[66] See Kälin and Künzli, *Universeller Menschenrechtsschutz*, 153–159. For a more detailed account, see Bettina Vollmer, *Die Geltung der Menschenrechte im Staatsnotstand: Eine völkerrechtliche Analyse der Rechtslage in Deutschland, Spanien und dem Vereinigten Königreich* (Baden-Baden: Nomos, 2010).

[67] This is also mentioned by Nickel, "Rethinking Indivisibility," 996.

exigencies of the situation."[68] Among the fundamental human rights from which "no derogation . . . shall be made"[69] are Article 2 (right to life), except for deaths resulting from lawful acts of war, Article 3 (prohibition of torture), Article 4.1 (prohibition of slavery), and Article 7 (no punishment without law). The International Covenant on Civil and Political Rights contains a more generous set of nonderogable rights. Article 4.1 reads, "In time of public emergency which threatens the life of the nation," states parties "may take measures derogating from their obligations under the present Covenant to the extent strictly required by the exigencies of the situation."[70] However, according to Article 4.2, Articles 6 (right to life), 7 (prohibition of torture), 8 (prohibition of slavery and servitude), 11 (prohibition of imprisonment for inability to perform a contractual obligation), 15 (no punishment without law), 16 (right to recognition as a person before the law), and 18 (right to freedom of thought, conscience, and religion) may not be suspended. Similar provisions are found in the American Convention on Human Rights,[71] the Arab Charter on Human Rights,[72] and the European Social Charter.[73] Although these provisions cannot provide us with a theoretically satisfactory answer to the question of which rights are to be considered more important or urgent for what reasons, the fact *that* legal practice contains a certain canon of nonderogable rights serves to confirm the assumption that the idea of equal weighting of human rights is not tenable.[74]

At this point, then, we are faced with the fundamental question of the standard by which a plausible weighting of human rights could be made. One prominent proposal has been made by Henry Shue.[75] Shue suggests that among human rights there is a special class of rights that are so fundamental that without them it would be impossible to enjoy or use any other human rights. Shue calls this class of human rights basic rights: "Rights are basic in

[68] See Article 15, para. 1 and 2 of the Convention for the Protection of Human Rights and Fundamental Freedoms, of November 4, 1950.

[69] Ibid.

[70] See Article 4 of the International Covenant on Economic, Social and Cultural Rights.

[71] See Article 27, para. 1 and 2 of the American Convention on Human Rights, of November 22, 1969.

[72] See Article 4 of the Arab Charter on Human Rights, of September 15, 1994.

[73] See Article 30 of the European Social Charter, of October 18, 1961. However, this is merely a derogation clause that does not specify nonderogable rights.

[74] See Teraya Koji, "Emerging Hierarchy in International Human Rights and Beyond: From the Perspective of Non-derogable Rights," *European Journal of International Law* 12, no. 5 (2001): 917–941. For a more detailed treatment, see Ian D. Seiderman, *Hierarchy in International Law: The Human Rights Dimension* (Antwerp: Intersentia, 2001).

[75] Shue, *Basic Rights*.

the sense used here only if enjoyment of them is essential to the enjoyment of all other rights. This is what is distinctive about a basic right. When a right is genuinely basic, any attempt to enjoy any other right by sacrificing the basic right would be quite literally self-defeating, cutting the ground from beneath itself."[76] As this quotation makes clear, basic rights should not be understood as rights that are intrinsically more valuable than others.[77] Rather, they form the basis or foundation upon which other rights are built. Thus other rights can be enjoyed only *on the basis of* these rights. According to Shue, therefore, basic rights must have categorical priority over other rights because their exercise is a necessary condition for the exercise of all other rights.[78] Their content can thus be determined by asking which rights must be assumed in principle if the meaningful exercise of other rights is to be possible at all. According to Shue, exactly four such rights can be identified: the right to physical security,[79] the right to subsistence,[80] the right to political participation, and the right to freedom of movement. These rights, according to Shue, constitute the essential, though not the only possible,[81] canon of basic rights. They are, therefore, rights about which it can be said in general that "they are not everything, but everything without them is nothing."[82] The possibility of exercising a right as such, whatever it may be, therefore necessarily presupposes that people are simultaneously able to exercise the basic rights.

To evaluate this claim, it is important to understand what Shue means when he speaks of the enjoyment of a right. Upon closer examination, this turns out to be not entirely clear. Let us approach the question carefully, starting with the definition of moral rights that Shue quotes at the beginning of his book. There Shue writes, "A moral right provides (1) the rational basis

[76] Ibid., 19.

[77] Ibid., 20.

[78] Ibid., 19–20. As Shue stresses, this holds for the relationship between basic rights as well. Here, too, the exercise of one presupposes the simultaneous enjoyment of all of the others: "Thus the enjoyment of the basic rights is an all-or-nothing matter. Each is necessary to the other basic ones as well as to all non-basic ones. Every right, including every basic right, can be enjoyed only if all basic rights are enjoyed" (178).

[79] According to Shue, the right to physical security designates the right "not to be subjected to murder, torture, mayhem, rape, or assault" (ibid., 20).

[80] "By minimal economic security, or subsistence, I mean unpolluted air, unpolluted water, adequate food, adequate clothing, adequate shelter, and minimal preventive public health care" (ibid., 23).

[81] "Security, subsistence, social participation, and physical movement are almost certainly not the only basic rights. The right to due process, or to a fair trial, for example, could surely be established by . . . [a similar] argument" (ibid., 91).

[82] I borrow this formulation from Wolfgang Kersting, *Theorien der sozialen Gerechtigkeit* (Stuttgart: Metzler, 2000), 27, although he uses it in a different sense.

for a justified demand (2) that the actual enjoyment of a substance be (3) socially guaranteed against standard threats."[83]

To better understand the components of this definition, we can follow Thomas Pogge and identify three conditions that must be met for a person P to have a moral right to X in Shue's sense:[84]

(A) P actually enjoys X—formally: A(PX).
(B) P's enjoyment of X is socially guaranteed against standard threats—formally: B(PX).
(C) P enjoys X as a right—formally: C(PX).

Condition (A) merely states that P must actually be able to enjoy X, that is, the substance of the respective right. According to Shue, the claim that P has a right to physical security is true only if P actually has the possibility of remaining physically unharmed. This possibility must not only exist in fact, but must also be guaranteed by social arrangements (B). Shue emphasizes, however, that these arrangements refer only to "standard threats," by which he means, in principle, foreseeable and remediable threats that would impair P's enjoyment of X.[85] Thus one cannot expect that P's enjoyment of X can be protected against all threats,[86] so that it would theoretically be possible to satisfy conditions A and B independently of each other. Accordingly, despite the existence of social arrangements, P's physical security could still be compromised if, for example, P suffers physical harm as a result of an earthquake. Conversely, it would also be possible for P to enjoy physical security in the absence of social arrangements, for example if P were protected by private bodyguards.[87] But a right to physical security remains unfulfilled, according to Shue, "until [social] arrangements are in fact in place for people to enjoy whatever it is [X] to which they have the right."[88]

But even the fact that the enjoyment of X (A) is socially guaranteed (B) does not mean that we can already speak of a right to X. For this to be

[83] Shue, *Basic Rights*, 13.
[84] See Thomas Pogge, "Shue on Rights and Duties," in Beitz and Goodin, *Global Basic Rights*, 114.
[85] See Shue, *Basic Rights*, 33: "The social guarantees that are part of any typical right need not provide impregnable protection against every imaginable threat, but they must provide effective defenses against predictable remediable threats."
[86] Ibid., 17: "I am not suggesting the absurd standard that a right has been fulfilled only if it is impossible for anyone to be deprived of it or only if no one is ever deprived of it. The standard can only be some reasonable level of guarantee."
[87] Ibid., 16.
[88] Ibid.

the case, the crucial condition C must also be fulfilled. Accordingly, we can speak of a right to X only if the contributions that others must make to fulfill conditions A and B are understood as duties (C_1) owed to P (C_2), and if the contributions and understandings in question are culturally embedded (C_3).[89] To illustrate that conditions A and B can be met without condition C, consider the example of a person P whose physical security is guaranteed only because others feel sorry for her. In this case, C_1 would remain unfulfilled. C_2, on the other hand, would remain unfulfilled if P's physical security P were guaranteed only because others consider it a sin to physically harm P and refrain from doing so because of their sense of guilt before God. Alternatively, P's physical security could be guaranteed by a benevolent monarch whose benevolence is not shared by his successors, in which case C_3 would remain unfulfilled.[90] These examples show that the enjoyment of X, even if socially guaranteed, does not automatically mean that X is enjoyed *as a right*. A person P's moral right to X would therefore be satisfied only if all three of the above conditions were met— this can be formally expressed as ABC(PX).

However, Pogge uses the example of the aftermath of Hurricane Katrina to draw our attention to an important point. He argues that it is perfectly possible to enjoy something as a right (C) without this necessarily leading to an actual (A) or socially guaranteed enjoyment of X (B): "Many residents of New Orleans did not actually enjoy access to clean water, and no social arrangements were in place against standard threats to such access. Nonetheless, Condition C was arguably met: it was widely accepted throughout the U.S. that the state owed a duty to the residents of New Orleans to ensure secure access to clean water for them."[91] The importance of this reference becomes clear when we consider the formulation that Shue uses in connection with his basic rights thesis. He emphasizes that a right R_X can be considered basic if and only if the enjoyment of R_X is a necessary condition for the enjoyment of all other rights. But what exactly is meant by "the enjoyment of a right"? Shue answers this question as follows: "We do sometimes speak simply of someone's 'enjoying a right,' but I take this to be an elliptical way of saying that the person is enjoying something or other, which is the substance of a right, and, probably, enjoying it *as* a right. Enjoying a right to, for example, liberty normally means enjoying liberty. It may also mean

89 Pogge, "Shue on Rights and Duties," 116.
90 Ibid.
91 Ibid., 116–117.

enjoying liberty in the consciousness that liberty is a right."[92] According to Pogge, "the enjoyment of a right" at this point can be interpreted in several ways. If we follow the above statement and translate it into formal terms, then Shue could mean that P's enjoyment of her right to X is equivalent to A(PX) or, "probably," AC(PX), or even ABC(PX). According to Pogge, in order to evaluate Shue's thesis, each of these combinations must be examined individually.[93]

Thus the first possible interpretation of the thesis is that all those rights are basic rights whose substance must be enjoyed in order for the substance of all other rights to be enjoyed. The claim that R_X is a basic right would therefore mean that it would be impossible for any person P at any time t to enjoy the substance Y of any other right R_Y without also enjoying X. Thus, $A(PY)_t$ is given only if $A(PX)_t$ is given. We should keep in mind that Shue tries to qualify exactly four rights as basic, namely the rights to physical security, subsistence, political participation, and freedom of movement. According to Pogge, however, none of these rights can be regarded as basic on the first interpretation, since even without freedom of movement or political participation, for example, one could still have the actual possibility of being free from torture and thus enjoying the substance of the right to physical security. "And, conversely, while one is being tortured, one may actually be enjoying the substance of some other right, for example adequate nutrition."[94]

A second possible interpretation of Shue's thesis is that only those rights whose substance must be enjoyed *as a right* in order for the substance of all other rights to be enjoyed *as a right* can be called basic. Accordingly, R_X would be basic if it were impossible for anyone to enjoy the substance of another right as a right at any time t without also enjoying X as a right at that time. Thus $AC(PY)_t$ is given, only if $AC(PX)_t$ is given. But even in this case, Pogge argues, none of the rights identified by Shue can be qualified as basic. For there is nothing inconsistent in the idea that a person regularly participates in elections and enjoys this participation as a right, even though she does not enjoy physical security or subsistence as a right. Pogge uses the example of the nobles in a feudal society: "The nobles are in power and they periodically elect a monarch from among themselves. They recognize one another's moral claim to partake in the elections and would fiercely resist

92 Shue, *Basic Rights*, 15.
93 Pogge, "Shue on Rights and Duties," 117.
94 Ibid., 118.

any effort to disenfranchise any from among themselves. Yet, they recognize no claim to contribute to one another's personal security; in this regard they each depend on their own resources and expect one another to do so."[95] Pogge's argument here is that each of the nobles in this scenario can participate politically and enjoy that participation as a right, even though they enjoy neither personal security nor subsistence *as a right*. The example thus shows that even on the second interpretation of Shue's thesis, the right to physical security or subsistence cannot be qualified as basic.

According to Pogge, however, a third interpretation of Shue's thesis is possible: only those rights whose substance must be enjoyed in order for all other rights to be fully enjoyed can be called basic. A right is fully enjoyed when the substance of the right is actually enjoyed (A) in a socially guaranteed way (B) and *as a right* (C). Thus R_X would be a basic right if and only if it is impossible for any person to fully enjoy R_Y at any time t without also enjoying X. Thus $ABC(PY)_t$ is given only if $A(PX)_t$ is given. Indeed, this is precisely the interpretation that Shue seems to have in mind when he seeks to qualify the rights to physical security and subsistence as basic: "Security and subsistence are basic rights, then, because of the roles they play in both the enjoyment and the protection of all other rights. Other rights could not be enjoyed in the absence of security or subsistence, even if the other rights were somehow miraculously protected in such a situation."[96] The fact that Shue speaks only of "security" and "subsistence" in the last sentence and not of "rights to security and subsistence" indicates that it is only the substance of those rights whose enjoyment is required for other rights to be enjoyed as such. The criteria by which a right can be qualified as basic would thus be relaxed to a certain extent.

However, according to Pogge, this does not really help us. To illustrate this, he cites the example of the right not to be arbitrarily deprived of one's nationality (Article 15).[97] He asks us to imagine a situation in which this right has long been guaranteed in the constitution of a country, enforced by its national courts, and affirmed by its population, so that in this country a person P has never been arbitrarily deprived of her nationality. Therefore, we can assume that P is able to enjoy the substance of this right in the full sense, that is, to actually enjoy it in a socially guaranteed way and as a right. If we follow Shue's thesis, it would be impossible for P to enjoy this right without

[95] Ibid., 119.
[96] Shue, *Basic Rights*, 30.
[97] Pogge, "Shue on Rights and Duties," 121.

also being able to enjoy physical security, subsistence, political participation, and freedom of movement. According to Pogge, however, this claim is not tenable. We could plausibly assume, for example, that P has been kidnaped and is being so badly beaten and starved by her captors that she is neither physically unharmed nor adequately nourished and, in addition, is unable to move freely or engage in political participation. But in this situation, according to Pogge, there is no reason to assume that P is no longer able to fully enjoy her right to a nationality. In fact, in this situation, P might be more than willing to give up her nationality in order to end her torment. However, this would probably be so irrelevant to her captors that it would not even occur to P to offer to give up her nationality. Therefore, Pogge argues, this situation shows that it is possible to enjoy a right in the full sense without presupposing the substance of all those rights that Shue tries to show are basic. These observations lead Pogge to conclude that the attempt to identify certain rights as basic in Shue's sense is doomed to failure.[98]

At this point, however, we must ask whether Pogge's explanations are actually sufficient to discredit Shue's thesis. As the above examples show, Pogge's strategy is to identify particular situations in which it may indeed be possible to enjoy certain rights without being deprived of other basic rights or their respective content. A closer look at Pogge's critique, however, reveals that it is valid only if we limit the temporal dimension of each of the situations under consideration and focus only on individual, temporary moments or a limited period of time during which people suffer from an actual denial of basic rights. Returning to his example of the kidnaped person, the snapshot presented by Pogge does indeed show that P enjoys her right to a nationality while at the same time being deprived of food and physical security. But if we now extend this situation of deprivation into a longer-term or permanent condition, it quickly becomes apparent that it would be impossible to exercise any of the other rights on a long-term or permanent basis because the prolonged deprivation of food and physical security would pose such a threat to P's existence that she would presumably not be able to survive for long, and thus would no longer be able to enjoy any right at all. Pogge's strategy for refuting Shue's thesis thus relies on freezing in time the moment when P is still able to enjoy the right to a nationality.

But if we allow that moment to thaw into a continuing situation, his strategy ceases to work. Once we are dealing with a permanent condition,

[98] Ibid., 122.

we have to agree with Shue on the point that certain rights that serve as a precondition for the enjoyment of all other rights must be defined as basic. These rights derive their basic character from the fact that their long-term curtailment threatens our very existence. It is precisely this point that Shue emphasizes when he describes the fundamental importance of the rights to subsistence and physical security:

> No one can fully, if at all, enjoy any right that is supposedly protected by society if he or she lacks the essentials for a reasonably healthy and active life. Deficiencies in the means of subsistence can be just as fatal, incapacitating, or painful as violations of physical security. The resulting damage or death can at least as decisively prevent the enjoyment of any right as can the effects of security violations. . . . And, obviously, any fatal deficiencies end all possibility of the enjoyment of rights as firmly as an arbitrary execution. . . . So the argument is: when death and serious illness could be prevented by different social policies regarding the essentials of life, the protection of any human right involves avoidance of fatal or debilitating deficiencies in these essential commodities. And this means fulfilling subsistence [and security] rights as basic rights.[99]

As this quote shows, the rights to subsistence and physical security can be considered basic precisely because their exercise is a necessary condition for the protection of human existence. It is precisely this connection that gives them their basic character, since the most basic condition for the exercise of any right is obviously to be alive. Conceptually, therefore, we can conclude that a right can be defined as basic precisely when its exercise is a necessary condition for the protection of human existence, or when its nonexercise poses a direct existential threat.

This conclusion also leads to the insight that not all of the rights identified by Shue as basic can actually be qualified as such. For example, the lack of political participation does not pose a direct threat to human existence as such, so a corresponding right cannot be described as basic. However, as will become clear in what follows, different rights can contribute more or less directly to the protection of human existence, so that the right to political participation, among others, also plays an integral, if not basic, role in the protection of human existence.

[99] Shue, *Basic Rights*, 24–25.

Let us try to explain this idea in more detail by first recalling the course of our argument so far. In the previous section, we tried to clarify the thesis that the purpose of human rights is to protect human needs from threats. This purpose is justified by the fact that any threat to human needs is also a threat to human existence, since human needs are the necessary and universal conditions of human existence. In this sense, needs represent the various dimensions in which human existence can be threatened. Since such threats vary according to time, place, and social conditions, they can, as we have seen, take a wide variety of forms. This led us to conclude that human rights are not abstract axioms but institutions constructed in response to experienced or observed threats. The content of human rights is thus not predetermined but evolves over time in response to threats to human needs.

In this context, however, we have also found that the threats to and violations of human needs not only take very different forms but also vary greatly in their intensity. Different threats can impair human needs to different degrees. This observation led us to conclude that different human rights can also contribute to the protection of human needs to different degrees. While the *content* of human rights is bound up with the existence of certain threats, the question of the *weights* to be attached to them depends on the severity of the respective threats. Accordingly, the more serious the threat against which a human right is to be protected, the more relevant it is, and hence the higher its priority, where the severity of a threat is directly related to the extent to which it contributes to the impairment of a human need.

If we now wish to arrive at a systematic hierarchization of human rights, it seems helpful to return to the model we encountered in the classical *maqāṣid* theory. If we follow this model, we can identify, at a first level, a category of human rights corresponding to those threats that so seriously impair a person's needs as to threaten his or her very *existence*. Obvious examples are threats such as manslaughter, food shortages, toxic pollution, natural disasters, deadly diseases and epidemics, but also mental illness, trauma, and living conditions that can drive people to suicide. In other words, they are threats that can harm people so badly "that their death either occurs or is probable or at least is accepted."[100] In terms of content, as explained in the previous section, the related human rights claims are addressed to the state, obliging it to refrain from causing such threats, to prevent them through practicable measures, and to assist in the event that they occur. The importance

100 Pollmann, "Von der philosophischen Begründung zur demokratischen Konkretisierung," 18.

of these claims is linked to the fact that they serve to protect human existence, the preservation of which is the necessary condition for the exercise of all other rights. Following Shue, we can therefore also speak of basic or, in the terminology of *maqāṣid theory*, necessary (*darūriya*) human rights.

While Shue's thesis limits itself to a binary division of human rights into basic and nonbasic rights, it seems reasonable to subdivide rights in a more differentiated way along the lines of the *maqāṣid* model. Accordingly, in addition to the necessary human rights, another category of human rights can be identified that go beyond the protection of mere existence and enable a *dignified life*. Thus these human rights demand a qualitatively superior form of human life with respect to threats that are not necessarily life-threatening, but so severely impair a person's needs that his or her life is almost physiologically and psychologically intolerable. Relevant examples are threats such as slavery, poverty, homelessness, oppression, marginalization, and all forms of humiliation and discrimination. The second category of human rights, which can be called required (*ḥājiya*) human rights following the *maqāṣid* model, thus serve to counteract those threats that allow only for a life lived under degrading conditions.

The required human rights also provide a basis for the exercise of a third category of rights, which in analogy to the *maqāṣid* model, can be called ameliorative (*taḥsīniya*) human rights, and which are intended to enable people to live not just a decent life but a *good life*. Thus, while the level of necessary human rights—in the area of health, for example—is concerned with taking vital measures to protect human health and the level of required human rights serves to enable a decent provision of healthcare, the level of ameliorative rights aims to ensure "the enjoyment of the highest attainable standard of physical and mental health."[101] In this sense, the European Social Charter, for example, calls upon states parties to "accept as the aim of their policy, to be pursued by all appropriate means, both national and international in character, the attainment of conditions in which . . . everyone has the right to benefit from any measures enabling him to enjoy the highest possible standard of health attainable."[102] What all three of the above-mentioned categories have in common is the goal of ensuring the protection of human needs. What distinguishes them is the relative strength of the human rights they contain.

[101] Article 12 of the International Covenant on Economic, Social and Cultural Rights.
[102] Part 1, Article 11 of the European Social Charter, of October 18, 1961.

Metaphorically, this model can be compared to the structure of a hospital, which pursues the normative goal of protecting human health. Since health can be threatened by a variety of different diseases, the hospital is divided into different departments (internal medicine, surgery, psychiatry, neurosurgery, etc.), each focusing on different dimensions or areas in which human health may be compromised. Because the severity of these impairments can vary with the severity of the disease, each department is further divided into different wards, each of which contributes to the protection of human health at different levels of intensity. Within this institutional framework, life-threatening illnesses and injuries are treated in the intensive care unit, which aims to ensure the patient's survival through appropriate intensive medical measures. Once the patient's condition has been stabilized, he or she is transferred to the step-down unit, where further therapeutic measures are taken to promote and accelerate the process of rehabilitation and recovery. In order to prevent possible relapses and to counteract a recurrence of the disease, prophylactic measures are taken within the framework of outpatient care to strengthen and improve the patient's state of health.

As this example illustrates, the different wards and their associated treatments are classified according to their levels of urgency for the protection of health. It is also apparent that the patient is able to achieve a different level of health in each ward. The possibility of enjoying a higher level of health presupposes that the more basic level of health has already been ensured, since any threat to the more basic level is also a threat to the higher level. Accordingly, the wards that facilitate the respective levels of health are arranged in an ascending *grounding relationship*, with the intensive care unit serving as the foundation for the step-down unit, while the latter serves as the foundation for the outpatient care unit.

The same grounding relationship can be observed in the case of the different levels of human rights. Here, the necessary human rights form the basis for the required human rights, whereas the latter form the basis for the ameliorative human rights. This grounding relationship should alert us to the fact that the fulfillment of more basic rights is a prerequisite for the effective, or even the possible, exercise of higher-level rights. Just as it would be of little use to a patient with a life-threatening illness to be treated with, say, heat therapy, it would be of little use to a starving person to be able to run in the next parliamentary election. Similarly, it would be of little use to a person suffering from oppression or discrimination to be able to participate in the cultural life of society, and someone who has not learned to read will correspondingly be unable to make use of his or her freedom to conduct scientific research. As these examples show, any impairment of the more basic rights inevitably implies an impairment of the higher-level rights, giving rise to the imperative to ensure the fulfillment of the former in order to enable the effective exercise of the latter.

It therefore makes sense to postulate a hierarchy of human rights, inasmuch as it provides us with a scale of urgency and priority by which politics must be guided in fulfilling its task of realizing human rights and the related goal of protecting needs. Such an orientation is also necessary, not least because the realization of human rights is directly linked to costs and the use of scarce resources.[103] In order to guarantee the effective exercise of human rights, resources must be allocated in such a way that the realization of the necessary human rights is ensured first, so that, building on this, the realization of the required human rights and, finally, the realization of the ameliorative human rights can be made possible. However, this does not support the mistaken assumption that the realization of higher-level human rights is optional or even dispensable when resources are scarce. Rather, resource scarcity requires that the state either generate or release the necessary resources and use them in such a way[104] that *all* levels of human rights can be fulfilled in order to enable people to achieve progressively higher levels of existence, from mere survival to a decent life to a good life.

It might be objected at this point that the conception of human rights outlined here makes a theoretical claim that goes far beyond our practical understanding of human rights. According to this objection, human rights have a minimalist character and should at most enable a decent life. The claims of human rights cannot extend to the good life, for the simple reason that the question of what exactly constitutes a good life depends on personal preferences and interests, and thus must be answered by each person for himself or herself. Independently of this, it can also be objected that, especially in view of the scarcity of resources, it makes more sense to limit the claim to human rights in order not to make it utopian even on a theoretical level.

103 See Stephen Holmes and Cass R. Sunstein, *The Cost of Rights: Why Liberty Depends on Taxes* (New York: Norton, 1999).

104 Therefore, one can also speak of a violation of human rights if a government merely provides its population with minimal services and puts the rest of the public funds "in its own pocket." As a result, the state loses its ability to provide both a higher quality and a more long-term guarantee that human rights will be fulfilled. Therefore, we must contradict Griffin when he writes, "A government that saw to it that its citizens reached the minimum acceptable welfare demanded by human rights but then diverted all the rest of the nation's wealth to itself would not thereby violate human rights." Griffin, *On Human Rights*, 283n34.

Regarding the first assertion, it should be noted, first, that it is based on an understanding that cannot be reconciled with the version of human rights codified in international law. In any case, it seems questionable to what extent one can speak of minimalism when the relevant legal documents grant human beings the right to enjoy the arts and to participate in scientific progress and its benefits.[105] Nor is there any trace of minimalism in the rights to rest and leisure and to regular paid vacation,[106] to work, including technical and vocational guidance and training,[107] to the continuous improvement of living conditions,[108] to the enjoyment of the highest attainable standard of physical and mental health,[109] and to the widest possible access to free higher education and to a system of financial support designed to achieve this end.[110] The aim of all these rights is obviously to enable people to enjoy a standard of living that goes beyond a decent life.

The second assertion must be accepted to the extent that the claim of human rights cannot be to guarantee people a good, successful, or happy life. This objection, however, ignores the fact that the claim of the conception of human rights defended here is not to ensure an individually perfect life, but to make possible a good life in general. As we have seen, its substantive frame of reference is limited to the indispensable and universal basic conditions of human existence, which it undertakes to protect as best it can in order to provide a secure *basis for human development.* In response to the objection concerning scarce resources, it should be emphasized that the grounding relationship described provides a guideline that should be followed in principle when it comes to the distribution of resources. It can be observed here that a considerable share of resources is invested in those measures and institutions that are needed to secure the more basic rights claims.[111] This can

[105] See Universal Declaration of Human Rights, Article 27.

[106] Universal Declaration of Human Rights, Article 24.

[107] See International Covenant on Economic, Social and Cultural Rights, Article 6.

[108] International Covenant on Economic, Social and Cultural Rights, Article 11.

[109] International Covenant on Economic, Social and Cultural Rights, Article 12.

[110] International Covenant on Economic, Social and Cultural Rights, Article 13.

[111] This, as Shue notes, holds not only for those rights that on the classical conception are described as positive rights, but also for those rights that are mistakenly described as negative: "At the very least the protection of rights to physical security necessitates police forces; criminal courts; penitentiaries; schools for training police, lawyers, and guards; and taxes to support an enormous system for the prevention, detection, and punishment of violations of personal security. All these activities and institutions are attempts at providing social guarantees for individuals' security so that they are not left to face alone forces that they cannot handle on their own. How much more than these expenditures one thinks would be necessary in order for people actually to be reasonably secure (as distinguished from merely having the cold comfort of knowing that the occasional criminal is punished after someone's security has already been violated) depends on one's theory of violent crime, but it is not unreasonable to believe that it would involve extremely expensive, 'positive'

be comparted to the intensive care unit of a hospital. Compared to the other units, it bears the largest share of personnel costs because, unlike the other units, it is staffed with highly qualified doctors and specially trained nurses and is equipped with a variety of technical devices that require appropriate monitoring. By comparison, the step-down unit accounts for a much smaller share of the personnel costs, and its technical equipment, although no less extensive, is qualitatively more limited. Both statements are even more true for the general care unit, so that the consumption of resources is lowest here. Suppose, however, that it also accounts for a significant portion of the total resources consumed. Would this be a reason to consider the general care unit dispensable? The staff of the step-down unit would emphatically deny this, because in the long run it would lead to an increased workload there as well. The role of the general care unit is to take precautionary measures to prevent the onset of disease, and to take appropriate measures to contain and reverse the progression of disease once it has taken hold. In this sense, it helps to relieve the pressure on the step-down unit and must therefore be seen as an investment that helps to prevent the patient's condition from worsening, thus avoiding even greater resource consumption and costs. The same relationship exists between the step-down unit and the intensive care unit. This should draw our attention to the fact that the different wards are not only in an ascending grounding relationship to each other but also in a countervailing *flanking relationship*. Regardless of the question of resources, this follows from the fact that in each case the higher ward fulfills the function of a protective zone for the lower ward by preventing a disease from potentially becoming more acute, thus contributing to the strengthening and stabilization of the patient's overall health.

To return to the reference to human rights at this point, we can see that the respective levels not only ground each other in the ascending direction but also flank each other in the descending direction. Thus, the higher-level rights help to consolidate and reinforce the general level of protection by either preventing or limiting the occurrence or progression of a threat. As Nooke observes, it is of no help to "someone who is struggling to survive if, instead of giving her something to eat or providing her with health care, we point to her guaranteed right to express her opinion or her right to vote. And yet it would be better for everyone if, before they starve to death, they could

programs." Shue, *Basic Rights*, 37–38. For an example of a list of the various costs and expenditures, see the table in Holmes and Sunstein, *The Cost of Rights*, 234–236.

safely draw public attention to their situation and peacefully protest against social exclusion."[112] Likewise, democratic participation rights can serve to create the political framework to hold state officials accountable when they disregard rights. This is not to say, of course, that the value of civil liberties and democratic participation derives solely from their function in protecting human security.[113] Of course, they also enable people to see themselves as free and equal members of society, and thus also serve to protect their needs for recognition and belonging. Different human rights can thus contribute more or less directly to the protection of different needs. For example, the right to participate in the benefits of scientific progress could contribute to a better and more effective exercise of freedom of expression and assembly. This was impressively demonstrated during the Arab Spring, which was triggered in no small part by the accessibility of social networks on the internet. The relevance of scientific progress and the resulting technological achievements is also a function of the opportunities created, for example, in the areas of healthcare and education. Better educational opportunities, in turn, could contribute to the eradication of poverty, which could lead to the elimination of forced or child labor. As these examples show, there is an extraordinarily complex relationship between the various threats and the associated human rights response mechanisms that can only be sketched here. Working out this relationship in detail would require empirical research and knowledge of a wide range of scientific disciplines that would enable us to establish a systematic relationship between the threats to the various spheres of life and their impact on human life.

[112] Günter Nooke, "Universalität der Menschenrechte—Zur Rettung einer Idee," in *Gelten Menschenrechte Universal? Begründungen und Infragestellungen*, ed. Günter Nooke, Georg Lohmann, and Gerhard Wahlers (Freiburg: Herder, 2008), 32.

[113] This argument is made by Thomas Christiano, "An Instrumental Argument for a Human Right to Democracy," *Philosophy and Public Affairs* 39, no. 2 (2011): 142–176.

Conclusion

In this book, I have explored the question of whether it is possible to develop a conception of human rights that can satisfy the normative requirements of universality and Islamic legitimacy in equal measure. Underlying this question is an attempt to disentangle the idea of human rights from a field of tension in which it is located in contemporary Islamic discourse. This tension is a function of the requirement that human rights must enjoy Islamic legitimacy—that is, they must be anchored in the edifice of Islamic law and thought—while they must also be able to command universal agreement, that is, they must be justifiable independently of the Islamic faith.

The reconstruction of this field of tension in the present study has taken the form of an analysis of the Islamic discourse on human rights, which has been examined contextually and systematically. From a contextual perspective, I have been able to establish that a major motivation of this discourse is to prove that Islam does not need foreign moral "teachings," since, depending on the view defended, it is either said to be morally complete in itself and thus has no need of foreign ideas of human rights, or even to have originally invented human rights. From a systematic point of view, I have surveyed the spectrum of Islamic human rights discourse and to arrange it according to a criterion that explains the differences in content and methodology of the answers to the question of the compatibility of Islam and human rights. I have distinguished four Muslim argumentative stances and analyzed their content: first, the argument of *rejection*, which asserts that human rights do not agree with Islam and must therefore be rejected; second, the argument of *incompatibility*, according to which Islam cannot be reconciled with human rights; third, the argument of *appropriation*, which assumes that human rights are valid only "within the framework of Islamic law"; and finally, the argument of *assimilation*, which seeks to demonstrate that Islam and human rights can be reconciled without any problem.

To explain these contrasting assessments of human rights, I have argued that claims about the compatibility of Islam and human rights depend essentially on the underlying conceptions of Islamic law. To this end, in the

Human Rights Between Universality and Islamic Legitimacy. Mahmoud Bassiouni, Oxford University Press.
 DOI: 10.1093/oso/9780197753897.003.0015

preliminary contextual analysis, I distinguished two conceptions of Islamic law, which I termed "static" and "dynamic." While the *static* conception of law is characterized by the rejection of a historical-critical view of the Islamic legal tradition, the *dynamic* conception assumes that Islamic legal norms are bound to specific times and places and that Islamic law is therefore capable of development. On this basis, I defended the thesis that the assessment of the compatibility of Islam and human rights in Islamic human rights discourse changes with an increasingly dynamic understanding of law. The more dynamic the position of Islamic law, the more likely it is that Islam and human rights can be reconciled.

What the reconstruction of Islamic human rights discourse has revealed is, first, that there is a very wide spectrum of opinion among Muslims when it comes to the question of the compatibility of Islam and human rights. Contrary to what is often assumed, there is no single Islamic position on human rights. What is striking about the Islamic discourse, however, is that it is primarily concerned with ridding itself of the stigma of being the "human rights problem child." Because of this reactive dynamic, the discourse has not yet been able to make an independent and theoretically valuable contribution to the general understanding of human rights. This is particularly evident in the case of the justification of human rights. The central assumption that human rights are given by God or have a divine foundation leads to the problematic conclusion that human beings are not entitled to them as such but only because they are creatures of God. As a result, respect for human rights becomes primarily a ritual duty to God, while the moral duty to individual human beings remains secondary and somehow only follows from the primary religious duty. This inevitably leads to another problem. For if human rights are to be respected only because faith makes this an obligation, then people of another faith, or of no faith at all, would have no binding reason to respect human rights at all. The problem with the Muslim justification of human rights is therefore that it wants to establish universal human rights without basing its justification on a foundation that could command universal agreement, and thus without being able to obligate all people equally to respect human rights.

On the theoretical level of justification, therefore, human rights must be justified independently of the Islamic faith in order to guarantee their universal validity. From a Muslim perspective, the problem arises that the acceptance of human rights is directly linked to the ability to establish an affirmative Islamic relationship to them, that is, to legitimize human rights from within the edifice of Islamic law and thought. This has to do, first, with the fact that human rights are normative claims that grant individuals a certain scope for action, but also prescribe a certain mode of action and thus encroach on the moral terrain claimed by religion. This problem is aggravated by the fact that the idea of human rights is part of an identity discourse in which they are often presented as "Occidental Christian values" to which other cultures must adapt. In order to avoid the appearance that accepting human rights means merely adopting supposedly "Western" ideas, therefore, it must be possible to derive and justify human rights from within the Islamic tradition.

In sum, the development of the Muslim understanding of human rights is situated in a field of tension between two different normative demands: the demand for universality and the demand for Islamic legitimacy. The question that this dilemma raised for me was therefore whether it is possible to formulate a conception of human rights that both enjoys Islamic legitimacy and can command universal agreement.

In order to answer this question, in the third part of the book I delved somewhat deeper into Islamic legal theory and dealt with a concept in the history of ideas that has emerged in connection with the justification of Islamic legal and revealed norms. The core idea of this conception is that Islamic legal norms have not been revealed arbitrarily or without reason but are aimed at the realization of certain objectives (*maqāṣid*) that the legislator, that is, God, wants to achieve by enacting them and which are therefore to be realized in a timeless manner. According to the classical jurists, based on an inductive analysis of legal norms, exactly five such legal purposes can be identified: the protection of life (*nafs*), reason (*ʿaql*), religion (*dīn*), offspring (*nasl*), and property (*māl*). These are basic human needs, the protection of which is indispensable for human existence. A consensus on this can be reached independently of religion, they argue, because reason is capable of recognizing these basic goods as worthy of protection even without the guidance of revelation, on the basis of an empirical consideration of human reality. This is nothing more than securing the basic conditions of human existence (*ḍarūrat al-khalq*).

In terms of how these five basic needs are protected by Islamic law, the classical jurists developed an interesting taxonomy, which I took up again in the last part of the book to develop a conception of human rights on this basis. In principle, the jurists argued that anything that serves to protect these five basic needs is a good (*maṣlaḥa*), while anything that prevents the protection of these basic needs is an evil (*mafsada*), the elimination of which is simultaneously a good. However, since not all goods contribute equally to the protection of the five basic needs, the jurists further distinguished three hierarchical levels of goods, each of which serves to protect the needs to a different extent. Necessary goods (*ḍarūriyāt*) counteract those evils that directly prevent the protection of a need and thus endanger human existence as such. Required goods (*ḥājiyāt*) counteract those evils that severely impair the protection of a need and thus prevent human beings from enjoying a tolerable existence. Finally, ameliorative goods (*taḥsiniyāt*) counteract those evils that can prevent a good life and indirectly endanger the protection of a need. A common feature of the goods on all these levels is that they relate to the protection of the five basic needs. They are distinguished by the fact that they enable increasingly sophisticated forms of human existence, from survival to a tolerable life to a good life.

The reconstruction of the classical *maqāṣid* theory was followed by a chapter in which I addressed some points of criticism and open questions. The main question was whether the basic needs identified by the jurists meet their postulated requirements of necessity, universality, and empirical ascertainability. Based on an analysis of the various justifications, I concluded that they do not, and that the classical theory of Islamic legal purposes is in need of both theological and philosophical revision if it is to live up to its own claims. Before presenting my own thoughts on the subject, I first discussed contemporary Islamic legal discourse and examined fourteen different proposals for reconceptualizing Islamic legal purposes. Central to the modern discourse is the argument that the restriction of Islamic legal purposes to five basic needs is historically and socially conditioned, and that therefore new legal purposes worthy of protection today must be determined in the light of social developments.

However, the modern legal discourse turns out to be quite arbitrary in this respect, since practically every author has a different idea of what goods should be protected in today's world. Accordingly, I criticized the modern discourse for failing to deal with the classical theory of legal purposes in sufficient detail, since the five basic needs of the classical theory are neither arbitrary theological prescriptions nor needs arising from a particular historical or social necessity. Rather, according to the classical argument, they are empirically ascertainable, necessary, and universal basic conditions of human existence. Therefore, I emphasized the need to understand the premises of the classical theory in order to arrive at a coherent and methodologically sound revision of the *maqāṣid* rather than one based on wishful thinking or arbitrary determinations. In other words, to avoid the latter error, we need to identify needs that meet the criteria of necessity, universality, and empirical demonstrability. This enables us to create a basis for legal reasoning that meets the requirements of universal agreement and Islamic legitimacy mentioned at the beginning. The basis of human needs enjoys Islamic legitimacy because its protection is the purpose of Islamic law, and it can command universal agreement because human needs represent a universal canon of values even independent of religious considerations. Thus, this is a foundation of legal reasoning that is also religious but is not essentially religious.

In order to specify this basis, the fourth part of the book focused on the concept of human needs. The first step was to offer a more precise specification of the concept of needs and to distinguish it from similar concepts (interests, preferences, desires, etc.). I defined the concept of need as referring to the universal, objective, and necessary conditions of human existence. "Universal" in this context expresses the fact that needs exist among all human beings regardless of historical or cultural differences; human needs are objective in the sense that their existence can be studied empirically. Finally, the criterion of necessity limits the concept to those needs without which human existence would be threatened.

In an attempt to determine what specific needs human beings have, I examined a variety of theories that address the topic of human needs in the context of various scientific disciplines. Specifically, I examined theories from motivational psychology, sociology, and peace and conflict studies. Based on an evaluation of these different theories, I identified five categories of needs, namely the needs for health, safety, belonging, recognition, and meaning. Given the centrality of these needs to human existence, I attempted—following the theory of Islamic legal purposes—to conceptualize human rights on the basis of human needs.

I began by postulating that a concept of human rights must meet three criteria. First, it should explain the moral relevance of human rights; that is, it should be able to explain why it is important for human beings to have certain rights. Second, it should specify how the content of human rights can be determined and which rights are involved. Third, it should do so in a way that is understandable and, in principle, acceptable to all people.

This led to a critical analysis of a number of prominent contemporary conceptions of human rights in terms of their ability to meet these three criteria, including those of John Rawls, Charles Beitz, Rainer Forst, James Griffin, and John Tasioulas. On the basis of this critique, I argued that human rights can most plausibly be understood as institutions for the protection of basic human needs. According to this thesis, the moral relevance of human rights can be explained by the fact that they serve to protect elementary and necessary needs without which human existence would be threatened. These are needs that exist independently of subjective attitudes and are therefore ethically neutral and intersubjectively justifiable. Thus human needs in this sense constitute a basis for human rights that can command universal agreement and at the same time define their substantive frame of reference.

In an attempt to formulate this idea in more detail, I argued, following the theory of Islamic legal purposes, that human rights are norms that serve to protect human needs against corresponding threats. We can speak of a human right when we can show that it is capable of protecting a human need against a corresponding threat. I noted in this context that human rights are not addressed directly to individuals, but primarily to the prevailing political order, and that they impose three obligations on it: first, to refrain from actions that endanger human needs (duty of forbearance); second, to take measures to prevent threats from other, nonstate actors (duty of prevention); and third, to take measures to assist those who are victims of a threat through no fault of their own (duty of assistance). In this context, I noted that a human rights claim cannot be made for every threat, but only for those threats that are both foreseeable and capable of being remedied by practical measures on the part of the ruling political order. What measures are practicable may change over time. This led to the conclusion that human rights aspirations increase with technical and scientific progress, since this creates progressively better opportunities to protect human needs against relevant threats. At the same time, I noted that technological, economic, and environmental change is accompanied by ever new threats that endanger human needs in previously unknown ways. Since, according to the view defended here, the identification of the specific content of human rights depends on the existence of specific threats, it follows that the scope of human rights increases with the emergence of new threats. Thus I argued that the scope of human rights claims depends on two factors: the emergence of new threats and the emergence of new means of protection against threats. Thus the content of human rights is not predetermined but evolves over time with the threats to human needs and the means of protecting them.

Accordingly, I have rejected the description of the established canon of human rights as "preexistent." Rather, according to the view defended here, human rights must be understood as socially constructed mechanisms that emerged at different times and in response to particular practices and conditions that threatened and violated people's basic needs. Thus the process of the emergence of human rights is not top-down, starting from some higher authority or transcendental moral principle that leads to a particular canon of human rights independent of human experience. Rather, it begins with the observation or experience of certain practices or conditions that violate people's basic needs and are therefore perceived as morally unacceptable. In response, certain norms are constructed and formulated to protect people from the experienced threats. Our contemporary understanding of human rights is a product of this process. Accordingly, it would be a mistake to regard the current canon of human rights as closed, since new, previously unknown or unperceived threats may lead to the articulation of new rights.

While I have thus established a direct link between the question of the content of human rights and the existence of specific threats, I have also argued that the weight and associated priority of a human right is directly related to the severity of the threat against which that human right is intended to protect. The severity of a threat, in turn, is directly related to the extent to which it contributes to the impairment of human existence. Therefore, following the theory of Islamic legal purposes, I identified different levels of human rights according to their respective degrees of urgency.

As a first step, I identified a category of human rights that corresponds to those threats that so seriously impair a person's needs that his or her very *existence* is threatened. The associated human rights are addressed in terms of their content to the respective ruling political order and oblige it to refrain from causing such threats, to prevent them through practicable measures, and to assist in the event that they occur. The importance of these rights is bound up with the fact that they serve to protect human existence, the preservation of which is the necessary condition for the exercise of all other rights. Thus, in line with Henry Shue, we can also speak here of basic rights or, in the terminology of *maqāṣid* theory, of necessary (*ḍarūriya*) human rights. In addition to the necessary human rights, I have identified another category of human rights that go beyond the protection of mere existence and enable a *dignified life*. These human rights call for a qualitatively superior form of human life with respect to those threats that, while not endangering human existence, so seriously impair a person's needs that his or her life is physiologically and psychologically virtually intolerable. The second category of human rights, which I have called required (*ḥājiya*) human rights following the *maqāṣid* model, thus serves to counteract those threats that would allow only a life lived under degrading conditions. At the same time, the required human rights also provide a basis for the exercise of a third category of rights, which I have called ameliorative (*taḥsīniya*) human rights in analogy to the *maqāṣid* model. This name is explained by the fact that the specific purpose of this category of human rights is to improve the protection of human needs in such a way as to enable people to live not just a dignified life but a *good life*.

The three categories of human rights are linked by their common purpose of ensuring the protection of human needs. What distinguishes them is the strength of their respective contributions to the protection of human needs. I pointed out that the fulfillment of the more basic rights is a precondition for the effective or even possible exercise of the higher-level rights. This grounding relationship therefore implies that any impairment of the more basic rights is also an impairment of the higher-level rights, which gives rise to the imperative to ensure that the more basic rights are fulfilled in order to enable the effective exercise of the higher-level rights. From a practical point of view, therefore, it makes sense to postulate a hierarchy of human rights insofar as it provides us with a scale of urgency and priority by which to guide policy in its task of realizing human rights. From a theoretical perspective, it leads us to problematize the related propositions that human rights are indivisible and all have equal weight, since not every violation of the higher-level rights necessarily leads to an impairment of the more basic rights. Nevertheless, I pointed out that the violation of the higher-level rights represents a potential gateway for threats that could lead to the impairment of the more basic rights. In this sense, therefore, the higher-level rights serve to prevent or contain the emergence or aggravation of threats, thereby contributing to the consolidation and strengthening of the more basic rights. Accordingly, I was able to establish not only an ascending relationship of foundation but also a descending relationship of flanking between the various levels of human rights.

The interrelationships between these levels of human rights could only be sketched in the present book, and they require further theoretical reflection and empirical research. Therefore, the foregoing discussion by no means claims to have presented a complete conception of human rights. Nevertheless, by drawing on Islamic legal philosophy, it has developed a theoretical approach that has proved promising for systematically addressing and answering essential and unresolved questions in human rights theory. Thus the discussion of Islamic legal philosophy has not only offered an approach to human rights that is legitimate in Islamic terms. It has also provided important theoretical building blocks that can contribute to the construction of a critical conception of human rights that is informed by both history and current events and is capable of commanding universal agreement. With this book, I hope to have laid at least a theoretical foundation on which further reflection can build.

References

'Abd al-Fattāḥ, Muḥammad, ed. *Mukhtarāt Min Ṣaḥīḥ al-Aḥādīth al-Qudsiyya Ma' al-Arba'īn al-Nawawiyya.* al-Mansura: Dār al-Manāra, 2004.

'Abd al-Jabbār, al-Qāḍi Abu al-Ḥassan. *al-Mughni fī Abwāb al-Tawḥīd wa'l-'Adl.* 16 vols. Cairo: al-Mu'assasa al-Miṣriyya al-'Āmma li'l-Ta'līf w'al-Anbā', 1962–1966.

Abid, Lise J. "Die Debatte um Gender und Menschenrechte im Islam." In *Facetten islamischer Welten: Geschlechterordnungen, Frauen- und Menschenrechte in der Diskussion,* edited by Mechthild Rumpf, Ute Gerhard, and Mechtild M. Jansen, 143–162. Bielefeld: transcript, 2003.

Abid, Lise J., *Menschenrechte im Islam.* Bonn: Huda Schriftenreihe, 2001.

Abou el Fadl, Khaled. *And God Knows the Soldiers: The Authoritative and Authoritarian in Islamic Discourses.* Lanham, MD: University Press of America, 2001.

Abou El Fadl, Khaled, "Cultivating Human Rights: Islamic Law and the Humanist Imperative." In *Law and Tradition in Classical Islamic Thought,* Michael Cook et al., 167–183. New York: Palgrave Macmillan, 2013.

Abou el Fadl, Khaled. *The Great Theft: Wrestling Islam from the Extremists.* San Francisco: HarperCollins, 2005.

Abou El Fadl, Khaled. "The Human Rights Commitment in Modern Islam." In *Human Rights and Responsibilities in the World Religions,* edited by Joseph Runzo, Nancy M. Martin, and Arvind Sharma, 301–364. Oxford: Oneworld, 2003.

Abou el Fadl, Khaled. *Islam and the Challenge of Democracy.* Princeton, NJ: Princeton University Press, 2004.

Abou El Fadl, Khaled. "Shari'ah and Human Rights." In *Routledge Handbook on Human Rights and the Middle East and North Africa,* edited by Anthony Tirado Chase, 268–287. London: Routledge, 2016.

Abou el Fadl, Khaled. *Speaking in God's Name: Islamic Law, Authority and Women.* Oxford: Oneworld, 2001.

Abū Sulaymān, 'Abdul-Ḥamīd. *Azmat al-'Aql al-Muslim.* Herndon, VA: International Institute of Islamic Thought, 1991.

Abū Sulaymān, 'Abdul-Ḥamīd. *Crisis in the Muslim Mind.* Herndon, VA: International Institute of Islamic Thought, 1993.

Abū Sulaymān, 'Abdul-Ḥamīd. *Towards an Islamic Theory of International Relations: New Directions for Methodology and Thought.* Herndon, VA: International Institute of Islamic Thought, 1993.

Abu Zayd, Nasr Hamid. *Critique of Religious Discourse.* New Haven, CT: Yale University Press, 2018.

Afshari, Reza. "An Essay on Islamic Cultural Relativism in the Discourse of Human Rights." *Human Rights Quarterly* 16, no. 2 (1994): 235–276.

Aḥmad, al-Tāj Ibrāhīm Daf' Allah. "Ḥuqūq al-Insān fī al-Sharī'a al-Islāmiyya fī Ḍaw' Maṣadrīhā al-Qur'ān w-al-Sunnah." *Majallat Kulliyyat al-Tarbiyyah Jām'at al-Azhar* 34, no. 164 (2015): 471–520.

Alexy, Robert. "Menschenrechte ohne Metaphysik?" *Deutsche Zeitschrift für Philosophie* 52, no. 1 (2004): 15–24.

Alexy, Robert. *Theorie der Grundrechte.* Frankfurt: Suhrkamp, 1985.

Ali, Abdullah Yusuf. *The Meaning of the Holy Qur'an.* Beltsville, MD: Amana, 1989.

Ali, Kecia. *Sexual Ethics and Islam: Feminist Reflections of Qur'an, Hadith and Jurisprudence.* Oxford: Oneworld, 2006.

al-ʿĀlim, Yūsuf Ḥāmid. *al-Maqāsid al-ʿĀmmah lil Sharīʿa al-Islamiyya.* Herndon, VA: International Institute of Islamic Thought, 1991.

al-Alusi, Mahmud Shukri. "Ijtihad and the Refutation of Nabhani." In *Modernist Islam 1840–1940: A Sourcebook*, edited by Charles Kurzman, 158–171. Oxford: Oxford University Press, 2002.

ʿAlwān, Fahmi Muḥammad. *al-Qiyam al-Ḍarūriyya wa Maqāṣid al-Tashrīʿ al-Islāmi.* Cairo: al-Hayʾa al-Miṣriyya al-ʿĀmma li'l-Kitāb, 1989.

al-Alwani, Taha Jabir. *Issues in Contemporary Islamic Thought.* London: International Institute of Islamic Thought, 2005.

al-Alwani, Taha Jabir, and Imad al Din Khalil. *The Qur'an and the Sunnah: The Time-Space Factor.* Herndon, VA: International Institute of Islamic Thought, 1991.

Amanat, Abbas, and Frank Griffel, eds. *Shari'a: Islamic Law in the Contemporary Context.* Stanford, CA: Stanford University Press, 2007.

al-Āmidi, Sayf al-Dīn. *al-Aḥkām fī Uṣūl al-Aḥkām.* Beirut: Dār al-Kutub al-ʿIlmiyya, 2005.

Amirpur, Katajun. "Sind Islam und Menschenrechte vereinbar? Zeitgenössische Menschenrechtsbegründungen: Von der demokratieorientierten Deutung des Korans zur Akzeptanz außer-religiöser Werte." In *Facetten islamischer Welten: Geschlechterordnungen, Frauen- und Menschenrechte in der Diskussion*, edited by Mechthild Rumpf, Ute Gerhard, and Mechtild M. Jansen, 162–178. Bielefeld: transcript, 2003.

an-Naʿim, Abdullahi. *Decolonizing Human Rights.* Cambridge: Cambridge University Press, 2021.

an-Naʿim, Abdullahi A., ed. *Human Rights in Cross-Cultural Perspectives: A Quest for Consensus.* Philadelphia: University of Pennsylvania Press, 1991.

an-Naʿim, Abdullahi. *Islam and the Secular State: Negotiating the Future of Shariʿa.* Cambridge, MA: Harvard University Press, 2008.

an-Naʿim, Abdullahi A. "The Position of Islamic States regarding the Universal Declaration of Human Rights." In *Innovation and Inspiration: Fifty Years of the Universal Declaration of Human Rights*, edited by Peter Baehr, Cees Flinterman, and Mignon Senders, 177–192. Amsterdam: Royal Netherlands Academy of Arts and Sciences, 1999.

an-Naʿim, Abdullahi A. *Toward an Islamic Reformation: Civil Liberties, Human Rights, and International Law.* Syracuse, NY: Syracuse University Press, 1990.

an-Naʿim, Abdullahi, and Mashood A. Baderin, eds. *Islam and Human Rights: Selected Essays of Abdullahi An-Naʿim.* London: Routledge, 2010.

an-Naʿim, Abdullahi A., and Francis M. Deng, eds. *Human Rights in Africa: Cross-Cultural Perspectives.* Washington, D.C.: Brookings Institution, 1990.

Appiah, Kwame Anthony, and Henry Louis Gates, eds. *Identities.* Chicago: University of Chicago Press, 1995.

al-ʿAqīl, Layla. "Ḥuqūq al-Insān fī al-Qurʾān al-Karīm." *Majallat al-ʿUlūm al-Islāmiyya al-Dawliyya* 4, no. 3 (2020): 97–131.

Arendt, Hannah. *Eichmann in Jerusalem: A Report on the Banality of Evil.* New York: Viking Press, 1965.

Asad, Muhammad. *The Message of the Qur'ān.* Bristol: The Book Foundation, 2003.

Asad, Muhammad. *This Law of Ours and Other Essays.* Kuala Lumpur: Islamic Book Trust, 2000.

el-Assad, Nassir el-Din. "Politik auf der Grundlage göttlicher Autorität." In *Menschenbilder Menschenrechte. Islam und Okzident: Kulturen im Konflikt*, edited by Stefan Batzli, Fridolin Kissling, and Rudolf Zihlmann, 206–216. Zürich: Unionsverlag, 1994.

Asseburg, Muriel, ed. *Moderate Islamisten als Reformakteure?* Bonn: Bundeszentrale für politische Bildung, 2008.

Attia, Gamal Eldin. *Towards Realization of the Higher Intents of Islamic Law: Maqāṣid al-Shariʿah: A Functional Approach.* Herndon, VA: International Institute of Islamic Thought, 2007.

ʿAṭiyya, Jamāl al-Dīn. *Naḥw Tafʿīl Maqāṣid al-Sharīʿa.* Damascus: Dār al-Fikr, 2003.

Auda, Jasser. *Maqāṣid al-Sharīʿah: A Beginner's Guide.* Herndon, VA: International Institute of Islamic Thought, 2008.

Auda, Jasser. *Maqasid al-Shariah as Philosophy of Islamic Law: A Systems Approach.* Herndon, VA: International Institute of Islamic Thought, 2008.

el-Awa, Mohamed S. *Punishment in Islamic Law.* Plainfield, IL: American Trust Publications, 2000.

al-Azm, Sadik Jalal. *Is Islam Secularizable? Challenging Political and Religious Taboos.* Berlin: Gerlach Press, 2014.

al-Azmeh, Aziz. *Islams and Modernities.* London: Verso, 1993.

ʿAzwi, Muḥammad al-Ṭāhir. *al-Ghazw al-Thaqāfī wʾal-Fikri lil-ʿĀlam al-Islāmi.* Mīlah: Dār al-Huda, 1999.

Baderin, Mashood A. *International Human Rights and Islamic Law.* Oxford: Oxford University Press, 2003.

Baderin, Mashood A. "A Macroscopic Analysis of the Practice of Muslim State Parties to International Human Rights Treaties: Conflict or Congruence?" *Human Rights Law Review* 1, no. 2 (2001): 265–303.

Baehr, Peter, Cees Flinterman, and Mignon Senders, eds. *Innovation and Inspiration: Fifty Years of the Universal Declaration of Human Rights.* Amsterdam: Royal Netherlands Academy of Arts and Sciences, 1999.

Bagby, Ihsan Abdul-Wajid. "Utility in Classical Islamic Law: The Concept of Maṣlaḥa in Uṣūl al-Fiqh." PhD diss., University of Michigan, 1986.

Bajoghli, Narges. *Iran Reframed. Anxieties of Power in the Islamic Republic.* Stanford, CA: Stanford University Press, 2019.

el-Baradie, Adel. *Gottes-Recht und Menschen-Recht.* Baden-Baden: Nomos, 1983.

Barlas, Asma. *"Believing Women" in Islam: Unreading Patriarchal Interpretations of the Qurʾan.* Austin: University of Texas Press, 2002.

Batzli, Stefan, Fridolin Kissling, and Rudolf Zihlmann, eds. *Menschenbilder Menschenrechte: Islam und Okzident: Kulturen im Konflikt.* Zürich: Unionsverlag, 1994.

Bauer, Oanne R., and Daniel A. Bell, eds. *The East Asian Challenge for Human Rights.* Cambridge: Cambridge University Press, 1999.

Bayat, Asef. *Revolutionary Life: The Everyday of the Arab Spring.* Cambridge, MA: Harvard University Press, 2021.

al-Bayḍāwi, Nāṣir al-Dīn ʿAbd Allāh Ibn ʿUmar. *Minhaj al-Wuṣūl ila ʿilm al-Uṣūl.* Khartoum: Dār al-Fikr, 1980.

Beitz, Charles R. *The Idea of Human Rights.* Oxford: Oxford University Press, 2009.

Beitz, Charles R., and Robert E. Goodin, eds. *Global Basic Rights.* Oxford: Oxford University Press, 2009.

Bergsträsser, Gotthelf. *Grundzüge des Islamischen Rechts.* Revised and edited by Joseph Schacht. Berlin: de Gruyter, 1935.

Bernsdorf, Wilhelm. *Wörterbuch der Soziologie.* Stuttgart: Enke, 1969.

Bielefeldt, Heiner. "Muslim Voices in the Human Rights Debate." *Human Rights Quarterly* 17, no. 4 (1995): 587–617.

Bielefeldt, Heiner. *Philosophie der Menschenrechte: Grundlagen eines weltweiten Freiheitsethos.* Darmstadt: Primus, 1998.

Bilgrami, Akeel. "What Is a Muslim?" In *Identities*, edited by Kwame Anthony Appiah and Henry Louis Gates, 198–219. Chicago: University of Chicago Press, 1995.

Blackstone, William. *Commentaries on the Laws of England.* Chicago: University of Chicago Press, 1979.

Blunt, Wilfred. *The Future of Islam.* Dublin: Nonsuch, 2007.

Bölke, Dorothee. "Der islamische Fundamentalismus bei Peter Scholl-Latour, Gerhard Konzelmann und Bassam Tibi." In *Das Schwert des "Experten,"* edited by Verena Klemm and Karin Hörner, 200–228.Heidelberg: Palmyra, 1993.

Brentano, Lujo. *Versuch einer Theorie der Bedürfnisse.* Munich: Verlag der Königlich Bayerischen Akademie der Wissenschaften, 1908.

Buchanan, Allen. "The Egalitarianism of Human Rights." *Ethics* 120, no. 4 (2010): 679–710.

Burke, Edmund. *Reflections on the Revolution in France.* Edited by Frank M. Turner. New Haven, CT: Yale University Press, 2003.

Burton, John. *Conflict: Resolution and Provention.* New York: Macmillan, 1990.

Burton, John. *Deviance, Terrorism and War: The Process of Solving Unsolved Social and Political Problems.* Oxford: Martin Robertson, 1979.

Burton, John. *Global Conflict: The Domestic Sources of International Crisis.* Brighton: Wheatsheaf, 1984.

Büttner, Friedemann. "Der fundamentalistische Impuls und die Herausforderung der Moderne." *Leviathan* 24, no. 4 (1996): 469–492.

Caney, Simon. "Human Rights, Responsibilities, and Climate Change." In *Global Basic Rights,* edited by Charles R. Beitz and Robert E. Goodin, 227–247. Oxford: Oxford University Press, 2009.

Castellino, Joshua, and Kathleen A. Cavanaugh. *Minority Rights in the Middle East.* Oxford: Oxford University Press, 2013.

Center for Progressive Reform. *Regulatory Blowout: How Regulatory Failures Made the BP Disaster Possible, and How the System Can Be Fixed to Avoid a Recurrence.* White Paper 1007, October 2010. https://papers.ssrn.com/sol3/papers.cfm?abstract_id=1685606.

Charfi, Mohamed. "Die Menschenrechte im Bezugsfeld von Religion, Recht und Staat in den islamischen Ländern." In *Freiheit der Religion: Christentum und Islam unter dem Anspruch der Menschenrechte,* edited by Johannes Schwartländer, 93–118 Mainz: Matthias-Grünewald-Verlag, 1993.

Chase, Anthony Tirado. *Human Rights, Revolution, and Reform in the Muslim World.* Boulder, CO: Lynne Rienner, 2012.

Chomsky, Noam. "The United States and the Challenge of Relativity." In *Human Rights Fifty Years On: A Reappraisal,* edited by Tony Evans, 24–56. Manchester: Manchester University Press, 1998.

Christiano, Thomas. "An Instrumental Argument for a Human Right to Democracy." *Philosophy and Public Affairs* 39, no. 2 (2011): 142–176.

Clark, Mary E. "Meaningful Social Bonding as a Universal Human Need." In *Conflict: Human Needs Theory,* edited by John Burton, 34–59. New York: Palgrave Macmillan, 1990.

Coate, Roger A., and Jerel A. Rosati, eds. *The Power of Human Needs in World Society.* Boulder, CO: Lynne Rienner, 1988.

Cohen, Stephen B. "Conditioning US Security Assistance on Human Rights Practices." *American Journal of International Law* 76, no. 2 (1982): 246–279.

Coulson, Noel J. *A History of Islamic Law.* Edinburgh: Edinburgh University Press, 1964.

Democracy Now. "Asmaa Mahfouz and the YouTube Video That Helped Spark the Egyptian Uprising." February 8, 2011. https://www.democracynow.org/2011/2/8/asmaa_mahfouz_the_youtube_video_that.

Donnelly, Jack. *Universal Human Rights in Theory and Practice.* Ithaca, NY: Cornell University Press, 2003.

al-Drīni, Muḥammad Fatḥi. *al-Haqq wa Madā Ṣulṭān al-Dawla fī Taqyīdihi.* Beirut: Mu'assasat al-Risāla, 1984.

Duderija, Adis, ed. *Maqāsid al-Sharīʿa and Contemporary Muslim Thought: An Examination.* New York: Palgrave Macmillan, 2014.

Dwyer, Kevin. *Arab Voices: The Human Rights Debate in the Middle East.* London: Routledge, 1991.

Emon, Anver M. "On the Pope, Cartoons, and Apostates: Shari'a 2006." *Journal of Law and Religion* 22, no. 2 (2007): 303–321.

Ende, Werner, and Udo Steinbach, eds. *Islam in the World Today: A Handbook of Politics, Religion, Culture, and Society.* Ithaca, NY: Cornell University Press, 2011.

Eppler, Erhard. *Was braucht der Mensch? Vision: Politik im Dienst der Grundbedürfnisse.* Frankfurt: Campus, 2000.

Evans, Tony, ed. *Human Rights Fifty Years On: A Reappraisal.* Manchester: Manchester University Press, 1998.

Fadel, Mohammad H. "The Challenge of Human Rights." *Seasons* 5, no. 1 (2008): 59–80.

Fadel, Mohammad H. "Public Reason as a Strategy for Principled Reconciliation: The Case of Islamic Law and International Human Rights Law." *Chicago Journal of International Law* 8, no. 1 (2007): 1–20.

Fadel, Mohammad H. "The True, the Good, the Reasonable: The Theological and Ethical Roots of Public Reasons in Islamic Law." *Canadian Journal of Law and Jurisprudence* 21, no. 1 (2008): 5–69.

Fadel, Mohammad H. "Two Women, One Man: Knowledge, Power, and Gender in Medieval Sunni Legal Thought." *International Journal of Middle East Studies* 29, no. 2 (1997): 185–204.

Falaturi, Abdoldjavad. *Westliche Menschenrechtsvorstellungen und Koran.* Cologne: GMSG, 2002.

Farooq, Mohammad Omar. *Toward Our Reformation: From Legalism to Value-Oriented Islamic Law and Jurisprudence.* Herndon, VA: International Institute of Islamic Thought, 2011.

al-Fāsi, ʿAllāl. *Maqāṣid al-Sharīʿa al-Islāmiyya wa Makārimihā.* Beirut: Dār al-Gharb al-Islāmi, 1993.

El Figiery, Moataz. *Islamic Law and Human Rights: The Muslim Brotherhood in Egypt.* Newcastle: Cambridge Scholars, 2016.

al-Fīrūzābādi, Muḥammad Ibn Yaʿqūb. *al-Qāmūs al-Muḥīṭ.* Beirut: Dār al-Kutub al-ʿIlmiyya, 1995.

Forst, Rainer. "The Basic Right to Justification: Towards a Constructivist Conception of Human Rights." In Forst, *The Right to Justification: Elements of a Constructivist Theory of Justice,* translated by Jeffrey Flynn, 203–228. New York: Columbia University Press, 2012.

Forst, Rainer. "The Ground of Critique: On the Concept of Human Dignity in Social Orders of Justification." *Philosophy & Social Criticism* 37, no. 9 (2011): 965–976.

Forst, Rainer. "The Justification of Huan Rights and the Basic Right Justification: A Reflexive Approach." In Forst, *Justification and Critique: Towards a Critical Theory of Politics,* translated by Ciaran Cronin, 38–70. Cambridge, UK: Polity, 2014.

Forst, Rainer. *The Right to Justification: Elements of a Constructivist Theory of Justice.* Translated by Jeffrey Flynn. New York: Columbia University Press, 2012.

Forst, Rainer. *Toleration in Conflict: Past and Present.* Translated by Ciaran Cronin. Cambridge: Cambridge University Press, 2013.

Frankl, Viktor E. *Der Wille zum Sinn.* Bern: Hogrefe, 2005.

Frankl, Viktor. *Man's Search for Meaning.* New York: Pocket Books, 1985.

Freeman, Michael. "The Problem of Secularism in Human Rights Theory." *Human Rights Quarterly* 26, no. 2 (2004): 375–400.

Galtung, Johan. "The Basic Needs Approach." In *Human Needs: A Contribution to the Current Debate,* edited by Katrin Lederer, 55–125. Cambridge, MA: Oelgeschlager, Gunn & Hain, 1980.

Galtung, Johan. *Human Rights in Another Key.* Cambridge, UK: Polity, 1994.

Garaudy, Roger. "Die Menschenrechte und der Islam: Begründung, Überlieferung, Verletzung." *Concilium* 26 (1990): 119–128.

Gasiet, Seev. *Menschliche Bedürfnisse: Eine theoretische Synthese.* Frankfurt: Campus, 1981.

al-Ghannūshi, Rāshid. *al-Ḥurriyāt al-ʿAmma fi-l-Dawla al-Islāmiyya.* Beirut: Markaz Dirasāt al-Waḥda al-ʿArabiyya, 1993.

al-Ghazāli, Abū Ḥāmid. *The Book of Knowledge.* Translated by Nabih Amin Faris. New Dehli: Islamic Book Service, n.d.

al-Ghazāli, Abū Ḥāmid. *Iḥyā' ʿUlūm al-Dīn.* Beirut: Dār al-Maʿrifa, 1982.

al-Ghazāli, Abū Ḥāmid. *al-Iqtiṣād fī al-Iʿtiqād.* Ankara: Nur Matbaasi, 1962.

al-Ghazāli, Abū Ḥāmid. al-*Mankhūl min Ta'līqāt al-Uṣūl*. Edited by Muḥammad Ḥassan Hītu. Damascus: Dār al-Fikr, 1998.
al-Ghazāli, Abū Ḥāmid. *al-Mustaṣfa min 'Ilm al-Uṣūl*. Edited by Ḥamza Ibn Zuhayr Ḥāfiẓ. Medina: al-Jāmi'a al-Islāmiyya, n.d.
al-Ghazāli, Abū Ḥāmid. *Shifā' al-Ghalīl fī Bayān al-Shabah w'al-Mukhīl wa Masāliku al-Ta'līl*. Baghdad: Matba'at al-Irshād, 1971.
al-Ghazāli, Muḥammad. *Huqūq al-Insān bayna Ta'līm al-Islām wa I'lān al-Umam al-Muttaḥida*. Alexandria: Dār al-Da'wa, 1993.
Geertz, Clifford. *The Interpretation of Cultures*. New York: Basic Books, 1973.
Gewirth, Alan. *Human Rights: Essays on Justification and Applications*. Chicago: University of Chicago Press, 1982.
Gosepath, Stefan. "Sinn der Menschenrechte." In *Die Menschenrechte: unteilbar und gleichgewichtig?*, edited by Georg Lohman, Stefan Gosepath, Arnd Pollmann, Claudia Mahler, and Norman Weiß, 21–27. Potsdam: Universität Potsdam, 2005.
Gosepath, Stefan, and Georg Lohmann, eds. *Philosophie der Menschenrechte*. Frankfurt: Suhrkamp, 1998.
Greenberg, Nathaniel. *How Information Warfare Shaped the Arab Spring: The Politics of Narrative in Tunisia and Egypt*. Edinburgh: Edinburgh University Press, 2019.
Griffin, James. "Human Rights and the Autonomy of International Law." In *The Philosophy of International Law*, edited by Samatha Besson and John Tasioulas, 339–355. Oxford: Oxford University Press, 2010.
Griffin, James. *On Human Rights*. Oxford: Oxford University Press, 2008.
Gunn, T. Jeremy. "Do Human Rights Have a Secular, Individualistic and Anti-Islamic Bias?" *Daedalus* 149, no. 3 (2020): 148–169.
al-Hageel, Sulieman Abdul Rahman. *Human Rights in Islam and Refutation of the Misconceived Allegations Associated with These Rights*. Riyadh: Imam Muhammad Bin Saud Islamic University, 1999.
Hallaq, Wael B. *Authority, Continuity and Change in Islamic Law*. Cambridge: Cambridge University Press, 2001.
Hallaq, Wael B. *A History of Islamic Legal Theories: An Introduction to Sunnī Uṣūl al-Fiqh*. Cambridge: Cambridge University Press, 1997.
Hallaq, Wael B. "On Inductive Corroboration, Probability and Certainty in Sunnī Legal Thought." in *Islamic Law and Jurisprudence: Studies in Honor of Farhat J. Ziadeh*, edited by Nicholas Heer, 3–31. Seattle: University of Washington Press, 1990.
Hallaq, Wael B. *The Origins and Evolution of Islamic Law*. Cambridge: Cambridge University Press, 2005.
Hallaq, Wael B. "Was the Gate of Ijtihad Closed?" *International Journal of Middle East Studies* 16, no. 1 (1984): 3–41.
Halliday, Fred. "Relativism and Universalism in Human Rights: The Case of the Islamic Middle East." *Political Studies* 43 (1995): 152–167.
al-Ḥasani, Isma'īl. *Naẓariyyat al-Maqāṣid 'ind Imām Muḥammad al-Ṭāhir Ibn 'Ashūr*. Herndon, VA: International Institute of Islamic Thought, 1995.
Hassan, Riffat. "On Human Rights and the Qur'anic Perspective." *Journal of Ecumenical Studies* 19 (1982): 51–65.
Hasse, Jana, Erwin Müller, and Patricia Schneider, eds. *Menschenrechte: Bilanz und Perspektiven*. Baden-Baden: Nomos, 2002.
Hauser, Jan. *Vom Sinn des Leidens: Die Bedeutung systemtheoretischer, existenzphilosophischer und religiös-spiritueller Anschauungsweisen für die therapeutische Praxis*. Würzburg: Königshausen & Neumann, 2004.
Heer, Nicholas, ed. *Islamic Law and Jurisprudence: Studies in Honor of Farhat J. Ziadeh*. Seattle: University of Washington Press, 1990.
Hegel, Georg Wilhelm Friedrich. *Elements of the Philosophy of Right*. Edited by Allen Wood. Translated by H. B. Nisbet. Cambridge: Cambridge University Press, 1991.

Helmy, Yomna. "From Islamic Modernism to Theorizing Authoritarianism: Bin Bayyah and the Politicization of the *Maqāṣid* Discourse." *American Journal of Islam and Society* 38, nos. 3–4 (2021): 36–70.
Henning, Max. *Der Koran.* Stuttgart: Reclam, 1998.
al-Hibri, Azizah. "Muslim Women's Rights in the Global Village: Challenges and Opportunities." *Journal of Law and Religion* 15, nos. 1–2 (2000): 37–66.
al-Hibri, Azizah. "A Study of Islamic Herstory: Or How Did We Ever Get into This Mess?" *Women's Study International Forum* 5, no. 2 (1982): 207–219.
Hicks, Neil. "Does Islamist Human Rights Activism Offer a Remedy to the Crisis of Human Rights Implementation in the Middle East?" *Human Rights Quarterly* 24, no. 2 (2002): 361–381.
Hillesum, Etty. *An Interrupted Life: The Diaries 1941–1943 and Letters from Westerbork.* New York: Henry Holt, 1996.
Hippler, Jochen, ed. *Der Westen und die islamische Welt: Eine muslimische Position.* Stuttgart: Institut für Auslandsbeziehungen, 2004.
Hippler, Jochen, and Andrea Lueg. *Feindbild Islam oder Dialogue der Kulturen.* Hamburg: Konkret Literatur Verlag, 2002.
Hinsch, Wilfried. *Gerechtfertigte Ungleichheiten: Grundsätze sozialer Gerechtigkeit.* Berlin: de Gruyter, 2002.
Hobbes, Thomas. *Leviathan.* Revised student edition. Edited by R. Tuck. Cambridge: Cambridge University Press, 1996.
Höffe, Otfried. "Transzendentaler Tausch: Eine Legitimationsfigur für Menschenrechte?" In *Philosophie der Menschenrechte,* edited by Stefan Gosepath and Georg Lohmann, 29–47. Frankfurt: Suhrkamp, 1998.
Hofmann, Murad Wilfired. *Islam: The Alternative.* Translated by Christiane Banerji and Murad Hofmann. Beltsville, MD: Amana, 2003.
Hofmann, Murad Wilfired. *Religion on the Rise: Islam in the Third Millennium.* Beltsville, MD: Amana, 2001.
Holmes, Stephen, and Cass R. Sunstein. *The Cost of Rights: Why Liberty Depends on Taxes.* New York: Norton, 1999.
Hondrich, Karl Otto, ed. *Bedürfnisse im Wandel: Theorie, Zeitdiagnose, Forschungsergebnisse.* Opladen: Westdeutscher Verlag, 1983.
Hondrich, Karl Otto. *Menschliche Bedürfnisse und soziale Steuerung: Eine Einführung in die Sozialwissenschaften.* Reinbek: Rohwolt, 1975.
Honneth, Axel. *The I in We: Studies in the Theory of Recognition.* Translated by Joseph Ganahl. Cambridge, UK: Polity, 2012.
Honneth, Axel. *The Struggle for Recognition: The Moral Grammar of Social Conflicts.* Translated by J. Anderson. Cambridge, UK: Polity, 1996.
Hourani, Albert Habib. *Arabic Thought in the Liberal Age: 1798–1939.* London: Oxford University Press, 1962.
Hourani, George F. "A Revised Chronology of al-Ghāzalī's Writings." *Journal of the American Oriental Society* 104, no. 2 (1984): 289–302.
Hume, David. *A Treatise on Human Nature.* Oxford: Clarendon Press, 1960.
Ibn ʿAbd al-Salām, ʿIzz al-Dīn. *Qawāʿid al-Aḥkām fī Maṣāliḥ al-Anām.* Damascus: Dār al-Qalam, n.d.
Ibn ʿAshūr, Muḥammad al-Ṭāhir. *Maqāṣid al-Sharīʿa al-Islāmiyya.* Tunis: Dār al-Salām, 2009.
Ibn Ashur, Muhammad al-Tahir. *Treatise on Maqāṣid al-Sharīʿah.* Translated by Mohaned El-Tahir El-Mesawi. Herndon, VA: International Institute of Islamic Thought, 2006.
Ibn al-Ḥājib, Jamāl al-Dīn. *Muntaha al-Wuṣūl wʾal-Amal fī ʿIlmay al-Uṣūl wʾal Jadal.* Beirut: Dār al-Kutub al-ʿIlmiyya, 1985.
Ibn Khaldūn, ʿAbd al-Raḥmān. *Muqaddimat Ibn Khaldūn.* Edited byʿAli ʿAbd al-Wāḥed Wāfi. Cairo: Maktabat al-Usra, 2006.

Ibn Rushd. *The Distinguished Jurist's Primer.* Translated by Imran Ahsan Khan Nyazee. Reading: Garnett, 2006.

Ibn Rushd, Abū al-Walīd Muḥammad Ibn Aḥmad. *Bidāyat al-Mujtahid wa Nihāyat al-Muqtaṣid.* Beirut: Dār al-Maʿrifa, 2000.

Ibn Taimiyya, Aḥmad Ibn ʿAbd al-Ḥalīm. *Majmūʿ al-Fatāwa li Shaykh al-Islām Ibn Taimiyya.* Mansura: Dār al-Wafāʾ, 2005.

Ibn Taimiyya, Aḥmad Ibn ʿAbd al-Ḥalīm. *al-Siyāsa al-Sharʿiyya fī Iṣlāḥ al-Rāʿī w-al-Raʿiyya.* Beirut: Dār al-Afāq al-Jadīda, 1983.

Ibrahim, Mohamed. *Al Qurān aus Sicht des Uṣūl al Fiqh als erste Hauptquelle der Rechtsfindung im Islam.* Darmstadt: Averroes Institut für wissenschaftliche Islamforschung, 2007.

Ibrahim, Mohamed. *Islamische Scharia versus Menschenrechte?* Darmstadt: Averroes Institut für wissenschaftliche Islamforschung, 2007.

Ibrahim, Yasir S. "Muḥammad ʿAbduh and Maqāṣid al-Sharīʿa." *Maghreb Review* 32, no. 1 (2007): 2–30.

Ignatieff, Michael. *Human Rights as Politics and as Idolatry.* Princeton, NJ: Princeton University Press, 2001.

ʿImāra, Muḥammad. *al-Islām wa Ḥuqūq al-Insān: Ḍarūriyyāt, la Ḥuqūq.* Cairo: Dār al-Shurūq, 2006.

International Commission of Jurists, Rijksuniversiteit Limburg Centre of Human Rights, and Urban Morgan Institute for Human Rights. "The Maastricht Guidelines on Violations of Economic, Social and Cultural Rights." *Human Rights Quarterly* 20, no. 3 (1998): 691–704.

International Commission of Jurists, University of Kuwait, and Union of Arab Lawyers, eds. *Human Rights in Islam, Report of a Seminar held in Kuwait, December 1980.* Geneva: International Commission of Jursits, 1982.

Iqbal, Muhammad. *Letters of Iqbal to Jinnah: A Collection of Iqbal's Letters to the Qaid-l-Azam Conveying His Views on the Political Future of Muslim India.* Edited by Sh. M. Ashraf. Lahore: n.p., 1974.

Iqbal, Muhammad. *The Reconstruction of Religious Thought in Islam.* Stanford, CA: Stanford University Press, 2012.

Ishay, Micheline R. *The Levant Express: The Arab Uprisings, Human Rights and the Future of the Middle East.* New Haven, CT: Yale University Press, 2019.

Ismaʿīl, Fatima M. *al-Qurʾān waʾl-Naẓar al-ʿAqli.* Herndon, VA: International Institute of Islamic Thought, 1993.

al-Jabri, Mohammed Abed. *Democracy, Human Rights and Law in Islamic Thought.* London: I. B. Tauris, 2009.

Jackson, Sherman A. "Islam and the Promotion of Human Rights." *Telos* 203 (2023): 59–77.

Jackson, Sherman A. *Islamic Law and the State: The Constitutional Jurisprudence of Shihāb al-Dīn al-Qarāfī.* Leiden: Brill, 1996.

Jackson, Sherman A. "Literalism, Empiricism, and Induction: Apprehending and Concretizing Islamic Law's *Maqāsid al Sharīʿah* in the Modern World." *Michigan State Law Review,* Special Issue 6 (2006), 1469–1486.

al-Jawziyya, Ibn Qayyim. *Aʿlām al-Muwaqqiʿīn ʿan Rabb al-ʿĀlamīn.* Beirut: Dār al-Kutub al-ʿIlmiyya, 1996.

Joas, Hans, and Klaus Wiegandt, eds. *The Cultural Values of Europe.* Liverpool: Liverpool University Press, 2008.

Johansen, Baber. *Contingency in a Sacred Law: Legal and Ethical Norms in the Muslim Fiqh.* Leiden: Brill, 1999.

Johnston, David L. "Maqāṣid al-Sharīʿa: Epistemology and Hermeneutics of Muslim Theologies of Human Rights." *Die Welt des Islams* 47, no. 2 (2007): 149–187.

Johnston, David L., "ʿAllāl al-Fāsi: Sharīʿa as a Blueprint for Righteous Global Citizenship?" In *Sharīʿa: Islamic Law in the Contemporary Context,* edited by Abbas Amanat and Frank Griffel, 83–103. Stanford: Stanford University Press, 2007.

al-Juwayni, ʿAbd al-Mālik Abū al-Maʿālī. *al-Burhān fī Uṣūl al-Fiqh*. Edited by ʿAbd al-ʿAẓīm al-Dīb. Doha: Jāmiʿat Qaṭar, 1979.

Kadivar, Mohsen. *Blasphemy and Apostasy in Islam: Debates in Shi'a Jurisprudence*. Edinburgh: Edinburgh University Press, 2021.

Kadivar, Mohsen. "Freedom of Religion and Belief in Islam." In *The New Voices of Islam: Rethinking Politics and Modernity: A Reader*, edited by Mehran Kamrava, 65–97. Berkeley: University of California Press, 2006.

Kadivar, Mohsen. *Human Rights and Reformist Islam*. Edinburgh: Edinburgh University Press, 2021.

Kadivar, Mohsen. "Revisiting Women's Rights in Islam: 'Egalitarian Justice' in Lieu of 'Desert-based Justice.'" In *Gender and Equality in Muslim Family Law: Justice and Ethics in the Islamic Legal Tradition*, edited by Ziba Mir-Hosseini, Kari Vogt, Lena Larsen, and Christian Moe, 213–234, London: I. B. Tauris, 2013.

Kälin, Walter, and Jörg Künzli. *Universeller Menschenrechtsschutz*. Basel: Helbing & Lichtenhan, 2005.

Kalisch, Muhammad. "Muslime als religiöse Minderheit: Ein Beitrag zur Notwendigkeit eines neuen *iğtihād*." In *Muslime im Rechtsstaat*, edited by Thorsten Gerald Schneiders and Lamya Kaddor, 47–67. Münster: Lit, 2005.

Kalisch, Muhammad. "Vernunft und Flexibilität in der islamischen Rechtsmethodik." PhD diss., TU Darmstadt, 1997.

Kamali, Mohammad Hashim. *The Dignity of Man: An Islamic Perspective*. Cambridge, UK: Islamic Texts Society, 2002.

Kamali, Mohammad Hashim. *Freedom, Equality and Justice in Islam*. Cambridge, UK: Islamic Texts Society, 2002.

Kamali, Mohammad Hashim. *Freedom of Expression in Islam*. Cambridge, UK: Islamic Texts Society, 1997.

Kamali, Mohammad Hashim. *Principles of Islamic Jurisprudence*. Cambridge, UK: Islamic Texts Society, 2003.

Kamali, Mohammad Hashim. *Shari'ah Law: An Introduction*. Oxford: Oneworld, 2008.

Kamrava, Mehran, ed. *The New Voices of Islam: Rethinking Politics and Modernity: A Reader*. Berkeley: University of California Press, 2006.

Kassis, Riyadh Aziz. *The Book of Proverbs and Arabic Proverbial Works*. Leiden: Brill, 1999.

al-Kawākibi, ʿAbd al-Raḥmān. "Summary of the Causes of Stagnation." In *Modernist Islam 1840–1940: A Sourcebook*, edited by Charles Kurzman, 152–154. Oxford: Oxford University Press, 2002.

Kersting, Wolfgang. *Theorien der sozialen Gerechtigkeit*. Stuttgart: Metzler, 2000.

Khalil, Karima. *Messages from Tahrir: Signs from Egypt's Revolution*. Cairo: American University of Cairo Press, 2011.

Khallāf, ʿAbd al-Wahhāb. *ʿIlm Uṣūl al-Fiqh*. Cairo: Maktabat Dār al-Turāth, 1956.

Khan, Muhammad Zafrullah. *Islam und Menschenrechte*. Frankfurt: Verlag der Islam, 2004.

Klemm, Verena, and Karin Hörner, eds. *Das Schwert des "Experten."* Heidelberg: Palmyra, 1993.

Koji, Teraya. "Emerging Hierarchy in International Human Rights and Beyond: From the Perspective of Non-derogable Rights." *European Journal of International Law* 12, no. 5 (2001): 917–941.

Körner, Felix, ed. *Alter Text—Neuer Kontext: Koranhermeneutik in der Türkei heute*. Freiburg: Herder, 2006.

Krämer, Gudrun. "The Contest of Values: Notes on Contemporary Islamic Discourse." In *The Cultural Values of Europe*, edited by Hans Joas and Klaus Wiegandt, 338–356.Liverpool: Liverpool University Press, 2008.

Krämer, Gudrun. *Gottes Staat als Republik: Reflexionen zeitgenössischer Muslime zu Islam, Menschenrechten und Demokratie*. Baden-Baden: Nomos, 1999.

Kreide, Regina. *Globale Politik und Menschenrechte. Macht und Ohnmacht eines politischen Instruments*. Frankfurt: Campus, 2007.

Kuhn-Zuber, Gabriele. "Der Islam und die Universalität der Menschenrechte in der Kritik." In *Menschenrechte. Bilanz und Perspektiven*, edited by Jana Hasse, Erwin Müller, and Patricia Schneider, 307–331. Baden-Baden: Nomos, 2002.

Künzli, Jörg. *Zwischen Rigidität und Flexibilität: Der Verpflichtungsgrad internationaler Menschenrechte: Ein Beitrag zum Zusammenspiel von Menschenrechten, humanitärem Völkerrecht und dem Recht der Staatenverantwortlichkeit*. Berlin: Duncker & Humblot, 2001.

Kurzman, Charles, ed. *Modernist Islam 1840–1940: A Sourcebook*. Oxford: Oxford University Press, 2002.

Lederer, Katrin, ed. *Human Needs: A Contribution to the Current Debate*. Cambridge, MA: Oelgeschlager, Gunn & Hain, 1980.

Locke, John. *Two Treatises of Government*. Edited by Peter Laslett. Cambridge: Cambridge University Press, 1988.

Lohman, Georg, Stefan Gosepath, Arnd Pollmann, Claudia Mahler, and Norman Weiß, eds. *Die Menschenrechte: Unteilbar und gleichgewichtig?* Potsdam: Universität Potsdam, 2005.

MacIntyre, Alasdair. *After Virtue: A Study in Moral Theory*. Notre Dame, IN: University of Notre Dame Press, 1981.

Mahler, Claudia, and Norman Weiß. "Zur Unteilbarkeit der Menschenrechte—Anmerkungen aus juristischer, insbesondere völkerrechtlicher Sicht." In *Die Menschenrechte: Unteilbar und gleichgewichtig?*, edited by Georg Lohman, Stefan Gosepath, Arnd Pollmann, Claudia Mahler, and Norman Weiß, 39–46. Potsdam: Universität Potsdam, 2005.

Manzoor, Parvez S. "Human Rights: Secular Transcendence or Cultural Imperialism?" *Muslim World Book Review* 15, no. 1 (1994): 3–10.

Maritain, Jacques. *Man and the State*. Chicago: University of Chicago Press, 1998.

Maslow, Abraham H. *Motivation and Personality*. New York: Harper & Row, 1954.

Maslow, Abraham H. *Toward a Psychology of Being*. 3rd edition. New York: Wiley, 1999.

Masud, Muhammad Khalid. *Shatibi's Philosophy of Islamic Law*. Kuala Lumpur: Islamic Book Trust, 2005.

al-Mawardi, Abu al-Ḥasan. *al-Ḥāwi al-Kabīr*. Beirut: Dār al-Kutub al-ʿIlmiyya, 1994.

Mawdudi, Abul Aʿla. *Human Rights in Islam*. Leicester: Islamic Foundation, 1976.

Mayer, Ann E. "Current Muslim Thinking on Human Rights." In *Human Rights in Africa: Cross-Cultural Perspectives*, edited by Abdullahi A. An-Na'im and Francis M. Deng, 133–156. Washington, D.C.: Brookings Institution, 1990.

Mayer, Ann E. *Islam and Human Rights: Tradition and Politics*. Boulder, CO: Westview Press, 1991.

Melchert, Christopher. *The Formation of the Sunni Schools of Law, 9th–10th Centuries C.E.* Leiden: Brill, 1997.

Menke, Christoph, and Arnd Pollmann. *Philosophie der Menschenrechte zur Einführung*. Hamburg: Junius, 2007.

Merad, Ali. "Das islamische Bewusstsein vor dem Anruf der Menschenrechte." In *Freiheit der Religion: Christentum und Islam unter dem Anspruch der Menschenrechte*, edited by Johannes Schwartländer, 347–352. Mainz: Matthias-Grünewald-Verlag, 1993.

Merad, Ali. "Die sharīʿa—Weg zur Quelle des Lebens." In *Freiheit der Religion: Christentum und Islam unter dem Anspruch der Menschenrechte*, edited by Johannes Schwartländer, 392–393. Mainz: Matthias-Grünewald-Verlag, 1993.

Mernissi, Fatema. *Islam and Democracy: Fear of the Modern World*. Translated by Mary Jo Lakeland. New York: Basic Books, 2002.

Miadi, Zineb. "Gleiche Rechte für Mann und Frau im Koran." In *Menschenbilder Menschenrechte: Islam und Okzident: Kulturen im Konflikt*, edited by Stefan Batzli, Fridolin Kissling, and Rudolf Zihlmann, 89–103. Zürich: Unionsverlag, 1994.

Mill, John Stuart. *Utilitarianism*. In Mill, *Utilitarianism and On Liberty: Including Mill's "Essay on Bentham" and Selections from the Writings of Jeremy Bentham and John Austin*, edited by Mary Warnock, 181–235. Malden, MA: Blackwell, 2003.

Miller, David. *National Responsibility and Global Justice.* Oxford: Oxford University Press, 2007.

Mir-Hosseini, Ziba. "Neue Überlegungen zum Geschlechterverhältnis im Islam: Perspektiven der Gerechtigkeit und Gleichheit für Frauen." In *Facetten islamischer Welten: Geschlechterordnungen, Frauen- und Menschenrechte in der Diskussion*, edited by Mechthild Rumpf, Ute Gerhard, and Mechtild M. Jansen, 53–81. Bielefeld: transcript, 2003.

Modirzadeh, Naz K. "Taking Islamic Law Seriously: INGOs and the Battle for Muslim Hearts and Minds." *Harvard Human Rights Journal* 19 (2006): 191–233.

Morsink, Johannes. *The Universal Declaration of Human Rights: Origins, Drafting and Intent.* Philadelphia: University of Pennsylvania Press, 1999.

Morsink, Johannes. "World War Two and the Universal Declaration." *Human Rights Quarterly* 15, no. 2 (1993): 357–405.

Moser, Simon, Günter Ropohl, and Walther Zimmerli, eds. *Die "wahren" Bedürfnisse oder: Wissen wir was wir brauchen?* Basel: Schwabe, 1978.

Müller, Lorenz. *Islam und Menschenrechte: Sunnitische Muslime zwischen Islamismus, Säkularismus und Modernismus.* Hamburg: Deutsches Orient Institut, 1996.

Mumisa, Michael. *Islamic Law: Theory and Interpretation.* Beltsville, MD: Amana, 2002.

Münch, Ingo. *Die deutsche Staatsangehörigkeit: Vergangenheit—Gegenwart—Zukunft.* Berlin: de Gruyter, 2007.

Mutua, Makau. *Human Rights: A Political and Cultural Critique.* Philadelphia: University of Pennsylvania Press, 2002.

al-Najjar, Abd al Majid. *The Vicegerency of Man between Revelation and Reason: A Critique of the Dialectic of the Text, Reason, and Reality.* Herndon, VA: International Institute of Islamic Thought, 2000.

Naqvi, Syed Nawab Haider. *Perspectives on Morality and Human Well-Being: A Contribution to Islamic Economics.* Leicester: Islamic Foundation, 2003.

al-Nashshār, ʿAli Sāmi. *Nash'at al-Fikr al-Falsafi fī al-Islām.* Cairo: Dār al-Maʿārif, 1977.

Nassery, Idris, Rumee Ahmed, and Muna Tatari, eds. *The Objectives of Islamic Law: The Promises and Challenges of the Maqāsid al-Sharīʿa.* Lanham, MD: Lexington Books, 2018.

Netherlands Scientific Council for Government Policy. *Dynamism in Islamic Activism: Reference Points for Democratization and Human Rights.* Amsterdam: Amsterdam University Press, 2006.

Nickel, James W. *Making Sense of Human Rights.* Malden, MA: Blackwell, 2007.

Nickel, James. "Rethinking Indivisibility: Towards a Theory of Supporting Relations between Human Rights." *Human Rights Quarterly* 30, no. 4 (2008): 984–1001.

Nooke, Günter. "Universalität der Menschenrechte—Zur Rettung einer Idee." In *Gelten Menschenrechte Universal? Begründungen und Infragestellungen*, edited by Günter Nooke and Georg Lohmann, 16–46. Freiburg: Herder, 2008.

Nooke, Günter, and Georg Lohmann, eds. *Gelten Menschenrechte Universal? Begründungen und Infragestellungen.* Freiburg: Herder, 2008.

Numani, Shibli. *Al-Farooq: The Life of Omar the Great.* Delhi: Adam, 1996.

Nyazee, Imran Ahsan Khan. *Outlines of Islamic Jurisprudence.* Islamabad: Advanced Legal Study Institute, 2000.

Nyazee, Imran Ahsan Khan. *Theories of Islamic Law: The Methodology of Ijtihād.* Islamabad: Islamic Research Institute Press, 1994.

Opwis, Felicitas. *Maṣlaḥa and the Purpose of the Law: Islamic Discourse on Legal Change from the 4th/10th to 8th/14th Century.* Leiden: Brill, 2010.

Opwis, Felicitas. "Schariarechtliche Stellungsnahmen zum Drogenverbot." *Die Welt des Islam* 39, no. 2 (1999): 159–182.

Osman, Samia. "Die Stellung der Frau im Islam und im Okzident." In *Menschenbilder Menschenrechte: Islam und Okzident: Kulturen im Konflikt*, edited by Stefan Batzli, Fridolin Kissling, and Rudolf Zihlmann, 50–68. Zürich: Unionsverlag, 1994.

Pogge, Thomas. "Shue on Rights and Duties." In *Global Basic Rights*, edited by Charles R. Beitz and Robert E. Goodin, 113–130. Oxford: Oxford University Press, 2009.

Pogge, Thomas. *World Poverty and Human Rights*. Cambridge, UK: Polity, 2008.

Pollmann, Arnd. "Die Menschenrechte: Teilbar und ungleichgewichtig!" In *Die Menschenrechte: Unteilbar und gleichgewichtig?*, edited by Georg Lohman, Stefan Gosepath, Arnd Pollmann, Claudia Mahler, and Norman Weiß, 29–37. Potsdam: Universität Potsdam, 2005.

Pollmann, Arnd. "Von der philosophischen Begründung zur demokratischen Konkretisierung: Wie lassen sich Inhalt und Umfang der Menschenrechte bestimmten?" *Zeitschrift für Menschenrechte* 1 (2008): 9–25.

Powers, Paul R. *Intent in Islamic Law: Motive and Meaning in Medieval Sunni Fiqh*. Leiden: Brill, 2005.

Poya, Abbas, and Maurus Reinkowski, eds. *Das Unbehagen in der Islamwissenschaft: Ein klassisches Fach im Scheinwerferlicht der Politik und der Medien*. Bielefeldt: transcript, 2008.

al-Qaraḍāwi, Yūsuf. *Approaching the Sunnah: Comprehension and Controversy*. Herndon, VA: International Institute of Islamic Thought, 2006.

al-Qaraḍāwi Yūsuf. "'Awāmil al-Si'a w'al-Murūna fī al-Sharī'a al-Islāmiyya." In *Wujūb Taṭbīq al-Sharī'a al-Islāmiyya w'al-Shubuhāt Alati Tuthār Ḥawl Taṭbīqiha*, edited by Manā' al-Qaṭṭān, 69–140. Riyadh: Jāmi'at al-Imām Muḥammad Ibn Sa'ūd al-Islāmiyya, 1984.

al-Qaraḍāwi, Yūsuf, *Madkhal li Dirāsat al-Sharī'a al-Islāmiyya*. Cairo: Maktabat Wahba, 2009.

al-Qarāfi, Shihāb al-Dīn. *Kitāb al-Furūq: Anwār al-Burūq fī Anwā' al-Furūq*. Beirut: Dār al-Kutub al-'Ilmiyya, 1998.

al-Qarāfi, Shihāb al-Dīn. *Sharḥ Tanqīḥ al-Fuṣūl*. Beirut: Dār al-Fikr, 2004.

al-Qaṭṭān, Manā', ed. *Wujūb Taṭbīq al-Sharī'a al-Islāmiyya w'al-Shubuhāt Alati Tuthār Ḥawl Taṭbīqiha*. Riyadh: Jāmi'at al-Imām Muḥammad Ibn Sa'ūd al-Islāmiyya, 1984.

Quṣīla, Ṣāleḥ Zayd. "Ḥuqūq al-Insān fī al-Tasawwur al-Islāmī w-al-Wāqi' al-Insānī." *Majallat al-Ustādh al-Bāḥith li-l-Dirasāt al-Qanūniyya w-al-Siyāsiyya* 4, no. 2 (2019): 674–699.

Rabb, Intisar A. *Doubt in Islamic Law: A History of Legal Maxims, Interpretation and Islamic Criminal Law*. Cambridge: Cambridge University Press, 2015.

Rahman, Fazlur. *Islam and Modernity: Transformation of an Intellectual Tradition*. Chicago: University of Chicago Press, 1982.

al-Raisūni, Aḥmad. *Naẓariyyat al-Maqāṣid 'ind al-Imām al-Shāṭibi*. Herndon, VA: International Institute of Islamic Thought, 1995.

Ramadan, Said. *Islamic Law: Its Scope and Equity*. London: Macmillan, 1961.

Ramadan, Tariq. "A Call for a Moratorium on Corporal Punishment—The Debate in Review." In *New Directions in Islamic Thought: Exploring Reform and Muslim Tradition*, edited by Kari Vogt, Lena Larsen, and Christian Moe, 163–174. London: I. B. Tauris, 2009.

Ramadan, Tariq. *Islam: Le Face à Face des Civilisations: Quel Projet Pour Quelle Modernité?* Lyon: Tawhid, 1996.

Ramadan, Tariq. *Islam, the West and the Challenges of Modernity*. Leicester: Islamic Foundation, 2001.

Ramadan, Tariq. *Radical Reform: Islamic Ethics and Liberation*. Oxford: Oxford University Press, 2009.

Ramadan, Tariq. *To Be a European Muslim: A Study of Islamic Sources in the European Context*. Leicester: Islamic Foundation, 1999.

Ramadan, Tariq. "The Way (*Al-Sharia*) of Islam." In *The New Voices of Islam: Rethinking Politics and Modernity: A Reader*, edited by Mehran Kamrava, 65–97. Berkeley: University of California Press, 2006.

Ramadan, Tariq. *Western Muslims and the Future of Islam*. Oxford: Oxford University Press, 2004.

al-Rashīdī, Badr, Muḥammad Fawzy Ḥāmed, and 'Alī Sājed. "al-Ḥurriyāt wa Ḥuqūq al-Insān bayn al-Islām w-al-Mawāthīq al-Dawliyyah li-Ḥuqūq al-Insān." *Majallat al-'Ulūm al-Islāmiyya al-Dawliyya* 5, no. 1 (2021): 143–176.

Rawls, John. *The Law of Peoples.* Cambridge, MA: Harvard University Press, 1999.
al-Raysuni, Ahmad. *Imam al-Shatibi's Theory of the Higher Objectives and Intents of Islamic Law.* Herndon, VA: International Institute of Islamic Thought, 2005.
Raz, Joseph. "Human Rights without Foundations." In *The Philosophy of International Law,* edited by Samatha Besson and John Tasioulas, 321–337. Oxford: Oxford University Press, 2010.
al-Rāzi, Fakhr al-Dīn. *al-Maḥsūl fī 'Ilm 'Uṣūl al-Fiqh.* Beirut: Mu'assasat al-Risāla, 1997.
Renan, Ernest. *Discours et Conférences.* Paris: Calmann Lévy, 1887.
Renan, Ernest. "Islam and Science." In Renan, *What Is a Nation? And Other Political Writings,* translated and edited by M. F. N. Giglioli, 264–280. New York: Columbia University Press, 2018.
Renan, Ernest. "The Share of the Semitic People in the History of Civilization." In Renan, *Studies of Religious History and Criticism,* translated by O. B. Frothingham, 109–167. New York: F. W. Cristern, 1964.
Reus-Smit, Christian. "On Rights and Institutions." In *Global Basic Rights,* edited by Charles Beitz and Robert Goodin, 25–48. Oxford: Oxford University Press, 2009.
Rieffer-Flanagan, Barbara Ann. "Rhetoric versus Reality: American Foreign Policy and Religious Freedom in the Middle East." In *Routledge Handbook on Human Rights and the Middle East and North Africa,* edited by Anthony Tirado Chase, 317–328. London: Routledge, 2016.
Riḍa, Muḥammad Rashīd. *al-Waḥy al-Muḥammadi.* Beirut: Mu'assasat 'Izz al-Dīn, 1985.
Rohe, Mathias. *Islamic Law in Past and Present.* Leiden: Brill, 2015.
Ropohl, Günter. "Bedürfnisforschung und soziotechnische Praxis: Ein vorläufiges Resümee." In *Die "wahren" Bedürfnisse oder: Wissen wir was wir brauchen?,* edited by Simon Moser, Günter Ropohl, and Walther Zimmerli, 111–133. Basel: Schwabe, 1978.
Rousseau, Jean-Jacques. *Emile or On Education.* Translated and edited by Allan Bloom. New York: Basic Books, 1979.
Rumpf, Mechthild, Ute Gerhard, and Mechtild M. Jansen, eds. *Facetten islamischer Welten: Geschlechterordnungen, Frauen- und Menschenrechte in der Diskussion.* Bielefeld: transcript, 2003.
Rymer, Russ. *Genie: A Scientific Tragedy.* New York: Harper Collins, 1993.
Sachedina, Abdulaziz. *Islam and the Challenge of Human Rights.* Oxford: Oxford University Press, 2009.
Sachedina, Abdulaziz. "Review of Abdullahi An-Na'im, *Toward an Islamic Reformation: Civil Liberties, Human Rights and International Law.*" *International Journal of Middle East Studies* 25, no. 1 (1993): 155–157.
Saeed, Abdullah. *Interpreting the Qur'an: Towards a Contemporary Approach.* London: Routledge, 2006.
Saeed, Abdullah, and Hassan Saeed. *Freedom of Religion, Apostasy and Islam.* London: Routledge, 2016.
Said, Edward. *Orientalism.* New York: Vintage Books, 1979.
Schacht, Joseph. *An Introduction to Islamic Law.* Oxford: Clarendon Press, 1964.
Schmitz, Barbara. "Bedürfnisse und Gerechtigkeit." Habil., University of Basel, 2008.
Schneiders, Thorsten Gerald, and Lamya Kaddor, eds. *Muslime im Rechtsstaat.* Münster: Lit, 2005.
Schopenhauer, Arthur. *The Essays of Arthur Schopenhauer.* Vol. 5: *The Art of Controversy.* Translated by T. Bailey Saunders. University Park: Penn State Electronic Classics Series, 2005.
Schopenhauer, Arthur. *The World as Will and Representation.* Translated by E. F. J. Payne. New York: Dover, 1969.
Schulze, Reinhard. "'Orientalistics' and Orientalism." In *Islam in the World Today: A Handbook of Politics, Religion, Culture, and Society,* edited by Werner Ende and Udo Steinbach, 755–766. Ithaca, NY: Cornell University Press, 2011.

Schwartländer, Johannes, ed. *Freiheit der Religion: Christentum und Islam unter dem Anspruch der Menschenrechte.* Mainz: Matthias-Grünewald-Verlag, 1993.

Seiderman, Ian D. *Hierarchy in International Law: The Human Rights Dimension.* Antwerp: Intersentia, 2001.

Selye, Hans. *Stress in Health and Disease.* Boston: Buttersworths, 1976.

Sen, Amartya. *Identity and Violence: The Illusion of Destiny.* New York: W. W. Norton, 2006.

Sen, Amartya. *Poverty and Famines: An Essay on Entitlement and Deprivation.* Oxford: Clarendon Press, 1983.

Senghaas, Dieter. *Wohin driftet die Welt? Über die Zukunft friedlicher Koexistenz.* Frankfurt: Suhrkamp, 1994.

al-Sharfī, 'Abd al-Majīd. *al-Islam bayn al-Risāla wa'l-Tarīkh.* Beirut: Dār al-Talī'a, 2008.

al-Shāṭibi, Ibrahīm Ibn Mūsa. *al-Muwāfaqāt fī Uṣūl al-Aḥkām.* Beirut: Dār al-Ma'rifa, 1996.

al-Shawkāni, Muḥammad Ibn 'Alī. *Irshād al-Fuḥūl ilā Taḥqīq al-Ḥaqq min 'Ilm al-Uṣūl.* Riyadh: Dār al-Faḍīla, 2000.

al-Sheha, Abdul Rahman. *Misconceptions on Human Rights in Islam.* Riyadh: n.p., 2001.

Shestack, Jerome J. "The Philosophic Foundations of Human Rights." *Human Rights Quarterly* 20, no. 2 (1998): 201–234.

Shue, Henry. *Basic Rights: Subsistence, Affluence, and U.S. Foreign Policy.* Princeton, NJ: Princeton University Press, 1996.

Simmons, Alan John. *Justification and Legitimacy: Essay on Rights and Obligations.* Cambridge: Cambridge University Press, 2001.

Sites, Paul. "Needs as Analogues of Emotions." In *Conflict: Human Needs Theory,* edited by John Burton, 7–33. New York: Palgrave Macmillan, 1990.

Soroush, Abdolkarim. *Reason, Freedom, and Democracy in Islam: Essential Writings of Abdolkarim Soroush.* Edited by Mahmoud Sadri and Ahmad Sadri. Oxford: Oxford University Press, 2000.

Stein, Tine. *Himmlische Quellen und irdisches Recht: Religiöse Voraussetzungen des freiheitlichen Verfassungsstaates.* Frankfurt: Campus, 2007.

Steinbach, Udo. "Die Menschenrechte im Verständnis des Islam." *Verfassung und Recht in Übersee* 8, no. 1 (1975): 47–59.

Sternkopf, Thorsten. *Bildung gegen Afrikas modernen Fluch: HIV-Prävention: Pädagogische Aufgabe in der Entwicklungszusammenarbeit.* Marburg: Tectum, 2007.

Tabandeh, Sultanhussein. *A Muslim Commentary on the Universal Declaration of Human Rights.* London: F. J. Goulding, 1970.

al-Taftazāni, Sa'd al-Dīn Mas'ūd Ibn 'Umar. *al-Talwīḥ 'ala al-Tawḍīḥ.* Beirut: Dār al-Kutub al-'Ilmiyya, n.d..

Taha, Mahmoud M. *The Second Message of Islam.* Syracuse, NY: Syracuse University Press, 1989.

Talbi, Mohamed. "Religionsfreiheit—eine muslimische Perspektive." In *Freiheit der Religion: Christentum und Islam unter dem Anspruch der Menschenrechte,* edited by Johannes Schwartländer, 53–71. Mainz: Matthias-Grünewald-Verlag, 1993.

Talbi, Mohamed. "Religionsfreiheit—Recht des Menschen oder Berufung des Menschen?" In *Freiheit der Religion: Christentum und Islam unter dem Anspruch der Menschenrechte,* edited by Johannes Schwartländer, 242–260. Mainz: Matthias-Grünewald-Verlag, 1993.

Talbi, Mohamed. "Zum Problem der *umma* und der sharī'a in der islamischen Welt heute." In *Freiheit der Religion: Christentum und Islam unter dem Anspruch der Menschenrechte,* edited by Johannes Schwartländer, 387–391. Mainz: Matthias-Grünewald-Verlag, 1993.

al-Tarmānīni, 'Abd al-Salām. *Ḥuqūq al-Insān fī Nazar al-Sharī'ah al-Islāmiyya.* Beirut: Dār al-Kitāb al-Jadīd, 1976.

Tasioulas, John. "Are Human Rights Essentially Triggers for Intervention?" *Philosophy Compass* 4, no. 6 (2009): 938–950.

Tasioulas, John. "Human Rights, Universality and the Values of Personhood: Retracing Griffin's Steps." *European Journal of Philosophy* 10, no. 1 (2002): 79–100.

Tasioulas, John. "Taking Rights out of Human Rights." *Ethics* 120, no. 4 (2010): 647–678.

Taylor, Charles. *Multiculturalism: Examining the Politics of Recognition*. Edited by Amy Gutmann. Princeton, NJ: Princeton University Press, 1994.

Tibi, Bassam. *Die fundamentalistische Herausforderung: Der Islam und die Weltpolitik*. Munich: Beck, 2002.

Tibi, Bassam. *Im Schatten Allahs: Der Islam und die Menschenrechte*. Düsseldorf: Ullstein, 2003.

Tibi, Bassam. *Islam and the Cultural Accommodation of Social Change*. Translated by Clare Krojzl. Boulder, CO: Westview Press, 1990.

Tibi, Bassam. "Wie Feuer und Wasser." *Der Spiegel* 3 (1994): 170–172.

al-Tirmidhī, al-Ḥakīm Abū ʿAbdallāh. *al-Ṣalāh wa Maqāṣiduha*. Cairo: Dār al-Kitāb al-ʿArabī, 1965.

Toney, Jeffrey H., Hank Kaplowitz, Rongsun Pu, Feng Qi, and George Chang. "Science and Human Rights: A Bridge towards Benefiting Humanity." *Human Rights Quarterly* 32, no. 4 (2010): 1008–1017.

Tugendhat, Ernst. *Vorlesungen über Ethik*. Frankfurt: Suhrkamp, 1993.

United Nations Human Rights Committee. *General Comment No. 31: The Nature of the General Legal Obligation Imposed on States Parties to the Covenant*. 2004. https://www.refworld.org/legal/general/hrc/2004/en/52451.

ʿUthmān, ʿAlī ʿĪsā. *Falsafat al-Islām fī al-Insān*. Beirut: Dār al-Adab, 1986.

Vogt, Kari, Lena Larsen, and Christian Moe, eds. *New Directions in Islamic Thought: Exploring Reform and Muslim Tradition*. London: I. B. Tauris, 2009.

Vollmer, Bettina. *Die Geltung der Menschenrechte im Staatsnotstand: Eie völkerrechtliche Analyse der Rechtslage in Deutschland, Spanien und dem Vereinigten Königreich*. Baden-Baden: Nomos, 2010.

von Jhering, Rudolf. *Der Zweck im Recht*. Leipzig: Breitkopf & Härtel, 1884.

von Jhering, Rudolf. *Law as a Means to an End*. Translated by Isaac Husik. Boston: Boston Book Company, 1913.

Wadud, Amina. *Qur'an and Woman: Rereading the Sacred Text from a Woman's Perspective*. Oxford: Oxford University Press, 1999.

Wadud, Amina. "Qur'an, Gender and Interpretive Possibilities." *Hawwa—Journal of Women of the Middle East and the Islamic World* 2, no. 3 (2004): 316–336.

Waltz, Susan. "Universal Human Rights: The Contribution of Muslim States." *Human Rights Quarterly* 26, no. 4 (2004): 799–844.

Walzer, Michael. *Thick and Thin: Moral Argument at Home and Abroad*. Notre Dame, IN: University of Notre Dame Press, 1994.

Weeramantry, C. G. *Islamic Jurisprudence: An International Perspective*. Kuala Lumpur: The Other Press, 2001.

Weiss, Bernard G. *The Search for God's Law: Islamic Jurisprudence in the Writings of Sayf al-Din al-Amidi*. Salt Lake City: University of Utah Press, 2010.

Weiss, Bernard G. *The Spirit of Islamic Law*. Athens: University of Georgia Press, 2006.

Wellman, Carl. *The Proliferation of Rights: Moral Progress or Empty Rhetoric?* Boulder, CO: Westvew Press, 1999.

Wichard, Johannes C. "Recht und Religion im islamischen Recht." *Verfassung und Recht in Übersee* 30, no. 4 (1997): 533–544.

Wichard, Johannes C. *Zwischen Markt und Moschee: Wirtschaftliche Bedürfnisse und religiöse Anforderungen im frühen islamischen Vertragsrecht*. Paderborn: Schöningh, 1995.

Wickham, Carrie Rosefsky. *The Muslim Brotherhood: Evolution of an Islamist Movement*. Princeton, NJ: Princeton University Press, 2013.

Wielandt, Rotraud. "Menschenwürde und Freiheit in der Reflexion zeitgenössischer muslimischer Denker." In *Freiheit der Religion: Christentum und Islam unter dem Anspruch der Menschenrechte*, edited by Johannes Schwartländer, 179–209. Mainz: Matthias-Grünewald-Verlag, 1993.

Windelband, Wilhelm. *A History of Philosophy: With Especial Reference to the Formation and Development of Its Problems and Conceptions*. Translated by J. H. Tufts. New York: Macmillan, 1901.

Wirtz, Ursula, and Jürg Zöbeli. "Das Trauma der Gewalt." In *Hunger nach Sinn: Menschen in Grenzsituationen: Grenzen der Psychotherapie*, edited by Ursula Wirtz, 114–169. Zürich: Kreuz, 1995.
Wolterstorff, Nicholas. *Justice: Rights and Wrongs.* Princeton, NJ: Princeton University Press, 2008.
Wong, Paul T., and Bernard Weiner. "When People Ask 'Why' Questions and the Heuristics of Attributional Search." *Journal of Personality and Social Psychology* 40, no. 4 (1981): 650–663.
Würth, Anna. *Dialogue mit dem Islam als Konfliktpräventation? Zur Menschenrechtspolitik gegenüber islamisch geprägten Staaten.* Berlin: Deutsches Institut für Menschenrechte, 2003.
Young, Walter. "Stoning and Hand Amputation: The Pre-Islamic Origins of the Ḥadd Penalties for Zinā and Sariqa." PhD diss., McGill University, 2005.
Zayd, Muṣṭafa. *al-Maslaḥa fī al-Tashrīʿ al-Islāmi.* Cairo: Dār al-Fikr al-ʿArabī, 1954.
Zimbardo, Philip G., Robert L. Johnson, and Vivian McCann. *Psychology: Core Concepts.* Boston: Pearson, 2012.

Index

For the benefit of digital users, indexed terms that span two pages (e.g., 52–53) may, on occasion, appear on only one of those pages.

Note: Figures are indicated by an italic *f* following the page number.

contemporary conception of *maqāṣid*, 163–68
contemporary context of Muslim human rights
  authoritarian state practices and, 19–20
  international human rights, 8, 13–14
  introduction to, 8, 9–10, 11–12, 13
  Western human rights policies, 14–18, 15*f*
Convention on the Elimination of All Forms of Discrimination against Women (CEDAW), 14
Convention on the Rights of the Child, 238–39
corporal punishment (*ḥudūd*), 59–60, 76–77, 82, 86–88, 90–91, 95, 97–100, 150, 161–62, 163, 167
criterion of necessity, 157–58, 274
criterion of universality, 157, 161–62
cultural identity, 1, 2–4, 6, 71
cultural imperialism, 3–4
cultural relativity, 62, 105
cultural self-assertion, 6, 80
cultural sovereignty, 13–14

dār al-ḥarb (realm of war), 32–33
dār al-islām (realm of Islam), 32–33
ḍarūriyāt. *See* necessary goods (*ḍarūriyāt*)
Declaration on the Right to Development, 249–50
decolonization, 13–14
deliberative democracy, 72
democracy
  advocating for, 2–3, 14–16
  claims of injustice and, 242–43
  conflict between Islam and, 62, 65
  cultural imperialism and, 3–4
  deliberative democracy, 72
  establishment of, 6
  social democracy, 168–69
  spiritual democracy, 168
dignity (*karāma*), 72, 74–75, 77–79, 87–88, 106–7, 127–28, 142–44, 164–65, 172–76, 195–96, 203–4, 276–77
duty of forbearance, 235–36, 238–39, 275
duty of prevention, 235–36, 239–41, 275
dynamic conceptions in Islamic law, 8, 53–55, 54*f*, 58–59, 270–71

economic rights, 13–14
esteem needs, 214–15
ethical norms (*aḥkām khulqiyya*), 29
European Convention on Human Rights, 254–55
European Social Charter, 254–55
evolutionary approach, 87–89

Fadel, Mohammad, 99–100
faith-based assumptions, 103–4
faith norms (*aḥkām i'tiqādiyya*), 29
Falaturi, Abdoldjavad, 16–17
fixed norms (*thābit*), 30–31
flexible norms (*mutaghayyir*), 30–31
food shortages, 237–38, 248–49, 263–64
Frankl, Viktor, 222–24
freedom of religion, 59–60, 72, 88–89, 186–87, 190–91
freedom of thought, 62, 254–55
fundamentalism, 14–16, 57–58, 68, 105–6

Galtung, Johann, 226–28, 228*f*
Gasiet, Seev, 210–24
gender equality, 59–60, 77–78, 89–90
al-Ghazāli, Abū Ḥāmid, 149–50, 151, 157–58, 160–61, 164–65, 231–32
al-Ghazāli, Muḥammad, 70–71, 171–72
Gosepath, Stefan, 185–86
gradualism (*tadarruj*), 90–91
Griffin, James, 183–84, 199–205
grounding relationship, 265–66, 267–68, 277

ḥadīth tradition, 40–41, 49–50, 70–71
ḥājiyāt. *See* required goods (*ḥājiyāt*)
Halliday, Fred, 57–58
Hassan, Riffat, 77–78
Hauser, Jan, 222
hermeneutical approach, 92–96
Hinsch, Wilfried, 240–41
historical context of Muslim human rights
  introduction to, 8, 21
  Muslim identity and, 22–23
  Qur'an and, 23–26
  religious understanding and, 23–26
Hobbes, Thomas, 181
Hofmann, Murad, 16–17, 24–26, 84–85
Holocaust, 243–46
Hondrich, K. O., 209–10
Honneth, Axel, 219–21
ḥudūd punishments. *See* corporal punishment (*ḥudūd*)
human existence (*ḍarūrat al-khalq*)
  conditions of, 147, 148*f*, 149–50, 157–58, 178–79, 210–11, 229–30
  levels of, 147, 148*f*, 149
  protection of human needs and, 231–33, 262–64, 267–68, 272–77
  rights of, 173
  summary of, 272
human interactions (*mu'āmalāt*), 93–94
human needs
  belongingness needs, 214

defined, 208–11
esteem needs, 214–15
interpersonal relationships and, 220–21
introduction to, 9–10, 208
Islamic law (*sharīʿa*) and, 111–12
love needs, 214
motivational psychology and, 211–16
objective-universal interpretation of, 209–11
peace and conflict research in, 224–28
physiological needs, 212–13
safety needs, 213
self-actualization needs, 211–12, 215–16
social recognition needs, 46–47, 218–20
sociohistorical perspective on, 216–24
subjective-historical interpretation of, 209–11
See also human rights as protection for human needs
human rights
autonomy and, 200–5
claims, 16–17, 200–1, 227, 237–39, 242–43, 263–64, 275
consensual justification of, 185–90
defined, 183
dignity (*karāma*) as, 72, 74–75, 77–79, 87–88, 106–7, 127–28, 142–44, 164–65, 172–76, 195–96, 203–4, 276–77
instrumentalization of, 16–17, 98–99
interests and, 205–7
introduction to, 183–85
justification and, 195–99
moral relevance of, 9–10, 184–85, 207, 231, 274–75
normative agency, 199–205
sacralization of, 73–75
sovereignty and, 190–95
violations of, 16–17, 186–87, 191, 202–3, 234–36, 239–41
Western human rights, 8, 13, 14–18, 15*f*
Western human rights policies, 14–18, 15*f*
See also historical context of Muslim human rights; Islamic human rights; theological context of Muslim human rights
human rights as protection for human needs
asymmetrical interdependence, 252, 253
human existence and, 231–33, 262–64, 267–68, 272–77
introduction to, 9–10, 181–82
priorities and interdependencies, 249–69
purposes of Islamic law (*maqāṣid al-sharīʿa*) and, 231–33
remediable threats, 241–42, 257
strong interdependence, 252–53
strong supporting relation, 251–52
threats to, 233–49, 236*f*
weak interdependence, 252, 253
weak supporting relation, 251–52
Huntington, Samuel, 14–16

Ibn al-Ḥājib, 149–50
Ibn Khaldūn, 11–12
Ibn Rushd, 43–44
Ibn Taimiyya, 23–24, 66–68, 160–61, 165–66
Ibn ʿAbd al-Salām, 151
Ibn ʿAshūr, Muḥammad al-Ṭāhir, 169–72, 173
identity construction, 2–4
identity discourse
cultural identity, 1, 2–4, 6, 71
historical context of, 22–23
human needs and, 224–28
Islamic human rights as, 1–10
identity preservation, 2–3, 4
Ignatieff, Michael, 186–87
ijtihād (effort), 24–26, 34–37, 43–44, 53, 92–93
incompatibility argument. *See* rejection and incompatibility arguments
instrumentalization of human rights, 16–17, 98–99
intellectual authority, 46–50
intellectual dependence, 37–39, 43–44, 46
intellectual legitimation, 38–39, 46
intentional approach, 89–92
intentions (*maqāsid*). *See* purposes of Islamic law (*maqāṣid al-sharīʿa*)
internal legitimacy, 107, 195–96
international concern, 192–94
International Covenant on Civil and Political Rights (ICCPR), 14, 254–55
international human rights, 8, 13–14, 61, 88, 97–100, 107, 186–87, 191
international justice, 13–14
international law, 32–33, 69–70, 107–9, 185–86, 189, 190, 193–95, 267
interpersonal relations (*muʿāmalāt*), 24–26, 30–35, 32*f*, 49, 53, 121, 135–38, 140–41, 158–59, 160–61
interpersonal relationships, 220–21
Iqbal, Muhammad, 23–24, 36–37, 168–69
Iranian Green Movement, 19–20
Islamic Council of Europe, 70–71
Islamic culture, 1–2, 6, 62, 66–67, 69
Islamic human rights
copyrights and, 70–73
defined, 80–81
as identity discourse, 1–10
Islamic legitimacy and, 7–8, 109, 179–80, 270, 272, 273–74

Islamic human rights (*cont.*)
Islamization of, 76–81
sacralization of, 73–75
summary and perspective, 8–9, 101–9, 104*f*
summary of discourse, 270–78
universal conception of, 111–14
See also contemporary context of Muslim human rights; historical context of Muslim human rights; human rights
Islamic jurisprudence (*fiqh*), 24–26, 28–30, 33–35, 37–38, 68, 78–79, 97–98, 111–12, 117–19, 161–62, 169–72
Islamic law (*sharīʿa*)
appropriation argument, 270
assimilation argument and, 82–83, 88, 91–92, 93–94, 98–99, 270
blind obedience (*taqlīd*), 24–26, 35–46
classic explanatory models, 35–37
differentiation of, 30–34
dynamic conceptions in, 8, 53–55, 54*f*, 58–59, 270–71
human needs and, 111–12
human rights and, 6
incompatibility argument and, 66–68
intellectual authority, 46–50
Islamization human rights and, 76–81
political authority, 46–50
rejection and incompatibility arguments, 8–9, 58–59, 61–62, 63–68, 64*f*, 270
stagnation in, 8, 21–22, 24–26, 34–50, 52*f*, 58
as system of norms (*aḥkām*), 24–26, 28*f*, 28–30, 50–51, 132*f*, 160–61
theological context of Muslim human rights, 28–34
See also purposes of Islamic law (*maqāṣid al-sharīʿa*)
Islamic legal purposes (*maqāṣ id al-sharīʿa*). *See* purposes of Islamic law (*maqāṣid al-sharīʿa*)
Islamic legitimacy, 7–8, 109, 179–80, 270, 272, 273–74
Islamic modernism, 22–26
Islamic values, 3–4, 24–26
Islamization human rights, 76–81
Islam of identity, 3–4
Islam of truth, 3–4

Jamal al-Dīn al-Afghāni, 24–26
justificatory narrative, 5–7, 118, 195–99, 271

Kadivar, Mohsen, 93–94
Kamali, Mohammad Hashim, 173
Khaled Abou el Fadl, 93–94, 156–57
al-Khamlīshi, Aḥmad, 171–72
Koran, 36–37, 62
Krämer, Gudrun, 3–5
Kreide, Regina, 188–89, 242–43

Law on the Revocation of Naturalization and the Annulment of German Citizenship, 244–45
Leviathan (Hobbes), 181
Locke, John, 78–79, 112, 181
love needs, 214

Maastricht Guidelines, 250
Mahfouz, Asma, 19–20
Manzoor, Parvez, 16–17
maqāṣid al-sharīʿa. *See* purposes of Islamic law (*maqāṣid al-sharīʿa*)
maqāṣid theory. *See* purposes of Islamic law (*maqāṣid al-sharīʿa*)
Maritain, Jacques, 185–86
Maslow, Abraham, 211–16
Mayer, Ann E., 61, 78–79
Miadi, Zineb, 78–79
Mill, John Stuart, 208–9
Miller, David, 241–42
moral orders, 186–89
moral relevance of human rights, 9–10, 184–85, 207, 231, 274–75
moral right, 195–96, 200–1, 233–34, 256–58
Morsink, Johannes, 243–45
motivational psychology and human needs, 211–16
Muslim Brotherhood, 19–20
Muslim consciousness, 1–2
Muslim legal thought, 37–38, 39–40, 43–44, 46, 50–51, 130–31

Naqvi, Syed Nawab Haider, 163–64
necessary goods (*ḍarūriyāt*), 124–25, 131–35, 133*f*, 146–48, 232, 233, 263–64, 272–73, 276–77
Netherlands Scientific Council for Government Policy, 107
Nickel, James, 188–89, 251–52
normative agency, 199–205
Nyazee, Imran, 164–65

objective-universal interpretation of needs, 209–11
Organization of Islamic Cooperation (OIC), 13–14
Orientalism, 27

penal norms (*ḥudūd*), 132, 161–62, 163, 165, 167, 170

physical violence, 233–36, 236*f*
physiological needs, 212–13
Pogge, Thomas, 257–61
political authority, 46–50
polygamy, 84–85, 86, 88, 90–91
pragmatic approach, 97–100
principles, defined, 32–33
Proclamation of Tehran, 249–50
protection of human needs
  human existence and, 231–33, 262–64, 267–68, 272–77
  See human rights as protection for human needs
protection of life (*ḥifẓ al-nafs*), 122–25, 126, 129, 146, 150, 152, 156–57, 162, 164–65, 167, 175, 272
protection of reason (*ḥifẓ al-ʿaql*), 123–24, 150, 153–54, 155–56, 162, 167, 172
protection of religion (*ḥifẓ al-dīn*), 123–24, 129, 150, 157–62, 164–65, 167, 172, 175
Protocol of San Salvador, 249–50
purposes of Islamic law (*maqāṣid al-sharīʿa*)
  classical conception of, 9, 146–62
  human needs and, 184–85, 231–33
  intentions (*maqāsid*), 118–19, 139–45
  introduction to, 9, 55, 113–14, 115–16
  Islamic legal purposes (*maqāṣ id al-sharīʿa*), 9–10, 121, 165, 171–72, 176–79, 273, 274–76
  Qur'an and, 115–17, 117*f*, 119–20, 127–28, 135–36, 138–39
  reasoning by analogy (*qiyās*), 116–19, 117*f*
  Sunnah and, 115–16, 119–20, 142
  See also classical conception of *maqāṣid*; Islamic law (*sharīʿa*)

al-Qaraḍāwi, Yūsuf, 171–72
al-Qarāfi, Shihāb al-Dīn, 149–50, 151
Qur'an
  appropriation argument and, 70–71
  assimilation argument and, 82, 83–100
  classical conception of *maqāṣid*, 165–70, 171–75
  historical context of Muslim human rights, 23–26
  incompatibility argument and, 65
  purposes of Islamic law (*maqāṣid al-sharīʿa*), 115–17, 117*f*, 119–20, 127–28, 135–36, 138–39
  theological context of Muslim human rights, 30–35, 39–41, 43–44, 49–50, 52–54

racist discrimination, 202–3
al-Raisūni, Aḥmad, 163–64
Ramadan, Tariq, 16–17, 98–99, 173–80, 177*f*
Rāshid al-Ghannūshi, 16–17
ratio legis, 54, 140–41
Rawls, John, 190–93
reasoning by analogy (*qiyās*), 116–19, 117*f*
Reflections on the Revolution in France (Burke), 182
rejection and incompatibility arguments, 8–9, 58–59, 61–62, 63–68, 64*f*, 270
religion, defined by Tibi, Bassam, 63–66
religious freedom. *See* freedom of religion
remediable threats, 241–42, 257
Renan, Ernest, 21
required goods (*ḥājiyāt*), 125, 132–34, 146–49, 232–33, 272–73
Riḍa, Muḥammad Rashīd, 24–26, 166–68
Rightly Guided Caliphs, 39–40
right of God (*ḥaqq Allah*), 159–61
rights of human beings (*ḥaqq al-ʿabd* or *ḥaqq al-ādamī*), 5–6, 67–68, 137, 138–39
rights of legal agents (*ḥaqq al-mukallaf*), 5–6
right to justification, 195–99
ritual norms (*ibādāt*), 24–26, 29–31, 34, 49, 132, 135–36, 159–61
Rosati, Jerel A., 225–26

Sachedina, Abdulaziz, 106–7
safety needs, 213
Schacht, Joseph, 27, 35–36
self-actualization needs, 211–12, 215–16
Sen, Amartya, 240–41
sexist discrimination, 202–3
sharīʿa. *See* Islamic law (*sharīʿa*)
al-Shāṭibi, Ibrahīm Ibn Mūsa, 130–40, 133*f*, 146–47, 149–51
al-Shawkāni, Muḥammad Ibn ʿAlī, 151
Shue, Henry, 255–57, 258–62
shūra principle, 72, 166–67, 187
slaves/slavery, 79, 90–91, 96, 165, 167–68, 189, 190–91, 248–49, 254–55, 264
social democracy, 168–69
social emancipation, 195–96
social justice, 19–20, 90–91
social recognition needs, 46–47, 218–20
social respect, 220
societal norms, 30–31
Soroush, Abdolkarim, 3–4, 23–24
sovereignty and human rights, 190–95
spiritual democracy, 168
stagnation in Islamic *sharīʿa*, 8, 21–22, 24–26, 34–50, 52*f*, 58
strong interdependence, 252–53

strong supporting relation, 251–52
subjective-historical interpretation of needs, 209–11
Sunnah
  appropriation argument and, 70–71
  assimilation argument and, 83–84, 85–88, 92–93
  purposes of Islamic law (*maqāṣid al-sharīʿa*), 115–16, 119–20, 142
  theological context of Muslim human rights, 32–33, 34–35, 36–37, 39–41, 43–44, 49, 52–54
system of norms (*aḥkām*), 24–26, 28*f*, 28–30, 50–51, 132*f*, 160–61

Taha, Mahmoud Mohammad, 87–88
taḥsīniyāt. *See* ameliorative goods (*taḥsīniyāt*)
taqlīd. *See* blind obedience (*taqlīd*)
Tasioulas, John, 205–6
Taylor, Charles, 219–20
theological context of Muslim human rights
  introduction to, 8, 27
  Islamic jurisprudence (*fiqh*) and, 28–30, 33–35, 37–38
  Islamic *sharīʿa* and, 28–50
  Qur'an and, 30–35, 39–41, 43–44, 49–50, 52–54
theoretical justification, 7
Tibi, Bassam, 62, 63–68, 64*f*
torture protection rights, 186–87, 189, 200–1, 205–6, 247–49, 253–55, 259
trust (*amāna*), 37–38, 75, 142, 166–67, 214–15, 234–35
al-Ṭūfi, Ibn al-Subki, 151
Tugendhat, Ernst, 198–99
Two Treatises of Government (Locke), 181

unchangeable norms, 32
unintelligible norms (*aḥkām ghayru maʿqūlat al-maʿna*), 30–31
universal agreement, 111, 113–14, 179–80, 184, 231, 270, 271–72, 273–75, 277–78
universal conception of Islamic human rights, 111–14
Universal Declaration of Human Rights, 70–71, 72–73, 185–86, 191, 238–39, 242–46
Universal Declaration of Human Rights (UDHR), 16–18, 106–7
universal goods (*kulliyāt*), 149–50, 151, 231–32
  ameliorative goods (*taḥsīniyāt*), 125, 126, 133–40, 146–47, 233, 264, 272–73
  necessary goods (*ḍarūriyāt*), 124–25, 131–35, 133*f*, 146–48, 232, 233, 263–64, 272–73, 276–77
  required goods (*ḥājiyāt*), 125, 132–34, 146–49, 232–33, 272–73
Universal Islamic Declaration of Human Rights, 70–71
Universal Islamic Declaration of Human Rights (1981), 69–71, 74
UN World Conference on Human Rights, 249–50
urgent rights, 190–91

Vienna Declaration, 250
virtue ethics (*ilm al akhlāq*), 29

Walzer, Michael, 186–87
weak interdependence, 252, 253
weak supporting relation, 251–52
Western human rights, 8, 13, 14–18, 15*f*
Wielandt, Rotraud, 79
Windelband, Wilhelm, 38